the FAITH
and the POWER

the inspiring story of the first Christians
& how they survived the madness of Rome

a first century history by

James D. Snyder

Pharos
Books

The Faith and the Power:
The inspiring story of the first Christians and how they survived the madness of Rome; a first century history, by James D. Snyder.

© 2002 by James D. Snyder. All rights reserved.
Published by Pharos Books
8657 SE Merritt Way
Jupiter, Florida 33458-1007

Cover and interior design and production by Pneuma Books
Set in Adobe Palatino 10 /13.

First Printing. Printed in the United States of America
10 09 08 07 06 05 04 03 02 01   10 9 8 7 6 5 4 3 2 1

Publisher's Cataloging-in-Publication
(*Provided by Quality Books, Inc.*)

Snyder, James D.
    The faith and the power : the inspiring story of the first Christians and how they survived the madness of Rome : a first century history / by James D. Snyder. --1st ed.
    p. cm.
    LCCN 2001119030
    ISBN 0-9675200-2-9

1. Church history--Primitive and early church, ca. 30-600-History.
2. Church and state--History. 3. Chritianity and other religions--Judaism.
4. Judaism--Relations--Christianity 5. Christianity and other religions--
Roman. 6. Rome--Religion. 7. Rome--History--Tiberius, 14-37.
8. Rome--History--Caligula, 37-41. 9. Rome--History--Nero, 54-68.
I. Title.

BR166.S69 2002   270.1
                                                    QBI01-701165

The Faith and the Power is dedicated to all those who perished
in the terrorist attacks of September 11, 2001,
to the surviving families who may now question God's purpose for us,
and to the equally grieving families of men who thought God's favor
could be gained by suicidal devastation.

I do so knowing that the hatreds torturing the Middle East today are
exactly the same as those that inflamed Judea and many provinces of the
Roman Empire some two thousand years ago.

It is my hope that all who read this history will conclude that if a small
band of people, armed only with acts of love and charity,
can light a beacon for the world to follow, a rededication to these basic
tenets can melt the mountains of darkness and hate that exist today.

The painting on the front cover is a
Eucharist scene, ca. early 3rd century,
from the Catacomb of Priscilla,
the wall of the altar chamber.
h14.5" × w92".

ACKNOWLEDGMENTS

This book reflects help and insights from two perspectives. One is the benefit of comment and criticism from historians and clergymen who have made a lifetime of learning about the first century.

Among them my special thanks goes to Dr. John Freely, Professor and author on Mediterranean history, The University of the Bosphorus, Istanbul; Dr. Fred Mench, Professor of Classics, Richard Stockton College of New Jersey; Dr. Philip Jenkins, Distinguished Professor of History and Religious Studies, Pennsylvania State University; Dr. Paul L. Maier, Professor of Ancient History, Western Michigan University; Dr. C. Patrick Shaffer, Senior Pastor, First Presbyterian Church of Tequesta, FL; and Dr. Paul W. Walaskay, Professor of Biblical Studies, Union Theological Seminary, Richmond, VA.

Equally valuable were comments from friends and family who read advance copies from the viewpoint of Christian laypersons who simply want to know more about an era that was surely one of history's most turbulent and traumatic. Was the story interesting? Told clearly? For helping to smooth the rough spots I thank Lois Arntzen, Fred Buss, Tucker Grinnan, Doug Kindschi, Virginia Willoughby, my sister Christine Moats and wife Sue.

Finally, I acknowledge the constant help of the book designing and editing team of Brian and Nina Taylor from Pneuma Books, whose Christian principles are aglow in their daily work.

TABLE OF CONTENTS

PREFACE

THE REMAINDER OF THE FIRST CENTURY after the crucifixion of Jesus was more than the commonly named "Apostolic Age." It may have been the most turbulent and terrifying period in all history. It was also an era that — more than any other since — shaped the destinies of Christianity, Judaism and world civilization for 2000 years to come.

Why, then, does it remain such a murky period to even the most avid of history readers? When this question first piqued my journalist's curiosity more than 20 years ago, little did I know then that it would eventually absorb me in the works, sites and bedrock of first century Christianity.

One of the barriers facing anyone who wants to know more about this period is that chronology — any historian's most basic tool — is obscured by ancient writers and their maddening lack of attention to it. The Book of Acts, for example, tells its story sequentially but never mentions dates as we would recognize them. Likewise, the 21 epistles of the New Testament are arranged with scant regard to chronology, and scholars still debate when many of them were written.

The Romans didn't help much. Rather than assigning numerals to years, they commonly identified events as happening "in the consulship" of two or more senators who may or may not have left us something more than their names.

The second barrier to a fuller understanding of this period is the narrow perspective of the Biblical text. The writers of the New Testament were understandably focused on telling the story of Christian community. And since these books were often dictated, then transcribed into many copies by paid scribes, they tended to be efficient but often frustratingly brief.

It wasn't the task of the first gospel writers to report in the broader context of events happening all around them in Jerusalem, Antioch, Alexandria and other centers of the Roman Empire. But when one consults the other histories of this period, the Christian tapestry gains even more color and texture. I refer to the contemporary Jewish historians Josephus and Philo, and to Roman writers such as Tacitus, Suetonius and Dio Cassius. Supplementing these essential sources are an array of ancient glitterati ranging from the philosopher-playwright Seneca to the early Christian Bishop Eusebius to the Roman poets Lucan, Livy and Martial.

The reward from all this added reading is that the first century Christian story — that Apostolic Age — becomes more powerful, understandable and believable than when told by Biblical sources alone.

I'VE SEEN MY JOB as sorting out and condensing the ancient sources so that you'll be spurred along in your discovery rather than frustrated as though you were left alone to dig through a 2,000 year-old archeological site with a teaspoon. Thus, I would like to begin with a few general suggestions to frame your mindset before you begin Chapter 1.

The first concerns the material world of 2000 years ago. Many people today seem to view their ancient counterparts as some sort of neo-cavemen who carved on crude stone tablets and walked about in loincloths. By all means do remove from the scene gunpowder, computers, air conditioning, jet travel and the like, but don't go too far with this exercise. People then had nails, winches and pulleys, intricate artwork, elaborate plumbing, huge apartment complexes, massive ships and stadiums with more seating than today's largest superdome. Books were often elaborately illustrated, and Rome alone had 25 public libraries in which to enjoy them. Every way that we see hair coiffed, permed or spiked today had already been done by Romans and emulated throughout their client kingdoms.

The same mindset applies to the way people thought and interacted. The more I delved into the ancient sources, the less distance there seemed between 20 centuries of human behavior. Men winked at pretty girls, mothers scolded their children at the dinner table, teenagers scrawled the same graffiti on bathroom walls, old men sat around telling lies about their war exploits and young dandies borrowed beyond their means to buy the trendiest clothes and bet on the horses.

Having said all that, one should note that the social structure was much more rigid and far more apt to dictate one's future. One of every three humans was a slave. For the others, social class and family background counted most, so that the son of a tanner would as surely follow him into the trade guild as would the son of a patrician into a life of leisure that actually proscribed him from taking part in the disdained world of commerce.

Overlaying these dictates were those of the religious world. The first Christians contended not only with the rigidities of Jewish ritual, but with a pantheon of state-sanctioned gods and the various priesthoods that profited from their many temples and sacrifices. But no less important to the average citizen in the Roman world was the need to be constantly attentive to one's many household god-spirits. And woven throughout the fabric of society were uncountable soothsayers, witches, magicians and messiahs. To an early Christian apostle, these purveyors of suffocating superstition were every bit as daunting as a cohort of Roman soldiers.

To these conceptual suggestions, I have added some practical aids in this book to make your reading easier:

- ~ Chapters are arranged in chronological order. Years are stated numerically (A.D. 60, etc.) even though all but a few ancient writings did not identify years by number.
- ~ Maps are supplied in the appendix and distances in miles are used liberally in the text to help show how difficult it was for Paul to walk across the Roman province of Asia (in today's southwestern Turkey) or how relatively convenient it was to board one of many ships for the 1,700 mile crossing from Rome to the shores of Judea.
- ~ Cities, provinces and other locations are listed by their ancient names, but, where possible, with the modern names in parenthesis upon first mention. A table in the appendix correlates ancient and modern place names for further reference.
- ~ I have reduced footnotes principally to those that identify the ancient source of a long quote. I have tried to omit lengthy scholarly asides that so often detract from the main story.

The subject of money is also worth some discussion here, simply because people in the Roman world — yes, even the Christians — thought and fought about it just as much then as they do today. Although many client states had their own coinage (for example, the Jewish *shekel*), the prevailing monetary units were the Roman *as, sesterce* and *denarius*. In general, four *as* comprised a *sesterce* and four of these a *denarius*. It took roughly 6,000 *denarii* to make a silver *talent*.

For convenience sake, one might roughly equate a *sesterce* to today's U.S. quarter (25 cents) and the denarius to $1. But precise comparisons are frustrating for several reasons. Cash was less crucial to ancient economies because most households produced more of their own goods and bartered for trade than today. Although the *as* (6.25 cents by the above reckoning) would buy six loaves of bread, it doesn't follow that an *as* should be valued at $6 just because today's stores may sell bread for $1 a loaf. The reason is that the value of human labor was more akin to that in today's least developed economies. A typical Roman soldier, for example, earned 900 *sesterces* a year. And to further complicate comparisons, the value of that pay would have been worth more in A.D. 31 and perhaps one-third less 50 years later. The reason: inflation took its toll then as it does now.

JUST AS ONE can't fully understand World War II by starting with the attack on Pearl Harbor, the story of the first Christians after Jesus doesn't begin at the crucifixion. Two men who were long since dead at the onset of our story probably had more to do with shaping events of the first century than any of the characters who lived through it.

The first is Octavian Cæsar Augustus, who died peacefully and gracefully in A.D. 14, or more than a decade before Jesus began his ministry. His deeds and persona are important to keep in mind, because of the way they contrast with what Rome did to itself in the rest of the first century. For 55 years Augustus employed his considerable charisma and cunning to preside over relative peace and prosperity. With his steel blue eyes and Apollo-like looks, he could charm a room with a smile or wilt a rival with an icy stare. Although a few members of his own family were banished (mostly on valid grounds for outrageous behavior), Augustus tolerated public criticism well and no citizen lost a night's sleep worrying that Prætorian guards would come to snatch him up for making a careless remark.

During these 55 years, government was reorganized, new temples built and old buildings recovered with marble. The people got an annual accounting of public finances and the treasury accumulated a surplus. When leading citizens left the emperor portions of their estates as a gesture of respect, he usually repaid the sum with interest to their children when they became of age. And when Augustus passed away at age 77, he left an orderly will, an inventory of his achievements, an uncontested successor and a farewell gift of some $20 million for the citizens of Rome.

Yet, Cæsar Augustus left something else as well. The builder of the Golden Age of Rome left an empire so large and intricately organized that it exceeded the leadership and management skills of the lesser mortals who followed him. And these people nearly destroyed the entire Roman Empire as a result.

Just as the persona of Augustus lingered in Rome, the legacy of Herod the Great could be seen in the spectacular building projects that graced Judea long after his death in 4 B.C. — from the colonnaded streets of Beirut to the gleaming man-made harbor of Cæsarea to the massive, marbled temple at Jerusalem. Outwardly, no two more different men could be found on earth than Octavian Cæsar Augustus and Herod the Great. One was clean-shaven and slight of build, with a regal calm. The other was a burly, bearded Semite whose moods could swing from outlandish generosity to fits of vile temper. He could be the most charming and obsequious of client kings or a ruthless ruler in his own right who would even kill his wife and sons.

Herod's rise may have been the more remarkable because he came from Idumea, an Arabic district south of Jerusalem that was a part of Judea in name only. For an Arab from Idumea to become king of the Jews was an audacious feat in itself. The reason is that most first century Jews knew Idumea as the successor to ancient Edom — the same kingdom that had rudely refused Moses and his wandering exiles permission to traverse on their way to Canaan. They were also the same treacherous jackals, who had, 500 years before, encouraged the Babylonians to destroy Jerusalem so they could join in the plunder. Yet, Idumeans could be useful to the Jews because the Jewish kingdom needed compliant clients to provide border protection against Egypt to the south. Herod's grandfather was a strong chieftain and willing ally for the right price.

But Rome, which ruled the Jews, had an even broader strategic need for such services. To the east lay Parthia, successor to the legendary Persian Empire. Although still a loose confederation spread over vast treeless stretches, Parthia could, when aroused, muster the only fighting force that could rival Rome's. And because the Roman client states along the eastern Mediterranean were both scattered and quarrelsome, Parthia regularly preyed on their people, herds and croplands.

In 62 B.C. the Roman governor-general Pompey tried to fix the problem by welding all of the smaller client states from Antioch to the Egyptian border into the new province of Syria. When he picked the compliant Hycrannus

II to rule the Jewish lands within the new province, it was too much for an envious brother named Aristobulus. Rallying a mass of fiery nationalists, he seized the temple, uprooted Hycrannus, and, I would suppose, made ready to cast his lot with Parthia. But now an angry Pompey stormed back to Jerusalem with a full legion, captured Aristobulus and sent him back to Rome to be paraded as a showpiece in the public celebration, or triumph, that followed.

This time Pompey set out to "balance"— or minimize — the power of the quarrelsome and unruly Jews throughout the new province. To this end he carved out, or isolated from Jewish rule, most of the cities that consisted chiefly of Hellenistic (ethnic Greek) populations. It meant denying Jewish rule over the already Hellenized cities along the Phoenician Mediterranean and Gaza strip. Because there were many ethnic Greek cities in the central hinterland, Pompey created the state of Samaria, which had the effect of splitting the Jewish stronghold of Galilee in the north from its counterpart Judea in the south. Then in the arid lands that stretched up and down Syria east of the river Jordan, Pompey created the Decapolis, a loose league of 10 Hellenistic city-states. Left in charge of the gutted but still-wealthy Jewish population centers was the newly-restored Hycrannus II. He returned, however, not as king, but as ethnarch — a term meaning "prince," but one that Roman provincial administrators came to use as they saw fit.

Herod's father Antipas had risen to become chief minister to Hycrannus. Now, although the ethnarch's powers receded, his Idumean advisor became increasingly active. Pompey, for instance, had wanted to invade and subdue Idumea. Antipas was the go-between who skillfully helped avoid it, then became the mediator of Roman and Arab interests. Several years later, Antipas — with the 25-year-old Herod at his side — rushed troops to reinforce Julius Cæsar during his march to Egypt. Four years afterward, when Julius Cæsar was murdered in Rome, it was the 29-year-old Herod who raised money in Galilee for the armies of his assassins, Brutus and Cassius. But when these were defeated in battle by Mark Anthony and Cæsar's 19 year-old nephew, Octavian, Herod again switched his allegiance to the victors.

Now came the decision that defined the rest of his life. The Parthians at last decided to invade Judea, hoping again to exploit the chaos caused by the Roman civil war. Much of the Jewish elite welcomed the prospect of a new form of servitude that might mean less tribute and taxes. But Herod was one of the a few leaders in the region to declare for Rome — and in so doing he bound himself forever to its fortunes.

To bolster his cause, Herod's immediate hope lay in Egypt where Cleopatra had cast her lot with Mark Anthony and the Romans. In a daring dash to Egypt, he borrowed a ship from the queen and sailed off for Rome in dangerous late autumn seas in order to appeal personally for support. He needn't have worried about it, because Anthony and the young Octavian, with their pressing need for an energetic ally in Judea, greeted the young Herod like a lost cousin. With great ceremonial gusto, the joint consuls then escorted him arm in arm to the Senate, which was ready to award him troops and money.

Herod now needed a title to match his lofty new status. Because he was either all or part Idumean, he could not become Jewish high priest. The Roman joint consuls quickly settled on a title that would soon lead to the reassembly of Judea's parceled domains into one political unit again.

The title was king.

Like Octavian Cæsar, Herod was to reorganize the government gristmill and preside over more than 40 years of internal peace — or, to be more precise, the absence of open civil war. And again like Cæsar Augustus, he became the greatest builder his nation had ever known. In addition to the public works already mentioned, the new King wasted no time erecting what one might call "fortified palace-resorts" at Ascalon, Jericho, Masada, Sepphoris and Herodium.

Yet, blocks of stone do not define or unite a people. The kingdom held together by Herod's guile until 4 B.C. was as fragile as the one crafted by the genius of Augustus. Herod's death left feuding family factions, fractious religious sects, disputed borders and covetous neighbors. The more the strife, the more Rome would yank on the reins of its unruly eastern buffer state. And the more pressure from Rome, the more tightly the Jewish leadership would attempt to police and pacify its noisiest factions.

In the Passover of A.D. 30, Jesus and his followers fell victim to that chain of events. But they also brought about a resurrection that ignited something that even the Roman Empire could not contain.

~J.D.S.~

A.D.
30–32

IN MAY OF A.D. 30 the most devout followers of Jesus gathered in Jerusalem in the upper room of a large public house or private villa to contemplate their future lives without him.

At the time they had no collective name other than God Fearers or Jesus Followers. Their message was most often called The Way.

How many of these Jesus Followers existed by the time of the Passover in A.D. 30? Overall, the number of those who were baptized by John the Baptist or declared themselves followers of Jesus during his ministry must surely have numbered many thousands. Galilee, for example, was full of towns with populations of 10,000 or more and the crowds that followed Jesus were often in the thousands. Jerusalem serves as another yardstick. The city at this time had a permanent population of around 1 million, which more than doubled each spring with the infusion of Passover pilgrims. For the city's governing authorities to perceive a serious threat to their control, the numbers of presumed believers that lined the streets and shouted hosannas for the new Messiah surely must have exceeded 10,000. However, the big question is how many still called themselves followers after the crucifixion and how many melted away in fright like rainwater down a desert gully.

The immediate world surrounding Jerusalem — the Roman province of Syria — probably contained 5 million more Jews, Hellenes, retired Roman soldiers and other transplants from nearly every Roman province on the Mediterranean rim. Many lived in the walled port cities that served the lively shipping trade up and down the Syrian coast. But most lived in clustered villages and went out by day to till their crops and orchards.

In all, the Roman Empire in A.D. 30 embraced some 40 provinces and perhaps 54 million residents. Of these, about 7 million were Jews, now scattered from their original homeland to cities from Spain to Babylon.

No matter who they were, the person who could most influence their lives — be it with a decree, a tax, a new political appointment, or sudden arrest — was one man who had already ruled from afar for 17 years.

IN A.D. 30, in his 71st year, Tiberius Cæsar Augustus was entrenched in a refuge that reflected his weariness and wariness of Rome. Far from the imperial palace on Palatine Hill, three miles off the Cape of Surrentum (Sorrento), was the rocky isle of Capri, the private preserve of just a few noble families. Today, as then, one can disembark at the island's only natural harbor and trek southward through ascending orchards and stony outcrops. At the highest and southernmost point is a breathtaking thousand-foot cliff overlooking Surrentum to the east and the sweeping, blue Bay of Naples to the north.

There, Tiberius built his terraced Villa Jovis and from there he ruled until his death at 78 with only occasional forays onto the mainland. The villa offered a natural protection from assassins, but it also symbolized the emperor's distain of and detachment from a people he despised as much as they did him. Tiberius was sick of Rome's dirty streets, the Senate's inane sycophancy and the thankless burden of governance itself. His naturally serious demeanor had by now turned sour and sullen.

Yet, some might have understood Tiberius and sympathized with his plight. His servitude to Rome began at age four when the young emperor Augustus became captivated by his mother Livia and compelled her to divorce her husband — even though she was carrying another son (Drusus) at the time.

From the time he became of age, the imperial stepson dutifully served Augustus, be it as personal emissary to investigate grain trade irregularities in Rome or commanding legions on the most contentious frontiers of Parthia and Germany. His only refuge had been his devotion to his wife, Vip-

2

sania, but even here imperial needs intervened. Tiberius was forced to divorce Vipsania "for the good of Rome" and marry the emperor's daughter Julia. Yes, part of it was Livia's insistence on positioning her son more securely in contention to succeed Augustus. But in the bargain, the emperor hoped to police his daughter's fondness for wine and sexual adventures.

The other light in Tiberius' life had been Drusus, his younger brother and military comrade in arms. But within a few years Drusus had died mysteriously in a German encampment and Julia had proven so unruly that her father banished her for life to a forlorn island.

Now Tiberius had no one save his busy stepfather and ambitious mother. But lest he be perceived as contending for the successorship with Augustus' two younger grandsons by a former marriage, Tiberius, now a tall, erect, proven military commander in the presumed fullness of his powers, stunned his parents by departing for the balmy isle of Rhodes with no more than a few household servants. There he lived alone for eight years as quietly as possible for a celebrity émigré.

That, however, would never do for his mother. At Livia's repeated instance, Tiberius was coaxed back again to Rome on the understanding that he could avoid public office. But within a few years both of Augustus' grandsons had died and Tiberius was again the hard working heir-apparent. And when Augustus died in A.D. 14, his stepson became the man who, in his own words, felt "as though I have just picked up a wolf by the ears."

The new emperor was then 56, and with an aging, but no less ambitious mother eager to be proclaimed Rome's first "Augusta" and rule at his side. After seeing that the Senate deified his stepfather and ensconced him in the round family mausoleum that still stands among Rome's crumbling antiquities, Tiberius embarked on several years of frugal administration and proper relations with a wary Senate. Quiet and courtly, the new emperor went out of his way to eschew honors and proposals that temples be erected in his name. He insisted that he was to be treated as a "mere man" and showed irritation when a senator would flatter him in a speech or approach his carriage in a subservient posture.

But in time Tiberius also came to be viewed by the populace as Rome's version of Ebenezer Scrooge. The image was reinforced by the very presence of his opposite — his handsome, outgoing stepson and most likely successor. Germanicus, the eldest son of the emperor's deceased brother, Drusus, was adopted by Tiberius and became his chief military commander whenever rebellion broke out in Gaul, Germany and other conquered provinces. The more glory the popular, young father of nine gained in his troubleshooting assignments, the more Tiberius would see *Give us Germanicus!* scrawled on the walls of buildings as he passed by in his litter.

At age 62, Tiberius might have welcomed displays of public confidence in this loyal heir-apparent. But it's also true that Germanicus had once botched a troop mutiny in Germany — pacifying his ragged, underpaid legionaries only by so many concessions that the treasury had trouble paying for them. Germanicus constantly had to be reigned in from launching overly expensive conquests and once brought his troops into Egypt in disregard of the long-standing rule that no senator enter Rome's prized breadbasket without the emperor's express permission.

In A.D. 19 Germanicus was suddenly dead at age 34 — struck down by some unknown malady while visiting Syria. Well, the emperor's emissary, Calpurnius Piso, had also been a guest in Germanicus' camp just beforehand and rumor soon flashed around the Mediterranean rim that Piso had poisoned the young general at a banquet. If so, on whose orders?

For days on end, the entire Roman Empire mourned with incense and loud wailing at losing this charming, charismatic Roman equivalent of Alexander the Great. Tears flowed as crowds gathered to watch Agrippina, his weary, grief stricken widow, shuffle down the gangplank of a Syrian ship with three of her children — the youngest, six year-old Gaius Caligula, reminding everyone of their fallen hero. And as they began the slow funeral march to Rome, hundreds from all walks of life joined in the cortege.

And they began to talk as they marched. Where were Tiberius and his mother Livia? Yes, they'd written that they had stayed in Rome so as not to deflect from Germanicus' last glory, but was it really because joining the mourners would expose their guilt?

Tiberius never escaped the constant comparisons to his predecessor, and now this tragedy triggered more of them. Was Tiberius merely frugal like Augustus? No, he was a skinflint. Was he merely taciturn? No, he was morose — a misanthrope. Was it his disdain of maudlin flattery that made him wave off people who approached his litter? No, it was really his fear of assassination.

Tiberius had won neither the hearts of the Senate nor people of Rome, and it would seem that somewhere around this time he stopped caring about it. The emperor ceased his regular appearances in the Senate and soon treason trials were flourishing. So was a growing network freelance informants eager to catch some patrician or knight in an imperial sleight so as to be awarded a slice of the victim's estate.

As Tiberius approached age 65 he was ready to welcome the ambitions of a man who would quickly become "the partner of my labors" and in the process structurally change the way Rome chose and deposed its emperors. In A.D. 22 Tiberius appointed a new commander to head the Prætorian Guards, the elite corps that protected the imperial palace, put down any major disruptions in the city and provided military splendor at parades and festivals. Lucius Ælius Sejanus, a handsome, skillfully diplomatic young officer from one of Rome's best equestrian families, was able to cover his fierce ambitions with a hard-working dedication to fulfill the emperor's every need.

At the time Sejanus was appointed, Prætorian units were barracked throughout Rome like so many fire brigades — each accountable to their local commanding officer. Within a year, Sejanus had moved about these officers, bribing and otherwise winning their personal loyalty in exchange for even more luster to come under his patronage. During his second year Sejanus called upon Tiberius with an "administrative" plan. Feeding and equipping all those Prætorian garrisons was costly and inefficient, he noted. Wouldn't it make more sense — and improve morale — if all 14,000 or so soldiers were quartered in a single complex just outside the city walls? Just imagine the efficiencies stemming from a single parade ground and a common rostrum from which imperial orders could be read to one and all.

Tiberius bought the idea, and soon Sejanus commanded a single fighting force that could combat trouble anywhere in Rome — or start it, as history would show. The Prætorian prefect was now ready for his next move. In A.D. 26 he waited until Tiberius was in one of his melancholy moods, deploring the pile of dispatches piled up for his perusal and ruminating about his simpler, sunny days on Rhodes. Besides, his astrologers were indicating that he might not have much longer to live.

Well, why *not* find a sunny place like Rhodes? Sejanus intoned. Why not somewhere around every rich Roman's favorite playground, the Bay of Naples? Or, just to keep the crowds away, why not the sparkling Isle of Capri? Sejanus and his men could set up a post on the mainland and courier dispatches back and forth to the island. They could also interview the crushing number of ambassadors, senators and other supplicants who came seeking the emperor and row his chosen few back and forth.

One spring day in A.D. 26 Tiberius and small entourage of senators, old cronies, astrologers and entertainers left the imperial Palace overlooking the noisy Roman Forum and headed southwest in the guise of going to dedicate some temples in Campania. They did. But afterwards, the party departed from Surrentum to a newly expanded, renovated villa on Capri, never to return to Rome.

Sejanus was now the gatekeeper, and of course everyone from senators to governors to ship builders to those seeking tax collection contracts in the provinces would vie to see him — and pay for the privilege. He, a mere knight, was now entertained by patrician senators, and soon his statues were appearing in theaters and temples alongside the emperor's.

It's doubtful that Tiberius realized the full extent of his protector's new persona in Rome, but then the younger Drusus may have warned him. Drusus was the emperor's only son and his logical heir if it weren't for the fact that he personified the idle, rich Roman dandy and took little interest in government. He hated Sejanus, however, and had once slapped him across the face in a public argument and had never apologized.

Sejanus, always the outwardly dutiful, modest imperial servant, had borne Drusus' ire in silence, but the episode made his next plan all the more delicious. Drusus had married Livilla, a younger sister of the illustrious Germanicus. Livilla lived an unhappy life, both from grief over her brother and disgust at how her husband neglected her for horses and harlots. So when Sejanus came calling with his arsenal of charms, Livilla willingly received them. Soon the two were in a love pact: Sejanus would divorce his own wife and disown his two children if Livilla would find a way to poison Drusus. Then he would ask Tiberius for her hand, the old man would make him regent (if he didn't die first) and the two would become the de-facto rulers of Rome.

Soon Drusus succumbed to a mysterious wasting disease. Not long after his elaborate state funeral, and at approximately the time Jesus was crucified in far-off Jerusalem, the emperor received the letter that would hopefully culminate all the dreams and ambitions of Ælius Lucius Sejanus. Although he would gladly live the rest of his life "working, like any soldier for the emperor's safety," the letter read, Sejanus had hoped that he had "gained the greatest privilege — to be thought worthy of a marriage link with your house." Thus, "please bear in mind," he implored, "that if you should seek a husband for Livilla, consider your friend, who would gain nothing but prestige from the relationship."

In time Tiberius replied in an equivocating letter. Although larded with praise for his efficient commander, the emperor noted that Livilla and her mother Agrippina (the publicly adored widow of Germanicus) were already at loggerheads, and that such a marriage would "virtually split the imperial house in two." But be of good cheer, it concluded obliquely, for "I have other plans for you that are better not to mention at this time."

So Sejanus took a detour and set to work splitting the imperial house on his own. He soon convinced Tiberius that Agrippina was enlisting conspirators in a plot to crown her eldest son, Nero Cæsar. In a few months Præ-torians carried Agrippina off to exile on one rocky, bird-stained island and her Nero Cæsar on to another. A second son was thrown into a Roman jail and kept near starvation. Military comrades of Germanicus were given orders, signed by Tiberius, to commit suicide as were friends of the family and, mixed up in the process, various rivals of the Prætorian prefect himself.

Sejanus' only mistake was in underestimating the fearsome power that an emperor wielded in Rome, even if he happened to be an elderly recluse. Nor did he reckon how easy it is for an emperor to find another willing Sejanus. This is because sometime in late A.D. 30 Tiberius learned who had killed his son Drusus. How? A common version is that one day a maid in the imperial household on Palatine Hill was collecting trash from various rooms with instructions to retrieve and remove the ink from expensive papyrus so that it could be reused. Soon she found herself holding discarded drafts of letters Livilla had intended for Sejanus protesting his sudden aloofness and demanding to know when he would marry her. When she began to read references to the poisoning of Drusus, the alarmed maid stopped and marched straightaway to Antonia, the widow of Tiberius' brother and de-facto head of the immediate household. Antonia was always loyal to Tiberius, and so it wasn't long before she smuggled a letter to the emperor past Sejanus' gatekeepers that told him all he needed to know.

Tiberius was the sort who enjoyed extracting revenge with slow torture. It probably began with a letter to Sejanus saying that he was planning to adopt him as his grandson. Therefore, he had arranged his marriage to — not Livilla — but her teenaged daughter Helen! And he confided that this would lead to a new role for his "partner" in the future.

Sejanus never flinched. He thanked the emperor for his decision, which, after all, gave him the same objective even though it meant discarding Livilla and divorcing his own wife.

Now, having played one cruel joke, Tiberius took his time arranging another. In the spring of A.D. 31, as the followers of Jesus prepared for their first Passover without him, the Roman Senate was told to convene, not at its usual meetinghouse in the Forum, but at the temple of Apollo, which nearly abutted the palaces of Augustus and Tiberius on Palatine Hill. Sejanus was approaching the temple that morning when he was surprised to be greeted by his second in command, Nævius Sertorius Macro, and a small detachment of Guards from the Prætorian barracks. Macro replied cheerfully that Tiberius had sent him a letter to deliver to the Senate.

"Hmm, why didn't he ask *me*?" an unsettled Sejanus wondered aloud.

"Ah, because the letter is *about* you," the smiling Macro confided with

7

a wink. "I think you're about to be named Protector of the People and our next emperor."

With that, an elated Sejanus strode into the temple beaming. Macro entered almost unnoticed behind him and handed the letter to the presiding consul. Already, word of the "Protectorship" was spreading, as senators buzzed together and looked up at Sejanus with fawning salutes and nods of congratulations.

The emperor's letter began with the phony apology about poor health preventing his return to Rome, then swerved directly into a crescendo of charges against his Prætorian prefect. Erecting statues on his own behalf. Putting enemies to death. Then, even plotting against the writer himself. Indeed, the real reason for the emperor's not coming to Rome was that he didn't feel safe enough to travel in the company of his own Guards. He had no choice but to ask for the immediate arrest of Sejanus.

Now one could hear boos and hisses build among the men who until then would have been elated had Sejanus but smiled in their direction. The presiding officer, who alone had been included in the little game with Macro, called out the name of Sejanus sternly from the rostrum. Sejanus merely sat slack-jawed.

The consul called out again.

"Me? You mean *me?*" Sejanus stammered at last.

Now the seats around him were quickly being vacated. Other senators suddenly became indignant accusers. Macro's guards were summoned and the dazed Sejanus was marched off towards one of the dingy prisons that lay just outside the Forum. The crowd that always loiters about the Senate quickly picked up the scent and followed the victim with a pelting of mud and rotten vegetables.

Sometime that afternoon Sejanus was beheaded and the rest of his body left to be hacked apart and abused by the rabble. Three days later, when tradition required the remains to be dragged into the Tiber with a hook through the throat, only half the body remained and the skull was being used as a ball in a public gymnasium. And the streets were still littered with the broken limbs of the many statues of the man who had aspired to join the pantheon of Roman emperors.

But did this now bring tranquility? It only demonstrated who was the more treacherous between Tiberius and Sejanus. What followed was a new wave of treason trials and executions — this time against anyone thought to be a friend of Sejanus or beneficiary of his favors. It also extended to his political appointees in the provinces. And when news filtered into far-away Parthia about chaos in Rome, King Artabanus II saw it as further evidence that an aged, weakened Tiberius was losing his grip on his empire.

Just a few years before, Artabanus had been bullied by no less than the late Germanicus into confirming Roman sovereignty over the traditionally Parthian kingdom of Armenia. Now his eyes turned again toward Armenia. His boldness served as a cue for the rulers of smaller Arab client states that bordered on Roman Syria — and specifically Judea. This in turn forced the governor of Syria and his regional procurator of Judea to tighten their control of the Jewish power center, Jerusalem. And at the end of this domino chain were the rebel prophet Jesus and his tenacious followers. As the surviving adherents of The Way met in Jerusalem in the midst of the post-Sejanus persecutions, the Jewish temple authorities were tense and watchful. Other messianic pretenders had appeared in town and were executed for heresy, only to see their followers quickly melt away. Yet these people were back again, proclaiming a resurrection and a new beginning for Jews everywhere.

STANDING at the massive wooden gates of the largest, most thickly-walled temple fortress on earth, one would wonder why the protectors of Judaism would be overly concerned about a small, apparently peaceful sect of just a few hundred followers.

Was there a structure anywhere in the world more marbled and gleaming than the new temple at Jerusalem? There on the highest hill in the city which the smaller temple of Solomon once graced, atop a platform of massive but perfectly-cut stone blocks, stood a huge complex of outer buildings, courts and cloisters. At the entrance were giant doors bedecked with golden vine and grape clusters. The inner walls were hung with the largest Babylonian tapestry ever made. Outside, the gold-plated, white-marbled walls were so striking that pilgrims and tourists could see them from miles away as they wound their way up to the historic city.

In the large colonnaded outer court one would see men buying lambs, rams, birds and bullocks for various purification or thanksgiving rites. Seated inside the long colonnades were moneychangers, ready to convert any of the world's currencies into the shekel of Tyre (the busy port city to the northwest), the only coins acceptable for temple offerings.

In the middle of this massive Court of the Gentiles, as most called it, stood a walled rectangular building, running east to west and containing the Inner Precinct. Inside these high walls, roughly one-half the space was occupied by the Court of Women, which included 13 chests, each shaped like a ram's horn trumpet, to receive the various offerings. Several times a day the money in the rams' horns was transferred to one of the numerous treasury chambers built into the temple's inner forecourt. The Shekel Chamber, for instance, contained the half-shekel annual fee imposed on all Jewish men. The Chamber of Utensils housed the great store of gold and silver vessels for use in worship services. But there was also a Chamber of Secrets — so called because its function was to dispense money quietly to those who were poor, but "of good family."

The remainder of the Inner Precinct contained the shielded Court of the Priests, so named because only clergy could enter it. This enclosed the Sanctuary, and at the top of the T-shaped building, the Holy of Holies.

The temple was not only the center of Jewish religious life, but a symbol of the highly volatile mixture of people who lived in southern Syria. Yes, the majority were Jews, but in this region of barely 150 miles in length and half as wide dwelled Romans, Jews, Greeks, a Jewish royal family, a priesthood and three religious sects with political differences as well. Added to these were a constant influx of pilgrims and merchants. Hovering on the outskirts of Jerusalem were gangs of outlaws that ranged from political rebels to highway bandits.

Of these converging forces, Rome was the most important, but this did not mean that the Jewish-Roman bond was strong or friendly. Yes, there were reasons why this should have been so. Rome and its Syrian province certainly needed the support of Judea as a borderland. The Armenians to the north were no less menacing than the Parthians to the east, and the Arabs to the south seldom offered more than a symbolic nod of vassalship.

Judea also needed to be embraced for its shrewd merchants and protected for its economic contributions to the empire. Judean linen produced the whitest and softest of garments. Its balsam was used for everything from medicines to fodder on funeral pyres. And a rich Roman's dinner table would surely include Judean dates, wine and olive oil.

Thirdly, Jews were different than, say, Celts or Sythians because the latter tended to live in one region. Jews, although not originally at their own choosing, had formed strong communities in all corners of the empire and beyond. In the last census of Augustus there were some 4.6 million Roman citizens and an estimated 54 million persons of all kinds throughout the empire. Of the latter, roughly one in eight were Jews. The Jewish population of Alexandria alone was estimated at 500,000. Thus, for all of these reasons, Roman rulers had made concessions to Jews they wouldn't have considered for others. For example, the military police force was garrisoned in Cæsarea, some 60 miles from Jerusalem, so that the eagles atop its banners wouldn't be seen by people whose religion tolerated no images. Moreover, Jews were exempted from service among the Roman auxiliary troops, due in part to their proscription against fighting on the Sabbath.

Yet, these very concessions — along with the uniqueness of Jewish customs — fostered widespread enmity. Romans snickered at the male circumcision ritual. Many were affronted that Jews refused to attend games in the theater, that they cited their dietary laws as an excuse for declining a dinner invitation, and that they worshipped a god with no name or form yet would pay not even a passing nod to the shrines of other peoples. This, in turn, contributed in Tiberius' time to the uneasy suspicion that the Jews would again welcome the Parthians if an enticing opportunity arose.

The temple symbolized this division just as it reflected Jewish glory. To Romans nothing was more insolent than to observe a religious temple in the process of being rebuilt into an impregnable fortress. And nothing was more irritating than to watch enormous Jewish wealth being amassed daily from the taxes and ritual fees imposed by temple priests on millions of Jews around the world.

But the Jews had their own good reasons why the bonds to Rome were in such constant tatters. Nothing was more hatefully symbolic of the yoke they lived under than the Fortress of Antonia that loomed ominously over the temple. Built by Herod to please his Roman patron, the 375-foot-long colossus housed a fortress, barracks and prison.

Its three towers rose up from the massive building with porticos that looked out directly over the large Court of the Gentiles. It meant that a Roman detachment, up from Cæsarea to police a festival, could maintain constant surveillance on almost everything going on inside the temple complex.

The Jewish-Roman relationship alone might have made a cauldron boil, but there were many more ingredients to be added to the stewpot that was Jerusalem. The second was a truncated royal family and fragmented rule. Herod created the problem by having ten wives and so many sons as to befuddle even a census taker. Added to this confusion was the fact that while Herod was mainly Idumean, his chief wife, Mariamme, represented the Jewish royal Hasmonean line. Another wife was Samaritan. The leading Jewish families viewed Idumeans and Samaritans with equal disdain. The predictable result of having this poisonous concoction of people all living within one household was an endless profusion of bickering, plots and conspiracies in which countless offspring and relatives were taken off by a king who could be heard raging "No one will escape who thirsts for my blood!"

It was perhaps Augustus himself who best summed up the situation when hearing of yet another son's execution. "It is safer to be Herod's pig than his son," the emperor lamented.

In the end it was not a plot that killed the aging despot after 36 years of rule, but a growing, agonizing "rage" in his lower quarters that his physicians' baths and balms could not overcome. The constant palace turmoil in Jerusalem had so undermined Augustus' confidence that he divided the old king's lands into three jurisdictions in 4 B.C. Archelaus, whose mother was a Samaritan, was named ethnarch over Judea and Samaria. Next, Galilee to the north and Perea, an elongated strip of land on the east bank of the Jordan, went to another son, Antipas, along with the still-lower title of tetrarch. Thirdly, Gaulanitus and Trachonitus, two even smaller districts just south of the venerable city of Damascus, were given to another son, Philip.

At the time of Tiberius, both Philip and Antipas were still ruling — and competently, by all accounts. Antipas, known as a fair and peaceful man, had managed to keep the rambunctious Galileans in check by killing two birds with one stone. To show his devotion to the emperor, he built an entirely new city on the southern shores of Lake Galilee and named it Tiberias. To coax leading Galilean families to live there he gave them land and even built some of them fine houses at his own expense.

But Archelaus had not fared well in Judea and Samaria. The two largest pieces of Herod's former kingdom had gobbled up more than their fair share of taxes, and now with a reduced domain, the new ethnarch was compelled to curtail many of this father's public works programs, which in turn caused unemployment and unrest.

And the fact that Archelaus was half Samaritan and half Idumean didn't help his standing with the Jewish populace. In 5 B.C., his first Passover as ethnarch, crowds in Jerusalem rioted. Archelaus panicked, called to the Roman garrison for help, and some 3,000 people lost their lives either fleeing or fighting back. Soon the uprisings had spread to the entire region and the governor of Syria was forced to move in with a large Army. Order wasn't restored until part of the temple had been set afire and its treasury looted.

Looted? Or justifiably "appropriated" by the Romans to pay for the high cost of an unplanned police action? In either case, it's clear that all this turmoil was too much for Augustus. The emperor ordered the hapless Archelaus to take up a new life of exile in southern Gaul and brought Judea and Samaria under direct Roman administration. After a census to determine the proper tax base, the province would then be administered by a series of military prefects, or procurators.

Let us now add some more spices to the stewpot called Jerusalem. We have next the high priest of the temple, the symbol of the Jewish religion, protector of all temple rites and embodiment of the Jewish character. Among the traits that a good Jew should be known for were love of family, personal dignity, adherence to Mosaic Law, tithing to the temple and — almost as important — avoidance of degenerate outside influences.

In its ancient and purest form, the priestly caste centered on a few families, such as the descendants of Zadok, who had been high priest a thousand years earlier under David and Solomon. Closely interwoven with these were the Levites, who were charged with maintaining the temple, including the provision of music and money changing services as well as disposition of hides from all sacrificial animals. Together, members of these powerful, elite families traditionally made up the ruling council, or Sanhedrin.

But the rule of Herod had altered that pattern and created new tensions. By the time of Tiberius, the Hasmonean hold on the priesthood had been broken several times by Herod, his successors, and now the Roman procurators, so that the number of priestly families were more numerous and no longer united by the same ancient ties.

The Sanhedrin had also changed — or had been shattered. King Herod had begun his reign by murdering most of its members and reserving important decisions to his own circle of advisors. He then enticed the return of many of the wealthy families who had been carried off to Babylonia in the Diaspora more than 500 years before. Now accustomed to life in an eastern court, they were more amenable to Herod's Hellenized way of life than the rigid traditionalists they replaced.

The Sanhedrin of Tiberius' day had expanded to 71 members, yet its responsibilities had been severely curtailed. Although the wealthy priestly families still dominated, they now formed what amounted to a party known as the Sadduccees. Increasingly questioning their authority and rivaling their power was a newer school of thinkers called Pharisees. Many were sages and teachers. Few were wealthy and most, as one record shows, plied such common trades as stonemason, charcoal burner and public letter writer. Rather than focus their lives on temple ritual, the typical Pharisee adhered to a detailed set of religious laws governing his daily conduct. Of these, the most important were tithing and maintaining purity of dietary habits and personal cleanliness.

Another difference between the two chief sects is that Pharisees believed in life after death. A priest of the day wrote that Pharisees "believe that souls have an immortal vigor to them, and that under the earth there will be rewards or punishments, according as they have lived virtuously or viciously in this life; and the latter are to be detained in everlasting prison."

In contrast, he added, Sadduccees believe "that souls die with the bodies." Nor, he said, "do they regard the observation of anything besides what the law enjoins them; for they think it an instance of virtue to dispute with those teachers of philosophy whom they frequent."

A smaller, softer voice in Jewish life were the Essenes, men who renounced wealth and women to live apart in wilderness compounds for the most part. There they rejoiced in being free of all the travails and tensions that swirled about. Suffice it to say that they shunned temple rites and tended to remain out of the center of the storm.

Our pot is now boiling, but we have still more herbs and spices to add. Let us now stir in the Greeks who inhabited either whole towns or enclaves in Jewish cities, who sneered at the strange customs of Jews and felt outraged that they were considered *am ha-aretz*, meaning that a pious Jew who accidentally touched them would have to undergo a purification ritual.

Now add some Syrians, Egyptians, the endless stream of traders and a half million slaves. Then assume it is Passover time in April or perhaps the Festival of Feasts 50 days later and we can add at least a million more persons to the city. With most of them either elbowing one another at the temple or fighting for attention at the taverns or standing in line for the latrines or listening to fiery speeches by rebels and would-be messiahs, the cauldron now begins to bubble and hiss.

The final ingredient is but one man, yet quite enough to ignite the whole potion as if it consisted of pure pitch. And this is the Roman procurator. Yes, Rome's objectives were his, too — order and taxes — but a procurator brought his own persona and agenda as well.

The first three procurators under Augustus and Tiberius were not necessarily cruel or violent, even though all did disrupt Jewish life by arbitrarily changing high priests as often as suited their own ends. But a sharply different era would unfold in A.D. 26 with the appointment of Pontius Pilate. Because Tiberius, unlike his predecessors, was known for keeping governors and procurators in office for extended terms, and because the emperor had just gone off to Capri hoping to avoid being pestered by far-off personnel problems, this ill-tempered and insensitive bully would hold his office for ten tumultuous years.

In Pilate's very first year he decided to test Jewish law by sending a large contingent of his troops from Cæsarea to Jerusalem for winter quartering. Moving by night, the column entered the city with Tiberius' effigies parading alongside the ensigns. Because Jewish law forbade even the making of images, other procurators had taken care to remove all such effigies before entering Jerusalem.

As dawn broke the next morning and the Jews of Jerusalem yawned and looked out their windows, they were astounded to see Roman images poking out from atop the Fortress of Antonia. Their protests to the commanding officer went unheeded. Angered even more, a disheveled deputation of religious leaders and hangers-on walked the 60 miles to Cæsarea and beseeched Pilate himself for permission to remove them. For five days they persevered in their pleas and lamentations. Each day they were refused on grounds that removing the images would be an affront to Tiberius Cæsar.

By the sixth day the procurator was seething. When he heard the Jews from Jerusalem were at the barracks doors again, the procurator ordered his soldiers to have concealed weapons at the ready when he came to sit on his judgment seat to hear the day's cases. When the Jews came to petition him again, he signaled the soldiers to surround them and draw their swords. Now Pilate informed them that they faced immediate death if they didn't stop bothering him and go home.

But the procurator had not expected what came next. The Jews threw themselves on the ground. Laying their necks bare to the swords of Roman soldiers, they vowed that they would accept death willingly rather than have their laws transgressed. In a surprising decision, Pilate relented and commanded that the images be carried back to Cæsarea.

But Pilate hadn't had an epiphany about respecting Jewish customs. For some months he had been planning to build a new aqueduct to bring more water to Jerusalem, and the procurator sent more men to seize a cache from the temple to pay for it. This time, many thousands of people gathered to plead that he abandon the idea and restore the money.

It was also a festival time, and some impassioned orators hurled insults at Pilate in the course of denouncing the aqueduct project. But, unlike the episode at Cæsarea, Pilate offered no warning this time. Soldiers in disguise had circulated among the crowd, and on Pilate's signal they unsheathed their swords and hacked a great many to pieces before the terrified Jews dispersed. Among them were many Galileans, who were often in the forefront of sedition in their homeland and rioting at festivals. And in this case, one account has it that the soldiers "mingled the blood (of the Galileans) with their sacrifices."

SOME 50 DAYS after the crucifixion of Jesus — probably May 25, A.D. 30 — approximately 120 close adherents to The Way were back in Jerusalem among the pilgrims streaming in for the Festival of Weeks — or simply "Pentecost" — that marked the end of the grain harvest. The eleven disciples probably occupied the same "upper room" in which they'd met with Jesus. The rest made do in private houses and public inns. During the days they prayed together at the Portico of Solomon in the Temple. But as dusk came on they would meet in groups for a common meal, no doubt using the same room where the disciples stayed and where Jesus had asked them to share bread and wine in remembrance of the fateful day that lay ahead.

Pilate had long since returned to Cæsarea, and none of this activity could have been enough to arouse temple authorities. For one thing, those of The Way were hardly wealthy or powerful or otherwise noteworthy as individuals. Almost all were small shopkeepers, craftsmen, women, unemployed laborers and even slaves. And they had to spend more time scraping together the means of survival than they could inciting rebellion.

Perhaps the city officials had also come to realize in the eerie calm following the calamitous Passover of the previous year that the message of Jesus these people prayed over was hardly seditious. After all, he had told the temple authorities himself that Cæsar was entitled to his taxes and temporal allegiance. Nor had he encouraged slaves to rebel against their masters. Indeed, he had taught his followers to love their neighbors as themselves and to turn the other cheek should anyone strike them.

But Rome and Jerusalem were wrong. What began to take place was perhaps as imperceptible to them as a tide changing. When the tide of history changes, most of us are too busy working, eating and sleeping to notice the moment an advance ceases and the receding begins. But something like this is what began to happen in Jerusalem. First, it is clear that these early followers of The Way had no doubt that they had witnessed miracles. The Galileans who joined Jesus at the beginning were not attracted by wealth or promises of conquest. They could have left him during any of the years that led up to this Passover, but always they remained devoted because of the healings and other miracles they saw almost daily. Those who had seen Jesus only at the Passover in Jerusalem had also witnessed miracles — from his healings to the disappearance of the sun as he expired on the cross.

Secondly, a great many people had seen Jesus reappear afterwards. Crowds had cheered as he had entered the holy city for Passover, and many thronged about as he taught in the temple. Just as many had seen him taunted as he staggered through the packed streets of Jerusalem beneath his heavy timber cross and then witnessed the agonizing death of the crucified. One such eyewitness was the disciple John, perhaps the youngest of the twelve who were with Jesus from the beginning of his ministry. Writing in his own gospel more than 60 years later, he testified that when he and Peter had come early to the limestone cave that served as his tomb, they had found it empty and had gone away in confusion and grief. Soon afterward, John reported, two of Jesus' women followers had come to prepare his body according to the proper Jewish rites. Upon also finding the tomb empty, they had begun to sob uncontrollably when suddenly standing before them was a man whom they at first mistook as a gardener. But they soon realized it was Jesus. After he consoled and reassured them, they ran back to the other followers to report what had happened.

John wrote that on the evening of the same day the followers were hiding from the Jewish authorities in a locked room somewhere when suddenly they found Jesus standing amidst them. John says that Jesus calmed their fears, then gathered them closely and breathed on them in order to "receive the Holy Spirit" so that they could go out and forgive the sins of others.

At one point in their early flight from the Jewish authorities, the small band of Jesus' followers eventually reassembled at Mount Olivet, about a day's journey from Jerusalem. There, John reported, Jesus again appeared in their midst and charged them to return to Jerusalem. When asked if that meant he would restore the kingdom to Israel, Jesus said it was not for men to know what events and what dates God has fixed by his authority. But he declared that they would receive power from the Holy Spirit to be his witnesses in Jerusalem, Judea and "to the end of the earth." Only experiences like these can explain why this group of faithful followers, almost all of them Galileans, soon returned to Jerusalem with a new and powerful resolve.

Indeed, it was only by returning to Jerusalem — as had Jesus — that The Way could appeal to the Jewish people and their leaders. Now that their witness to the resurrection had vindicated Jesus' claims, they felt authorized to urge it vigorously upon the leaders and people. The Way did not seek merely to win scattered individuals. In Jesus they now saw the fulfillment of God's promise to Israel.

There was a third force as well that changed the tide. Some of these same fishermen, tradesmen, slaves and sinners began to display the power of healing.

If you are looking for a 21st century explanation, you will not find it here. One can just report what respected and reliable people wrote. And this brings us to the Pentecost of May A.D. 30. After scattering from the Passover and spending many days in confusion, then returning to preach and pray in the stronghold of organized Judaism, the Feast of Weeks marked a new turn.

The followers were meeting in the same "upper room" as usual when something like a gale of wind swirled down on them, and they recognized it as the Holy Spirit. Soon they were all speaking loudly in a cacophonous chorus of different tongues. Pilgrims and travelers began to gather on the street below to see what the commotion was all about. Some scoffed that it was a drunken rabble, but the morning hour was much too early to make that a logical reason. Others might have compared the noise to the hysteria that would grip crowds during the rites of Bacchus or the frenzy some people worked themselves up to when the goddess Cybele was paraded through the streets at her festivals. But just as many in the street below began to believe they were hearing a din of foreign tongues, because the crowd now included Parthians, Mesopotamians, Egyptians, Romans and others there at Festival time. And many swore in amazement that these unlettered Galileans were shouting in their own native languages.

Before long one of the Galileans stood on the upstairs porch and began to address the people below. Peter, appearing with the ten others who had been with Jesus since the beginning, declared that what they were hearing had all been foretold by the Jewish prophet Joel when he said in part:

> And in the last days it shall be that God declares,
> that I will pour out my Spirit upon all flesh,
> and your sons and your daughters shall prophesy,
> and your young men shall see visions,
> and your old men shall dream dreams;
> yea, and on my menservants and maidservants in those days
> I will pour out my Spirit and they shall prophesy.[1]

Peter until then had been a fisherman, untutored in rhetoric. But with a newly discovered passion he boldly proclaimed that Jesus had worked God's wonders on earth, had been unjustly crucified and had been raised from the dead. "Let all the house of Israel therefore know assuredly that God has made him both Lord and Christ, this Jesus whom you crucified."

Peter went on to urge people to repent and to "save yourselves from this crooked generation." And when he then beseeched them to repent and be baptized in the name of Jesus for forgiveness of their sins, it is said that more than 3,000 people did so that day.

From then on the numbers who prayed in the temple every day multiplied. So did miracles performed by the disciples. Many followers, believing that Jesus would return momentarily, sold all their possessions and distributed them to those in need. They invited others into their homes and gladly shared their meals with them.

Life would also change for leaders of The Way. At or just before this time the disciples had brought their ranks back to twelve, choosing one Matthias by lot to replace the fallen Judas. Moreover, there had also evolved a group of "elders" who were simply known as The Seventy, no doubt emulating the same number who served as advisors and adjudicators to Moses in the desert days or to the high priest of Jesus' day.

The need for a ruling body of seventy confirms that the number of converts in Jerusalem had grown considerably. At the same time, the twelve apostles were finding it too burdensome to preach as well as see to the tasks of distributing food, clothing and the like to their followers. So they met and formed a Council of Seven, headed by a young, energetic Hellene named Stephen, to administer their affairs so that they could devote all their time to spreading the word.

Now Peter and others were spending even more time each day preaching at the temple in the Portico of Solomon. Reports of their healings were so widespread that it is impossible to dismiss all of them as fabrications. The following is typical, however. Peter and John were going to the temple at the ninth hour when a man, lame from birth, was carried to the gates to take up his daily position as an alms seeker. Seeing the two apostles of Christ about to enter the gates, he asked for alms. As Peter fixed his gaze at him, John said, "Look at us." When the man did so, perhaps expecting to receive a coin, Peter said, "I have no silver or gold, but I give you what I have. In the name of Jesus Christ, walk."

Peter took him by the right hand and immediately his feet and ankles were strong. Leaping up, he walked and entered the temple with them, praising God all the way. Many people there knew him, for he was over 40 and had been at his begging station for many years. Several people followed the three to the Portico of Solomon, where Peter began urging them to repent and show the same faith that made the beggar well.

Why did the disciples choose to preach at the temple when they might have chosen a place farther from the eyes of the authorities? One of many reasons would be that at the temple they would find people free from their daily cares and in a frame of mind more suitable for preaching and discussion. However, a more powerful reason is that the disciples saw the risen Jesus as the rightful Lord of the Jews and one who would come soon to assume control of the temple. In short, the temple was the central place of Jewish religious life and they had every right to be there.

But, yes, these new preachers did draw unwelcome attention, for on the same day he healed the crippled beggar, Peter's preachings were officially challenged. It was now early evening, and the crowd around the disciples had swelled to about 5,000 when the head of temple security, followed by several priests and Sadduccees, abruptly scattered everyone and took Peter and John off to prison.

The next morning the two apostles found themselves confronting Ananias the high priest and several members of the Sanhedrin. "By what power did you do this?" they wanted to know.

Peter answered firmly: "If we are being examined today concerning a good deed done a cripple, then let it be known that it has been done in the name of Jesus Christ of Nazareth, whom you crucified, whom God raised from the dead. By him this man is standing before you well." And he went on to preach that salvation of all could come only through Jesus.

On one hand, the Jewish elders were taken aback by Peter's boldness and self-assurance. On the other hand, they quickly realized that he was uneducated and from some rustic backwater fishing village in Galilee. After leaving the defendants so they could confer in private, the elders agreed that it was impossible to deny the healing because it was witnessed by so many. So they agreed simply to chastise the two defendants against preaching again in the name of Jesus.

Summoned back and told this, Peter and John quickly retorted, "We cannot but speak of what we have seen and heard." By this time a crowd of Jesus' followers had begun to gather outside. So with another threat not to preach again, the elders let the disciples go.

Now the number of believers multiplied like never before, and many from surrounding cities would bring their sick to the Portico of Solomon to be healed by the disciples. Even those who feared the authorities too much to go there would carry their sick out into the streets in hopes that Peter would walk by and cast his shadow on them.

At seeing the crowds increase, the leaders of the Sadduccees grew more incensed than ever. So this time they had Peter and John thrown into the common prison. Late that night, the gospels say, an angel of God opened the prison doors, telling the two disciples, "Go to the temple and speak to the people all the words of this life."

They did so and were there by daybreak, teaching again. When the Sanhedrin gathered later that morning to decide the fate of the two men they thought were in jail, the temple security police astounded them by reporting that, although the prison doors were locked with guards standing outside, they found no one inside. Then someone rushed into the meeting hall to report, "The men you put in prison are standing in the temple and teaching the people!"

When the two were at last brought before the Sanhedrin and asked why they persisted, Peter answered that "we are witnesses to these [deeds of Jesus] and so is the Holy Spirit whom God has given to those who obey him."

By this time the elders would have condemned the upstarts to death had they not been stopped by Gamaliel. As both head of the temple rabbinical college and one of the Sanhedrin's most respected members, Gamaliel asked that the defendants be removed so the council could again confer privately. Once they were alone, Gamaliel calmed his colleagues by citing similar threats in prior years and what had become of them given a little patience by the elders. He recalled a rebel named Theudas, who had once attracted some 400 brigands, all of whom had scattered eventually once Theudas was killed. Then he recalled Judas, a famous Galilean strongman who, just after Herod's death, had incited a rebellion because Augustus had ordered a census. Again, said Gamaliel, "once he perished, all who followed him soon scattered."

Gamaliel's advice was to "Leave these men alone. If this undertaking is of men it will fail," he said. "But if it is of God, you will not be able to overthrow them."

The perplexed Sanhedrin members could think of nothing better, so they took Gamaliel's advice and let Peter and John go — but only after a severe beating. This, however, the disciples bore with resolution, rejoicing that they had been deemed worthy enough to suffer in the name of Jesus. They continued preaching every day, and more people than ever came to hear them.

BEFORE WE leave this early period, here is a postscript to ponder. Did word of Jesus' deeds — or at least his Passover "disturbances" — ever reach Tiberius on his rocky perch 1,700 miles away? It's an intriguing question that scholars have largely ignored. Logic alone would indicate that it was probably so. At this time, the Roman governing network abroad was anchored by a hundred or so client kings, provincial governors, procurators, senatorial proconsuls and military post commanders. If each one sent reports back to Rome on an average of once a week, the emperor might find himself confronted with a dozen-plus dispatches a day in addition to the various petitions from everyone from client kings to Roman citizens.

A formidable reading task, yes, but not overwhelming for an emperor with a bevy of secretaries and petitions clerks. The question then becomes: would Pontius Pilate, the man in charge of controlling the religious center of seven million Jews and the richest temple on earth, be likely to report on major events there — namely the turbulence created by a charismatic preacher during the Passover of A.D. 30 and Pilate's successful quelling of a possible rebellion?

Quite probably, yes.

A second answer is that Eusebius himself says so. Eusebius was the bishop of Cæsarea from A.D. 313 until his death in 339. He lived through the last days of Christian persecutions and during the critical period when the emperor Constantine declared himself a Christian and intimated that his subjects had better do so as well if they knew what was good for them. Eusebius was a prolific writer, known best for his *History of the Church*, and his works reveal an earnest, fair-minded scholar trying faithfully to record and synthesize the writings of church pioneers as he looked back over 300 years. Writes the bishop:

> The story of the resurrection from the death of our Savior Jesus, already the subject of general discussion all over Palestine, was accordingly communicated by Pilate to the Emperor Tiberius. For Pilate knew all about Christ's supernatural deeds, and especially how… he had risen from the dead and was now generally believed to be a god. It is said that Tiberius referred the report to the Senate, which rejected it. The apparent reason was that they had gone over the matter before, for the old law said that no one could be regarded by the Romans as a god unless by vote and decree of the Senate. The real reason was that no human decision or commendation was required for the saving and teaching of the divine message. In this way the Roman council rejected the report…but Tiberius made no change in his attitude and formed no evil designs against the teachings of Christ.[2]

Tertullian, a Roman-Christian scholar writing nearly a hundred years before Eusebius, takes it further by insisting that:

> Tiberius, when a report [of Jesus and his teachings] reached him from Palestine, where it originated, communicated it to the Senate, making it clear to them that he favored the doctrine. The Senate, however, because it had not examined the doctrine for themselves, rejected it. But Tiberius stuck to his own view and threatened to execute any who accused the Christians.[3]

On one hand, there is no particular reason to contest the integrity of Eusebius or Tertullian. Moreover, Tiberius was an eager devotee of prophecies and astrological predictions. On the other hand, because Tiberius was also in the midst of a ruthless purge that devoured senators week after week, it is difficult to imagine any proposal — or even harmless whim — that the cowed conscript fathers would not indulge.

However, the notion of Tiberius at least *knowing* about Jesus is made more plausible when one considers the relative ease of communications within the empire.

Consider first that the imperial palace in Rome (even with Tiberius absent) was a beehive of gossip and information for the whole Mediterranean world. Client kings routinely sent their children as hostages to be reared in the royal household and steeped in Roman culture. Dinner on any given evening would witness the future rulers of places like Parthia, Cappadocia, Gaul and Judea jostling and joshing one another at tables as their elders dined nearby on couches. There, the adult Roman rulers and their guests traded the Empire's most precious commodity — news from the provinces that would enable them to be first to fatten their purses or fend off any threats to their dominions.

Now consider how this information network might have learned of a related event — the death of John the Baptist. In the latter twenties A.D., the elite social circle on Palatine Hill included two grown grandchildren of Herod the Great: the clever, entertaining Herod Agrippa I and his haughty, ambitious sister, Herodias. One day Herod the Great's son, Antipas, the ethnarch of Galilee and Perea, arrived on one of his many visits to Rome and fell head over heels for Herodias. No matter that she was the daughter of his half-brother, which made her a niece. And no matter that he was already married to the daughter of Aretus, the Arabian king of neighboring Nabatea.

Passengers could take their pick of dozens of ships sailing from Italy to Cæsarea, and travelers soon spread word through Judea that Antipas was about to discard his Arabian wife and put Jewish croplands squarely in the path of revengeful Nabatean marauders. Even worse, Antipas was defying Mosaic Law to marry his niece, and this was too much for John the Baptist. John, the wandering hermit-prophet who appeared from the desert to baptize the repentant in the Jordan River and herald the Messiah's arrival, now thundered to hundreds on the riverbank that Herodias and Antipas deserved God's vengeance for their contemptible affront on God's law. And he repeatedly demanded that they repent of their sins.

Instead, Antipas had John clapped in the prison at Mecherus, at the outer reaches of his realm, to keep him as far as possible from his followers. All this came at the height of John's ministry and in the same year (A.D. 28 or 29) that he had baptized Jesus in the Jordan.

Not long after John was thrown in the dungeon, Herodias made good on her end of the bargain by traveling from Rome to Perea along with her teenaged daughter Salome. Since her new husband's birthday fell soon afterwards, she sponsored a sumptuous banquet to honor the occasion. When the meal was completed and the entertainment began, Antipas gazed at the fetching Salome and asked if she would dance for him on his birthday. When Salome demurred, her new stepfather, doubtless flushed with wine, blurted out that he would honor any request if she would only take a little whirl about the floor.

At this point Herodias leaned over to Salome and whispered something in her ear. It must have been so because it would be difficult to imagine an innocent young thing forming such a horrible thought: She would dance if her step-father would promise to produce the head of John the Baptist on a serving platter.

Salome — or rather, Herodias — soon got her wish that night. The king would regret it in blood spilled many times over, as will be seen later. But the purpose here is to demonstrate that, with Jewish royals constantly flitting back and forth between Rome, how likely it was that such a shocking episode would have wound up as a delicious tidbit at the table in the Palatine palace of Tiberius.

If the Romans had discussed the fate of John the Baptist in A.D. 29, then why not the astounding miracles — and fate — of Jesus of Nazareth just a year later?

A.D.
33–36

By A.D. 33 Tiberius had turned 74. The longer he lived, the more he clung to his rocky retreat, the more he relied on astrologers for advice and the more rumors swept Rome about his compulsive perversions. One story whispered about was that the emperor commandeered local children and compelled them to frequent his daily bath. Other stories emerged from visitors about long tortures performed on captives until finally discarding them into the blue sea below, where marines waited in an open boat and dashed their brains to pulp with oars. All that Romans knew for certain was that the purges of everyone associated with the fallen Sejanus only intensified, with the new Prætorian prefect Macro now the eager instrument of terror. The Roman historian Tacitus writes that in the year A.D. 33 not a day passed without at least one execution a day — sometimes 20.

It was a massacre. Without discrimination of sex or age, eminence or obscurity, there they lay, strewn about — or in heaps. Relatives and friends were forbidden to stand by or lament them, or even gaze for long. Guards surrounded

them, spying on their sorrow, and escorted the rotting bodies until, dragged into the Tiber, they floated away or
grounded — with none to cremate or touch them. Terror
had paralyzed human sympathy. The rising surge of brutality drove compassion away.[4]

Or as graffiti in the streets of Rome would sum it up:

No more the happy Golden Age we see;
The Iron's come, and sure to last with thee.
Instead of the wine he thirsted for before,
He wallows now in floods of human gore.[5]

Agrippina and her eldest son barely clung to life in exile, but Tiberius continued to lash out at the ghost of Germanicus. As already reported, Drusus
Cæsar, Agrippina's second eldest son, had been kept in wretched near-starvation in an attic somewhere in or near the Palatine palace. The reason was
simply that had Sejanus been able to thwart Tiberius and launch a claim to
the throne, the emperor was ready to rally the people by proclaiming the
son of Germanicus as his new heir-apparent. Now Drusus Cæsar was no
longer needed.

For eight days he had staved off death by gnawing the stuffing of his
mattress. All the while, two slaves were ordered to harass and strike him
whenever he tried to move about his room. They also recorded the victim's
last hours.

Feigning madness, Drusus Cæsar screamed apparently
delirious maledictions upon Tiberius. Then, despairing of
his life, he uttered an elaborate and formal curse: that for
deluging his family in blood, for massacring his daughter-in-law, nephew and grandchildren, Tiberius would
pay the penalty due to his house — to his ancestors and
descendants.[6]

The death of Drusus was followed by the self-starvation of his mother Agrippina in her treeless rocky islet not far from the gaze of Tiberius in his Villa Jovis.
It is ironic — or perhaps a self-fulfilling prophecy — that now living on
Capri with the emperor was none other than Gaius Caligula, the youngest
of the Germanicus-Agrippina male offspring. The only other possible successor
was Tiberius Gemullus, the son of the Drusus whom Sejanus and Livilla had

poisoned to death. But Gaius Caligula was 21 and Tiberius' grandson Gemul-lus a mere child of seven. And if anyone had asked the rabble of Rome whom it preferred, the resounding cheer would be, "Give us Gaius!"

Born in the German winter quarters of Germanicus' legions, he soon grew to a toddler who would remind the Roman soldiers of the children they had left at home. When one of them made Gaius a pair of miniature military boots, he soon became known more by the nickname of Caligula, the Latin word for "Little Boots." Overindulged by soldiers, an equally fawning poet would later write,

> Born in a camp, reared with soldiers, he;
> A sign assured he would a ruler be.[7]

But Tiberius and his handful of cronies on Capri undoubtedly had a dif-ferent view of this gawky, blond but already thin-haired young man. He was a master in the art of survival. His grandfather Drusus, brother of Tiberius, had been poisoned. So had his father Germanicus and his uncle Drusus, the emperor's son. Of his eight siblings, three had died in infancy. His two re-maining brothers were imprisoned and starved to death by Tiberius. All this he watched quietly, just as he did when his mother was exiled, when she pleaded for freedom after the death of Sejanus, and finally when she aban-doned all hope and allowed herself to waste away by starvation.

What Gaius *did* do was cater to every mood and whim of his host on Capri. One wag summed it up by saying that "there never was a better slave or a worse master." Even Tiberius himself would make cruel jokes that he was "rearing a viper for the Roman people and a python for the world."

The reign of terror that swept Rome happened to coincide with a financial crisis that reverberated throughout the Roman Empire. Its roots probably went back to Augustus' theory that minting more money and keeping in-terest rates low would stimulate business and prolong prosperity. Tiberius, in time, became convinced that the best guarantee of national stability is frugal government spending. So he never sponsored public games and re-stored only two buildings during his entire reign. He kept veterans waiting for their retirement bonuses (which led them to mischief in the provinces) and delayed sending provincial appointees their salaries (which made them more susceptible to bribes from client rulers and merchants).

The result by A.D. 34 was a treasury surplus exceeding 2.7 billion sesterces. The other side of the coin was a dearth of circulating currency, worsened by an outflow of money eastward for everything from Egyptian wheat to

Judean linen. Prices fell and interest rates rose. Debtors began suing lenders, citing a long-standing but much ignored law that had capped interest rates at 5%. Financial houses, for fear of prosecution, practically ceased all lending activities but continued to call in overdue loans.

The Senate, long since transformed into suffering sycophants and incapable of innovation, only worsened the situation. It voted that to check the flow of capital abroad, two-thirds of every member's personal wealth must be invested in Italian land. But once again the sheep had managed to shear themselves. Senators found themselves calling in loans and foreclosing on mortgages in order to raise cash to buy Italian land. When two major banks suddenly announced bankruptcy, they sent back tidal waves that capsized businesses from Tyre to Alexandria to Carthage that had depended on them for working capital.

To his credit, the emperor finally signaled from Capri that he would intervene by creating a group of temporary state banks and distributing a hundred million sesterces in the form of three-year, interest-free loans. This halted the upward pressure on interest rates, which coaxed money out of hiding places and gradually restored business confidence.

The biggest casualties of the financial panic were Jews — and for the most bizarre of reasons. For many years, it was almost fashionable for well-bred Roman women to embrace Judaism (probably along with pagan religions) because they were attracted to its high moral standards and emphasis on family values. In A.D. 34 a certain young financier in Judea (his name isn't recorded) was deported on several counts of fraud. He next turned up in Rome as a "rabbi" who tutored wealthy women in the laws of Moses — and the wealthier the better. Novitiates were required to send as much gold and jewels by ship to the temple in Jerusalem in order to demonstrate their ardor for Judaism. The rabbi and three equally unsavory characters would then intercept the precious cargo before it was loaded and spend the proceeds in who knows what debaucheries.

This went on unnoticed by Roman officialdom until the rabbi enrolled one Fulvia, described by Tacitus as a "woman of great dignity." But her exceedingly wealthy husband was also an old crony of Tiberius, and when word spread that four drunks were bragging in taverns about Fulvia being their biggest mark to date, the emperor received a quick, direct appeal for help.

Tiberius characteristically overreacted to perceived threats against his own welfare, and his response to Fulvia's plight was no different. He not only had the evildoers tracked down and arrested, he also ordered all Jews banished from Rome for good measure. Whether the emperor may have also seen Jewish bankers as contributors to the financial crisis and found the "rabbi" an excuse to unleash revenge is probable but impossible to prove. But this is fact: as the Jewish population was packing up and preparing to leave its quarter along the Tiber River, the Senate consuls had 4,000 Jewish men rounded up and sent off to the island of Sardinia for a road building project.

AT THE OTHER end of the Mediterranean basin, rivals of Rome were divining the economic and political omens: an emperor who was hated, the Senate decimated by repression, an economy shaken by chaos and Jews in official disfavor. All of above certainly appealed to Aretus, the king of Nabatea, which clung to the length of fertile Judea and Perea, only 30 miles from Jerusalem in places, before it gave way to miles of hilly desert to the south and west. As explained a chapter ago, it was Aretus who had wed his daughter to Herod Antipas, ethnarch of Galilee and Perea, in a gesture of friendship to his Jewish neighbors. And it was that daughter who had been discarded and sent back home in disgrace after Antipas wooed and wed his niece, Herodias.

Aretus was insulted, but his daughter's tears fell at a most convenient time for revenge. The more feeble and erratic he perceived Tiberius to be, the bolder Aretus became. His first move was to assume control over part of the Decapolis, that loose collage of ten Hellenistic city-states that spread out along Galilee and Samaria east of the River Jordan. How especially sweet it was to occupy Damascus uncontested, adding to his arid dominions one of the world's oldest cities and richest east-west caravan trading centers. Now it was time to turn to Jewish Perea, whose prosperous palm and balsam groves were owned by Herod Antipas, the direct cause of his ire.

The above maneuvers were not lost on Artabanus III, king of the Parthian Empire, to whom Aretus was just one of many clients. If Aretus could muster 20,000 men for a fight, Artabanus could field perhaps 500,000 in the best tradition of his Persian forbearers, Cyrus and Xerxes. The Parthian had been smoldering ever since Germanicus marched out from Syria with two legions in A.D. 20 to persuade him not to invade his large neighbor, Armenia. But now the venerable king of Armenia had just passed away, and Artabanus decided it was time to make his move to claim this large land of steppes, nomads and their prize horses for Parthia.

All this military activity had a direct impact on both the Jews and Christians of Palestine. As ever, grain for troops would be needed from breadbaskets like Galilee. Recruits for Rome's auxiliary corps would be needed from Samaria (which, unlike neighboring Judea, supplied mercenaries for armies of all persuasions). The Jewish hierarchy in Jerusalem would need to show solidarity for Rome and avoid signs that its loyalties might (as in the past) be up for sale to the Parthians. And Roman occupiers could help their own cause by exhibiting a kinder, gentler attitude.

But Pontius Pilate didn't seem to read the same signs. Pilate's base of operations was Cæsarea, some 350 miles south of Antioch, capital of Roman Syria. Tiberius hadn't sent a governor to Antioch in several years and it's likely that the procurator saw all of lower Syria as accountable to no one but himself. Moreover, Tiberius' recent banishment of Rome's Jewish population would have certainly reinforced Pilate's view that the people of Palestine deserved the harshest of policing to keep them in line.

Samaria lay closest to Pilate's barracks in Cæsarea, and its people were as vexatious as they were befuddling. Samaritans were stubborn types who alone clung to the belief that Moses actually deposited the Ark of the Covenant (containing God's sacred laws) on their own Mount Gerizzim rather than in Judea as the Jewish temple priesthood preached (and which scholars today confirm). In time the differences had widened and hardened. Samaritans didn't pay the temple tax, feuded with their Jewish neighbors over property borders and fought so regularly at the drop of an insult that when Jews from Galilee journeyed south to Jerusalem for their various festivals, they usually made a wide eastward detour around the place just to avoid trouble.

Now then, there was a small town named Tirathaba at the base of Mount Gerizzim and one can imagine the excitement when a stranger arrived and announced with great theatrics that he had found where the sacred relics of Moses were buried. He would even lead them up the mountain to uncover them! Indeed, a large crowd was getting ready for the pilgrimage when it was observed by Roman soldiers making their way along the military road to nearby Cæsarea.

The pilgrims were probably still assembling in Tirathaba that afternoon when they saw dust clouds raised by the hoofs of horses charging up from Cæsarea. When the cavalry cohort rode into sight, Pilate himself was in the lead. Without asking any questions, the Romans began flailing their swords at the shocked and paralyzed Samaritans. When some drew their swords, even more were hacked down in the street. The others were rounded up and herded into a farmer's goat pen. There Pilate ordered every man, woman and child executed at once.

This happened in Pilate's eighth year as procurator. He would serve two more, but this episode would prove to be his undoing, because it happened just as Tiberius was in the process of sending, at last, a governor to Syria, and one who was as handy at diplomacy as Pilate was with a sword.

Lucius Vitellius was already known as Rome's foremost politician in A.D. 35. He would go on to serve other emperors and father one himself. But in this year the sagacious senator was known both as consul and frequent, fawning drinking crony of Tiberius on Capri. With his consulship drawing to a close, the emperor thought him just the man to become governor of Syria in Antioch and to quell the ambitions of the Parthian king Artabanus — be it by bribery or military force.

Once outside the confines of Capri and secure in Antioch with his broad imperial mandate, Vitellius began to sway his new clients with his well-polished talent for flattery, charm and empathy. Among his first tasks was to pacify angry Samaria, the wellspring of recruits for his auxiliary troops. So when an anxious delegation came calling to protest Pilate's massacre at the foot of Mount Gerizzim, one can imagine Vitellius reaction: "What's this? Struck down without a hearing? How many again? How gruesome! Tell me no more. I'll certainly see that you are received in the court of the emperor himself to present your case."

And so off went Pontius Pilate to Rome to face charges of abuse and corruption. Neither Biblical nor Roman writings offer further details other than that the procurator was recalled in A.D. 36, never to surface again in recorded history.

Vitellius then turned to the critical Jewish heartland, traveling to Jerusalem during the time of the Passover. Upon entering the city he announced to tumultuous cheers that its inhabitants would be released from taxes on all fruits bought and sold. Then, almost before the applause had died down, he removed the high priest Caiaphas (who had sent Jesus to the cross) and replaced him with the more politically friendly Jonathan. Then, to assure Jonathan's instant popularity, he restored to the Jews the right to have permanent possession of the high priest's vestments.

This was perhaps a trivial concession to a Roman, but not to a Jew. The vestments were a combination of breeches, inner garment, girdle and head covering with ribbons, bells, buttons and fringe all symbolizing the history of Jewry since Genesis. The garments had been seized by Herod the Great some 50 years before and kept by his guards in the Tower of Antonia. Fearing that they might be used to rally the people to revolt, Herod had allowed the high priest access to the vestments only on three annual festivals. Later, when Rome decided to govern Judea directly, its procurators had also kept custody of the garments. Seven days before a festival they were delivered to the high priest by a captain of the guard, who would retrieve them the day afterward. In all, a humiliating display of Rome's utter control.

Now, this new governor was signifying a new beginning in Roman-Jewish relations by giving back the dignity of Judaism.

ONE OF THE reasons that had motivated the Apostles in Jerusalem to select the Council of Seven was that the brethren of Hellenized backgrounds claimed that their widows and poor were not being included in the regular distribution of food and other necessities. As such, the seven persons who administered affairs for the early Jesus followers were mostly of Greek-speaking communities and backgrounds. And their leader Stephen soon became more than a manager of affairs. He, too, became imbued with the Holy Spirit and began to preach The Way and heal people who came before him.

At the same time, there was something about young Stephen that aroused the ire of the Jewish authorities even more than had Peter and John. It was probably in part that he was strikingly handsome and partly that he preached in Greek and won many non-Jews for The Way.

A clash was inevitable, and it happened one day when Stephen was preaching in one of the Hellenized temples that bore names such as Synagogue of the Freedmen and Synagogue of the Cilicians. He must have been fiery and abrasive in his youthful zeal, because his words had already incensed members of these congregations before. On this particular day he soon had the elders on their feet contesting various claims about Jesus. They were especially agitated when Stephen referred to Jesus' prediction that the temple would soon be destroyed. They also interpreted his words to mean that the laws of Moses were no longer valid.

Shortly thereafter, hostile elders from several synagogues sought out Stephen and dragged him before the chief temple priests. When asked to account for himself, Stephen was no less zealous amongst the temple elders than he had been to the elders of Jerusalem's synagogues. In a long dissertation that must have struck them as patronizing, he traced the history of the earliest Jewish patriarchs through Moses to the days of Solomon and David, all things the priests knew by heart. Then he lashed out: "You stiff-necked people, uncircumcised in heart and ears, you always resist the Holy Spirit! As your fathers did, so do you. Which of the prophets did not your fathers persecute? And they killed those who announced beforehand the coming of the Righteous One, whom you have now betrayed and murdered, you who received the law as delivered by angels and did not keep it."

The more Stephen railed at them, the more rigidly irate his priestly interrogators became. He then gazed upward and said, "Behold, I see the heavens opened and the son of man standing at the right hand of God..."

But he was not allowed to finish. Their tempers erupting in a single roar, the elders rushed upon Stephen, dragged him outside the city gates and stoned him one by one. Stephen did not resist, but prayed to Jesus to "receive my spirit" just as he died.

On that same day, the Jewish authorities released all their pent-up frustration on the troublesome heretics of The Way. The temple police went from house to house of known adherents, dragging off men and women to prison. Many more were warned by friends and fled from wherever there was Jewish authority, some even to Damascus far to the northeast.

One of the leaders of this repression was a temple worker named Saul, who was probably in his early or mid-twenties. It was he who cleared the way for the angry priests when they brought Stephen outside the gates, and he who guarded the outer garments that had been flung at his feet by those who hurled the lethal rocks. Perhaps he cast one himself.

Once the Jesus people had fled, temple authorities grew concerned that they might have only succeeded in spreading a plague, that the exiles would simply infect other synagogues in major cities. Obviously, not many of the regular temple security guard could be spared: their job was tough enough keeping order in Jerusalem. Thus, it's likely that the Sanhedrin deputized several of its younger, hardier priests and administrative officials and dispatched them in small groups to the leading synagogues in the major cities.

Among them none would have been more zealous than the young, fiery Saul. He led a contingent to Damascus, armed with letters to its leading synagogues authorizing them to bind and bring back as many of the renegade leaders as they could find. Many years later a much older Saul would write of "how I persecuted the church of God violently and tried to destroy it...so extremely zealous was I for the traditions of my fathers."

From Jerusalem, Damascus required a dusty trek of some five days. As Saul himself would later confirm in letters, he was approaching Damascus on that hot, dusty road when suddenly he was enveloped in such a stunningly bright light that he felt himself knocked to the ground. As he groped about on the ground and regained his senses, he heard a voice saying to him, "Saul, Saul, why do you persecute me?"

And the terrified young man stammered, "Who are you, Lord?"

"I am Jesus, whom you are persecuting," came the voice. "But rise and enter the city and you will be told what to do."

The small group with Saul stood speechless. They heard the voice but saw no one else. Saul finally staggered to his feet and opened his eyes. But he could see nothing.

Saul's companions led him by the hand into Damascus. There he sat dazed and without sight for three days, neither eating nor drinking.

Acts reports that the voice of Jesus also came to a follower named Ananias at his home in Damascus. "Rise up," the voice told Ananias. "Go to the street called Straight and inquire in the house of Judas for a man from Tarsus named Saul; for he is praying there and has seen [a vision of] a man named Ananias come in and lay his hands on him so that he might regain his sight."

But Ananias answered, "Lord, I have heard from many about this man, how much evil he has done to your saints at Jerusalem and that he has authority from the chief priests to bind all who call upon thy name."

But the voice of Jesus said to him, "Go, for he is a chosen instrument of mine to carry my name before the Gentiles and kings and the sons of Israel. For I will show him how much he must suffer for the sake of my name."

So Ananias found Saul just as Jesus had said. Laying his hands on the sightless young traveler, he said "Brother Saul, the Lord Jesus who appeared to you on the road by which you came has sent me that you may regain your sight and be filled with the Holy Spirit."

And immediately "something like scales" fell from Saul's eyes. He got up and could see again. And after he had taken some food, he was baptized.

Saul then spent several days in Damascus with followers of The Way. He appeared in the synagogues to exalt Jesus as the son of God. And all who heard him were astounded, saying, "Is this not the man who came here to find Jesus followers and take them in fetters back to the chief priests?"

But this same enthusiasm for Jesus caused the leading Jews of Damascus to beseech King Aretus' governor in Damascus to have Saul captured and killed. Rumors were that he was being kept hidden somewhere by his new friends. So the governor ordered his guards at the city gates to tighten their scrutiny of all strangers who entered and left Damascus.

Days passed with no visible sign of the Jewish fugitive. Then, late one night Saul was quietly beckoned from his cramped hiding place and escorted to the home of a Jesus follower who lived in a tenement that formed part of the city's eastern wall. There, in the darkness of night, Saul was helped into a large basket and slowly lowered down the wall by a rope. And there he escaped by the back roads used by local farmers and herdsmen.

Meanwhile, the believers who had scattered from Jerusalem had indeed begun to do just as the temple authorities feared. They appeared in synagogues throughout Judea and Samaria telling of the resurrected Jesus and The Way. One Philip, who had been one of the Council of Seven with Stephen, took up residence in a Samaritan city and found himself with the Holy Spirit. Soon reports spread of Philip making "unclean spirits" come out of the possessed, "crying with a loud voice" as they did. The Book of Acts reports that "many who were paralyzed or lame were healed," and that Philip was soon followed by "joyous multitudes."

When the apostles remaining in Jerusalem heard that Samaria was accepting Jesus, Peter and John traveled there to pray that these people, too, might receive the Holy Spirit. Among the people was a man named Simon, who had become famous as a magician but who had joined the throngs who had accepted Jesus. When he saw Peter perform his first baptisms there and give people the Holy Spirit by laying his hands on them, Simon approached the apostle and offered to pay him well if he, too, could receive these powers. But Peter turned to him and said, "Your silver perish with you because you thought you could obtain the gift of God with money!" Repent of this wickedness, he said, "and pray to the Lord that if possible, the intent of your heart may be forgiven you. For I see that you are in the gall of bitterness and in the bond of iniquity."

Soon afterward Peter and John headed back for Jerusalem, stopping at many Samaritan villages along the way to preach the gospel. Philip continued evangelizing up and down the coast from Gaza to the south and as far north as the towns just before Cæsarea.

For Peter, John and the other disciples, new repressions by the Jewish authorities represented a threat and an inconvenience, but their basic mission had not really changed. A far greater force for change in their lives would come in the person of Saul.

WHO WAS this mysterious, not yet trustworthy, convert to The Way? Perhaps the young Saul was only beginning to answer this question for himself that first night alone as he walked along a rough desert road, the walls of Damascus receding in the distance. The night air was crisp and cold. The moon and stars loomed large over the mountains to the west. Except for the sounds of distant dogs or goats, Saul was alone in absolute silence.

No doubt he was frightened and uncertain of his destination. At the same time he probably found the stillness almost invigorating. After all, he had been at the center of a tempest in Jerusalem and had created another one when he entered Damascus. Now he was alone under the heavens to grapple with the brief experience that had transformed his life. What had happened? What did it mean? Where was he headed?

But even before this, it may be better to start with the question: who was this passionate young man Saul *before* Damascus?

Scholars agree that Saul was probably born eight or ten years after Jesus, in the last years of Augustus. He was raised in Tarsus, the cosmopolitan capital of Cilicia, beautifully situated on a lake about 130 miles northwest of Antioch. From there the lake flowed into the River Cydnus, which ran south for 12 miles until it reached a bay that would link Tarsus to Mediterranean commerce. The seaport was worthy enough to have been chosen by Cleopatra when she sailed in with her gold-plated fleet some 50 years before Saul's birth.

And because Tarsus itself straddles the road that cuts through the Taurus Mountains, the city has been a well-traveled caravan stop since the days of the Hittites. Because of the road and the water, the city had long been a jumble of Jews, Asians, Syrians, Persians, Phoenicians, Greeks, Romans and sailors from everywhere.

Saul's father, one tradition has it, bought his Roman citizenship with money made by selling large quantities of tents to various armies. Another theory: Saul's father was one of thousands of Cilicians to be granted instant citizenship by Mark Anthony (no doubt in the fullness of inebriated generosity) when he and Cleopatra met in his home town of Tarsus to consummate their lavish seduction of one another.

Both stories have the ring of truth about them. Certainly the apostle Paul wrote of himself as a tentmaker, and it's logical that his father would have been one as well. Indeed, the cilicium cloth used then in the best tents, sails and awnings throughout the empire derived its name from the word "Cilician" because Cilicia produced the best goat hair for making them. And since busy caravan routes were the best places to sell tents, one can walk about today's silted up ruins and have little trouble vectoring in on the probable neighborhood where Saul's father and his fellow guildsmen plied their trade.

Inheriting his citizenship at birth, the child, after being circumcised on his eighth day, would be known by the usual two names: Saul to the Jews and Paul to his Hellenized neighbors. Paul (as he will be called henceforth) was born into the tribe of Benjamin and named for Saul, the brave, impulsive and violent first king of Israel. The Benjamanites were known as fearless fighters who always stood in the front of Jewish battle lines. They had earned this honor because they were the first to cross the Red Sea when Moses led the Jews in their exodus from Egypt.

As a child Paul no doubt played in streets full of Greek students, Stoics,

Cynics, priests of Cybele and even worshipers of Sandan, the god of vegetation. One can see Paul as a young boy, holding the hand of his mother, with her head covered and face veiled, as they passed by thickly made-up street women with their high-tiered hair, and their perfumed male counterparts, all gesturing obscenely as they traded raucous insults. But it seems evident that Paul's life as a young boy was centered on the synagogue. There he would have started his studies in the House of the Book, the Jewish center for instruction in reading, writing and The Law. This would have led to memorizing the whole of The Law and, presumably, to early training to become a rabbi.

And a Pharisaic rabbi as well. Pharisaism and its reputation as being preoccupied with the rule of Mosaic Law can be better understood by a look at its genesis. Pharisaism arose in the years that preceded the revolt of the Maccabees against Rome around 100 years before Paul's birth. At the time, Hellenistic rulers in major cities were exerting growing pressure on Jews to forego circumcision, eat pork, renounce their sanitary laws and surrender copies of their Mosaic Law. But some rigidly refused, instead detaching themselves from the rest and devoting themselves to living and preserving The Law handed down by Moses. If The Law was an expression of God's will, they reasoned, then man might hope to carry it out so completely that God could ask no more of him.

In time, others would argue that Pharisaism had evolved into, not a fulfilling religious experience, but a slavishly meticulous routine. Nonetheless, it is logical that Paul's family found strength by clinging to this tradition in the profane and culturally cacophonous Tarsus, and that they would press this legacy on their son, Paul.

As such, it would best explain why Paul departed for Jerusalem, probably around age 20, and perhaps not many months after Jesus had been crucified. Because Paul later wrote to one of his churches that he had studied under Gamaliel, one must assume that he was enrolled in the House of Interpretation, or rabbinical college. Gamaliel was a grandson of Hillel, perhaps the most famous of all rabbis, and he led a busy life as a leader of both the college and the Sanhedrin. He represented the more liberal approach that his grandfather had espoused. Some years later it was even said that "When Rabban Gamaliel the Elder died, regard for the Torah ceased and purity and piety died."

To have "studied under" Gamaliel may have meant that Paul was merely one of perhaps a thousand students who were enrolled at the college. However, Paul was to write in another letter that he had, during the time The Way was gaining ground in Jerusalem, "advanced in Judaism beyond many of my own age among my people." Thus, it's likely that Paul was just completing his studies or had recently done so and had been assigned to a position in temple administration reserved for young men of exceptional promise.

But so specialized and sophisticated was the organization of temple affairs that it would be impossible to speculate on the actual position Paul might have held. Temple administration was supervised by a permanent staff that specialized in such matters ranging from collection of tithes and management of private funds deposited for safekeeping to such chores as the offering of birds, shutting of gates, preparation of incense and baking of shewbread. Moreover, the supervision of daily ritual was an enormous task in itself. A typical day began with a procession of priests carrying a pitcher of water from the Pool of Siloam and pouring it on the altar. Animal sacrifices took place for eight-and-a-half hours each day. Priests were also needed constantly for the private offerings to pray for cure from illness, to mark a family reunion and the like. If an offering were made after confession of a civil wrong, a temple official was needed to collect the full restitution plus 20%.

During major festivals, the permanent staff was bolstered by the arrival of priests and Levites from surrounding cities. During Passover the high priest typically supervised some 200 chief priests, 7,200 ordinary priests and 9,600 Levites. Priests and Levites were each assigned to one of 24 "courses." Each priestly course, or clan, which was organized according to its region, drew lots to determine what tasks they would perform in assisting the regular temple priests with sacrifices and other aspects of worship. Levite clans were organized by skill, so that some within each group provided a service such as music or gatekeeping or cleaning of the temple mount. No less than 200 Levites were deployed each day just to open and shut the massive temple gates.

One story has it that Paul was employed by the temple guard, and another that he was a broker in hides of sacrificed animals. Both tales are dubious simply because they don't seem like logical pursuits for a newly graduated rabbinical scholar. It may well be that Paul received hides from time to time, just as the visiting priestly clans were given animal skins they could sell in order to defray their travel expenses. If so, it would be another good reason why Paul would take up his father's trade of tentmaking and leatherworking to sustain himself both as a student and as traveling missionary.

All that is known from Paul himself about the period immediately after his life-changing trip to Damascus is that he stayed in "Arabia" for three years, at least some of it spent in a return to Damascus, before he saw Jerusalem again.

Some say he stayed in the wilderness contemplating the events that had driven him there. Some say he preached his new faith throughout the Hellenistic towns of the Decapolis. Some say he plied a tentmaker's trade to keep body and soul together. The fact that we know so little would confirm that he was mostly alone.

It is logical that Paul did all of the above. In the beginning he may have gained work as a tentmaker in some quiet village. After all, he was — at least for many months — a fugitive sought by authorities in both Jerusalem and Damascus. And with the armies of the Nabatean Aretus constantly moving across the land to and from various maneuvers, it is unlikely that Paul would choose a conspicuous place.

Wherever it was, he would no doubt spend nights under the bright stars praying for guidance in sorting out the meaning of his experience on the road to Damascus. An impulsive, emotional person can change his life in an instant, but a thinker must have time to reconstruct the knowledge and values that are the foundation of his inner world. Paul had been swept away from his moorings and had nothing to cling to but a vision and a voice.

One hears far more afterthoughts about what happened on the road to Damascus than Paul probably had himself. A common theory is that Paul's experience was no doubt evidence of a person with epileptic seizures. "The light you mention was probably the bright aura that people with seizures usually experience before they are struck to the ground," one medical writer explained.

Yet, if Paul had such an affliction, why did he not attribute the experience to just another seizure? If it was his first such episode, why did not all the subsequent ones fill him with doubts about the veracity of his experience with Jesus?

And what about this Ananias, who was also visited? Did two men mistakenly hear the same voice? How were these strangers accidentally guided to meet at the same place and why did both know exactly what to do when they met?

Others have said that Paul's sense of guilt about Stephen was so overwhelming that it caused him to be "possessed" in the same way that initiates into the ecstatic Dionysian mysteries would emerge with a glassy-eyed frenzy that made ordinary villagers want to dart into doorways for protection as they whirled and staggered down the street.

Well, yes and no. Paul had not been "converted" to a cult or religion with rites and priests because The Way lacked both. But Paul had indeed become "possessed" in that he had surrendered his being and his destiny to a higher power. He was to write often that he had become "a slave of " and "a prisoner of" Jesus Christ. He said that God had been "infused in my weakness" and "when I am weak, then I am strong." He would write, too, that "God in foolishness is wiser than men" and "God in weakness is stronger than men."

The most convincing aspect of Paul is simply that, from the moment he saw the brilliant light and heard the voice on the road to Damascus, he never once expressed a doubt or looked back longingly on his previous life. Rather, Paul's early contemplation of his "reborn" status probably centered on three questions:

First, how did his revelation relate to The Law that he had been memorizing since boyhood? Suddenly, all the painstaking prescriptions for daily living that Paul had spent so many years acquiring and debating were dissolved into a few simple concepts. Repentance. Redemption. Salvation. Love. Faith. Forgiveness. Hope. Tolerance. Charity.

Second, was Jesus the messiah of Hebrew scripture? If so, was he the all-powerful, mighty warrior who would deliver the Jews from the yoke of their oppressors? Or was he the "suffering lamb" of Isaiah in Jewish scripture who would bring eternal salvation to even the sickest and weakest person who believed in him?

Third, what was Paul's role in this to be? Should he preach his new belief? To whom?

Answering the last question was probably the easiest of all for Paul. He could still recite the words of Jesus some 26 years later when he stood on trial before a Jewish king:

> Rise and stand upon your feet, for I have appeared to you for this purpose: to appoint you to serve and bear witness to the things in which you have seen me and to those in which I will appear to you, delivering you from the people and from the Gentiles — to whom I send you to open their eyes, that they may turn from darkness to light and from the power of Satan to God, that they may receive forgiveness of sins and a place among those who are sanctified by faith in me.[8]

To answer the first two questions and to gird one's mind with the resources necessary to convey those answers to skeptical strangers could easily have taken a year or two. Whatever the duration, there is no doubt that Paul emerged believing that his spirit had been set free and that he was embarked on a great voyage to spread joyous news. One can now picture him around A.D. 36 as he began to attract curious crowds in Petra, the Nabatean capital, and in cities of the Decapolis such as Philadelphia and Gerasa. Soon he would be approaching the familiar gates of Damascus, where he would build on the brief friendships with his courageous friends in The Way and deliver his new message without fear or compromise.

A.D.
37-40

ONE MAN'S FORTUNES were remarkably intertwined with the Romans, Christians and Jews of this period. He directly influenced the lives of everyone from three Roman emperors to the apostles James and Peter. So it is time for a proper introduction to Herod Agrippa I, a grandson of Herod the Great and a Romanized opportunist without peer.

Again, we must delve back into the legacies of Herod the Great and Cæsar Augustus. Herod excelled at imagining and/or detecting plots and sparing absolutely no one — even his sons and favorite wife — his lethal retribution. After the king had executed two sons, Alexander and Aristobulus IV, allegedly for planning to take him on a one-way hunting trip, Herod found it rather awkward to have their children running about underfoot and through his conscience, so he sent them off to the household of Augustus to be reared as cultivated as client nobility should be. The brightest stars among them were Herod Agrippa I and his sister Herodias, the offspring of Aristobulus.

And a stimulating adolescence it was for the young Agrippa. Not only was he dressed in royal purple and tutored with the princes of Gaul, Sicily, Parthia and the like, but he was fast becoming a favorite of everyone from

Augustus himself to the brother-generals Drusus and Tiberius to Drusus' sons Germanicus and his lame, stuttering brother, Claudius. Antonia, the proud daughter of Mark Anthony and wife of Drusus, was so besmitten with the witty, impish Jewish prince that he was as much a fixture in her immediate household as her own, less endowed son, Claudius.

There was only one problem. When Herod died and his kingdom was carved up for other sons to run, there was little legacy for Agrippa and his sister — only the generosity of their hosts. This made for bad chemistry, for Agrippa was already in the habit of giving his school chums lavish presents, only to have angry creditors later nipping at his heels.

As Agrippa married and plotted his rise in patrician society, he developed a pattern that eventually became obvious to all around him. He would charm a friend into a "temporary" loan for, say, 5,000 drachmæ. He'd then use a chunk of the loan to wine and dine someone else higher up the social ladder. When that "mark," as they say in the scam world, would lend him perhaps 15,000 drachmæ, Agrippa would pay off the first loan of 5,000 and begin courting a new friend in the next social strata.

Before long, friends were calling in their old loans and prospective ones were avoiding Agrippa at social engagements. Now in his late thirties, despondent and destitute, Agrippa sailed back to Judea with only his wife, Cypros, and a long-time manservant. From there he drifted aimlessly, winding up in an abandoned garrison outpost in the Idumean desert of his grandfather. There he locked himself up and threatened suicide as Cypros wailed outside his door. So desperate was the long-suffering wife that she secretly sent a letter to Antipas, the tetrarch of Perea and Galilee, pleading for some sort of patronage job to help the couple get back on their feet.

Antipas was now married to Agrippa's haughty sister Herodias (whose whisper had brought her the head of John the Baptist). So, the fair-haired darling of patrician Rome was in a shambles and had to come to his sister's little backwater ethnarchy for his next meal? Well, of course they would help a family member in trouble, but in a way that would clearly put him in his proper place. A letter went back to Cypros saying that the relatively new city of Tiberias on the Lake of Gennesaret (Sea of Galilee) had a vacancy for a chief magistrate, or what would amount to a city manager. The post was Agrippa's if he would ask for it.

One can imagine the struggle Cypros and the manservant waged in dragging to this rural Jewish market town the man who had entertained 50 Roman senators and half the imperial household in a single evening. He came with teeth clenched, and his stay didn't last long. When the two couples found themselves together at a banquet in the port city of Tyre, Agrippa was soon into his cups and berating his benefactor for paying him a bureaucrat's pittance that couldn't support a decent lifestyle. Antipas roared back that his ungrateful, ne'er-do-well brother in-law ought to be happy just to have enough food on his plate.

Agrippa stormed out into the night with his confused wife and servant straggling behind him. All he knew was that there would be no more hand-outs from Antipas and no more Tiberias. First came a stay in Antioch with the governor of Syria; but after charming his way into the ruler's confidence and being asked to help him judge a land dispute between two cities, Agrippa was shown the door for allowing one of the petitioners to grease his palm.

Now came many days of desperation and depression as the three made their way down the Judean coast from one seedy inn to another. At one point Agrippa managed to borrow enough to charter a small skiff. But when he sailed it into a seaport that night, he was startled to hear his name called out by a group of Roman soldiers. One of them unfurled an official scroll and read loudly that one Herod Agrippa was to be detained in custody until he had repaid 300,000 silver drachmæ he had borrowed from the imperial treasury in Rome several months before.

Agrippa, always the prince, replied haughtily that the amount would of course be delivered the next day. And instead of having to spend the night in a cold jail, Agrippa promised not to escape if his party were allowed to stay aboard ship.

But as soon as all was dark and quiet in the harbor, Agrippa cut his slips and quietly glided his little ship out to sea. Down the southern corner of the Mediterranean they sailed until they had reached Egypt and had tied up in the busy commercial harbor of Alexandria. His last hope was Alexander, the alabarch (technically tax collector) for the large community of 500,000 Jews who lived in the Roman Empire's second largest city.

Well, Alexander, too, had learned about Agrippa's ways, but he was touched when the long-suffering, faithful Cypros dissolved her imperial dignity in tears and begged for help. After a pause, the alabarch said he would lend her enough so that the prince could get back to Rome and petition Tiberius personally to help him rebuild his life. But on one condition: Cypros couldn't give her husband any of the money aboard ship, for he'd surely find a way to spend it in the middle of the sea!

Within a few weeks Agrippa indeed found himself on Capri, and his reception was cordial as Tiberius recalled the times when he had been amused and charmed by the Jewish princeling who lived in the household of Augustus. Agrippa went to bed his first night on Capri secure that his fortunes were turning at last.

He awoke the next day to encounter a much different Tiberius. The emperor informed him icily that he'd just been reading a regular report from the procurator in Judea. Part of it mentioned the capture and escape of one Herod Agrippa over an unpaid debt for 300,000 drachmæ.

As Agrippa, now officially a fugitive, stood stunned before Tiberius, the thought must have crossed his mind that others had been tossed over the thousand-foot cliff for far less. However, the emperor merely informed Agrippa coldly that he would no longer be welcome in his presence until the debt to the treasury was repaid.

Now Agrippa faced certain ruin. And yet, there might just be one more possible oasis in his desert of disgrace. He went back to Rome and straight to Antonia, the emperor's revered sister-in-law and truly Agrippa's surrogate mother in the days of Augustus. When he left her gates he had a loan for 300,000 drachmæ, which Tacitus tells us she gave out of regard for the kindnesses Agrippa had shown her lame, stammering son Claudius during their school days together. Indeed, when nearly all of the other children thought Claudius perhaps retarded, his friend from Judea had been his inseparable companion and defender. Perhaps only he knew at that time that the brother of dashing Germanicus was no fool.

Agrippa's world suddenly brightened considerably. Tiberius received the 300,000 drachmæ and surprised even Agrippa by stating that he'd make an excellent companion for his 22 year-old adopted grandson, Gaius Caligula. Indeed, the emperor added that Agrippa "should always accompany him when he went abroad" (meaning anywhere outside of Capri).

Well, now, someone to be seen in the royal presence every day would require proper raiment, a retinue of retainers and enough resources to keep an imperial heir-apparent amused. This time Agrippa commanded respect when he sought a private appointment with Thallus, a freedman who oversaw finances for the imperial household. The result was a loan for 1 million drachmæ. This allowed him to repay Antonia and regain her confidence, with 700,000 drachmæ left over to repay the alabarch in Alexandria and pay lavish obeisance to Gaius.

But, no, this isn't the happy ending one might have expected. One summer evening in A.D. 36 Agrippa and Gaius were rumbling about the rough roads of Capri in a carriage. Sitting up front at the reins was Eutychus, a freedman who performed many odd jobs for Agrippa. The prince, no doubt his flattery honed to fine form by now, said he was praying to the gods that Tiberius would soon "go offstage" and leave the matter of governance to the far more worthy Gaius.

No doubt this wasn't the first time Eutychus had heard something like this, and the carriage driver probably thought little of Agrippa's remark at the time. But it would loom much larger a few days later when Agrippa accused his servant of stealing some of his clothes. Perhaps guilty as charged, the freedman somehow managed to escape Capri, only to be arrested several days later in Rome. Rather than accept his punishment, Eutychus blurted out that he had information relating to the emperor's "security and preservation." This alone compelled the prefect of Rome to have him bound and returned to Capri.

Wherever the emperor went, so did his retinue — even including prisoners and petitioners who remained clustered at a respectful distance for the spare moment when the princeps might decide to hear their cases. So it was a hot August day when Tiberius arrived from Capri to visit Antonia in her villa at Tusculum, about 12 miles outside Rome. Agrippa was there, and when Antonia asked him what had happened about that rascally fellow who'd run off with his clothes, the prince huffed and blustered that he couldn't understand why his charges had gone unheard. Moreover, they learned that the man was on the property in chains along with others who had been brought to be near the emperor's beck and call. So, at dinner that night they pestered Tiberius to hear the case before he retired.

The emperor had already left the house and was easing into his sedan chair when Antonia came out behind him and asked again if he'd just summon his guards to bring the chained Eutychus for a quick resolution to the matter. Tiberius was both tired and reluctant. Chances are he already knew the essence of Eutychus' defense and didn't want to cause Agrippa's patroness any embarrassment. "Please don't ask me to do this," he said wearily. "If guilty, he (Eutychus) has already suffered enough punishment by his confinement. But if the accusation appears to be true, Agrippa may find that out of a desire to punish a freedman, he rather brings punishment on himself."

When Antonia persisted, Tiberius heaved a sigh and bade his bearers set him down. "Oh Antonia," he said heavily, "the gods are my witnesses that what I am about to do comes not at my own inclination, but because of your petitions. " With that he ordered Macro, the Prætorian prefect, to bring out the prisoner.

The freedman had by then many weeks in which to practice and embellish the scene in the carriage with Gaius and Agrippa. "Oh my lord," he bewailed with arms gesturing. "This Gaius and Agrippa were riding in a carriage as I drove and this Agrippa said 'Oh that the day would come when this old fellow would die and name thee governor of the habitable earth! For then this other Tiberius [the emperor's seven year-old grandson] would be taken off by thee and the earth would be happy, and I happy also!'"

The discourse was so literal that it rang with reality. Tiberius was silent for a moment, then turned to Macro and pointed to Agrippa standing among his retainers. "Bind that man," he said stonily.

We now arrive at the winter of A.D. 37. As the first shoots of spring popped up around Rome in mid-March, Herod Agrippa was enduring his sixth month of confinement in a Prætorian prison — and faring far better than his compatriots. Antonia, no doubt feeling some guilt for Agrippa's fall from the pinnacle of power, had won Macro's assurance that he would be allowed to bathe each day and receive his friends and attendants.

Meanwhile, Tiberius, back on Capri, had come down with a cold he couldn't shake. Now 78, the emperor did everything to make his regular appearances and shoo away physicians, for one of his favorite sayings was that no man who has survived his first 30 years should ever need a doctor. But as his visible signs weakened, the emperor (perhaps his astrologers) decided that the air or omens on Capri were unfavorable. Or perhaps he sensed the end was coming and wanted to be nearer his roots. Whatever the cause, Tiberius had himself rowed across the Bay of Naples to Cape Misenum, where he settled into a wealthy senator's villa.

There, the emperor continued to appear at small dinner parties and tried to maintain an image of stability, but his mind now was preoccupied with thoughts of death and succession. His natural grandson, Tiberius Gemellus, was but a frail boy of nine or ten. Claudius, the brother of Germanicus, was gaining minor renown as a historian in his middle age, but how could this stuttering cripple wear the mantle of Augustus? This left only the eager Gaius Caligula, now 25 and the obvious choice to anyone but the few who witnessed his erratic and erotic behavior on Capri. Gaius, however, had long since made a mutual promotion pact with Macro — one that would lead to a palace guard controlling the selection of an emperor and beginning a tradition that would plague Rome for the next 32 years.

The old man soon lapsed into a comatose state and on March 14 his breathing seemed to cease. Gaius, surrounded by a hushed but excited crowd, actually slipped the imperial ring from Tiberius' finger and prepared to rule Rome. But just then the "deceased" raised his head, blinked his eyes and asked for food. Gaius stood open mouthed, frozen in fear. The retainers outside the emperor's bedchamber immediately recomposed themselves in a posture of prayer.

But enough was enough. It was Macro who calmly walked into the bedroom and unceremoniously smothered with a pillow the wolf that had made the world cower for 22 years, five months and three days.

Tiberius had always seemed to enjoy tantalizing his subjects by announcing plans to visit this or that mainland location, only to cancel the trip on some astrologer's advice. So when news of his death first spread throughout Italy, people were too wary to celebrate. But when they could see that Gaius had actually set out on the road from Misenum to be formally crowned in the Senate of Rome, near delirium spread in his path. Although Gaius was dressed in mourning garb and escorting the body of Tiberius, unrestrained crowds lined the road with torches and makeshift altars, calling out to him as their "star," their babe" and their "nursling."

By the time word of the old man's demise reached Herod Agrippa in his gentlemanly confinement near Rome, it was to report one of the very first decrees that Gaius had issued in Misenum. Agrippa was to be freed from prison and allowed to return to his former residence in Rome. And shortly after the elaborate state funeral for Tiberius, and after the Senate had unanimously granted the new emperor absolute power, Gaius summoned his old comrade to a morning reception. There, the former deadbeat, fugitive and accused traitor was given a ceremonial head shaving and saw his raiment changed back to royal purple. Then Gaius put a royal diadem on his friend's head and proclaimed him king of Trachonitis and Gaulanitis, a fertile region just northeast of Galilee. Finally, he gave Agrippa an unusual keepsake: a long chain of gold symbolizing freedom from the chains he had worn as a prisoner of Tiberius.

This was just one example of the new ruler's generosity and unstinting effort to heal the wounds of repression that had cast a gloomy cloud over the world's epicenter for over 20 years. The emperor's reticent Uncle Claudius, now 47 and never allowed to hold government office, was made joint consul. His grandmother Antonia was granted every honor given to Augustus' wife, Livia. Senators cheered as Gaius announced that he would formally adopt Tiberius' grandson Gemellus. "What greater blessing could there be than that a single soul should cease to be laden with the heavy burden of sovereignty and should have one who would be able to relieve and lighten them?" he postured to the conscript fathers. "And I," he assured, "will be more than a guardian, tutor and teacher."

The winds of change blew everywhere. Exiles were recalled, and the emperor himself traveled to the forlorn isle where his mother had been banished and returned her ashes to the Mausoleum of Augustus along the Tiber. Likewise, Gaius reinstituted local elections, recalled some banned books and resumed imperial sponsorship of gladiatorial shows. Scarcely anyone escaped the new emperor's munificence in the first few months — from the citizens of Rome each receiving a gift of 300 sesterces to a lavish banquet for 600 senators at which men received expensive togas and their wives elegant red scarves.

Then after nearly seven months — in October, A.D. 37 — the hand went off the tiller and the ship ran aground. Gaius was struck down with a mysterious malady that immobilized Rome's bright new hope with crashing headaches, chills, nausea and sleepless nights. Historians have vied to explain the cause, but the only clue may be that Gaius did have bouts of epilepsy as a child. As his life seemed to hang in the balance, Romans prostrated themselves at the palace gates, offering their own lives if the gods would spare Gaius. At the Empire's farthest reaches, the Jewish philosopher Philo wrote from his home in Alexandria that "No one remembers any single country or single nation feeling as much delight at the accession or preservation of a ruler as was felt by the whole world in the case of Gaius — both when he succeeded to his sovereignty and when he recovered from his malady."

Gaius did recover in a few months, but the empire did not. For this episode seems to have marked the abrupt return of crushing repression at the hands of an absolute ruler who was as cruel as he was mentally unstable.

The first to feel it was Macro. As the man who had with his two strong hands more to do with the emperor's ascent than anyone else, the Prætorian prefect considered himself Gaius' closest advisor. He felt it his duty to admonish the young man whenever he nodded off during a banquet speech or lingered too long chatting with his favorite chariot driver while venerable Senate leaders were being kept waiting for an audience. But soon Gaius was cutting Macro off in mid-sentence. "How can they who were but common citizens have the right to peer into the counsels of an imperial soul?" he spat at the older man during one widely overheard tantrum. "Yet in their shameless effrontery, they who would hardly be admitted to rank as learners dare to act as masters who initiate others into the mysteries of government!"

From then on the relationship was never to be the same. Nor was it for the hapless Tiberius Gemellus. In A.D. 38, barely a year after adopting the youngster, Gaius was openly complaining that his "son" was an oppressive nuisance. And one day the boy was greeted by an officer of the Guard bearing orders to kill himself with his own hands (this, because it was unlawful for a royal to be slain by others).

Alas, the poor lad lacked the skill to do the deed, for he had never seen anyone killed and had not yet been trained in any martial exercises. Trembling but brave, he stretched out his neck to the officers and asked that they dispatch him. But when they said they were forbidden to do so, the boy resolutely took the sword himself and asked them to point out the most vulnerable spot that he could strike and end his miserable life. And thus the pitiful lad became his own murderer by passing his first and only lesson in martial arts.

Even so, people around the Mediterranean rim clung to their hope for a better era.

They even managed to accept the demise of young Tiberius Gemellus by rationalizing something like this: It is both a danger and a distraction to a monarch to be burdened with worrying about the whims and wiles of a possible competitor. An immutable law of nature is that sovereignty cannot be shared. Even if Gemellus had remained a faithful supplicant, he would have attracted partisans, which could have led to division and warfare. Yes, it certainly was a sad occurrence, but undoubtedly one best for the empire.

Thus encouraged, Gaius moved down the list of his imperial nuisances. Next was Macro. As Tiberius showed Sejanus, a man can perform favors for another on such an epic scale that they can never be repaid. And that is unbearably threatening to one who must control all events. So Macro and his entire household were slaughtered in a single day — May 24, A.D. 38 — only 14 months after the death of Tiberius.

Other close supporters were taken off-stage as well. The common reason for all may be that they were impediments to an overriding ambition: the more unstable Gaius became, the more he was seized by a egomaniacal drive to be thought of by the world as a living god.

Augustus, at the height of his powers, had allowed only one city (Pergamum) to build a temple in his name and sacrifice to his statue — and only because it was jointly dedicated to the city of Rome. Tiberius bristled at the mere notion of his living divinity. But only five months into his reign, Gaius Caligula had given signs of things to come when he allowed a deputation of Greeks to build temples to him in four major cities. Other provinces saw this as a signal to compete to see which could erect the biggest temple and conduct the most lavish sacrifices.

From this point on it almost seemed as if the emperor were competing with the gods on Mount Olympus themselves by assuming their roles and exceeding their achievements. Thus, he would typically attend the theater attired in the costume of his current godly foe. He might appear as Herakles with lion skin and club, or perhaps as Dionysus wearing ivy, thyrsus and fawn's skin.

People in Rome soon grew accustomed to seeing their emperor riding in his carriage in the dress of Apollo. Or one might see him in the temple on Capitoline Hill whispering in the ear of Jupiter's statue. In time he had built a ramp that extended from his palace on Palatine Hill down to the temple of Castor and Pollux, which stood in the Forum below. Now he could parade down the walkway and into the temple, taking his place between the divine brethren so as to be worshipped among them. In another temple appeared his own golden, life-sized statue, dressed each day in the clothing worn by the living emperor. Wealthy citizens vied to become priests of the cult and to make daily sacrifices of flamingoes, peacocks, pheasants and the like.

Gaius had no more brothers, but three of Germanicus' daughters were quite alive and married. By this time, the people of Rome were well conditioned to absorb the shock when it became known that Gaius practiced open and enthusiastic incest with all of his sisters. Again, popular opinion adapted conveniently to his needs. Once a person proclaims himself a god, the reasoning went, it follows that the only humans worthy of his sexual confidence should be those of his own earthly flesh.

As to all those temples of worship, it was reasoned that because Orientals and other barbarians accepted their rulers as divine, an emperor must be seen as equally so in order to command their respect in his conduct of diplomacy.

As for explaining Gaius' own thought process, here is an insight by way of the Roman historian Dio Cassius. He quotes the emperor as having said: "The shepherds who care for herds of animals are not themselves oxen, goats and lambs, but men to whom is given a higher destiny. In the same way I am who in charge of the best of herds — mankind — must be considered to be different from them and not of human nature, but to have a greater and diviner destiny."

JEWS WERE directly in the crosshairs of Caligula's madness. In only one instance did it work in favor of a Jew — the newly crowned king of Trachonitis and Gaulanitis. After spending several months in Rome at the new emperor's side, Herod Agrippa had scarcely arrived in his new kingdom when it became clear that Caligula's generosity was not sitting well at all with his sister Herodias. Here was the deadbeat brother returning as a king — a *king* if you will — while her husband Antipas, a living *son* of Herod the Great, was relegated to the status of a backwater tetrarchy! And the very idea of Agrippa and Cypros regally bedecked and flaunting the emblems of royal authority all about Palestine was more than she could endure.

Perhaps the aging Antipas didn't even care anymore, but the younger, ambitious Herodias was soon berating him daily about it. Finally she swore she would not continue living unless they went to Rome and pled for equal status. "And let us spare no pains nor expenses." she vowed. "To what better use could they be put than obtaining a kingdom?"

Within a few weeks Antipas and Herodias were in patrician Rome's favorite vacation spa of Baiæ on the Bay of Naples, where Gaius was basking in one of his sumptuous villas. When the big moment came and the couple was ushered into a reception room, they were dumbfounded to see Herod Agrippa's top freedman, Fortunatus, waiting as well. As ever, the walls had ears during Herodias' outbursts back in Galilee and word had reached her brother in neighboring Trachonitis. While the tetrarch and Herodias were selecting their finest garb for their entourage, Agrippa had sent his freedman alone on the fastest ship he could find out of Tyre.

Fortunatus had arrived with some sumptuous gifts, and he also knew what to say as Gaius suddenly entered the room. Antipas' petition was simply that he felt entitled to have his tetrarchy upgraded to a kingdom. But Fortunatus brought more interesting information: Antipas was conspiring with the wily King Artabanus of Parthia to take most of Syria from Gaius. "Please ask him to deny that he already has armor sufficient for 70,000 men stored in his armory at Jerusalem," said the freedman coolly.

"Is this true?" asked the emperor, looking down his nose with a frown.

Well, it was true that Antipas had stored arms, but probably to fight off the marauding Nabatean, Aretus, and probably with the approval of the Roman governor in Antioch. But Antipas had reacted with too many seconds of stunned silence and then began explaining so tentatively that his guilt was evident enough for Gaius. Not having much time for such matters anyway, he took away Antipas' tetrarchy on the spot and ordered the couple banished to Lyons — a new city being carved from a forest in Gaul and not a very nice place for those used to soft and effeminate lives. And just before they departed into historical obscurity, the emperor delivered the cruelest blow: he announced that their tetrarchy would be incorporated into the kingdom of Herod Agrippa.

Agrippa, however, may have been the only Jew who fared well under Gaius Caligula. In A.D. 38, as the concept of becoming a living god began to possess the emperor, the more irritated he became with Jews in general. As peoples around the world scurried to build temples and display their worshipful supplication, centers of Jewish population did nothing — obviously because their laws prevented them from worshipping men or erecting idols. Jews would offer prayers *for* an emperor — that is, pray to God that Gaius have a long life — but they would not pray *to* him.

In time, vandals and pranksters would taunt Jews by breaking into their synagogues and erecting crude statues of Gaius. But Egyptian Alexandria was the city that caused an explosive reaction throughout the empire, and here is why. First, the approximately 500,000 Jews who lived there were more than any city outside of Jerusalem. Second, normal population growth had already pushed the Jewish "quarter" (probably 40% of the city) against its neighbors and caused fights over real estate. Third, Egyptians, who had already spent 3,000 years deifying everything from pharaohs to cats and crocodiles, were quite happy to welcome the emperor Gaius into their pantheon of gods.

So the tinderbox was ready, and all it needed was the torch supplied by the emperor's Egyptian chamberlain. Helicon was probably as clever as Agrippa, but his rise into the emperor's palace began as a street urchin who sold scrap for his master. So amusing, versatile and adept at eavesdropping was Helicon that he kept fetching higher and higher prices at slave auctions until a Roman knight had bought him as a gift for Tiberius. The old man had no tolerance for a jester's flattery, but Gaius loved it, and soon Helicon was his constant attendant.

At about this time, Gaius — or perhaps even Helicon — had begun to envision a grand tour in which an imperial fleet would glide down the eastern Mediterranean, stopping in its harbors to visit the emperor's images in their leading temples and to be worshipped as their living god. The climactic moment would come in Alexandria, the city that entombed Alexander the Great, where the triumph would be complete. And if Helicon's lucky streak continued, he might return one day to govern the people who once waved him off the streets as they passed by.

The only problem with these plans was that 40% of the city's population didn't welcome the idea of a living god. This would never do, and for days on end his chamberlain would remind the emperor that Jews were still the only people who hadn't prayed *to* him. In time this displeasure was communicated to the local leaders of Alexandria, who quickly made the most of it. With a brutal rage, a mob overran homes of Jews, expelling families and stealing whatever furniture and valuables they could carry off. Within days, throngs of burned-out, destitute Jewish families were subsisting in the streets without food. So the leaders of the rabble next herded them into a very small portion of their former quarter so that they were now penned up like so many cattle. It was now blistering hot in mid-August, and there the victims endured until they finally broke loose and scrambled into the streets. Pelted with rocks as they went, they ran for the outskirts, where they existed in graveyards and fields while constantly harassed by gangs of young ruffians.

Flaccus, the Roman governor of Alexandria, was implored to restore order, but Helicon had anticipated it and taken care of the matter in advance. Flaccus had been appointed by Tiberius, and he received word that he might be removed from the richest governorship in the Roman Empire if he were perceived to favor the enemies of Gaius Caligula. So when Flaccus did nothing to police the Hellenes, they became even bolder. Horses dragged Jews down the splendid, three-mile long Canopic Way until the cobblestones made them unrecognizable. Organized attacks were made on Jewish meetinghouses, with many demolished to their foundations.

When the first news of these atrocities reached Gaius, it came by way of letters from Alexandrians in the Roman government. The reports were couched in such a way that a fair judge could only conclude that the violence was caused by insolent Jews who had opposed the people's attempt to pay homage to their beloved emperor. And if Gaius wanted to learn more, Helicon was at his ear to supply it.

It had taken Jewish elders of Alexandria a long time to fathom the reason for the pogrom and who had ignited it. When the trail led to the emperor's chief gatekeeper, they knew that it was futile to appeal through normal channels. Their only option was to send a delegation (then called an "embassy") directly to Gaius and wait outside his residence until such time as he might beckon them.

And so, one summer day in A.D. 39 Gaius was inspecting a villa and gardens his mother had left him on the rural west side of the Tiber — probably in the very section now called the Vatican. Outside the hedge-lined walls waited a gaggle of foreign ambassadors and supplicants. Among them were three Jews from Alexandria, including the brother of the alabarch, a philosopher named Philo to whom historians are indebted for keeping a dairy of his experience. When the Jewish envoys were finally ushered in, they found Gaius disarmingly cordial and cheerful. After listening briefly to their appeal, he nodded understandingly and said only, "I will hear your case in full when I get a good opportunity."

With a good-bye wave, the group was dismissed as another took its place. Philo's younger companions were elated: surely the emperor's sunny disposition meant that their case would prevail. But not Philo. The senior-most member worried privately that Gaius had already been captivated by the other faction in Alexandria and was merely prolonging the torment of the Jewish community there.

Soon summer had turned to autumn. One day the ambassadors were waiting outside the walls of yet another imperial estate when a fellow Jew they knew in the area rushed up to them, gasping for breath. Clearly in an apoplectic state, he pulled the little band off to one side and asked, "Have you heard the news?"

As Philo reports in his diary: "When we shook our heads, he began to speak, but a flood of tears streamed down his eyes. He tried to speak a second and third time, until one of our party finally said, 'If you have facts that are worth so many tears, at least let us share your sorrow, for we have become inured to misfortune by now.'"

"Our temple is lost!" the man blurted out. "Gaius has ordered a colossal statue of himself to be set up within the inner sanctuary. It is to be dedicated to himself in the name of Zeus!"

Wrote Philo: "We simply stood there, speechless and powerless in a state of collapse with our hearts turned to water."

The Jewish delegation spent days in agonizing discussion, and the result of it was this: they could not predict or control what an all-powerful megalomaniac might do. They knew only that they had no choice but to uphold their ancient laws. "So be it," Philo had concluded at their last meeting. "We will die and be no more, for the truly glorious death, met in defense of The Law, might be called life."

It was now very late autumn and the envoys managed to sail on one of the last ships bound for Egypt. The weather was stormy, but Philo sensed that a worse storm might be waiting on land.

It was, but not just in Alexandria. As the much-discussed imperial tour of Egypt began to harden into a real plan with a timetable, Gaius Caligula and his inventive chamberlain Helicon began to conclude that the Jews of Alexandria weren't the biggest barrier to their success. An imperial entourage would have to travel in a convoy of warships. But an emperor's court couldn't be subjected to rough open seas like passengers on a grain ship. They'd need to glide down the coast and spend evenings in friendly harbors where they could take on the best of provisions and display their splendor to adoring subjects. Assuring a peaceful Phoenician-Judean coastline would best be achieved by pacifying — by whatever means necessary — the very center of Jewish culture.

In the summer of A.D. 39 the recently-installed governor of Syria received a detailed formal letter with instructions to mount a show of military might in Judea — and a war, if need be. The governor was to muster two Roman legions, escort a colossal statue of the emperor to Jerusalem, and see that it was erected in the Jewish temple.

By now Vitellius had been replaced as governor by Petronius, a man known both for his even temper and sound administrative ability. Petronius was also a loyal imperial servant, and that fall he marched his two best legions 240 miles down the coast to Ptolemais, where he would quarter them in the winter before making a show of strength at nearby Jerusalem.

But as Petronius reached Ptolemais and began plotting the details of his mission, the more daunted he became by the probable consequences. He realized that a people who blanched even at the prospect of seeing imperial standards and images within its walls was no doubt ready to sacrifice thousands of lives to defy the erection of a giant statue of Gaius Caligula dressed as Zeus. The notion went against his own sense of justice, but it also threatened the survival of his legions. For Jews were spread all over the world. If delegations from hundreds of synagogues could trek over seas and mountains each year to bring annual tribute to the temple, might they not rush from every quarter of the empire to defend it? Yes, Roman reinforcements could rally from other provinces, but might Petronius and his legions be wiped out before they arrived? Worse yet, what if the Jews of Galilee and Judea refused to plant their crops or burned them in the fields? What kind of provisioning would this leave for an imperial flotilla? And who would be killed for failing to provide it? Petronius first, *then* the Jews.

As the governor tortured himself with these unhappy options, he did find one that offered at least some escape — or at least delay. Gaius had not said he was sending a statue from Rome. Nor did he order Petronius to remove and transport any of the existing statues throughout the eastern provinces. This implied that one should be built anew. Volatile Judea certainly wasn't the place for it, so he ordered that it be done far up the coast in Sidon — and by skilled craftsmen who would be encouraged to take all the time they needed to properly glorify the imperial image.

In the winter of A.D. 39 Petronius decided on trying to defuse the situation by inviting the leaders of Jerusalem to a meeting on neutral territory. He calmly stated the emperor's wishes and almost begged them to accept their lord and master's orders and to consider the dire consequences of doing otherwise. As one account records, "Besmitten by his first words, they stood riveted to the ground, incapable of speech. Then, as a flood of tears poured from their eyes as from fountains, they plucked the hair from their beards and wailed as if the dead were bring mourned."

As the Jewish elders left for Jerusalem, Petronius had no inkling as to whether they would heed his words, whether they would cease to plant their crops or even take up arms. Back in Ptolemais a few days later, the governor's forward scouts reported a strange, incredible sight approaching in the plain from the south. What had at first seemed a large cloud of dust was instead a vast crowd of people. The governor would soon learn that when the elders had returned to Jerusalem, they had issued an appeal to Jews from every city to stream out and supplicate themselves to Petronius. Now as they drew closer to the military camp, the Romans could see they were totally unarmed.

When Petronius beckoned the elders in front to approach him, it was evident that they had been rolling in the dust. Their eyes were streaming with tears and their hands were set behind them as if pinioned. "We are a peaceful people," cried out one. "We are unarmed and present our bodies as easy targets. We have prostrated ourselves before you — and to Gaius — so that you may either save us all from ruin or send us all to perish. Our houses, lands, furniture, money and cherished possessions we will willingly give over. But we would think ourselves gainers and not givers if we could receive but one thing in return — that no violent changes should be made to the temple and that it be kept as we received it from our ancestors. If we cannot persuade you, we give ourselves up for destruction so that we may not live to see a calamity worse than death."

The spokesman added as a "final prayer" that, rather than request the governor to disobey his master's orders, they be allowed to send a delegation to Rome in hopes of persuading the emperor directly.

Petronius and even his most hard-bitten officers were moved nearly to tears. They retreated beyond earshot of the Jews and held a long private discussion. Then Petronius returned. The crowd pressed in, breathing in an almost spasmodic rhythm. "I cannot grant your request for an embassy," he said solemnly. However, he, as governor, would write Gaius a letter that, while neither accusing the Jews nor reporting their tearful entreaties, would merely inform the emperor about some unforeseen delays, such as the need to construct a statue and to gather in winter grain crops before risking hostilities.

Gaius had the letter within a month, and began fuming as soon as he had read the first words. "Good Petronius, you have not learned to harken to an emperor," he exploded. "Your excessive offices have puffed you up with pride. You have known Gaius only by reputation, but you will soon know him by experience. You concern yourself with institutions of the Jews, the nation which is my worst enemy, yet you ignore the imperial commands of your sovereign! Even if the Jews destroyed all the crops in Judea, are not neighboring countries so many and so prosperous as to compensate for the deficiency of one?"

Having vented his anger, Gaius composed himself and turned to his ever-present chamberlain Helicon. "But why should he who is to reap this reward know my intentions in advance?" he said impishly. "I have stopped talking but I haven't stopped thinking."

Governors who command legions weren't to be aggravated unnecessarily, so it was a calm and diplomatic reply that Petronius received from his master as the first signs of spring came to Galilee in A.D. 40. When he summoned the Jews to a second meeting some 30 miles from his military camp, so many thousands showed up that the nervous Romans took care to ring the supplicants with legionaries poised to attack if necessary. The meeting began with a stonier, sterner governor rising from his judgment seat to read what seemed like a decree. The emperor, he said, had reaffirmed his command. "And it is fit that I, who have obtained so great a dominion by his grant, should not contradict him," Petronius added.

A mournful wail began to rise up from the masses before him, but Petronius held up his hand and bade them listen. "Yet," said he, "I do not think it just to have such a regard for my own safety and honor as to refuse to sacrifice them for the preservation of you who are so many in number — nor for your law, which has come down to you from your forefathers."

By now the crowd was struck dumb as it began to anticipate the governor's intent. "Therefore," he said, "I will send another letter to Gaius to let him know what your resolutions are. I will assist in your case as far as I am able. But if Gaius decides to turn the violence of his rage upon me, I will rather undergo all that danger that may come to my body and soul rather than see so many of you perish."

After those words — never before heard by a Jew from a conqueror — the elders had no choice but to urge their people to go home, plant their crops and pray for the best. The land was in the throes of a drought at the time. Just as the Jewish throng was departing the camp of Petronius, there were thunderclaps and the heavens opened up with a cooling rain. The governor could only shake his head and say, "God takes care of the Jews."

So did Herod Agrippa, in his own unique way. Just before the Jews had first sought out Petronius about the impending statue, Agrippa had embarked on a leisurely return to Rome to keep his hand in affairs there. Upon arriving, he promptly went to the emperor's morning reception to pay his usual homage. Agrippa expected to be welcomed back warmly, but Gaius had no sooner entered among his courtiers when he began staring straight at his old friend with a smoldering anger. Agrippa searched his mind for something he'd done wrong and quickly concluded that this was simply his turn to be the day's butt of the imperial bully.

Gaius quickly observed the king's anxiety and said "Let me release you from your perplexity, Agrippa. Yes, I have been speaking to you with my eyes. Your excellent and worthy fellow citizens, who alone of every race do not acknowledge Gaius as a god, appear to be courting even death with their recalcitrance. When I ordered a statue to be set up in your temple, they marshaled their whole population and marched forth from the city, supposedly with a petition, but actually to counteract my orders!"

Statue? Temple? The emperor was about to continue his assault when Agrippa, gasping for breath, turned blood red, then deathly pale, then livid again. His limbs convulsed and he would have toppled to the floor had not some bystanders caught him. People moved back to give him room, then a stretcher was summoned and Agrippa was carried home in a comatose condition.

As the bearers scurried off with their limp cargo, Gaius threw up his hands and looked heavenward. "If Agrippa, who is my dearest friend and bound to me by so many benefactions, is so under the dominion of his nation's customs that a few words against them make him swoon into near death, what can we expect of others who are *not* under the influence of any counteracting force?"

Agrippa lay in his deep coma for more than a day. When he finally opened an eye, his mood was no less dour, nor would he take food. "All it would do," he told his anxious retainers, "is to assuage my hunger so that I could live to surrender this miserable nation." Eventually he took a bite, a sip of water, and said sadly, "Now I have nothing to do but make my petition to Gaius about our present situation."

He picked up a stylus and began to write in the sycophantic style he had mastered as well as any citizen of Rome. In a long and rambling appeal, Agrippa poured out his thanks for all the favors that Gaius had done him, but matched them with a litany of deeds that had bound Jews to Romans over the centuries. Hadn't the divine Augustus and his family furnished the temple with golden vials, libation bowls and other marks of their respect? Had not Tiberius become "violent with anger" upon hearing that Pontius Pilate had attempted to bring the imperial ensigns inside the walls of Jerusalem?

After an appeal not to alter "the laws and traditions that have been passed from emperor to emperor," Agrippa turned to his personal dilemma. "You released me bound fast in iron fetters," he wrote, "but do not clamp me, my emperor, with still more grievous fetters. For those that were then unbound encompassed but a part of my body. Those which I see before me are of the soul and press on every part of my whole being"

And now the letter concluded with the rhetoric of a man on his knees. "You gave me a kingdom — the greatest gift of fortune a man can possess. But I do not beg to keep short-lived good fortune. I exchange all for one thing only, that the ancestral institutions of the Jews be not disturbed. For what would be my reputation among either my compatriots or all other men? Either I must seem a traitor to my people or no longer be counted your friend as I have been." The only way out, pled Agrippa, was through the mercy of the emperor in canceling his order to erect the statue.

The above comes from Philo's diary. Josephus, the pre-eminent historian of his day, suggests that Agrippa didn't bet his entire fate on one letter. In what certainly seems in character with this lifelong gambler, the king marshaled all the financial resources he could summon from wealthy Jews everywhere and staged a banquet for the emperor that, says Josephus, "was so far from the ability of others that Gaius himself could never equal, much less exceed it."

When this stupendous feast was in full swing and everyone was flush with wine, a very merry and maudlin emperor staggered to his feet and made the speech Agrippa had been hoping for. "I knew beforehand, of course, what great respect you had for me and what risks you took with Tiberius on my behalf," he gushed, extending his hand toward the resplendent King Agrippa. "I am therefore desirous to make amends for everything for which I have been deficient. Everything that might contribute to your happiness shall be at your service as far as my ability will reach."

No, my Lord, replied Agrippa. "It was out of no expectation that I have paid my utmost respects to you. The gifts already bestowed upon me are quite beyond the dreams of most men."

Gaius was astonished at his modesty, and pressed again, asking if there wasn't but a wish he could grant.

Agrippa had stretched the odds far enough. "Since you, O Lord, have insisted that I am worthy of your gifts, I will ask nothing for my own felicity," he intoned. "My petition is simply this: that you will no longer think of the dedication of that statue which you have ordered to be set up in the Jewish temple by Petronius."

Agrippa's life again hung in the balance. Had not a governor already received orders? Hadn't two legions already been provisioned and marched 240 miles to carry them out? Gaius was stunned. Also trapped, because he could not take back his offer in front of so many witnesses. So with a wave of his hand and a forced smile, he granted Agrippa's wish.

Days later he wrote Petronius: "If you have already erected my statue, let it stand. But if you have not dedicated it, do not trouble yourself further about it, but dismiss the army and go back to tend to other affairs, for I have no further need for erection of the statue. This I have granted as a favor to Agrippa, a man whom I honor so very greatly that I am not able to contradict what he would desire me to do for him."

Supposedly that would have been the end of it. But Helicon was there to remind the emperor that he'd been tricked. "Proof" of the slave's point was that the emperor's letter to Antioch was still at sea when the second letter from Petronius now arrived from the opposite direction. This was the one written after the governor's second encounter with the Jews. Perhaps he exaggerated conditions in Judea by picturing barren fields and a people ready to revolt if the statue weren't removed. In any case, the emperor was fuming all over again, and his reply dropped all pretense of diplomacy.

"Seeing as how you esteem the presents made to you by the Jews to be of greater value than my commands, and that you have grown insolent enough to be subservient to their pleasure," he wrote, " I charge you to become your own judge and to consider what you are to do now that you are under my displeasure. For I will make of you an example to present and all future ages that they may not dare to contradict the commands of their emperor."

Gaius now had a secret plan for the Jews, but he resolved that for the time being he would maintain an outward calm so that its execution would be all the more delicious when it came. Thus, in the summer of A.D. 40, when the Jewish ambassadors from Alexandria came calling again to press their case, the emperor seemed content simply to keep them in high anxiety.

The audience was hardly conducive to discourse. Gaius was pacing about a complex of gardens and villas, dictating a list of needed renovations as busy secretaries scribbled nearby. Philo's diary records that they encountered a "ruthless tyrant with a menacing frown on his despotic brow." Gaius stunned them with his first words: "Are you the god-haters who do not believe me to be a god — a god acknowledged among all nations but not to be named by you?"

"Oh, no, Lord," they cried as one. "We did sacrifice, not once but thrice — the first time at news of your succession, the second time when you escaped severe sickness and the third as a prayer for victories as a commander of the legions And we did not just pour the blood upon the altar and then take the meat home to feast on, as many do. No. We gave the victims to the sacred fire to be entirely consumed!"

"All right, all right," said the emperor impatiently. "You sacrificed — but to another. It was *for* me, but not *to* me."

The precious moments began to run off as water in a storm drain. The Jews would attempt to press their arguments for clemency (their enemies had also petitioned that their Roman citizenship be revoked) only to find themselves chasing the distracted Gaius as he went from room to room commenting on a painting or window in need of replacement.

"Why do you refuse to eat pork?" he broke in at one point. But when they would attempt a reasoned answer, he would ask "Eh, how's that?" Then he wandered off again and the Jews concluded that it was probably to fetch guards to take them off in chains. But seconds later he was back, and in a softer mood. With hands raised, as if addressing the gods above, he said, "They seem to be people more unfortunate than wicked. They are simply foolish in refusing to believe that I have the nature of a god." With that he strolled away again and the ambassadors found themselves free to leave.

Gaius Caligula could afford to toy with some envoys from Alexandria because he had something more important in mind. The emperor had already ordered that the statute under construction in Phoenecia be continued but left there in place as a decoy to keep the populace at bay. Meanwhile, an even larger gold-plated bronze likeness of himself would be cast in Rome under great secrecy. When the planned eastern voyage embarked, the golden monstrosity would be conveyed in a large grain ship to Cæsarea and transported up to Jerusalem. Once in place, the emperor himself would arrive and would lead a ceremony in which Herod the Great's unsurpassed temple would be renamed "The Temple of Gaius, the New Zeus Made Manifest."

FOR FOLLOWERS of The Way in Jerusalem, this period began in a less threatening atmosphere than any they had known thus far. The only explanation is as follows. When the Roman governor Vitellius granted the Jewish authorities more dominion over their own religious affairs, and when King Aretus of Nabatea decided not to press his ambitions on Judea following the death of Tiberius, temple officials felt their sacred institutions less threatened. Thus, they felt less need to observe or restrict the activities of those who might pose potential challenges.

And perhaps this is why one Paul, lately of Damascus and the Arabian desert, decided to march boldly back to the city that he had served just three years before as temple officer and persecutor of everyone associated with the prophet Jesus. One can imagine this energetic young man, emblazoned with the spirit of Christ, eager to enter the Holy City and use his newly reorganized zeal as a battering ram against the fortifications of disbelief. And naturally wanting to be at the heart of things, it is no surprise that he would offer his services directly to the leader of The Way.

Paul did so by first befriending one Barnabas, a Cypriot who was both gentle and respected among the followers as a man above reproach, one who could never be suspected of collusion with enemies of The Way. Soon Paul had been invited into the home of no less than Peter and his family, who had by now moved from Galilee to quarters in Jerusalem. It was in that home that Paul spent the next two weeks as a guest.

Nowhere is it written that Peter was instructed by Jesus or angels to accept this one-time persecutor of The Way; but if Paul was convinced by a voice to become a believer, one might surmise that Peter may have needed divine guidance to overcome his logical suspicions that the "new" Paul was but the "old" Paul up to some treachery. In any event, Paul must have spent these days mining from Peter's memory every event and word he had experienced with Jesus. He also spent time with James, the brother of Jesus, who had by now taken up residence in Jerusalem with the original apostles.

Paul accompanied Peter and James all over Jerusalem, "preaching boldly in the name of the Lord," as later letters describe it. And these sermons were no doubt crowned by relating Paul's astounding experience on the road to Damascus — to the point where he was accepted by Peter and most followers of The Way. And because Paul was fluent in Greek and they were not, Jewish leaders of The Way were no doubt willing to let Paul be their spokesman in spreading the word to Hellenistic audiences.

It also seems likely that the fire that burned within Paul ignited indignation among some of his audiences in both camps. Many of his Hellenized audiences were hearing about The Way for the first time, and it may be that Paul lashed out directly at their mysterious religious rites and idolatrous sacrifices. It also seems apparent that the sight of Paul still offended some of the Hellenic friends and followers of the slain Stephen. Thus, like his return to Damascus, it was only a few weeks before there again were plots against Paul's life.

So it was, then, that Barnabas and some of Paul's other new friends in The Way escorted Paul out of the holy city and over the 60-mile path to Cæsarea. Perhaps as they walked, they were able to reinforce the words that Paul himself had already heard on the road to Damascus: that his calling was not to be in Judea, but among the Greek-speaking pagans in cities quite beyond. They would have been able to cite the fact that some of Stephen's followers in The Way who had been scattered by the persecutions (of no less than Paul himself!) were now preaching in Phoenicia, Cyprus and Antioch. But perhaps they implied something else as well to Paul: that his colleagues would feel more comfortable about him with the passage of time — enough to produce evidence that he had indeed preached The Way and lived by his words.

One can picture a cloudy dark night at the man-made harbor in Herod's Cæsarea, when in another version of lowering Paul in a basket over the city walls, he was quietly put aboard a ship sailing for Tarsus on the high tide. Back he would go for the next two years. No doubt his feelings were tossed about like bilgewater in a storm as the ship lumbered its way 250 miles up the coast and finally into the mouth of the Cydnus River for its 12-mile entry into the busy harbor of Tarsus. Yes, the Cilician capital was the home he had left just a few years before, but it was as equally alien a place for his mission as had been the arid hills of Nabatea. Certainly Paul's father and family could not have been happy to know that the son they had sent off to become a rabbi was now returning full of zeal for a prophet who he called the son of God, and who had actually spoken to him in some sort of vision. Nor could his father even be permitted to sulk in private. Oh, no! His strange son would have joined him at work on the Street of Tentmakers, sharing his newfound zeal with his father's long-time colleagues while they stole sideward glances at the mortified old man.

Still, the primary objective of Paul's mission soon became the many others who seldom came near the Street of Tentmakers. In this sense, Tarsus presented Paul with the most dramatic challenge possible because most of its people contrasted sharply with the clear, pure waters of the river that rushed through the center of town. Lined along its banks were the temples representing a polyglot of pagan religions and wooded groves given over to every form of perverted sensuality.

Neither Paul nor those who have written about him ever described his impressions of Tarsus. But it is interesting to note how it was described by Apollonius, a leading philosopher and traveler. Apollonius was born about the same time as Paul in nearby Tyana. He had been brought there at age 14 to study under a leading scholar, but soon departed because

> ...he found the atmosphere of the city harsh and strange and little conducive to philosophic life, for nowhere are men more addicted to luxury than here. Jesters and full of insolence are they all; and they care more about their fine linen than the Athenians do wisdom.[9]

Paul came now, not to study, but to proclaim something he considered of momentous import. And nowhere else would he find people so pre-occupied with other religions and diversions. Their temples lined the walkway that followed the riverbank. Paramount among them was a complex that served the cult of Isis. This Egyptian mystery religion would have been gaining ascendancy in Tarsus at this time because Cleopatra had expanded and beautified the temple when she arrived there by barge to meet Anthony some 70 years before. Like peoples in many Roman cities, the citizens of Tarsus probably embraced this mother goddess because she, her husband Osiris and their son, Horus, formed a trinity that satisfied many yearnings of the human heart. Many a young mother could recite a part of the famous hymn supposedly sung first by Isis:

> I brought together woman and man, I appointed to women
> to bring their infants to birth in the tenth month. I ordained
> that parents should be loved by children. I laid punishments
> on those without natural affection towards their parents.[10]

To others Isis was the goddess of justice:

> I broke down the governments of tyrants. I made an end to
> murders. I compelled women to take the love of men. I
> made the Right stronger than gold and silver. I ordained
> that the True should be thought good...[11]

But as anyone initiated in the mysteries knew, Isis was also power.

> I am the queen of rivers and winds and the sea. I am the
> queen of war. I am the queen of the thunderbolt. I stir up the
> sea and I calm it. I am the rays of the sun. Whatever I deem
> shall come to an end.[12]

And so, Paul had to contend with hundreds of daily Isis worshippers and with thousands at festival times. As throughout the eastern provinces, he would see those who had been inducted into the mysteries parading through the streets, holding high the statue of Mother Isis, cradling in her arms the holy infant that she had borne her husband Osiris. And always, as part of the procession, Paul would hear the noise of sounding brass and the tinkling of the cymbals from the instruments initiates shook with their hands as they marched.

Further down the riverbank one could see the temple of the manly cult of Mithras, established from Parthia to Britain no doubt because it was the religion of so many Roman soldiers. Its devotees called themselves Sons of Light and followed Ormazd, the "Lord of Life," rather than the God of Death (Ahriman) and his Sons of Darkness. Paul, the rabbi, perhaps appreciated the fact that its initiation requirements were difficult, being based on knowledge of ancient law (or Avesta) and seven levels of achievement. As a follower of Jesus, he might have empathized with a mystic rite in which members ate bread and drank wine to remind themselves of the time when the god Mithras sacrificed a bull and created the first man and woman from its blood.

Many other cults vied to rule over all matters of fertility — from seeds of grain and grape to spawning fish, birthing cows and fecund girls. It was sometimes hard to tell them apart except for the stories of their origins. In Tarsus one could cite the temple that served the cult of Attis and Cybele. Attis was born of a virgin who became pregnant by eating almonds from a sacred tree. Attis was so beautiful that the goddess Cybele fell in love with him. Well, he replied that he really had his heart set on a daughter of the king of Galatia. The goddess was so infuriated that she decided to drive him mad, which she did indeed. He fled to the countryside in this crazed state where he emasculated himself at the foot of a big pine tree and bled to death. From those drops of blood sprang up violets, which were always associated with the name Attis in springtime. And every March 22 cult priests would preside over frenzied rites in which they tried to resurrect the dead lad from his eternal sleep.

But nearly unrivaled were the temples of Aphrodite. In fact, the most splendid of all was at Hierapolis, just 100 or so miles east of Tarsus. Wherever they might be, these temples to fertility were known best for the doves that constantly flew overhead, for the sacred fish that swam in their special pools inside the grounds and for the young girls who beckoned outside (to be further explained in a moment).

Might these religions and their rites have evoked Paul's sympathy? After all, they all struggled in their different ways to ease man's way through the pangs of birth, the ordeal of feeding one's family and the mysteries of death. Paul the Jew had known animal sacrifice. Paul the follower of Jesus could understand the resurrection of a god. Some religions had even supplied leaders of The Way with customs to which their own adherents could relate.

But sympathy from Paul of Tarsus? Hardly! He certainly knew enough of these rituals to refer to them when preaching, but to embrace any part of them? Never! Collectively, they stood for exactly what Paul opposed with all his might. He was only saddened that they hadn't heard the Word as he had; and sharing that Word filled him with energy and a sense of urgency. For who knew how long the world had to repent before Christ came again to take up the faithful?

Isis? A mere wooden statue whose mythical son had been pieced together from dismembered body parts! Mithras? The god was a myth. He never lived.

Jesus had lived — created by a loving God and not by the blood of a sacrificed animal. The Mithraic "Communion" service? Paul would be quick to point out that the bread and wine were accompanied by a hallucinogenic drug, extracted from the Hellebore plant, which made people leave their senses during their "religious" ceremony.

Attis and Cybele? One might lose his life for spying on one of these spring rites. Here is why. On March 22 a group of eunuch priests would cut down a pine tree, swath this "corpse" of Attis with violet wreaths and bury it in a grave. After two days of fruitlessly blowing trumpets to resurrect the dead tree, the priests would conclude that the only way to do so is to shed the blood of worshipers. So, to the endless din of drums, cymbals, castanets and horns, the "worshippers" whirled about the so-called grave, working themselves into a frenzy by gashing their bodies with knives, splattering the altar with their blood to give Attis the strength to rise again. The climax came when novices, awaiting the right to enter the priesthood, hacked off their own male members and threw them into the lap of the goddess Cybele, who watched by the grave.

All became quiet until the early hours of the next morning. Then a priest cried out and everyone (rather, all those who hadn't bled to death by then) would run out to the grave. There, amidst flares affixed to the branches of trees, they would discover the grave empty. Lo! The tree had been resurrected and all the "worshippers" were "saved" as well.

And finally, another look at those young girls who beckoned outside the temple of Aphrodite. The fertility goddess had her own ring of temple prostitutes, and in some areas — probably Tarsus — it was even decreed that no virgin could be married until she first gave herself to a stranger at the temple of Aphrodite. This is not the way the cult of Aphrodite began. It was legitimized and encouraged by the male priests who saw in it a way to compete with the brothels in harbor areas and to collect more temple taxes from all sorts of souvenir merchandise sold in their precincts.

Paul was ready to confront all such religions and priests. There is no record of what he had to say at that time, but we do know his views on the subject some 20 years later when he wrote his long letter to the Christian community of Rome. Regarding the nature of men, he said:

> Claiming to be wise, they became fools, and exchanged the glory of the immortal God for images made to look like mortal man or birds or animals or reptiles. Therefore, God gave them up in the lusts of their hearts to impurity, to the dishonoring of their bodies among themselves, because

they exchanged the truth about God for a lie and worshipped and served the creature rather than the Creator,
who is blessed forever![13]

At this point, we do not know exactly where or how Paul started his mission in Tarsus. But two pieces of evidence do indicate that that he indeed
began there. First, his later letters describe having endured the lash-the full
39 strokes-on five occasions. But since they don't mention any specific instance of scourging, it is reasonable to conclude that some of them were inflicted during these first years in or near his native city.

Secondly, Paul certainly proclaimed The Way in Tarsus, because within
two years Barnabas saw fit to journey there and ask him to undertake an
important mission in Antioch. When they met, Barnabas no doubt encountered a man who, though always of slight and stooped stature, was
toughened by scars and setbacks, yet emboldened by having reached into
the souls of men when he preached of love, forgiveness and salvation only
through God's grace.

Sometime around A.D. 39 Peter and a small group of disciples decided to
venture from their homes in Jerusalem and preach in surrounding Judea,
Samaria and Galilee. This may have been due, in part, to a formal decision
among the apostles to go forth to many lands and spread the gospel. It may
be, too, that their success in Jerusalem had again put the temple officials on
edge. That the authorities were already tense and nervous was probably
the result of a rippling across the Mediterranean that was caused by the emperor himself.

The pogrom in Alexandria had ignited many smaller but similar acts by
Hellene vandals and street bullies all up and down Palestine. These tensions
certainly would have reached their peak when the high priest heard the stun-
ning news that Gaius was to erect his statute in the very heart of Judaism.

With the despair that Jews felt after first going out through the desert to
petition Petronius, it is certainly logical to assume that many more would
be receptive to the message preached by the new sect called The Way.
There is no Biblical reference to such a direct connection to the impending
statue, but *Acts* makes it clear that people were eager to listen to Peter. Farmers, shopkeepers, women and other common Jews felt more downtrodden
than ever. The new emperor, who would liberate them from dreary depression
under Tiberius, the promising youth whose recovery they had prayed for
so earnestly just two years before, had revealed himself as oppressive as his
predecessor — and with an unexplained hatred for their own people.

Added to this was the fact that Roman taxes were being raised again and the increasing drought had made it more difficult to produce crops that could be converted into coins for tribute.

Thus, more people now cocked their heads and listened intently when Peter preached that God had revealed himself on earth not as a mighty, conquering messiah, but as a gentle, loving servant of man. Hope leapt anew in their hearts when they heard that salvation and eternal life were available to *all* believers — not just those who had the time and training to observe every jot and tittle of the Torah. And lo! Word spread that Peter had also worked miracles, just as some of them had witnessed Jesus performing then when they had been at the Passover feast some seven years before.

On one such occasion, Peter had come to Lydda, a town about 30 miles from Jerusalem on the road to Cæsarea, to encourage a group of believers that had already formed there. Upon arriving, he was asked to visit a man named Æneas, who had been paralyzed and bedridden for some eight years. When Peter entered his house, he gazed down on the man and said gently, "Æneas, Jesus Christ heals you. Rise and make your bed." Immediately the man rose- and word spread quickly throughout Lydda and neighboring Sharon as to what had happened, "and a great many gave themselves up to Jesus."

At the same time Peter was in Lydda, he was met by some followers who lived in Joppa, which was ten miles to the west on the seacoast. They had rushed the whole way, overcome with grief because one of their members had just died after suddenly being stricken ill. Her name was Tabitha, and she was cherished among the people for her acts of charity.

When Peter hastened to Joppa, he found the body of Tabitha in an upper room where it had been washed and laid in a bed. All around stood women weeping. In their anxiety to pay Tabitha tribute, they had displayed coats and other garments that she had made for her family and friends.

Peter stepped into the room and ushered everyone outside. He knelt down and prayed. Then turning to the body, he said, "Tabitha, rise." Her eyes opened, Acts reports. And when she saw Peter, she sat up in bed. He gave her his hand and lifted her up. Then Peter called out to the others waiting outside and they came in, astonished at seeing Tabitha standing with him in the center of the room.

Many more came to the cause of Jesus that day in Joppa, so many that Peter remained there several days, staying at the home of a tanner named Simon. During this time, and throughout the first years of The Way, Jews weren't the only ones to hear the gospel or to witness the healings of the apostles. But great barriers remained to their understanding and acceptance of this message. Peter, for one thing, spoke only Hebrew and the native Aramaic of Galilee. Doubtless he had picked up some Greek as well, being brought up among the Hellenistic towns of Galilee, but his smattering of words and phrases was probably far too rough and halting to use it in preaching to crowds. Secondly, common Jews simply didn't associate with Gentiles because their ancient dietary and sanitary laws proscribed too many restrictions to make it practical. Third, living apart bred ignorance, which, of course, only led to suspicion, rumor, enmity and the like between Jews and others. Thus, for all these reasons, it was not easy for most Gentiles to hear and accept the word of Jesus even if they might be so inclined. And if they *did* become believers, they could not share in common rituals, such as the taking of bread and wine. So, the preaching of the gospel to Gentiles had been left largely to disciples like Paul and the followers of Stephen.

All of the above explains why Peter had a shattering experience during his stay in the house of Simon. It was the sixth hour of the morning and Peter was hungry for breakfast. As the women were preparing the meal in the kitchen, he went to the housetop to pray as the glistening sea spread out to the west of him and the new sun rose to the east. It was then that *Acts* says he fell into a trance. He saw the heavens open and something descending from the sky that resembled a great sailing sheet. Gathered up inside it were all kinds of animals, reptiles and birds. The sail was let down, its four corners touching the ground. Then a voice called out: "Rise, Peter! Kill and eat."

But Peter said, "No, Lord, for I have never eaten anything that is common or unclean." But the voice came to him again, saying, "What God has cleansed, you must not call common."

The voice repeated the same message three times. Then the huge sheet, or sail, was taken up again and disappeared.

After the breakfast that followed, the apostle was still contemplating the meaning of this experience when three men stopped on the street outside Simon's house and called out to ask if a man named Peter was staying there. As Peter rose to look out, he again heard the voice that had accompanied the vision of the sail. "Behold, there are three men looking for you," it said. "Go down and accompany them without hesitation, for I have sent them."

When Peter did so and asked the men why they had come, they introduced themselves as servants of Cornelius, a centurion of the Italian Cohort who was posted at Cæsarea. Cornelius, they explained, had become a devout follower of The Way, along with his entire family. They added that the centurion was also known around Cæsarea as a man who always gave alms to the poor and who was just to the Jews who lived there. "Cornelius," they explained, "was directed by a holy angel to send for you to come to his house and hear what you have to say."

Peter might have suspected a plot, but the vision and voice had given him courage. The next day, Peter, the three servants and six of the brethren from Joppa departed on the 30-mile journey north to Cæsarea. When Peter arrived at the house of Cornelius in the shadow of the Roman military camp, he saw a group of Romans and other Gentiles gathered outside. He soon learned that the centurion had called his kinsmen and close friends to witness what he believed would be a momentous encounter. When Peter came into his presence, Cornelius fell at the apostle's feet in a posture of worship. But the alarmed Peter quickly lifted him up, saying, "Stand up. I, too, am but a man."

When they were inside and the centurion's kinsmen had crowded in with them, Peter rose and said, "You undoubtedly know how unlawful it is for a Jew to associate with or visit anyone of another nation. But God has shown me that I should not call any man uncommon or unclean. So when I was sent for, I came without objection. I ask, then, why you sent for me."

Cornelius explained. "Four days ago I was keeping the ninth hour of prayer in my house when, behold, a man stood before me in bright clothing. He told me 'Cornelius, your prayer has been heard and your alms have been remembered before God. Send therefore to Joppa and ask for Simon, who is called Peter. He is lodging in the house of Simon, a tanner, by the seaside.' And then the angel departed."

Peter spoke next. "Truly, I perceive that God shows no impartiality," he said. "Any nation and anyone who fears him and does what is right is acceptable to him. You know the word which was proclaimed throughout all Judea, beginning from Galilee, after the baptism which John preached, how God anointed Jesus of Nazareth with the Holy Spirit and with the power, how he went about doing good and healing all that were oppressed by the devil. For God was with him. And we are witnesses to all that he did both in the country of the Jews and Jerusalem. They put him to death by hanging him on a timber. But God raised him on the third day and made him manifest, not to all the people, but to us who were chosen by God as witnesses and who ate and drank with him after he rose from the dead.

"And he commanded us to preach to the people," Peter continued, "and to testify that he is the one ordained by God to be judge of the living and the dead. To him all prophets bear witness that every one who believes in him receives forgiveness of sins through his name."

Acts records that well before Peter had finished speaking, all those who were listening were seized with the Holy Spirit in the same way that the apostles had witnessed from their balcony in Jerusalem several days after the crucifixion. The circumcised disciples who had accompanied Peter were amazed that the gift had been poured out even on the Gentiles, for they were speaking in tongues and extolling God.

Then Peter declared, "Can anyone forbid water for baptizing these people who have received the Holy Spirit just as we have?" With that, he commanded them to be baptized, remaining in Cæsarea for several days to preach the word and baptize still others.

In time, Peter returned to Jerusalem. When he arrived, news of what had happened in Cæsarea had already reached the ears of what was now called "the circumcision party" among the Jewish brethren of The Way (in order to distinguish themselves from the Gentile converts). But when Peter gathered them together and patiently explained his vision in Joppa and that of Cornelius in Cæsarea, they sat in silence. Then, says *Acts*, they rose as one and they gave praise to God, saying, "Then to the Gentiles also God has granted repentance!"

In the months to come the despair throughout the Jews of Palestine grew deeper as the erection of Gaius' statue grew more inevitable. Resigned that they must die in opposing it, people fell into a torpor. Some walked about in sackcloth and others even abandoned the planting of their crops, as Petronius had feared. During these times the disciples were surely among them, urging them to repent now, for these were signs of the end days and Jesus would soon call the faithful to be with him in eternity.

As for the Hellenists, disciples from Cyprus and Cyrene were so successful that they had made great numbers of believers even in cosmopolitan Antioch, the Syrian capital, the Roman Empire's third largest city and the permanent headquarters of Petronius and his legions. A leader among those disciples was Barnabas, the Cypriot. So busy and demanding was his work that he needed assistance. Barnabas went to Paul in Tarsus and asked if he could join him as soon as possible. Paul did.

A new time had begun. Groups of believers were still meeting mostly in the homes of members, but they had in fact coalesced into "churches," or governing bodies for the selection of worship rituals, the collection of offerings and the distribution of alms to the poor and orphaned. And by now they had become easy in calling themselves by their new name...*Christians*.

A.D. 41 – JULY 44

THE LOWER THE SOCIAL CLASS, the more adulation Gaius Caligula could expect. Plebeians and slaves cheered the many games he sponsored, and on any given day the young emperor might appear on the portico he had built onto the old palace of Tiberius and toss handfuls of gold and silver pieces down into the Forum. No one dreamed of or built public works on so grand a scale — his latest flash of brilliance being a plan to construct a new city in the highest of the Alps in Gaul.

But to any equestrian, senator or palace servant, it was evident that Caligula was at best mentally unstable and sometimes even raving mad. He suffered from crashing headaches that caused his moods to swing wildly from morosity to flights of wild fancy. He scarcely slept, and would sometimes lurch among the colonnaded temples in the dead of night talking with statues. Or there might be nights like the one in which three leading senators were roused from their beds by imperial guardsmen, hustled off to the palace and deposited — trembling with fear — in a small theater of the palace used for intimate performances. Suddenly they heard a chorus of instruments from behind stage, and out sprang the emperor of the Roman Empire, clad in the tunic and shoes of a woman. He whirled about to the din of flutes and clogs. Then, after singing an aria in a female falsetto, he tiptoed offstage.

The audience of three applauded wildly. Then they found themselves sitting in agonizing silence, not daring to speak or move from their seats. The evening ended unceremoniously when a servant came out and told them it was time to go home.

Even at his best, Gaius was always the impish, prankish boy. One night at the theater of Pompey he had his servants distribute free tickets entitling the bearers to sit in the choice rows always reserved for senators and equestrians. When they arrived, they had no place to sit — much to the emperor's amusement.

When the actor was his favorite, Mnester the mime, Gaius would jump on stage and kiss him with passion. If anyone made the slightest sound when Mnester was dancing, Gaius had the offender dragged from his seat and scourged.

But on any given day a monster could appear as well. The same precocious prankster often enjoyed having people slowly tortured as he dined. During one dinner when a slave was brought to him for stealing silverware, Gaius ordered that the man's hands be cut off and slung around his neck while he was made to parade among the guests with a sign announcing his crime.

By the start of A.D. 41, Caligula's madness had polluted Rome and was both sapping and embarrassing the empire. The emperor's games, gifts and public works had already run through the 2.7 billion sesterces Tiberius and Augustus had amassed in the treasury. In a frantic effort to raise money, provincial rulers were ordered to strip foreign temples of valuable icons and statutes and ship them back for the emperor's safekeeping. In Rome, all sorts of new and bizarre sales taxes were imposed — including one in which prostitutes were supposed to collect a different sum for each position employed in an evening's acrobatics.

An emperor's tenure ultimately depended on his ability to placate the ruling classes, and for Gaius Caligula these had deteriorated to the worst of his relationships.

The downslide had accelerated in A.D. 40 when the emperor had departed Rome on what was to be a triumphant military march through the heart of Europe. He would pay a nostalgic visit to his father's old legionary camps in Upper Germany, then board a fleet for Britannia, on which he would set foot long enough to confirm Rome's long-held claim on this wild and unruly land.

But things literally got off on the wrong foot. Gaius learned en route that the German camp commander had been plotting with a leading senator to do him in upon arrival. Instead, the emperor sent a cavalry squadron in advance and dispatched the general before he could act.

After deciding that crossing the sea to invade Britain might not be wise when Rome's own legions in Germany might just be waiting on shore to prevent his return, Gaius decided to even an old score. Twenty-five years before, when the emperor was a small boy, his father Germanicus had barely been able to quell a near mutiny of legionaries in the German camps. Gaius now told his commanders that to show he hadn't forgotten the insult to his father, he wanted them to line up all the men in the parade ground and order the officers to decimate their ranks (i.e. kill every tenth man by sword). The commanders begged him to relent, but he would not budge.

As the soldiers heard the trumpet summoning them from their tents, someone had decided to level the killing field by spreading word that they should grab their arms in case of trouble. When Gaius saw hundreds of men running forth with their spears and swords in hand, he panicked and tore out of camp with the cavalry unit that had brought him from Rome.

Once out of danger, the slow march back gave the emperor plenty of time to seethe. One rider was sent ahead with word that Gaius expected a lavish triumph for his victory, but not at his own expense. By the time a group of senators walked out to receive him on the outskirts of Rome, Gaius had convinced himself that all of them had probably been in on the assassination plot in Germany and that all should be treated with the contempt they deserved. From almost that point on, Caligula resumed the treason trials of the Tiberian era. Deaths and confiscations of estates again became the order of the day. Some senators were disfigured with branding irons. Some were put in cages with wild animals or put to work building roads. Old patricians were made to run along side the royal carriage or to serve the emperor at his table, dispensing a napkin or clearing away his plates. And as these dinners began, Gaius made a practice of looking over the wives of guests, then commanding the fairest of them to submit to him in his private quarters. Then he'd return to the roomful of diners with the shame-faced woman in tow and comment on her performance to all within earshot.

The more the Senate and equestrian ranks were ravaged, the fewer men of ability remained to govern Rome's everyday affairs. But the financial crisis was still the worst of the maladies because it affected everyone in the empire. And now came the worst of the new taxes: Gaius revoked Roman citizenship that extended beyond its transference from fathers to sons. All grants of citizenship or property by Augustus and Julius Cæsar were nullified as being out of date. But all of the above could be bought back for a fee. Furthermore, all those who had increased their property holdings since the previous census were at once charged with making out false tax returns. Gaius himself would sit in judgment at the trials, announcing in advance how much money he intended to raise from each defendant.

At the onset of A.D. 41 there were any number of prominent Romans who wished that Caligula would not see his 30th birthday, but none who thought it possible. Neither did Cassius Cherea, one of the tribunes, or colonels, of the Prætorian Guard who took his turn in commanding the palace security detachment.

Cherea was probably in his early fifties at the time, a proud man who had earned his advancements in years of grueling assignments in faraway provinces. Although guarding an emperor should have been the culmination of his career, he hadn't expected to be pressed into collecting taxes and confiscating property from people who had been hounded into suicide. Because taxes had recently been doubled and because Cherea saw their back-breaking effect throughout Rome, he was often moved by pity to "forget" this man's debt or grant that one a delay. But Gaius had been told about it and began to berate the tribune as soft or weak in enforcing the law.

Soon the emperor hit upon a little game that was sure to get the proud Cherea's goat. As the tribune stood at attention awaiting the watchword of the day, Gaius would taunt him in obscene ways that brought guffaws from everyone standing around. Thus, when asked for the watchword, Gaius might give him "Priapas" (the god with the enormous penis) or another word for some part of the female anatomy.

Outwardly, this grizzled veteran bore his insults with stoic dignity. Inside he had become a wreck — but not just from the insults of a warped bully. Increasingly, Cherea and his men were being ordered to carry out atrocities in the name of maintaining order. Each January, when the chariot races were inaugurated in the Circus Maximus, it was traditional for the people to make various requests to the emperor, most of which were granted in the spirit of the new year. But in January of A.D. 41, when they beseeched Gaius to relent on some of his more onerous new taxes, the emperor angrily waved them away from the royal box. When they persisted, he ordered Cherea and his Prætorians to plunge into the crowd of petitioners and kill everyone they could catch.

The tribune's breaking point probably came with the torture of Quintilia. It seems that a senator named Timidius had reported that a political rival named Pompedius had made some insulting comments about the emperor. To bolster his case, Timidius added that the slanderous remarks had been made in the presence of Quintilia, the accused Pompedius' lover and one of the most beautiful women in Rome.

When arrested, Quintilia defiantly denied everything. Timidius implored Gaius to put her to torture. The emperor quickly assigned the task to Cherea, chiding him to go about it with as much fervor as possible in order to atone for his past "effeminacy." Quintilia gave him no room for compromise by declaring that he should be of "good courage" because she was prepared to bear up against anything he could inflict.

Cherea proceeded to put the poor woman through every cruel contrivance his prison could offer. But when it was over he realized that he had tortured his own soul even more than her body. After Quintilia was reduced to a gasping, bleeding, grotesquely contorted sack of broken bones, Cherea had her carried before Gaius and asked in his most imperturbable manner what the emperor wished next.

Gaius had been reading some documents at a desk. When he looked up at last, he was so shocked to see this beauty reduced to such a state that he immediately ordered both Quintilia and Pompedius freed of the charges. He even decreed that she be awarded a "gift" of 800,000 sesterces "to make honorable amends for keeping her glorious patience under such insufferable torments."

Cherea returned to the officers' barracks that day with his teeth clenched in hate. Until then, no Prætorian had ever expressed his private feelings about the emperor for fear of informers within his own ranks, but Cherea couldn't contain himself. "There is no doubt that we have done our job of guarding the emperor against conspiracies, because we have tortured some to such a degree that he himself pities them!" he raged to the few officers lounging about. "It is we who bring these tortures on Rome and all mankind because it is done with our own consent. Even though we have the power to put an end to the life of this man who has so terribly injured his subjects, we have become his executioners instead of his soldiers!"

By now the tribunes and officers were nodding but motioning Cherea to keep his voice down. He ignored them. "Every day we are polluted with the blood we shed," he spat bitterly. "Yet we do this only until somebody else becomes Gaius' instrument in bringing like miseries on ourselves!"

The result of this outburst was that Cherea and another defiant tribune, Cornelius Sabinus, agreed to seek out a leading senator and confess their dire predicament. The senator was Minucianus, known as the most honorable among the surviving patricians and also a logical successor because he was married to one of the childless Caligula's sisters. To their relief, Minucianus cried tears of joy when he heard their intentions, and within a few days a dozen more senators and prætorians had been enlisted in the secret confederation.

Days passed, often with Gaius appearing unguarded in the Forum or in the Temple of Jupiter Capitoline as he performed some official ritual. The conspirators met and met, but always their resolve was thwarted by some bad omen or strategic slipup. Cherea's frustration grew as plans for the emperor's departure for Egypt loomed near. Finally, it was clear that the only remaining opportunity would be at the Augustan Games. Staged in late January, the series of plays, songs and poetic recitations were held in the small outdoor theater on the Palatine that lay between the palace and the now-enshrined home of Cæsar Augustus. Attendees were chiefly neighboring patrician families along with their wives and chief household slaves. Gaius would sit among them, and his personal, inner guard of Thracian and German mercenaries could offer little protection in such a compact and crowded place.

All agreed that the deed would be dispatched on the first day. Yet, three days passed with conditions never being "just so," and a thoroughly exasperated Cherea assembled the plotters on the eve of the last day and dressed down a group that largely outranked him by birth and station. "Do you not see that Gaius is about to set sail for Alexandria?" he hissed. "Is it honorable to let a man who is the scourge of mankind go out of your hands and to a pompous triumph over land and sea? As for myself, I will not leave it to some Egyptian or other to kill him. I will expose myself to the dangers of this enterprise and bear its consequences cheerfully."

The next morning Cherea was at the palace of Gaius, ready to ask for the watchword. Outside in the adjoining theater the same crowd of noble households were chatting and greeting one another for another day's festivities. As he had for three days, Gaius appeared on stage to their applause and solemnly offered sacrifice to the deified Cæsar Augustus. Gaius seemed in good humor and the mood was light — made all the more so when some rare fruits were flung out to the audience. Many birds were released, too, and there were shouts of laughter as some of them dove among the spectators to vie for the fruit they were eating.

Cherea mulled the possibilities as he took his seat to watch the shows. The theater had two doors. The one on the left led to the public street. The one to the right was a covered walkway leading to the palace cloisters. It was divided into two partitions: one for actors to come and go from the stage, the other a way for the emperor and his guests to come and go with privacy.

The day's program led off with a tragedy starring Gaius' oft-time lover, the mime Mnester, and when it was over the emperor opined that he'd decided to retire for a bath and midday dinner, returning to the theater in late afternoon. Gaius rose to leave, and it was a lucky stroke for Cherea, standing in the shadows of the partitioned entrance to the palace. He had just about made up his mind to fall upon the emperor in his seat regardless of the carnage that would follow.

The emperor walked down the aisle toward the private passageway. He paused briefly at the partitioned actors' entrance and cocked his ear while some boys from Asia practiced hymns for rites to the Augustan priesthood. Then he turned up the partitioned private walkway.

Within a few yards Gaius encountered a stern-faced Cherea. The old tribune asked for the watchword. The emperor wiggled his fingers obscenely like a woman's legs and giggled at his cleverness. Suddenly Cherea jerked his sword upward from its scabbard and in almost the same motion hacked it down between the gape-jawed emperor's neck and shoulder.

Gaius staggered back and groaned with pain. Then he straightened up as if to flee, but the tribune Sabinus rushed out from behind Cherea and threw him down on one knee. Others rushed forward, and suddenly the narrow corridor was a hubbub of men slashing, stabbing, hurling epithets at the fallen Gaius and shouting encouragement to one another.

Then, as they could see the life draining from the ashen clump at their feet, all drew back as if each man realized the enormity of what he had done and the danger now facing him. Gaius' attendants had been waiting at the other end of the passageway and had already heard the commotion. Soon the wild, red-haired Germans and Thracians who made up the emperor's personal guard would come storming behind them.

The assassins bulled their way through the passageway with swords flailing. With Cherea shouting impromptu commands, they managed to barricade themselves in the house of Germanicus, which was a wing of the palace that had been added for Gaius' father and his family in the early days of Tiberius. At last they could gasp for breath and collect their wits.

The emperor's bodyguards knew nothing of Roman politics. All they knew was that their assignment paid more money than they had ever seen in Thrace or Germany, and now they faced the stark prospect of no pay at all. After storming in from the theater and seeing the bloodstained lump that had been their emperor, they went wild with rage, killing anyone from senators to servants who happened to step into the corridor.

Within a few minutes, all in the theater also knew what had happened. First, they sat in shock, unable to believe that anyone would have the power to kill the already deified ruler of the civilized world. They wondered how Rome might react. Common people had been inveigled with shows, gladiators, coins tossed from balconies and free distributions of fresh meat. Slaves, above all, had championed Gaius because they could count on his sympathy when they wanted to charge masters with abuses. Why? Because he rewarded them with one-eighth of the booty when they spied on their masters and disclosed unreported caches of wealth that could be confiscated.

But more immediately, the patrician crowd feared the frenzied and unpredictable bodyguards. Suddenly they gasped as Germans burst out of the passageway with the bloodied heads of their slain victims on the tips of their spears. Now the theater reverberated with bellowing wails of people begging for their lives, praying to God and pleading ignorance of everything that happened. But, after menacing the theatergoers with their swords, the Germans cooled down a bit and began to realize how small their numbers were. Might the Senate have them all killed if they slaughtered the spectators? After several minutes, they hastened to the protection of their barracks.

Meanwhile, dramas were unfolding in two other locations. The first was the palace itself, where Prætorians were searching for conspirators, unaware that some of their own comrades had led them. It seems that the emperor's uncle Claudius hadn't gone to the theater that day, or had left it early. At the time of the assassination he had been in one of the apartments that the approaching Prætorians were coming to ransack, and in a moment of panic he slipped onto a balcony and hid behind the curtains that hung before the door.

As Claudius cowered there, one of the Prætorians, prowling about at random, saw two feet sticking out from under the curtains. He swept them aside and instantly recognized the man who stood cringing before him. "Comrades!" he called. "Look what we have here: the brother of Germanicus! Let's hail him as emperor!"

What happened next was a blur as soldiers took turns hauling the dead emperor's petrified uncle in a makeshift litter to their barracks northeast of the city walls. There he spent the cold night, huddled between two sentries, still in fear of his own life and in no way expecting that the Senate would ever allow the despised monarchy to continue.

Indeed, the second drama that fateful day was in the Senate house itself. Nothing stirred men's hearts more than the romantic notion of resuming the republic that had existed before Julius Cæsar. Who didn't dream of a return to democracy governed by the collective wills of free men? But it was *how* to reconstruct that golden heritage that began to consume the Senate from mid afternoon all through the night. Who should be consuls? To whom would provincial governors report? Who would command the legions? Who would preside over the state religion?

As senators prattled and postured, Prætorians milled in and outside the Curia. The more they stood about shifting from one foot to the other, the more they muttered among themselves. Soon they were wondering in loud, sarcastic tones how the world could be led by a spineless, babbling, bickering legislature that had already swooned before two tyrants. And they wondered who would continue to pay their wages. Might those wages even be less than now?

Back at the Prætorian barracks, Claudius' spirits surely warmed as the morning sun rose and as soldiers and dignitaries filed in to declare their support. By midday, a delegation of stern senators entered the camp and asked to address Claudius. In a firm manner bordering on insolence, they warned him that he was but one man and should yield to the will of the many and let democracy take its course. Having closely observed the madness of Caligula himself, Claudius should be "eager to hate the heavy burden of tyranny." If he would but retire to a quiet and virtuous life, the Senate would award him "the greatest honors a people can bestow."

A stern message, indeed. But just then the senatorial envoys seemed to crack. Perhaps it was the sight of so many raucous soldiers surrounding them, but in next instant the senators were on their knees and pleading that if Claudius still insisted on assuming the throne, he should accept it only as given freely by the Senate.

In order to understand why they did so — and what Claudius said in response — it is necessary to add that among the delegation was none other than Herod Agrippa.

Yes, Agrippa had once again insinuated himself into a pivotal moment in history. In the midst of the chaos that had swept the theater after the assassination, the King of insignificant Trachonitis and Gaulanitis had the same instincts as the Prætorian soldier as to who should succeed Caligula. He ran into the palace seeking his friend for over 40 years and just managed to spot the terrified Claudius emerging from the palace, his chair teetering on the shoulders the some boisterous Prætorian soldiers. Agrippa managed to break through the mob long enough to tell Claudius in a desperate whisper not to give up the government if the Senate demanded it.

When Agrippa returned home to wash and change clothes, he received a note to hasten to the hilltop temple of Jupiter Capitoline, where the Senate was holding an extraordinary session (probably because it offered more privacy than the Senate house in the crowded Forum). There, Agrippa found the senators in the midst of discussing ways to raise an army to contest the Prætorians and Claudius. He heard men pledging money and even offering to free any slaves who would join the Senate in an army that would march on the Prætorians and end the hated monarchy.

Agrippa let them talk, then in time raised his hand to speak. He began by swearing that he was prepared to lose his life to defend the Senate's honor, but begged them to think twice about mounting a military conflict. "Against men who are skillful at war we must use men who do not know so much as how to draw a sword," he cautioned. "Thus, in my opinion we should send some persons to Claudius to persuade him to lay down the government. And I am ready to be one of your ambassadors."

Sometime before the delegation's arrival at the Prætorian camp, Agrippa managed to smuggle a note to Claudius telling him of the Senate's disorder. He urged his friend to reply in a conciliatory tone, but with imperial authority and dignity.

And so he did. Claudius said he didn't wonder why the envoys had no taste for another emperor. But under him, Claudius assured, they could expect equitable and moderate government. He would be ruler only in name, relying heavily on their cooperation and authority. He had seen so much misery himself, he added, that they could well trust him to rule judiciously. This struck home with the ambassadors, because the stuttering Claudius had been the endless butt of Gaius' jokes and jibes.

As the ambassadors were departing, the soldiers let up a great roar and swore an oath to Claudius. Another cheer went up when he decreed that every Prætorian would be given 15,000 sesterces. By nightfall the Senate was in session again, but only a hundred of the 600 members had bothered to drift back. The senators were still ruminating when dawn came, and it seemed as if only the obstinacy of the tribunes of Cherea and Sabinus cowed them into continuing. Outside, a mob of soldiers milled about, and when Cherea raised his hands to signal for silence, the throng raised a cacophonous din because they wanted no one talking against their monarchy and their plump bonuses. But the angry Cherea out-shouted them. Oh, was it an emperor they wanted? Well, he would go ask the watchword from Eutuchus (whom everyone knew as charioteer of the Green Team and a favorite of Gaius). What idiots they were to endure all the madness of Caligula only to turn their fate over to a stammering fool!

Some of Cherea's former comrades now had swords in their hands and menacing looks. Others went back to the Prætorian camp to hail Claudius. More senators drifted off and soon Cherea and Sabinus were nearly alone in the cold marble temple of Jupiter Capitoline. Their talk turned to whether they should kill themselves on the spot. Sabinus was ready, but Cherea said he wanted to learn the new emperor's intentions.

By the next day a more confident Claudius had been escorted back to the palace in which he'd been raised under Augustus and Tiberius. The chief remaining topic was what to do with the slayers of Gaius. None doubted that the deed had been a "glorious one," as one of them put it, but the killers posed a conundrum under Roman law. After all, Prætorian guardsmen swore an oath of fealty to their emperor and no one could escape the fact that the conspirators had violated their pledge. And how could Cherea go free when he had also spoken against the monarchy and Claudius? The only plausible accusation was that the old soldier had acted to avenge the personal insults of Gaius rather than from any concern for the nation's welfare.

And so, Cherea was led to his execution and bore it with an officer's dignity. He calmly inquired about the skill of the young soldier assigned to do the deed. After offering a suggestion or two, Cherea presented the young man with the very sword he had used to kill Gaius. He stretched out his neck and his head toppled after a single stroke.

What of Sabinus, who had struck the second blow on Gaius? For reasons that Roman writers have never explained, Claudius pardoned the tribune and restored him to his former command. But after a few weeks Sabinus could no longer live with himself or the glares of his troops. He fell on his sword and drove it up to the hilt.

Not surprisingly, one of Claudius' first acts as emperor involved his Jewish friend and champion. In the spring of A.D. 41 the emperor held a great assembly at the public rostrum in the Forum and proclaimed that his lifelong friend and recent benefactor would now add Judea, Samaria, Perea and Galilee — nearly all the lands of Herod the Great — to his kingdom. The only exception was that the small princedom of Chalcis (not far from Antioch) would go to his brother (inconveniently named Herod as well) along with the privilege of appointing high priests. With these territories, Herod Agrippa could expect an annual income of about 12 million drachmæ, or about two-thirds of what his grandfather could expect at the peak of his powers.

All this was consummated by a pact of friendship and two imperial decrees that would be equally important. The death of Gaius Caligula had so emboldened the oppressed Jews of Alexandria that they had risen up against their tormentors and inflicted so much damage that it was now the latter who were petitioning Claudius for relief.

The emperor's reply has been preserved intact. It reads in part:

> As for which party was responsible for the riot and feud (or, rather, if the truth must be told, the war) with the Jews, although your envoys...put your case with great zeal, never-

theless I was unwilling to make a strict inquiry, though guarding within me a store of immutable indignation against any who renewed the conflict; and I can tell you once and for all that unless you put a stop to this ruinous and obstinate enmity against each other, I shall be driven to show what a benevolent emperor can be when turned to righteous indignation.

Wherefore once again I conjure you that, on the one hand, the Alexandrians show themselves forbearing and kindly toward the Jews, who for many years have dwelt in the same city, and dishonor none of the rights observed by them in the worship of their god but allow them to observe their customs as in the time of the deified Augustus, which customs I also, after hearing both sides, have confirmed. And, on the other hand, I explicitly order the Jews not to agitate for more privileges than they formerly possessed, and in the future not to send out a separate embassy as if they lived in a separate city — a thing unprecedented — and not to force their way into gymnastic games, while enjoying their own privileges and sharing a great abundance of advantages in a city not their own, and not to bring or admit Jews from Syria or those who sail down from Egypt, a proceeding which will compel me to conceive serious suspicions. Otherwise, I will by all means proceed against them as fomenters of what is a general plague on the whole world.

If, desisting from these courses, you both consent to live with mutual forbearance and kindness, I on my side will exercise a solicitude of very long standing for the city, as one bound to us by ancestral friendship...Farewell.[14]

At this time, however, Jewish quarters all through the Hellene world were being vandalized and otherwise harassed wherever they found themselves in the minority. So Herod Agrippa pressed his good fortune once again and persuaded the much-obliged Claudius to restore the same privileges to Jews throughout the empire. The second decree added that:

It will therefore be fit to permit the Jews, who are in all the world under us, to keep their ancient customs without

> being hindered so to do. And I charge them also to use my kindness to them with moderation, and not to show a contempt of the superstitious observances of other nations, but to keep their laws only. And I will that this decree of mine be engraved on tables by the magistrates of the cities, colonies and municipal places, both those within Italy and those without it, both kings and governors, by the means of the ambassadors, and to have it exposed to the public for a full thirty days, in such a place where it may plainly be read from the ground.[15]

Having demonstrated that he was a loyal Roman, Herod Agrippa was eager to show that he was an observant Jew as well. After a few more months of helping Claudius settle in, the successor to Herod the Great was soon a fixture in Jerusalem offering all the proper temple sacrifices. Having been able at last to repay his many debts, Agrippa embellished his old ways of winning friends with great flourishes of generosity. Abolishing the annual tax on houses quickly endeared him to a great many working families. And like his grandfather, Agrippa began undertaking large public works projects, such as an elegant new theater, baths and porticos in the Phoenician city of Berytus (Beirut). For its dedication, Agrippa assembled more musicians and gladiators than had ever been seen in these parts. In one day at the new theater, 700 condemned criminals were pitted against a like number and virtually all were killed in hand-to-hand combat. The Jews of his own country would not have permitted it, but the Hellenes of Berytus roared without letup until the arena was awash in blood.

During his first year in Palestine, Agrippa showed remarkable skill in dealing with his major constituencies. As the historian Josephus wrote shortly afterwards, "He was not at all like the Herod who reigned before him; for that Herod was ill-natured and severe in his punishments. But Agrippa's temper was mild and equally liberal to all men. He was humane to foreigners and made them feel sensible of his liberality." But Josephus adds that he also "kept himself entirely pure" when it came to Jewish ritual so that "never did a day pass over his head without its appointed sacrifice."

There always to remind the king to enjoy his good fortune was a golden chain he had hung over the entrance to the temple treasury — the same one Gaius had given him upon his release from Tiberius' prison. He said it was there as an inspiration to all as to "how one fallen so low can regain the heights of dignity."

AT SOME POINT midway into his second year in Jerusalem, Herod Agrippa decided to purge the Jewish leaders of The Way. And by choosing to do so at the Passover festival, he intended to make his action as public as possible.

Why would this supposedly good-natured ruler single out this group at a time when he was trying so hard to consolidate support from all quarters? One simple answer is that this particular "sect" was not large enough to warrant any concessions from the king. At the same time, these Christians, as they were coming to be called, posed an increasing threat to his three most important interests: himself, the temple leadership and the Romans.

Regarding the temple leaders, Jerusalem had already seen three high priests during the king's young tenure. The exact reasons are lost, but one can guess that the king was unhappy with their politics. The latest appointment, one Simon, may have felt his duties impeded by the growth of the Christian sect, by its resistance to share in the duties of temple administration and its divergence from standard worship practices. For example, Jewish Christians would celebrate the Passover, but their prayers were for the forgiveness of the wrong done to their Messiah — and for his second coming. Moreover, the Christians of Jerusalem ceased slaughtering the Passover lamb because Jesus, the Lamb of their salvation, had already been sacrificed.

The perceived threat to the Romans and Agrippa himself were one and the same. A movement preaching the return of a messiah as king of the Jews was hardly a source of joy to an incumbent king. As for the Romans, the prospect of a growing religion that united Jews and Gentiles alike carried the seeds of sedition. At the very least, every Gentile who became a Jew might feel entitled to special privileges such as exemption from military service and various taxes. They might even build an empire within an empire!

On a more practical level, Agrippa by this time was seeking ways to demonstrate his loyalty to a new governor. When Claudius' new man in Antioch first visited Agrippa, he was alarmed to see hundreds of workmen building the outer walls of Jerusalem higher and thicker. Soon the king had a letter from Claudius advising him to "leave off the project."

Thus, the Christians offered a convenient way to advance all three goals. And no one stood in his way, because thanks to the Claudian edict, all Roman troops had been withdrawn, leaving Agrippa free to manage local affairs with his own army.

Once having concluded that the Christians were undesirables, it is not difficult to see why a king known as gentle and just could justify dispatching troops to arrest people in the midst of preaching love and mercy.

Indeed, had he hesitated to see 1,400 convicted criminals destroy themselves in a theatrical spectacle?

Peter, who had already survived one arrest, was an obvious target. Why Agrippa chose James, the son of Zebedee, as his first example seems unclear at first — but perhaps not after closer inspection.

According to the Gospel of Mark, James and his younger brother John were raised on the shores of Lake Galilee, some 20 miles from Nazareth, where Jesus grew up. Their mother, Mary Salome, may have been a relative, perhaps even a sister, of Jesus' own mother, Mary. The boys' father, Zebedee, was both a pious Jew and prosperous fisherman. He had a home, servants, and a second home in Jerusalem that he visited often. In fact, it's probable that Zebedee was more than a mere fisherman. He had a partner named Jona, and it may be that his trips to Jerusalem were the result of their supplying fish and other foods to that city. Jona, however, is more important to us as the father of two sons named Peter and Andrew.

It is plausible that Peter, Andrew, James and John all grew up knowing Jesus. At least some of them had also become believers in John the Baptist. One cannot know exactly when and why all four decided to drop everything they held dear and join Jesus in his wanderings, but one of many stories will suffice to explain why they *remained* with him. Sometime before A.D. 30, Jesus, who had already acquired his band of disciples by this time, was preaching at the edge of the Lake of Gennesaret early one morning and was being pressed hard by a crowd that had grown so large that the farthest away could neither see nor hear him. So Jesus commandeered Peter's fishing boat and asked the crew to keep it steady in the shallow shore waters as he spoke to the people from a short distance away.

Peter and his partners had already been out all night rowing, casting nets and having nothing to show for it. No doubt very fatigued and hungry when the sermon was over, the crew was about to wash their nets and head home for a meal. But then Jesus turned to Peter with what must have seemed like an irritating request. "Launch out into the deep and let down your nets," he said.

One can see Peter replying wearily, "Master, we've already worked all night — and for nothing." Besides, anyone in these lakeside towns knew that fish were active at night and not when the hot sun shone on the waters. "Nonetheless," sighed Peter perhaps with a trace of sarcasm, "at *your* word I will let down the net."

What happened then must have been momentous for a disciple who was also a fisherman. When they pulled the net back up they had taken in such a load of fish that the crew could scarcely haul it in. One wonders if that event alone didn't sustain Peter more in his dark, lonesome trials than any of the many miracles that he was to witness.

James and John, the sons of Zebedee, were part of that experience. While there is no mention of their father's reaction to joining Jesus, their mother, Mary Salome, became a devout follower as well. She followed the disciples on their last trip to Jerusalem and was one of the women who anointed the body of Jesus after it was removed from the cross.

Mary Salome's two sons were among Jesus' most zealous followers and among the three who appeared to be brought in to share his most intimate experiences. The three were Peter, James and John, all fishermen from Galilee. In what *Mark* records as the first time Jesus raised anyone from the dead, he took only these three with him across the lake and into a city of the Decapolis where the 12-year-old daughter of a synagogue leader had just died. There, in the elder's house with the family and three disciples looking on, Jesus took the girl's hand and said, *"Talitha cumi,"* which means "Arise, little girl," which *Mark* says she did. In another instance, Peter, James and John were the only disciples to accompany Jesus when he was transfigured on a mount as he met with Moses and the Jewish prophet Elijah.

At one point in his ministry Jesus began calling James and John the "Sons of Thunder." It was probably because they were zealous in their cause and preached in a strong, demonstrative manner or spoke in a way that caused thunderous torment in the souls of those who heard him.

On another occasion the prideful mother of James and John actually beseeched Jesus to decree that her sons would sit on his right and left when he came into his kingdom. Jesus refrained from rebuking her, but on the road to Jerusalem when James and John raised the matter again, he shook his head and said simply: "You know not what you ask."

Then said Jesus, "Are you able to drink from the cup I am about to drink, and to be baptized with the baptism I am about to be baptized with?' And instantly they replied "We are able!"

Not long afterwards, Jesus chose only Peter, James and John to be with him when he agonized in the garden of Gethsemane on his final night on earth. But those who had proclaimed themselves "able" to share in his "baptism," according to *Mark*, spent the night dozing and sleeping as Jesus confronted "the hour and power of darkness."

All this may have made James resolve never again to weaken should his own trial come. If so, it would explain why this "Son of Thunder" stood out among the apostles in Jerusalem and why he went with calm resignation when the soldiers of Agrippa took him away one night and killed him with the sword.

Peter, as if to confirm that he was more widely known, was seized and thrown into prison. It happened during Passover (the Feast of the Unleavened Bread), and it was Agrippa's intent to bring Peter out to the people the next day. As it had been with Pilate in Jesus' time, it was traditional for an eastern monarch to present a few imprisoned persons to the festive crowd and allow them to select one or two for freedom on the strength of their shouts — all, of course, to demonstrate the ruler's generosity. It would appear that Peter was to share the fate of Jesus, for no fewer than four squads of soldiers were rotated around the clock to make sure no one would try to free him.

All night long the Christians prayed for Peter's safe delivery. That he *was* delivered — and certainly with no help from Agrippa — is indisputable. And the only account is this one from *Acts:* In the dead of night Peter was sleeping between two soldiers, bound with two chains. Sentries outside were guarding the door of the prison cell. Suddenly a light shone all around and an angel of God appeared. He nudged the sleeping Peter in the side and said, "Get up quickly."

With that the chains fell off Peter's hands. "Dress yourself and put on your sandals," said the angel. As Peter did so, the angel said: "Wrap your mantle around you and follow me."

Peter still thought he was dreaming. But when the two had passed the first and second guard outside the cell, they came to an iron gate that separated the prison from the city. The gate opened of its own accord. They went out into the street and immediately the angel left him.

Peter stood open-mouthed in the dimly lit street before he began walking. He wound up in front of the house of Mary, mother of John Mark, whose home was undoubtedly used for Christian meetings and worship services. In any case, many people were inside, all in the midst of praying for Peter's safety.

Peter knocked. A maid came and listened to a voice asking to be let in. Recognizing it instantly as Peter's, she forgot to open the door, but ran joyously to tell everyone that Peter was standing outside.

"Either you are mad or it's his angel," someone said.

But when the knocks continued and they opened the door, they fell back in amazement to see it was indeed Peter. Motioning with his hand for them to remain silent, he described in whispers how an angel of the Lord had brought him out of prison. Then, deciding that the house of Mary was a place that would be searched first, Peter stole away and went into hiding.

The sentries did indeed come calling. And when they could not find Peter anywhere, Herod Agrippa had the soldiers examined by torture to determine if they had aided Peter. Then apparently finding no evidence there, either, he had them all put to death.

New Testament writings say only that Peter "went to another place" at this time. Indeed, no one seems to know for sure where Peter did go for the next three or four years. However, all this does suggest that Peter and at least some of the original disciples (whom I will now call apostles because all Christians were called disciples then) left Jerusalem during the persecution of Agrippa. The fact that the twelve apostles did not replenish their number this time (as they had upon the suicide of Judas Iscariot) further suggests that the group broke up at this time to begin preaching beyond Jerusalem.

It is also reasonable to assume that the apostles had to travel farther than they had done before. This is because all of Judea, Samaria and Galilee were again under control of one king — and one who had taken pains to build friendly relations with rulers in many neighboring lands who would gladly return any fugitives he requested.

Beyond that, the initial dispersion of the apostles can be divined only through conjecture and oral tradition (the latter of which generally gains more credibility with each new archeological discovery). Here, among the strata of tradition and lore are the most likely possibilities:

Peter may have spent time in Babylon preaching to the Jews of the Dispersion, for no city except Alexandria had a larger Jewish population. Some say he was in Rome during this time, but it's probable that the many friends of Agrippa would have prevented him from preaching openly if not actually delivering him back to the king.

Thomas is reported to have gone to Parthia, and then as far as India.

Bartholomew is also said to have journeyed to India and Parthia, later settling in Armenia.

Andrew also reportedly journeyed to the Black Sea region and preached among several cities along the coast.

Philip preached among several Greek cities — Hierapolis among them.

Simon the Zealot went to Gaul and the British Isles.

Thaddeus reportedly returned to settle in Edessa, a small state approaching Armenia some 500 miles north of Jerusalem. I say that he "returned" because the bishop Eusebius, who wrote so credibly from Cæsarea in the early fourth century, reports matter-of-factly that Jesus had received a letter from Abgar, the king of Edessa, stating that he was dying of a seemingly incurable disease, and imploring Jesus to come heal him. Jesus, says Eusebius, sent the disciple Thaddeus to cure the king, who gratefully became a Christian along with all his nobles. That Edessa remained a strong

Christian community for centuries afterward certainly lends credence to the bishop's report.

Despite the lack of details about the early whereabouts of the apostles, there is also absence of an equally important piece of information. That is, there is no written source nor oral tradition nor even hearsay that any of the original apostles ever rejected Jesus or retreated from his mission. Equally noteworthy is that The Way, a term falling into disuse by now, did not shrink or shrivel when Agrippa tried to slice its heart out in Jerusalem. In fact, new disciples came forth to fill the roles played by the dispersed original apostles. And not the least of them was another James, a brother of Jesus. A conservative orthodox Jew, he had at first refused Jesus' invitation to join his ministry. Perhaps he even opposed it. Now he came forward in Jerusalem to become the leader and spokesman for the Christians. And perhaps because he was pious in observing traditional Jewish worship, he was a tolerable substitute to the authorities for the unpredictable Peter and James.

Antioch, 350 miles north of Jerusalem, was large and nonchalant enough to absorb whatever disputes erupted within its many ethnic enclaves. And if any group threatened to disrupt the usual busy hum of life in the Syrian capital, two Roman legions were on hand to change their minds. All this worked to the advantage of Paul and Barnabas in the more than two years they spent there.

Founded some 400 years before by Seleucus, one of Alexander's generals, and named for his father Antiochus, the city became the western capital of the Seleucid Empire for some 250 years. When Pompey conquered Syria in 64 B.C., he made Antioch as its capital.

Indeed, Rome inherited a well-fortified city that marked its key line of defense against Parthia to the east. Seleucus had first built a naval base in one of the Mediterranean's best harbors. Located near the mouth of the river Orontes, it was protected to the north by Mount Pierus, which rises 4,000 feet and offered an impregnable natural fortification.

Having secured the sea, Seleucus next built the city itself some 20 miles inland on a bend where the Orontes breaks out of the valley and begins to race downhill to the sea. Just north of it the river valley, a lake and a plain assured a generous supply of grapes, olives, grain, fish and vegetables. To the west, the commercial and military highway led through Cilicia and across the province of Asia. To the east the highway reached all the way into Mesopotamia. And to the south lay the granaries of Syria and Palestine.

Seleucus laid out the city in a square and divided it in two parts: one for native Syrians and the other for his retired soldiers. Rome in turn continued the expansion when Julius Cæsar added several public buildings, a the-ater, an amphitheater and an extraordinary aqueduct that brought water from a source 45 miles to the southeast. Thanks to the generosity of Herod the Great, the broad, colonnaded main market road was paved with marble. Augustus and Tiberius added more public buildings and statues.

It was to this vibrant, cosmopolitan city that the Jewish Christian leadership in Jerusalem had sent Barnabas. His apparent mission was to verify word that the fleeing followers of the martyred Stephen had coalesced there and had established a growing, enthusiastic group of Hellenistic adherents to Jesus. But no doubt Barnabas, the Jewish Cypriot, was somewhat flustered in trying to communicate effectively with persons who were attempting to fit into a movement rooted in Jewish customs and law.

So it was natural that Barnabas should think of Paul in nearby Tarsus. After all, Antioch was but a larger, more crowded version of Paul's native city and an even broader stewpot of races and religions. Paul, almost as if in an apprenticeship, had been living among and speaking Greek to a polyglot of people, yet all without abandoning his Pharisee's moral code or sharpness in debate. So when Barnabas sailed the brief trip to Tarsus and found Paul, no doubt hunched over while stitching some skins, both knew that the time had come to engage in an important new mission.

One can also envision the sites that Paul and Barnabas saw as they pulled into the commercial harbor and walked to the great city along the fast-flowing Orontes. Clustered about the center city, to be sure, were tenements as dense and dark as any in Rome. But the original core that had been laid out by Alexander's army engineers was splendidly spacious. Built much like the town plan of Alexandria in Egypt, Antioch employed the popular Hippodamian system of broad streets cutting one another at right angles. The two main colonnaded thoroughfares intersected at the town center. There stood the baths and theaters, which were the center of life for a people known for their enjoyment of music and stage plays. The baths reflected this because inside were statues and frescos of Apollo, Olympos, Scythes and other deities all playing the Antiochenes' favorite instrument, the flute.

Throughout the city the most frequent adornments were temples and statues to Zeus, Apollo, Isis, Demeter, Aphrodite, Artemis, Athena, Hermes and a dozen more. But the largest statue was one of Tyche, representing the good fortune of Antioch. Seated on a rock symbolizing Mount Silpius, the robed goddess wore a turreted crown representing the walls and gates of the city. At her feet was a youth representing the river Orontes.

Still, the one sight Paul and Barnabas would have noticed more than any other as they passed along the Orontes was the sacred Grove of Daphne. This large riverfront oasis of grass, tall trees and temple buildings commemorated the nymph whom Apollo had attempted to rape — unsuccessfully because Mother Earth had heard Daphne's pleas for help and had changed her at once into a laurel tree in order to protect her. From its leaves Apollo made a wreath for his head, thus originating the tradition of the laurel crown.

The Grove of Daphne began as both a public park and a sanctuary in which fugitives, debtors and others could not be seized. But by the time Paul and Barnabas arrived, this "sanctuary" was known more for being dedicated to the pleasures of the flesh. Male and female prostitutes from all over the East frolicked through the woods, paying a fixed portion of their earnings towards the upkeep of the temple and ancillary buildings. In fact ancient authors used the "Grove of Daphne" as a catchphrase for any wicked place.

In many ways, Antioch represented all that raised hackles on the backs of conservative Romans. Whereas it was said that Alexandria combined the vanity of the Greeks with the superstition of the Egyptians, the Antiochenes combined every vanity, superstition and sensual excess from all over the eastern world.

When Barnabas had first arrived alone for his one-man "inquiry" the year before summoning Paul, he found that the Christians there already were led by dedicated disciples from places as diverse as his own native Cyprus. *Acts* mentions Lucius, a Cyrene, and Nicholaus, who was a native of Antioch and one of the seven who had served in Jerusalem with the martyred Stephen.

But there were others without Greek backgrounds. The early writings also mention Manæn (derived from the Hebrew name Menahem) who had been a childhood companion of Herod Antipas and probably came from a wealthy Jewish family. And there was Simeon Niger, who seems to have been a black immigrant from the western section of North Africa. In fact, there is a strong tradition that Simeon Niger was the same Simeon whom the Roman soldiers had pulled out of the crowd in Jerusalem a dozen years before and forced to carry the cross of Jesus through the streets. The experience had caused him to become a believer, and now he had become a leader among the Christians.

In any event, the people in Antioch who called themselves Christians were both diverse and growing in numbers. Surely the primary cause was the persecution of Stephen and the dispersion of his Hellenistic comrades. But since then some Jewish Christians had found themselves more comfortable in Antioch after the persecutions of Agrippa. And non-Jewish Christians felt the same because they had escaped the watchful eye of temple authorities and the smothering effects of temple ritual in their daily lives. And for much of this they could thank Peter, who, through his encounter with the family of the centurion Cornelius had affirmed that salvation through Jesus definitely included Gentiles.

But defining precisely *how* Gentiles were to behave was the question left to the Antioch church to sort out for itself. By the time Barnabas and Paul arrived a dozen years after the crucifixion, the young church at Antioch was a mirror of roughly four schools of thought that had already evolved in Christian centers of population.

The first group was Jewish Christians who insisted on total adherence to Mosaic Law. In fact, they came to be known as the "circumcision party." Providing them with a reservoir of potential believers was the fact that Antioch at the time had the largest Jewish community in northern Syria, with as many as 40,000 people occupying the city's southwestern quarter. Thus, Jewish Christians could count on receiving at least a polite hearing in most synagogues because their message was steeped in Jewish tradition: the God of Abraham, Isaac and Jacob had fulfilled his promises to his chosen people by sending them a Messiah, a fellow Jew, whom he had also raised from the dead.

A second group was comprised of Jewish Christians who did not insist on the painful circumcision ritual but who required non-Jewish converts to observe many of their traditional dietary and hygienic practices. Peter was best identified with this group, and so was James, the brother of Jesus, when he assumed leadership of the church in Jerusalem.

The third group was best represented by Paul of Tarsus. It spared Gentile converts from both circumcision and the observance of Jewish food laws. But neither did it require Jewish Christians to abandon any of their traditional practices.

The fourth and perhaps smallest group was the most radical. Identified with Hellenists such as Stephen, Philip and others of The Seven, these zealots for Christ saw no significance in observing any of the Jewish traditions. They regarded Judaism and Christianity as two distinct religions. Indeed, they believed that Christians could not breathe free in their new life unless liberated entirely from the beliefs and rites of those whose leaders had persecuted Jesus.

This is not to say that these groups formed altogether different sects and worshipped as separate entities. Although a house church in the Jewish quarter no doubt had a different complexion than one elsewhere, it would be more typical to find persons of all persuasions within one congregation as well as persons whose opinions were changing or still forming. After all, Christians everywhere were facing questions not always addressed by Jesus. How were they to provide for the poor? How much should they allot for the care of widows? How much of their personal wealth should they share among the Christian community? Should one punish a Christian caught stealing? How long might it be before Christ returned to earth for the Judgment? In the meantime, should they postpone pending marriages or delay having children?

It was in this atmosphere that Paul labored for longer than two years. And during this whole period, *Acts* always mentions his name after that of the gentle Barnabas. For by now the fiery preacher of Damascus and Jerusalem had learned to become a teacher and reconciler as well. And soon he would be called upon to employ all of these qualities at once.

IN A.D. 44 Claudius had taken care of a project that Gaius had botched. He completed the trip across the English Channel to Britain and stayed long enough to proclaim it for Rome without much opposition from the disorganized native clans. When word of the conquest reached the other side of the Mediterranean, Herod Agrippa was visiting Cæsarea and decided to organize a festival of shows and games in celebration.

The chief magistrates of the Phoenician cities of Sidon and Tyre no doubt thought that the happy event would be a good time to send a delegation to Agrippa to mediate some long-standing dispute. In any event, Agrippa was scheduled to address a crowd about the matter in the theater at the beginning of the festival's second day. As the royal entourage filed in to take their seats early that morning, the spectators were soon abuzz. They had seen that the king wore a resplendent garment made entirely of silver. As he moved through the aisles, the low angle of the sun sent ripples of reflected light through the theater while the points of the king's crown seemed to shoot out sparks of fire. When Agrippa stood to speak, people began to shout, "Oh look, it is not a man but a god." And orthodox Jews joined in with impious flattery. "Oh be merciful to us," one of them mocked. "For although we have but revered thee only as a man, we shall henceforth know thee as superior to mortal nature."

The historian Josephus has it that as Agrippa stood waiting for the shouts to quiet down, an owl swooped in and settled on one of the ropes above his head that was used to pull an awning of shade over the royal box when the sun got overhead. In a sickening instant, the grandson of Herod the Great recalled that during the night near Rome when he had stood so forlornly in chains after being arrested by Tiberius. One of his fellow prisoners had prophesied that Agrippa would go free and live in splendor until one day when an owl would perch over him and signal his end.

Only Agrippa or the owl could confirm this story. But historians do confirm that just then a severe pain began to stab at the king's stomach or chest. Instead of addressing the crowd, Herod clutched at his middle and turned to those in his party. "I, whom you are calling a god, am now commanded to be hurried away by death," he said, grimacing. "But I am bound to accept what Providence allots as it pleases God; for I have by no means lived ill, but in a splendid and happy manner."

With that the pain became more violent and the king was carried to his palace. Soon, those who had dressed in their finest for a celebration spectacle were wearing sackcloth and beseeching God for the king's recovery.

Inside the palace, as the stricken Agrippa lay in an upper chamber and looked down on people lying prostrate on the ground in prayer, he began weeping softly. After five days of no longer being able to bear the pain in his stomach and the foreboding he felt for the future of his people, Herod Agrippa gave up the ghost in his fifty-fourth year.

The government decreed days of public lamentations, and I would like to report that this complex-yet-compassionate man was universally mourned. The truth is that it took but a few hours for his fragile coalition of support to cave in. The orthodox Jews who had taunted him as a pompous, walking idol were just as jubilant as the Hellenists who resented Jewish rule over their cities. Even in Cæsarea itself and nearby Sebaste, people put garlands on their heads and engaged in wild drinking and dancing to celebrate Agrippa's passing. Despite the fact that five Roman regiments were stationed in Cæsarea, many of their ranks joined a frenzied mob that stormed into the Herodian palace and carted off everything from statues to furniture. Some reports add that even the king's daughters were abused in the rampage.

But the price for a few days of wild abandon in some cities would be extracted from all of Palestine a million fold in the years to come.

A.D.
JULY 44
– 46

TIBERIUS CLAUDIUS CÆSAR AUGUSTUS GERMANICUS was three years into his reign and probably enjoying life more than at any other time in his 54 years. Although no one had a more noble birthright — his mother was the daughter of Mark Anthony and his brother the legendary Germanicus — Claudius had been mocked, shunned, and passed over for all of his life until the Prætorian Guards had found him cowering behind a curtain just when they were looking for someone to crown emperor.

By now, Claudius was settling in on Romans and they were enjoying the contrast with Gaius. Certainly his stuttering, nervous tick and lame left foot were not the stuff of emperors, but one might guess them all to be the scars of infantile paralysis. His mental prowess had long since been proven: in the days when a patrician of his rank would have been consul or commander of a legion, Claudius had written a 20 volume history of the Etruscans, a biography of Augustus and tracts ranging from a defense of Cicero to an instruction manual on playing at dice (all of them now lost). Moreover, his years observing other emperors up close had produced a certain imperial majesty about him. Claudius was "tall of stature and full of frame," as Suetonius puts it, "with a lively countenance and handsome gray hair." And he would always rise to a dignified attention when approached by an official visitor.

The emperor's health, despite his abnormal mannerisms, remained excellent and certainly didn't slow down his lifelong pursuit of wine, food and women. Already divorced twice (not counting a betrothal in which the bride took ill and died on the eve of the wedding), he had recently married again to a woman of only 20. Valeria Messalina, a grandniece of Augustus, had given Rome an empress for the first time in 30 years. When she wasn't vying to be the most beautiful and admired woman in Rome, Messalina had borne the emperor two children: a daughter, Octavia, and a son, Germanicus.

Whereas Gaius had been preoccupied with his own godhead, Claudius the historian made his mark on Rome by re-instituting many ancient religious customs that had been allowed to lapse. His day-to-day interests lay more in the courts than the Senate. Where Caligula was bored by anything to do with judicial duties, Claudius showed a zeal for hearing individual cases and reforming the judicial process.

In court Claudius was so good-natured and approachable that at the end of the day lawyers would often grab onto the fringe of his robes as he left, begging him to hear one more case. One knight, enraged that Claudius would let several well-known prostitutes testify against him, once hurled his stylus and tablets into the emperor's face and cut his cheek badly. In another case when the emperor berated a lawyer for failing to produce a witness, the barrister spat back: "He's dead! Is that not a lawful excuse?"

That Claudius could spend so much time in court and even take a four-month excursion to Britannia was due largely to the growing use of skilled freedmen in government administration. Augustus had employed a few Greek or Hellenized ex-slaves to help with his correspondence. With Tiberius and his long stay on Capri, some of these freedmen assumed expanded duties, but their numbers were still limited. With the next emperor too engrossed in his deification to worry much about earthly affairs, more freedmen rose up to fill the breech of responsibility (but just as many were pruned by constant purges). Under Claudius, educated freedmen would eventually receive official titles and duties in financial and foreign affairs. They would also amass great wealth and exercise, collectively, as much power as the Senate itself. Indeed, their rise was doubtless because Claudius couldn't bring himself to trust the Senate fully after exposing its sympathy for the Republic in those all-night sessions that followed the slaying of Gaius.

In the very first years of Claudius these administrative assistants were clearly organized and controlled by the emperor. And they were kept in check because Claudius also relied heavily on a few friends from the Senate to help him govern. Chief among them was none other than Lucius Vitellius, the same man who had served Tiberius ably as governor of Syria and whose experience in Jewish affairs would again prove especially valuable.

All in all, Claudius had good reason to feel confident and even content in the way he governed during these first years. But he would be wrong had he felt the same way about his wife. Sadly, the same 23-year-old empress who by day looked so regal in her husband's presence turned into an alley cat by night. Apparently Messalina couldn't wait for her husband to snore off in his bed before she would be up and prowling about for anyone else's.

It's possible Claudius didn't know about any of this or that he was shielded from it, but it wasn't long before everyone else in Rome knew of Messalina's exploits to the point where a young satirist named Juvenal was raising eyebrows with a verse written in A.D. 44.

> Hear what Claudius had to put up with. The minute she heard him
>   snoring,
> His wife — that whore empress — who dared to prefer the mattress
> Of a stews to her couch in the Palace, called for her hooded
> Night-cloak and hastened forth, alone or with a single
> Maid to attend her. Then, her black hair hidden
> Under an ash-blonde wig, she would make straight for her brothel
> With its odor of stale, warm bedclothes, its empty reserved cell.
> Here she would strip off, showing her golded nipples and the belly
> That once housed a prince of the blood.[16]

It was just about this time that word of Herod Agrippa's sudden death came from Cæsarea. Any worries that Claudius retained about Herod's insolent move to re-fortify Jerusalem must have been erased by a floodtide of memories: two boys playing in the household of Augustus, suffering together the torments of Tiberius and Gaius, and mustering all their wits to secure Claudius the grand prize when it could have been denied at any moment by a Prætorian's sword.

The same dispatch from Judea informed the emperor as to the infamous celebrations by the people of Cæsarea and Sebaste. Now, with both grief and anger contending inside him, Claudius had to report both events to Herod Agrippa II. The king's 17-year-old son was living at the palace while completing his education. Out of loyalty and a sense of revenge, the emperor's first impulse was to send the son to Jerusalem at once as successor to all his father's lands. But Vitellius, the former Syrian governor, and all of the emperor's freedmen urged against it on grounds that the people were far too quarrelsome and divided for an inexperienced lad to hold together in one nation. At last it was decided to send one Cuspius Fadus, a freedman and experienced administrator, as procurator over Agrippa's entire kingdom until the son reached maturity.

So Fadus departed by early fall with three primary orders. The first was to punish the citizens of Cæsarea and Sebaste for dishonoring the king's family and household. The second was that the five disobedient regiments in Cæsarea were to be transferred to bleak Pontus on the Black Sea and replaced with a like number from Antioch. Thirdly, Fadus was to remove the high priest's control over the vestments used in temple sacrifices. Once again, as in the dark days of Pontius Pilate, the ritual garments would be stored in the Roman Fortress of Antonia and the high priest would have to endure the humiliation of asking a procurator or garrison commander for permission to use them.

Fadus would soon find that extracting meek apologies from the magistrates of Cæsarea and Sebaste perhaps the easiest of his tasks, for upon arrival in Palestine he encountered many tempests and troubles that had not been anticipated by any of his orders from the emperor. Virtually every town of any size again seethed with the old Hellenist-Jewish tensions, only this time with an added reason. The spring grain crop had been skimpy. Now, with no letup in sight to the drought, prophets and diviners were crossing the countryside predicting a great famine. This, of course, caused the wealthy to hoard and the poor to loot. It also gave impetus to brigands of common criminals, who hid themselves along the trade routes and preyed on travelers without discrimination.

If that weren't enough, Fadus was soon confronted with new and unexpected crises. To the east, Parthia was again in a state of internal agitation as its grandees rose up against the durable but difficult king Artabanus. If the long-time king were permanently dislodged, who knew where else his emboldened successor might strike. Yet, the Jewish state hardly presented itself as a united and stable force on Rome's eastern frontier. Fadus had scarcely arrived when the Jews of Perea, just east of Jerusalem, decided to make war on the chiefly Arabian city of Philadelphia (today's Amman), which lay on Perea's eastern border. Fadus, incensed that no one had bothered to consult the procurator about any disputes, arrested the leaders and had one of them executed.

One might not think that requiring some pieces of cloth to be given up would compare with the above challenges, but it was the one order Fadus worried most about. When it came time to receive the temple vestments from the high priest — for the Jews a most unpleasant ceremony in itself — the many other tensions afoot threatened to make this an explosive encounter.

Thus, when Fadus confronted the temple priests, he had behind him what the official records call a "great army" from Cæsarea and Antioch. Arduous as the long march must have been, the show of Roman strength was clearly a wise move because it stifled any notions of armed rebellion. It also put the procurator in a position of strength to appear gracious in responding to what came next: a plea from the temple priests to let them send ambassadors to beg Cæsar that they be allowed to retain the vestments. To this Fadus acquiesced, but only when the ambassadors promised to leave their sons with him as hostages.

The embassy afforded Claudius two opportunities: displaying his mercy at absolutely no cost and strengthening the position of the young Agrippa II, who still lived in his household. After the ambassadors had stated their case (but after a year had passed), the emperor decreed that they "may have the vestments...because I would have everyone worship God according to the laws of their own country."

THE TURMOILS of political and religious divisions were but diversions from the growing hunger pangs that gnawed at the stomachs of the people in lower Syria. When the Christian community in Antioch learned of the worsening famine, they made great efforts to collect food and money for their brethren in Jerusalem. It would also be a chance to display their respect for the church headed by James (the Just, as he was now called) and perhaps demonstrate that their bonds in Jesus were stronger than the differences between Hellenistic and Jewish cultures.

It attests to their growing respect in the Antiochene community that Barnabas and Paul were chosen to lead the delegation. There is no official record of whom they met with in Jerusalem or what took place, but Paul made an illuminating statement about it in a letter he wrote much later. Referring to the meeting with James the Just and the Jerusalem elders, he says "they shook hands with Barnabas and myself and agreed that as partners we would work among the Gentiles and they among the Jews. All they asked was that we should remember the needy in their group — the very thing I have worked to do."

Since no reference was made to Peter's presence, he doubtless remained a fugitive from the temple authorities, yet at the same time probably the most active apostle to Jews outside of Judea.

Another symbol of the new accord is that Barnabas and Paul returned to Antioch with a new companion, John Mark, the young son of the same Mary whose house Peter had gone to the night in Jerusalem when he escaped prison. Mark's presence was surely a symbol of the Jerusalem church's support and participation in what was unfolding in Antioch. And it may be that he was also sent because he could offer vivid first-hand impressions of Jesus' life and death. The Gospel of Mark says that a boy (Mark himself?) followed Jesus and some of his disciples into the Garden of Gethsemane on the night before the crucifixion. *Mark* says that when the soldiers rushed into the garden to grab the whole lot, the willowy lad left one of them clutching his cloak as he ran off clad only in his loincloth.

It would also seem that both churches were in agreement that it was time for the Antioch apostles to preach the gospel in communities quite beyond their present confines. *Acts* says that "after much praying and fasting," it was decided to send Barnabas, Paul and Mark to begin that mission in Cyprus once winter had yielded to the spring sailing season. Having already collected money from members for the famine relief, they demonstrated the depths of their conviction by again reaching into their purses to provide the missionaries enough of a stipend to meet their travel expenses.

Cyprus was a logical choice for a first missionary effort. Its closest point lay just 70 miles east of Seleucia, the port city of Antioch. Measuring 140 by 160 miles, it was the largest island in the Mediterranean, and located equidistant between the busy Roman provinces of Asia and Syria. A Roman province itself, administered directly by the Senate, fertile Cyprus was valuable both for its agricultural and mining exports. In fact, it was the latter that spawned the rise of a large Jewish community there when Augustus leased the highly productive copper mines of Cyprus to Herod the Great.

Barnabas was an equally logical choice as mission leader. Born in Cyprus, he surely had family and friends there ready to help the three travelers. Having lived in Jerusalem, he was personally acquainted with followers of the martyred Stephen who had fled to Cyprus and formed the beginnings of a Christian community there. Barnabas was known for his great heart and ideal temperament (his name means "Son of Encouragement") and must have been witness to Jesus' ministry. Indeed, some speculate that Barnabas was one of the candidates who were put forth when Matthias was elected to replace Judas Iscariot. Finally, he seems to have been the uncle of his new companion, John Mark.

And so, one can picture a spring morning in which elders of the Antioch churches escorted Barnabas, Paul and Mark in a barge down the Orontes to where it met the port city of Seleucia. There the three would have no trouble finding passage on one of the many 100-ton merchantmen that carried manufactured goods to Cyprus. Twice a week the ships would make the overnight run, returning to Syria with salt, fruit, wine, copper and other raw commodities.

The first stop in their overseas missionary career was the port of Salamis, the island's largest eastern city and a center for salt mining. There, one record says, "they proclaimed the word of God in the synagogues of the Jews," then worked their way southwestward along the coast toward Paphos, apparently without encountering any hostility. It would have been difficult not to have a cheery outlook during the Cypriot spring; the snow-capped mountains of the Troodos range loomed to the northeast and their slopes of pine forests radiated with the brilliant colors of wildflowers.

But cities are seldom tranquil, and such was the case when the three reached the population center of western Cyprus. Paphos was home to a cult of Aphrodite that worshiped a crude phallic cone rather than a sculpted statue. The sanctuary was served by a priesthood that compelled young virgins to prostitute themselves to passers by after being persuaded that it is better to suffer the pain of defloration with a stranger than with one's bridegroom. In any case, the practice produced a handsome income for priests and fine sport for the sailors and traders who called at the busy port. And shopkeepers did a brisk trade in silver amulets shaped like the Aphrodite phallus because they were said to ward off shipwrecks.

It was in this setting that the three missionaries were preaching when word came that Sergius Paulus would like to hear this message personally. Paphos was also the home of the Roman Senate's proconsul, and Sergius Paulus was known as a man of keen and curious intellect. He was anxious to test the wisdom of these travelers before his own resident intellectual, a seer and magician named Bar-Jesus, who seemed to perform everything from magic tricks to interpreting the stars.

By now, Paul had apparently assumed the role of preaching before large audiences. Not long after he had begun proclaiming the "good news" to this important Roman official and his entourage, Bar-Jesus could no longer stand either what he heard or the looming threat to his dominion — or both. He interrupted with a question, then again and again with this and that counterpoint. Paul had a short fuse to begin with, and he soon had enough of this sleight-of-hand-and-mouth scoundrel who made his living doing tricks and whispering tips to those who sought the proconsul's favor.

"You son of the devil!" Paul shouted, wheeling on the surprised Bar-Jesus with a pointed finger. "You enemy of all righteousness, full of deceit and villainy, will you not stop making crooked the straight paths of the Lord?"

Looking squarely at the startled sage, he railed, "Now, behold, the hand of the Lord is upon you, and you shall be blind and unable to see the sun for a time." Immediately Bar-Jesus staggered about and cried out for someone to lead him by the hand, for he could no longer see.

Some say Paul made a believer of the proconsul right then — and perhaps many in his court. One asks if Bar-Jesus himself wouldn't have become one, too, just as temporary blindness had transformed a young Jewish temple official while traveling to Damascus.

Whatever the case, the three missionaries seem to have concluded a successful stay in Paphos. It was now early summer when they decided to use the prevailing and pleasant "beam winds," as mariners called them, to sail 170 miles northwest to the mainland province of Pisidia. Passing by the main port of Attalia, the merchantman sailed on to the smaller harbor of Perga eight miles inland, where it probably had a load of timber to collect.

At a time of year when the heat in the lowlands was becoming stultifying and the marshes malarial, the three missionaries faced an arduous 95-mile climb up the Taurus Mountains to their destination, the major commercial center of Pisidian Antioch. Moreover, they now traveled among people who were neither as Greek nor cosmopolitan nor friendly as the Cypriots. In this, the Pamphyian region of the province, the people were more indigenous than Greek, and their begrudging use of broken Greek for commerce was further corrupted with local slang. All too many of them roamed the mountains in bands, preying on travelers. Thus, the missionaries probably did like others of that time and joined a trade caravan. In return for greater protection, they would be required to take their turn standing watch at night with their swords at their sides and listening to camels groan, horses snort and men snore.

However, when this leg of the trip set out, it included only two missionaries. *Acts* says simply that John Mark departed at Perga and took a ship back to his home in Jerusalem. Just why is left to guesswork. Some say the young man became sick, or maybe just homesick. Some say he resented the fact that Paul had emerged as the leader and behaved in an overbearing way. All that can be said for sure is that Mark didn't stop being a Christian, as his gospel bears out.

Several days later Paul and Barnabas emerged from their climb through mountain gorges and on to the high plains of central Anatolia. There they must have felt exhilaration at the cooler air, fertile fields and blue lakes that spread before them in the fullness of summer. Soon visible on a hill beyond was a town with the literal name "Antioch towards Pisidia." Founded by a Seleucid general for his pensioned veterans, it became a Roman colony around 150 years later when Augustus commandeered it to settle his own legionary veterans. Situated on the East-West military highway, Pisidian Antioch was now a frontier town of more than 100,000 Romans, Greeks, nomads, Jews and native barbarians, guarded by mounted troops who rode out from its walls regularly to skirmish with the bandits who menaced the countryside.

As ever, Paul and Barnabas headed first to a synagogue and therein Paul gave the first sermon reported in *Acts*. The Jewish meetinghouse that invited the missionaries in to say their piece was not much different than most found today in Israel. The one in Pisidian Antioch was probably a rectangular stone basilica with a row of columns running along each of three sides of the interior. Seats would have been arranged along the walls, with front rows for men and rear ones for women, or with a separate gallery for women. Against one of the shorter walls was an ark, or cabinet, containing sacred scrolls. At the opposite wall was a lectern. But worship wasn't the synagogue's only purpose, for many such buildings were used for education of the young and community meetings. Some even had guest rooms for travelers like Paul and Barnabas.

The religious ceremony began with the congregation reciting a creed, commonly called the Shema, as set forth in their sacred books. The first sentence began (as today): "Hear, O Israel: The Lord our God is one Lord; and you shall love the Lord your God with all your heart, and with all your soul, and with all your might."

Next, the ruler of the synagogue appointed someone to be the leader in a prayer consisting of 18 invocations and petitions. This being done, an attendant took a scroll of the Law out of the ark and a few men from the congregation read in Hebrew the passages that were selected for the particular day. After the readings came the sermon. However, it would also have been possible for any member to address the assembly upon the ruler's invitation.

On this Sabbath in Pisidian Antioch, the ruler of the synagogue turned to Paul and Barnabas and said, "Brethren, if you have any word of exhortation for the people, say it." Paul began with the same approach that he would use everywhere. He would quote ancient scripture by heart and relate how the word of the prophets had been fulfilled in the life and resurrection of Jesus Christ. After beginning thusly in Pisidian Antioch, he said:

> ...Before his [Jesus'] coming John had preached a baptism of
> repentance to all the people of Israel. And as John finished

his course, he said, "What do you suppose that I am? I am not he. No, but after me one is coming, the sandals of whose feet I am not worthy to untie."

Brethren, sons of the family of Abraham and those among you that fear God, to us has been sent the message of this salvation. For those who live in Jerusalem and their rulers, because they did not recognize him nor understand the utterances of the prophets that are read every Sabbath, fulfilled those by condemning him. Though they could charge him with nothing deserving death, yet they asked Pilate to have him killed. And when they had fulfilled all that was written of him, they took him down from the tree and laid him in a tomb.

But God raised him from the dead; and for many days he appeared to those who came up with him from Galilee to Jerusalem, who are now witness to the people. And we bring you the good news that God promised to the fathers; this he has fulfilled to us their children by raising Jesus; as also it is written in the second psalm, "Thou art my Son, today I have begotten thee."

And as for the fact that he raised him from the dead, no more to return to corruption, he spoke in this way: "I will give you the holy and sure blessings of David."

Therefore, he says also in another psalm, "thou wilt not let thy Holy One see corruption."

For David, after he had saved the counsel of God in his own generation, fell asleep, and was laid with his fathers, and saw corruption; but he whom God raised up saw no corruption. Let it be known to you, therefore, brethren, that through this man forgiveness of sins is proclaimed to you, and by him everyone that believes is freed from everything from which you could not be freed by the law of Moses.[17]

This was a startling message indeed. This visitor was declaring that a new Law had been established and that it had freed not just Jews, but everyone who believed in the resurrection of Jesus, from the imprisonment of their sins.

People left the synagogue in a hubbub. A great many were already asking the elders to invite the newcomers back the following week. But some were so caught up by the message that they followed Paul and Barnabas right out of the building and declared themselves believers in this gospel.

When the two missionaries returned to the synagogue the next week it seemed as if the whole city had crowded inside to hear them — including Gentiles, women, children and slaves — because Paul and Barnabas had spent the previous days with everyone who would listen.

To the synagogue elders, this kind of turnout was unprecedented. It was also disruptive to their accustomed routine and even menacing in a way. But Paul did nothing to calm the consternation he saw in their eyes. Rather, he spoke out boldly saying, "It was necessary that the word of God should be spoken first to you. But since you thrust it from you and judge yourselves unworthy of eternal life, behold, we turn to the Gentiles. For so the Lord has commanded us, saying 'I have set you to be a light for the Gentiles, that you may bring salvation to the uttermost parts of the earth.'"

When the Gentiles in the audience heard this, they cheered and some gave thanks to God. Afterwards, a great many followed Paul and Barnabas all over town, and as *Acts* states: "The word of the Lord spread all over the region." The missionaries probably stayed on for several weeks to instruct their new followers. But by then the elders of the synagogue had been able to meet often and digest what all this would mean to themselves, the synagogue and the families it served. After all, Paul had offered scant advice on how this new order would be administered. Besides, the elders feared that accepting all these outsiders into the Jewish community would overwhelm their resources and shatter their sacred traditions. And for *them* to join a brand new "religion" would not just corrupt the law of their forefathers but pitch it into the trash heap altogether. So they stirred up opposition to the apostles and prevailed on the city magistrates to send them away.

Acts relates that the missionaries symbolically "shook off the dust from their feet" at the scolding elders as they departed the city walls. Yet, at the same time they were "filled with the Holy Spirit."

It was now autumn. The two walked another 110 miles to the east and the smaller city of Iconium. Although the chief city of the Lycaonian province, Iconium was still within the influence of the much larger Pisidian Antioch. Again, Paul and Barnabas began by addressing the synagogue, then stayed several weeks preaching to Jew and Gentile alike. But this time the opposition grew even more intense. A delegation of Jewish elders from Pisidian Antioch eventually arrived and were actually in the midst of inciting the local Jewish leaders to stone the two apostles when they were warned in time to pack their few things and move on.

This time, with the first winter winds now swirling, the undaunted itinerant preachers walked south along the military highway and stopped only 30 miles away at Lystra. Known only as a town where big city merchants came to buy grain for the winter, Lystra was still smaller than Iconium and had no Jewish community to speak of. Worse for two Greek-speaking preachers, its people spoke an even more fractured dialect than anywhere they'd been in Pisidia or Lycaonia.

One might think Paul and Barnabas quite justified if they had intended to hole up in this peaceful, out-of-the way place until winter passed, but all evidence points to the contrary. Lacking a synagogue, they seem to have gone straight to the local marketplace (*agora*) and began to proclaim the gospel to everyone within earshot.

Gradually, they became a familiar albeit curious sight in the marketplace. But one event changed all that. It seems that Paul was addressing a fairly skeptical crowd one day when he took note of a crippled man in their midst. The fellow had been unable to walk since birth and was well known to the locals because his family carried him about town. Doubtless Paul had seen him often as well, because on that day he turned to the man in the middle of his sermon and said in a loud voice: "Stand up on your feet!"

And with that the man sprang up and walked. The crowd was flabbergasted because it knew this was no fakery by some traveling magician. Word spread all over town and people even began chanting, "The gods have come down to us in the likeness of men!" Soon they were calling Barnabas "Zeus" (no doubt because of the likeness) and Paul "Hermes" because he had delivered the words that cured their townsman. Before long some people rushed up to where the missionaries were staying and announced that the priest from the old temple of Zeus that stood in front of the town was bringing oxen and garlands to the city gate and was about to sacrifice to them. Could they come quickly?

What the priest probably had in mind was an ancient legend. It seems that Zeus and Hermes decided to visit Lycaonia disguised as humble travelers. After being scorned and turned away from the doors of rich and poor alike, they came to the cottage of a poor elderly couple where they were gladly given some country wine and bread. The gods were grateful, and before departing they turned the old couple's hovel into a splendid temple of marble and gold. The husband and wife were transformed into two immortal cypress trees that were still standing in front of the temple in Paul's day.

All the other Lycaonians who had spurned the gods were turned into frogs.

Perhaps if Paul and Barnabas had known the tale they would have had a good laugh over the whole thing. Instead the two rent their garments in anguish and rushed out to the city gate where a crowd had assembled. "Men, why are you doing this?" shouted the one they knew as Hermes. "We are also men like you. And we have brought you good news that you should turn from these vain practices to a living God who made the heaven and earth and the sea and all that is within them!"

Soon Paul was delivering a sermon on the temple steps. "In past generations God allowed all the nations to walk in their own ways," he said to the crowd. "Yet he did not leave himself without witness, for he did good and gave you from the heavens rains and fruitful seasons, satisfying your hearts with food and gladness."

Words like these gradually deflated their fervor, and the people went back to their homes. But not long after this affair another angry group of Jewish elders arrived in town from Pisidian Antioch and Iconium. This time, without asking permission from any authorities, they rushed to Paul in the marketplace and began pelting him with rocks, stones and curses. When he finally collapsed, bruised and bleeding, they thought him near death. So, since it was illegal to leave a corpse within the city walls, they dragged Paul outside the main gate and left him there. Then they fled because they feared that the civil authorities would arrest them.

Barnabas and the new disciples weren't far away. As soon as the persecutors had left, the Christians rushed out and managed to pull Paul to his feet. As it was growing dark, they had no choice but to half-carry him back into the city where they spent the night putting salve on his wounds and praying for his recovery. The next day, though Paul was still badly bruised, they were fearful of staying any longer, so Barnabas got him upright and they made their way east. In what must have been the 50 most painful miles of Paul's life, they finally arrived at the even smaller town of Derbe. It was no more than a dull frontier village, but Derbe may have been an ideal place for a sick man to recuperate and spend the winter.

One might ask why Paul wouldn't have continued his journey as soon as possible. Just another 125 miles away was his hometown of Tarsus, where he could have spent the winter snug in his parent's home or in the care of his many Christian brethren. But there is no evidence of it. And the only reason for that must be that Paul was determined to head right back where he came from as soon as winter ebbed and the icy roads were passable.

A.D. 47–48

CLAUDIUS WAS BY NOW A BUSY ADMINISTRATOR of the realm. During this period he revived construction of an aqueduct that would take 30,000 men eleven years to complete. He began building a new harbor at Ostia to speed off-loading of grain ships. Secular Games were held to mark the 800th anniversary of Rome's founding and a census was taken that counted 5,984,072 Roman citizens throughout the empire (but a total population of at least tenfold).

However, the emperor's favorite pastimes remained the reform of Rome's political, judicial and religious institutions. Claudius prevailed on the Senate to create a Board of Soothsayers so that "the oldest Italian art," as he called it, "would not die out through neglect." In the courts, no topic aroused more emotion than the emperor's attempt to revive an ancient law forbidding the acceptance of money or gifts for legal services. After an army of pleading lawyers surrounded his tribunal chair, he agreed to a limit of 10,000 sesterces per case.

Amidst all this, Claudius took it upon himself to assume the long-vacated position of censor and to personally conduct a formal review of the rolls of senators and knights. The 600 senators, for example, were each required to own property exceeding a million sesterces, have at least one son and be of "acceptable moral character." No one had purged the rolls in years and Claudius was convinced that the Senate had become inbred and insular. After he'd completed the excruciating winnowing out process (at great cost to his popularity) the way had been cleared to include nobles from Italy, Spain, Gaul and other provinces that once faced Rome in war.

Now then, one reason for describing all of the above is simply to suggest that the emperor's preoccupation with them may be the only way to explain how he could be so naively oblivious to the outrageous events that were happening in his own household.

Yes, Messalina. At first, his wife's nocturnal adventures had no effect on governance. But soon she was using her powers as empress to win a position for a lover or (as in one case) force a senator into suicide because she coveted his lavish gardens. Her ambitions reached a peak when she found herself entwined in bed and politics with one Gaius Silius, a young, single consul-designate.

Silius' rapid rise in the Senate was full of danger and intrigue. Perhaps he felt he was destined to live a brief but brilliant life because he had watched Tiberius and Sejanus condemn his father to death simply for being one of Germanicus' most loyal commanders. In any event, one day Messalina was worrying aloud about getting caught by Claudius, and Silius blurted out an audacious idea. "Let's simply drop all pretense of concealment," he told the young empress. "Why do we have to wait until the emperor dies of old age? Flagrant guilt requires audacity! I'm ready to marry you and adopt Britannicus (the son whose name had been changed from Germanicus after Claudius "conquered" Britain).

The daring and deceitful Messalina had clearly met her match. Here was fear, excitement, sex and intrigue all in one outrageous act, and she found it exhilarating.

What follows would seem to defy credulity except that the historians Tacitus, Suetonius and Dio Cassius all report it the same. Silius and Messalina waited until Claudius left for Ostia to look in on construction of its new harbor. No sooner was his small entourage out of sight than the bevy of wealthy and witty nobles who swirled about Messalina were invited to the palace of Claudius to witness her wedding to the consul-designate Gaius Silius. How they felt the festivities could elude the greatest gossip factory on earth is anyone's guess, but on this autumn day in A.D. 48 Messalina donned the wedding veil and sacrificed to the gods. Afterwards the happy couple hosted an obscenely lavish banquet and apparently consummated the marriage on a couch in full view while other guests took the cue to entertain themselves accordingly.

It seems that the only ones outraged by all this were the emperor's household staff. They had turned their heads often enough when men from senators to mimes and dancers would slink in and out of Messalina's bedroom, but this was too much. Their worst fear was that the uxorious Claudius might rationalize it as an ill-advised but harmless caper because it had not affected government affairs. But from their perspective, they saw Messalina as a schemer who was capable of assassination — of the emperor *and* themselves.

Soon a formal meeting was convened among the emperor's chief personal advisors. All were freedmen: Callistus, once the secretary to Gaius Caligula and one of the confederates in his assassination; Pallas, who served as financial secretary, and Narcissus, now secretary-general and probably the man closest to Claudius. Might they simply feign ignorance of the whole thing and secretly persuade Messalina to abandon Silius? No, this was too risky to themselves. The only course, they decided, was to send Narcissus directly to Ostia. He only hoped that the emperor would be quickly roused into action.

What Narcissus found instead was a man too dazed to comprehend.

The freedman tried more shock. "Are you aware that you have been *divorced*?" he scolded. " Her wedding to Silius has been witnessed by members of the Senate and army. The whole nation knows. Act promptly or her new husband controls Rome!"

Claudius summoned what friends and advisors he could at Ostia, men such as the prefect of the corn supply and the inseparable imperial companion, Vitellius. "Am, am I still emperor?" Claudius kept stammering. "Is Silius still a private citizen?"

The next day Messalina and Silius were still entertaining their friends in what seems to have become a marathon marriage festival. The autumn weather was mild and the bride was hosting a mock grape harvest on her grounds. Wine presses were churning and vats overflowing, surrounded by women capering and sacrificing. Messalina, with hair flowing, was brandishing a Bacchic wand. Silius stood beside her dressed in ivy wreath and buskins. Around them were besotted revelers. But all quickly sobered to attention when messengers began rushing up to say that Claudius knew all and was on his way back, bent on cruel revenge.

With that everyone scurried in all directions. Messalina took refuge in the Gardens of Lucullus, the same ones she had acquired at the cost of a senator's life. Silius retreated to the Forum, where he pretended to go about his business as though nothing had happened.

Within hours, Prætorians had rounded up nearly all of the participants save Messalina. At first she fled down into the valley of the Forum and to the house of the Vestal Virgins for sanctuary. There she begged Vibidia, the senior priestess, to seek the emperor's ear as Pontifex Maximus and beg his pardon. Failing that, would she beseech Claudius to see his wife face to face? At the very least, would she prevail on Claudius to receive young Octavia and Britannicus in his embrace?

The chief priestess must have said only that she would consider it, because the frantic Messalina now fled from the house, determined to intercept Claudius on his way from Ostia. Accompanied by just two female attendants, she darted from villa to villa along the Ostian Way begging for a carriage and driver to take her. All refused her, either because they loathed her or feared for their own skins. Finally, the empress was reduced to waving down a mule-driven cart hauling garden refuse and jumping onto its rear platform.

All was not going smoothly with Claudius, either. As his carriage with Vitellius and Narcissus lumbered along on the 25-mile return journey, the occupants decided that the tribune in charge of the palace guard probably couldn't be trusted because the "festivities" had, after all, taken place under his nose. Thus, Narcissus prevailed on Claudius to make *him* commander for one day as the only way to save the emperor's life. More vexing to the freedman was that Claudius spent the whole return trip in his carriage with his emotions veering from outrage ("How wicked of her! How sinful!") to tearful reminisces of happier times and worries about raising motherless young children.

As they neared Rome, Claudius was startled to see a woman jump down from an approaching mule cart and come scampering towards his carriage with arms waving. It was Messalina herself. Now she was running alongside and shouting his name between sobs. The carriage stopped and Messalina was on her knees weeping uncontrollably. "Oh please just listen to the mother of Octavia and Brittanicus," she begged. But Narcissus stood up and quickly shouted her down. Every time the tearful empress would gasp for breath to speak, the freedman would brandish a document he had brought Claudius summarizing her infidelities. Angrily, he commanded the driver to push on.

As they neared the city, Claudius saw some servants holding his children's hands along the roadside, but Narcissus again ordered the driver on. Then they spotted Vibidia, the senior Vestal Virgin, shouting sternly from the roadside that a wife should not be executed without being heard. Roaring back that Messalina would have a chance to clear herself, Narcissus waved her off with an admonition to "go and attend to your religious duties!"

Claudius merely sat dumbly in his carriage. Next to him, the usually resourceful Vitellius, former governor of Syria and clever advisor to three emperors, slumped limply in his seat. Narcissus the freedman was clearly in charge.

As the carriage ascended to the Palatine neighborhood, Narcissus thought of a way to stiffen the emperor's spine. On one of the side streets leading to the palace, he ordered the carriage to stop in front of a villa with high, vine-covered walls. Narcissus commanded the servants inside to open the gates. As they drove through, the freedman announced to Claudius that this was none other than a house Messalina had bought and furnished for Gaius Silius. Throughout the atrium the emperor saw statuary and heirlooms — even things Claudius had given Messalina — that had been taken there from his own palace.

Now Claudius came to life again, sputtering and spouting threats. With that, Narcissus ordered the carriage hasten directly to the Prætorian camp. Once inside the gates, Narcissus quickly scrambled everyone inside to attention. As to the reason for it, Claudius could only muster a short, stammering speech; he was both too angry and too embarrassed at not being able to prevent his own wife from causing the mess the guards were now having to clean up.

But Claudius didn't need much of a speech. His words were quickly drowned out by soldiers chanting that the offenders should be punished. All they wanted was his permission. Claudius gave it. And he didn't have too long to wait thereafter. The next commotion in the camp was that of Prætorians dragging Silius himself and some of his fellow revelers inside the gates and up onto the parade platform. Without demanding a trial or saying a word in his own defense, the handsome senator, now bound in chains, simply asked for a quick death. Now his supporters and wedding revelers were herded out in chains as well and pushed onto the platform. The last to be thrust among them was the palace tribune under whose auspices the festivities had been allowed to take place.

All remained silent except one. He was Mnester, the famous mime and ballet dancer, once the favorite partner in Gaius Caligula's perversions and now the playmate of Messalina. Tearing his clothes, Mnester shouted for Claudius to observe the many lash marks on his back. The others, he pleaded, had defied the emperor for money or ambition. But surely Claudius would remember that it was *he* who had ordered him to attend Messalina — even having him flogged for refusing the first request!

Again, the explanation lies in the emperor's infernal naivety and/or absent-mindedness. Because of the actor's seemingly inexhaustible supply of bedroom energy, Messalina had become obsessed with making Mnester her household pet. When he declined her offers, she actually went to Claudius with fluttering eyelashes and pleaded that the emperor command him to be her dancing coach (or something equally innocuous). Claudius complied, and When Mnester still dallied about it, she ordered him flogged and said it was on the emperor's orders.

In subsequent weeks when dinner party talk turned to the theater, someone invariably would ask Claudius why Mnester was not dancing. The emperor would always look surprised, wondering why *he* was being asked about Mnester. Eventually, his friends came to believe that Claudius really was ignorant of what was going on in the palace — behavior so salacious that it was even circulating among foreign kings and generals as evidence of Rome's vulnerability.

Now, at the Prætorian camp, Mnester displayed his scars to Claudius and shouted that he had been *compelled* to feed Messalina's passions in order to remain faithful to the emperor!

Claudius hesitated briefly — but all too long for Narcissus. The freedman took it as a sign of weakening, so he and the other advisors were at the emperor's ear again, whispering hotly that Claudius couldn't spare a ballet dancer after executing so many men of high birth and distinguished reputation. Besides, they said, the rogue had already committed so many perversities and crimes, who should care about having to prove that the latest ones were deliberate or not?

So Mnester's appeal was rejected. At that point Silius quietly stretched out his neck and was dispatched on the spot. The other wedding revelers were led off to a similar fate.

Only Messalina remained. After Claudius had returned to his palace and was soothed by dinner, he ordered that "the poor woman" (in his words) be brought in the next day to defend herself. Narcissus sensed that the emperor's anger was cooling, and no doubt memories of Messalina's considerable conjugal gifts would soon fill his mind as well. But now the stakes were too high. If Messalina were allowed to live, Narcissus clearly wouldn't — not after the way he had denounced the empress from the carriage that day.

With the dinner party in full swing and Claudius distracted by lively conversation, Narcissus quietly slipped away. After all, he was still commander of the Guard for the day. Ostensibly on the emperor's orders, Narcissus dispatched a tribune and some staff officers to go to the Gardens of Lucullus. Meanwhile, he commanded a slave to run there quickly to prevent Messalina from escaping and to remain until the soldiers had carried out his command.

When the slave arrived at the villa beside the gardens, he was admitted quickly in hopes he might have a message from Claudius. Inside he found Messalina weeping, her head in the lap of her mother, Domitia Lepida, one of Rome's foremost noblewomen. During the whole of her marriage to Claudius, Messalina had quarreled with and belittled her mother, but now the woman had been filled with pity and was, in fact, the only person to come to her daughter's comfort.

"Your life is finished," Domitia Lepida said softly, stroking her distraught daughter's hair. "All that remains is to make a decent end."

But Messalina still hadn't accepted her fate. She writhed about, churning over this and that possible way of appeal or escape when she heard the heavy knocks. Then she felt the force of the door breaking down and saw the soldiers storming in.

Messalina gaped in terror. Without further word, the mother calmly opened a drawer and offered her daughter a dagger. Messalina looked at it as though it were a serpent. She put it to her throat, but could not strike. Then she moved it to her breast, but her hand was as frozen as her stare.

The soldiers watched her for all of five or six seconds. In the next instant an officer ran her through.

Claudius was still at his dinner table when news came that Messalina had died. He did not even ask by whose hand. After an eerie pause, the emperor called for more wine and the conversation went on.

In the days that followed, Claudius exhibited no human feeling about the matter. No hatred. No remorse. No satisfaction. No distress. Not even a murmur when he saw little Octavia and Brittanicus dressed in mourning. Once at dinner he absent-mindedly asked where Messalina was, then caught himself and went on eating.

The Senate helped erase her memory from his by decreeing that Messalina's name and statues should be removed from all public and private sites. Narcissus was awarded an honorary quæstorship.

Claudius did say often that he had been unlucky in marriage and that he certainly didn't intend to fall into that trap again. But he did, and this time the effects would be felt throughout the Roman Empire.

WHEN PAUL AND BARNABAS finally left Derbe in the early spring of A.D. 47, they had managed to win believers and form a church even at this small junction on the Roman military highway. Healthy again, Paul was filled with renewed vigor and optimism.

And so, the two apostles decided to retrace their steps. They walked back along the same road to Lystra, Iconium and Pisidian Antioch. Incidentally, it was on the return trip to Iconium that someone recorded the only written description of Paul in existence. Although written around A.D. 160 (*The Acts of Paul*, incorporated into *The Apocryphal New Testament*), the description is consistent with the frescoes found in the Roman catacombs. It seems that a certain man named Onesiphorus, when he heard that the apostle was on his way, rushed out to the military highway with his wife and children in hopes of enticing him to stay with them.

> Titus had told him what manner of man Paul was in appearance; for he had not seen him in the flesh, but only in the spirit. And they went by the king's highway that leads from Lystra and stood expecting him, and looked upon them that came, according to the description of Titus. And they saw Paul coming, a man of little stature, thin-haired upon his head, crooked in the legs, of good state of body, with eyebrows joining, and nose somewhat hooked, full of grace; for sometimes he appeared like a man and sometimes he had the face of an angel.[18]

Paul and Barnabas doubtless accepted the offer of hospitality; it was their purpose to spend most of these visits fortifying the congregations they had already established. This they did by leading worship services, appointing elders and attempting to answer the dozens of questions that believers would raise about how to conduct their daily affairs.

Why didn't the same opponents mobilize to drive out Paul and Barnabas as they had done before? One answer is that the number of believers in each city was not in the hundreds, but perhaps in the dozens. Yet, they could not have numbered much less than this because each church had elders, and elders usually corresponded to the twelve that had served Jesus. Absent any historical text to explain it, one might only surmise that the apostles stayed away from the synagogues this time and the Jewish elders no longer felt in danger of losing their flocks. This would indicate that the great majority of the new church members were Gentiles.

By the time the missionaries had finished nurturing their new churches in the highlands, it may have been early autumn when they made the twisting, arduous trek down to the low plains of Pisidia. To retrace their steps completely, they would have sailed again to Cyprus, but they decided to break new ground in Perga and Attalia, the principal cities on the Pisidian coastal plain.

Then it was time to leave. Again, Paul could have walked aboard a merchantman in Attalia and used the northwest winds of the season to cruise some 250 miles to Tarsus. Instead, the missionaries sailed some 60 miles past Paul's home city and into the Syrian port of Seleucia, which they had left a year-and-a-half before.

Once in nearby Antioch, one wonders who reported with the greater enthusiasm, the two missionaries or the Christian leaders at the Syrian capital. The latter could cite great progress in the numbers of believers and they were thrilled to know that their investment in the mission had planted churches in Asia Minor.

This euphoria, however, was broken not long afterward when a small delegation of Jewish Christians arrived from Jerusalem — all Pharisees, it would seem. The Christian communities in Jerusalem and Antioch had kept in regular communication, and thus it was probably a glowing report of Paul and Barnabas' success that had struck a nerve among many of the brethren in the cradle of Christianity. The problem was the impression they had gained that most of the missionaries' converts in Cyprus, Pisidia and Lycaonia were not Jews, but Gentiles, and that scarcely any were circumcised or trained in Mosaic Law. Worse, they continued to eat anything at all — and often in the company of Jews.

This will never do, said the Jewish Christians. It certainly will not, Paul retorted at hearing their displeasure. Had it not been understood during his earlier visit to Jerusalem that *his* mission was to the Gentiles — that Peter and others would preach to the Jews? Did they not understand that being one in Christ left both groups free to practice their traditional customs when it came to temporal life?

All agreed civilly enough that another meeting of the church leadership was needed to settle the matter. Understandably, Paul and Barnabas were elected by the Antioch elders to state their case in Jerusalem, and off they went. It is noteworthy that whereas the Antiochenes might well have considered breaking relations with Jerusalem and forming their own branch of Christianity, they gave little thought to it. They, too, regarded Jerusalem as the "mother church." Many knew and loved James, Peter and the other Jewish apostles.

Jerusalem wasn't the only stop on this trip. The first writings show that Paul and Barnabas wound their way south through many towns of Phoenicia and Samaria, "reporting the conversion of the Gentiles and giving great joy to all the brethren." Nor was their greeting by the Jerusalem church in any way cool. *Acts* says that "they were welcomed by the church and the apostles and the elders, and they declared all that God had done with them."

But the purpose of the visit was, after all, a confrontation, and it was indeed the faction of Jewish-Christian Pharisees, these devout practitioners of Mosaic Law, who began by expressing their surprise and serious concern at learning of all the untutored Gentiles who were now calling themselves Christians. I should point out that the Christian Pharisees were not necessarily a majority. Nor, it turns out, had they actually been sent to Antioch as official ambassadors of the Jerusalem church. But they were a group large enough to be named the Circumcision Party, and James the Just, who presided, apparently thought their concerns certainly justified the meeting.

The concerns of the Pharisees were not frivolous, either. Focusing first on the subject of circumcision, they could point to the fact that the custom had not begun merely on the order of a king or prophet. No, they could show that the Book of Genesis, the first of the ancient Torah, quotes the very words of God himself as demanding that every descendant of Abraham — including foreigners who become members of his household — practice circumcision "throughout your generations" as "an everlasting covenant."

Beyond this was the fact that circumcision was the Jewish mark of identity — a sign of Israel's election as God's people. Throughout history, pious Jews had faced death bravely rather than deny the necessity of circumcision. Moreover, Jesus was a Jew and any true follower should be glad to bear the same identification in order to signify his faith. To be sure, Gentiles were welcome in the church, but they must be circumcised and observe Mosaic Law.

Next to speak was none other than Peter. This comes as a surprise in *Acts* because there had been absolutely no word of him after escaping Agrippa's jail and disappearing that night to "another place." Then again, some six years had passed, Herod Agrippa was dead and the renewed presence of a Roman procurator could provide some protection against the violent impulses of Jewish kings and temple priests.

"Brethren," said Peter, rising,

> ...you know that in the early days God made choice among you, that by my mouth the Gentile should hear word of the gospel and believe. And God, who knows the heart, bore witness to them, giving them the Holy Spirit just as he did to us; and he made no distinction between us and them, but cleansed their hearts by faith.

> Now therefore, why do you make trial of God by putting a
> yoke on the neck of the disciples which neither our fathers
> nor we have been able to bear?
>
> But we believe that we shall be saved through the grace of
> the Lord Jesus, just as they will.[19]

Next it was the turn of Paul and Barnabas; but it was Paul, of course, who rose. Just as circumcision was a bedrock belief of the Pharisees, it was an enormous boulder in the path of missionaries to the Gentiles. When an eight-day-old infant underwent this rite, one could only hope that his brief cries were the only pain he bore; but now consider what this procedure meant to an adult male. In the first part, called *milah*, the rabbi used a metal knife and cut away the outer part of the foreskin. Next was the *periah*, in which the *mohel*, or expert circumciser, used his thumbnail and index finger to tear the inner lining of the foreskin that had been left adhering to the gland. In the final step, the *mohel* took the penis into his mouth and cleansed the wound by sucking away the blood.

In an adult male the bleeding could be considerable and the pain both intense and prolonged. Indeed, just as devout Jews believe that anyone who was not circumcised will delay the arrival of the Messiah, Paul went as far as to say (no doubt only in moments of exasperation) that circumcision might well "cut you...off from Christ."

Nonetheless, there is no indication that Paul mentioned any of this in addressing the conference of church leaders. Trained as a Pharisee himself, he knew that his only hope of overcoming his protagonists lay in citing the Law as well. Nor would he want to sever the church's tie with the Judaism of Abraham and Moses.

In part, Paul's answer was that God's promise to Abraham preceded by centuries the giving of the Law to Moses. Therefore, the Law, which came later, could not annul that promise or replace *faith* as the basis of God's acceptance of men. The Pharisee Christians could point out that it was to Abraham whom God first gave the explicit command to circumcise both Jews and any foreigners who became members of their household. But Paul could counter that God, first of all, gave Abraham the *promise* and thus justified him on the basis of faith. Therefore, faith is more important than observing any particular rite.

Paul then turned to his second tenet. The coming of Christ had signaled the beginning of a new day in God's dealings with men. Yes, before this, all God's people were required to keep the Mosaic Law. Now, with the

Messiah's arrival, the period for God's people to live under the Law had ended. The first and central requirement is faith in Christ. And where that is found, through this "new covenant," the believer is acceptable to God and will be forgiven and blessed by him.

But the Scripture, Paul added, is not to be discarded. Indeed, it is full of promise and points to the day when the prophecies will be fulfilled and men will live under the new covenant.

When all had finished, everyone looked to James the Just for the last word. Who would have thought that it was only in Jesus' final year that James began to accept the true nature of his brother? Now he had long since given up his home in Galilee and become the center or ballast of the young church in Jerusalem — all without giving up his rigid adherence to Mosaic Law or his allegiance to the temple. More than any others, his piety and personality bound together all the believers.

James rose. "Brethren, listen to me," he said. "Simeon [Peter] had related how God first visited the Gentiles, to take out of them a people for his name. And with this the words of the prophets agree, as it is written:"

> After that I will return,
> And I will rebuild the dwelling of David, which has fallen;
> I will rebuild its ruins,
> And I will set it up,
> That the rest of men may seek the Lord,
> And all the Gentiles who are called by my name,
> Says the Lord, who has made these things known from of old.[20]

"Therefore," continued James, "my judgment is that we should not trouble those of the Gentiles who turn to God, but should write to them to abstain from the pollutions of idols and from unchastity and from [eating] what is strangled, and from blood." For, he added, these are the words of Moses and have been read every Sabbath in the synagogues for many generations.

It would seem that all those present agreed with this course. To reinforce what had been said, a letter was composed and two Jewish Christian leaders — Silas and Judas called Barsabbas — were chosen to accompany Paul and Barnabas back to Antioch to read its contents aloud. Here is the letter they read upon arriving:

> The brethren, both the apostles and the elders, to the brethren of the Gentiles in Antioch and Syria and Cilicia, greetings.

Since we have heard that some persons from us have trou-
bled you with words, unsettling your minds, although we
gave them no instructions, it has seemed good to us in assembly to choose men and send them to you with our
beloved Barnabas and Paul, men who have risked their
lives for the sake of our Lord, Jesus Christ. We have therefore sent Judas and Silas, who themselves will tell you the
same things by word of mouth.

For it has seemed good to the Holy Spirit and to us to lay
upon you no greater burden than these necessary things:
that you abstain from what has been sacrificed to idols and
from blood and what is strangled, and from unchastity. If
you keep yourselves from these, you will do well.
Farewell.[21]

The Antiochenes were clearly jubilant, and Judas and Silas stayed
there several days to help reinforce this new spirit of unity. Now, for
once, Jewish and Gentile Christians felt at much greater ease in each
other's company.

In time, however, the Jerusalem accord inevitably produced more questions — most of them about proper eating. Should Jewish Christians share
in Gentile Christian foods such as pork? Should they even sit at the same
table in which it is served? How could one be sure that the meat in a Gentile Christian's house church had not been sacrificed or strangled? Did
James and the elders really intend for Christians to dine at the same table?
Or were they to eat separately, each observing their own laws and customs?

In all likelihood most Christians in Antioch managed to circumvent
such indelicacies easily enough, just as we do today. If we are invited to someone's house for dinner and find something we don't like on the table, we
just do our best to overlook it (and the host is usually considerate enough
not to rub our nose in it). But if the host knows in advance that custom bars
us from certain foods, he usually has the courtesy not to offer it at all. Yet,
such questions did linger in Antioch, and the most serious of these was
whether Gentile and Jewish Christians should eat together in the first place.
And what brought the matter to a head was no less than a visit by Peter.

The apostle certainly hadn't planned it that way at all when he arrived
in Antioch one day not too long after the Jerusalem meeting. It would
seem that his intent was purely to promote harmony and reconciliation among
Christians. But Peter was put to the test soon enough. He must have felt pres-

sure from James (who continued his strict observance of Mosaic Law), because he declined to eat at the same table with his Gentile brethren. Paul was astonished at this — from the very man who had visited the family of Cornelius, the Roman centurion, and who had defended the Gentile cause in the meeting of church leaders. He was all the more incredulous when Barnabas voiced his agreement with Peter.

Paul overlooked his traveling companion for the moment: Peter had a higher ranking in the Jerusalem church. Paul, who writes that he rebuked Peter "to his face," did not cite the letter that had been read at Antioch, but stabbed right to the heart of the matter. If both Jew and Gentile can find salvation only in the grace of God through Christ, then Mosaic Law has no saving power for either party. Thus, it was not right for Peter to begin observing the Law again as though it were necessary to salvation. What is not necessary, said Paul, should not be made compulsory.

There is no record of what Peter said. In time, he probably relented, as we shall see later; but for the moment there was tension again in Antioch. And it hovered over the leaders there as they prepared to sponsor a second and more ambitious mission to the west. Paul was ready to go, of course. He would be expected to take Barnabas. Barnabas was willing and wanted to take John Mark again. But it was undoubtedly two points of friction — the "defection" of Mark from the last trip and the apparent unwillingness of Barnabas to share meals with Gentiles — that proved irreconcilable. Soon, Paul departed with Silas (the same "ambassador" from Jerusalem) to visit his new churches in Pisidia and to cultivate new ground in cities further west. Barnabas took Mark with him and headed back to his native Cyprus.

For Paul it was to be the second leg of a quest that would lead him to the capital of the Empire.

A.D. 49–50

THIS WAS THE PERIOD in which Claudius expelled the Jewish population from Rome — and with them, the Jewish Christians as well. In the official chronicles a decree that upended the lives of perhaps 40,000 people gets only routine mention, and it's very likely that the emperor himself — friend and protector of Judaism — had little to do with it. However, the incident serves as a clear example of Claudius' transition from active and sole emperor to collegial and passive ruler.

Indeed, nothing indicates that Claudius was ever again personally in charge of Rome from the day his freedman, Narcissus, took the reins of his carriage on the road from Ostia. For, after Messalina's death, the emperor invariably seemed dispirited and distracted while his palace secretaries exercised imperial power as if they had seized it by necessity. It also explains how, for example, the financial secretary Pallas was able to amass a personal fortune of more than 400 million sesterces after just seven years of service to his emperor.

Further proof of their power was that the freedmen could even choose another "emperor" — and with the approval of Claudius himself. This otherwise incongruous statement can be explained by recalling the emperor's vow never to marry again. The only heir to the throne was the eight-year-old Brittanicus. His father was eating and drinking to the point of being carried off to bed most nights. And so, it was logical for the emperor's chief advisors to begin asking themselves how long he would last. If Brittanicus came to the throne, how might he deal with those who were responsible for killing his mother? The solution: find Claudius a new wife, a strong helpmate in governing who would, of course, retain the current corps of advisors.

Before long the chief dinner topic, after Claudius was mellow with wine, centered on his impoverished love life. Was his lordship not lonely? Wouldn't a beautiful companion be welcome? He deserved it — and so did Rome because it loved seeing its emperor in the company of a lovely empress! Claudius, never one to see virtue in an empty bed, soon backed down from his vow and triggered a beauty contest of sorts, with each palace freedman championing his own contender.

The eventual winner was Pallas, with help from the venerable senator Vitellius. Their entry was none other than Agrippina II, eldest daughter of Germanicus, sister of the fallen Gaius Caligula, who at 33 still lived up to her reputation as one of Rome's most beautiful women. This, despite some harsh experiences that included the banishment of her mother, her own exile by Gaius, the horror of his own assassination and her determined climb back to the top of society. Finally, Agrippina was the widowed mother of a fairly attractive 12-year-old son. His name was Lucius Domitius Ahenobarbus, or simply Nero to his family.

Claudius was quite willing, and some say partly because he had already been given the opportunity to sample her favors. The only barrier was one of public perception: she was the emperor's niece.

One day Vitellius, the most sagacious of salons, entered the Senate and asked to be heard. After extolling the virtues of Agrippina and declaring what a joy it would be "for the nation to present the emperor with a wife," he turned to the awkward subject of marrying nieces. "In other countries it is regular and lawful," he intoned. "After all, unions between cousins have become more frequent with time. Customs change with circumstances, and this innovation, too, will take root."

Having quickly secured one edict beseeching Claudius to marry and another one legalizing marriages with a brother's daughter, Vitellius bade the senators join him in going to the palace to inform Claudius of their happy news.

Agrippina knew all about governance in a man's world and she thirsted to be part of it. And rather than recoiling at a woman's ambitions, the palace household felt immediate relief at having a decisive, sober, energetic person at the side of a ruler who had become as enigmatic as he was pliable. Pallas, however, had the most to gain because at some point during the "empress contest" he had become her lover as well.

Agrippina's primary goal at the time was to secure her status by betrothing her 12-year-old son to the emperor's daughter Octavia. He thus became Claudius' son-in-law. But because that was not exactly a direct line to the succession, Agrippina prevailed on Claudius to adopt the lad as his son. Ah, but that triggered another complication: Nero would now be betrothed to his own sister. The solution: offering a leading senator a choice governorship in exchange for adopting Octavia as his daughter!

At the same time, the boy Brittanicus fell under a sort of house arrest, forbidden by Agrippina to appear in public or be seen with his father. As Tacitus observed: "No one was hard hearted enough not to be distressed at Brittanicus' fate. Gradually deprived of even his slaves' services, he saw through his stepmother's hypocrisy and treated her untimely intentions cynically."

Having tended to the successorship, Agrippina now concentrated on two all-consuming passions: consolidating her political power and acquiring wealth by whatever means necessary. And this leads back to this chapter's beginning: the expulsion of Rome's Jewish population (and probably including one of its newer "sects" called Christians).

The records simply indicate that the banishment decree was prompted by "continuous disturbances at the instigation of Chrestus." Since the Christians were still perceived as a mysterious Jewish sect, it may be that they were made scapegoats in the conflict that was growing between Roman Jews and Roman Christians of both Jewish and Gentile origin.

How many Christians were in Rome and how long had they been there? Mid-first century sources are silent on the matter but offer several hints. Might the centurion who summoned Peter in Cæsarea have one day retired and returned to Rome? Did followers of Stephen come that far? Mightn't the throngs of tourists to Rome have included some of the 500 or so persons who had seen the resurrected Jesus?

Most importantly, what of Peter? His documented whereabouts are cloudy during the roughly six years after he escaped from Herod Agrippa's jail in A.D. 42. We know that he went to Antioch during this period and oral tradition is strong that he also came to Babylon and then Rome. Based on this pattern of preaching in the empire's largest Jewish population centers, one can reasonably ask that if Peter considered himself the chief apostle to the Jews, would he not have included those in the epicenter of the empire among his priorities?

To this one can add the following reason for going to Rome. *Acts*, as already related earlier, describes how one Simon the Magician came upon Peter healing believers in Samaria and offered money to infuse him with the Holy Spirit. Peter rebuked him, but this same Simon later showed up in Rome performing so many feats of magic and supposed healing that some Romans declared him a god and erected a statute to him in the Asclepieum (hospital) that stood on an island in the Tiber. When Peter learned that Simon was winning converts and plaudits in Rome, the tradition goes, he sailed there to expose the charlatan. And while in Rome, he preached the gospel and formed the first church before returning home.

Regardless of who was leading the Christians in Rome in mid-century, there is little doubt that their numbers were growing. As they did, it produced a two-fold effect on those around them. First, orthodox Jews felt threatened. They had no temple or strong priesthood as a core of strength. It was enough to attend their meetinghouses in peace, retain their special privileges under Roman law and keep suspicious Gentile troublemakers at bay. Seeing some of their flock become Christians not only diluted their ranks, but threatened to make them a minority within their own religion.

Second, other Romans were confused whenever they stopped to think about what was going on behind closed doors in the Jewish Christian enclaves of Trastevere and the Subura. Whatever happened in those synagogues or house churches was all part of a single religion that, to them, had its many murky sects and strange customs. What was one more sect? To official Rome, the only concern was that a new religion might experience sudden growth and become a threat to the state religion. And Claudius, historian and guardian of the traditional rites, knew only that he would not allow Rome's heritage to become jeopardized by the beguiling ways of imported mystery cults.

Adding to the confusion and suspicion may have been something of the Christians' own making: they commonly used the Greek *Anastasis Christou* when discussing the resurrection of Jesus. To most Greeks, the word *Anastasis* connoted "insurrection" as well as "resurrection." This suggested a messianic rebellion, a concept difficult for Christians to explain away considering that they also talked of "Christ the King" — a term that would scarcely fall lightly on the ears of a reigning monarch.

Claudius was doubtless persuaded to banish the Jews and their mysterious new sect on grounds that they threatened both the throne and Rome's sacred religious traditions, but the edict also coincided nicely with the financial ambitions of Agrippina and Pallas. That is, the sudden uprooting of some 40,000 Jews and a far lesser number of Christians offered a golden opportunity to confiscate wealth and property. Imperial agents, their true identities well shielded from their actual sponsors, would make the rounds offering to buy up what they could cheaply from the majority who were forced to close up their shops and trade stalls in the rush to depart. In the case of those who stayed and tried to melt into their traditional neighborhoods of Trastevere and the Subura (where almost all foreigners lived and plied their trades) the oppressors could rely on an unofficial corps of informers who lived off rewards for tracking down fugitives.

News of the expulsion must have puzzled the Jews in Palestine. Herod Agrippa II was still an honored guest in the household of Claudius and had just been favored with an extension of his future kingdom when he inherited the tiny city-state of Chalcis. The only explanation is that the rulers of Rome (i.e., advisors to Claudius) saw the Jews of their city through one pair of eyes and the Jews of Palestine through another. The former were one of many convenient tools in helping a new regime establish a financial base. The latter were needed as a stable border ally against new commotions on their eastern flank.

In A.D. 50 Syria had a new Roman governor in Gaius Cassius Longinus and a new procurator for Judea in one Cumanus. Parthia was again probing for possible Roman weaknesses, and in Palestine passions were roiling again over stifling taxes, absentee "Romanized" Jewish rulers, too many requisitions to feed the latest military excursion and too little left to feed a family. And as ever, a predictable flashpoint was the April Passover Feast in Jerusalem.

Cumanus, newly arrived and forewarned of possible trouble, may have overreacted by ordering a Roman regiment to stand at attention along the temple cloisters, ready to put down any sign of insurrection. All was going without incident when on the fourth day of the festival, someone in the crowd — or maybe mere boredom — provoked one of the soldiers standing watch on the portico of the Fortress Antonia to drop his breeches and wave his behind at the multitude below.

Those who saw what may have been history's first recorded mooning went into a rage. A Roman had insulted God in his own sanctuary! When reported to Cumanus, the procurator tried to calm the crowd by asking that they treat the incident as an isolated aberration. But when the vast crowd became all the more agitated, the procurator abruptly changed his stance. His soldiers were ordered to charge into the crowd. The huge Passover throng was already far more numerous than the city was built to accommodate. When people saw the soldiers running at them in full battle armor, they scattered in panic. But the exit passages were only so big, and as their fear took charge terrified Jews began to trample and suffocate each other, killing thousands and turning a supposedly glorious occasion into a collective mood of outrage and insurrection.

As (bad) luck would have it, at the same time one of the emperor's minor envoys was coming up to Jerusalem, perhaps with an imperial Passover greeting or message for Cumanus, when he was beaten and robbed by thugs as he approached within view of the city gates. When word of this reached the procurator, he ordered soldiers to ride out immediately and search neighboring villages for both robbers and any booty they could recover.

More likely the "searching" gave way to plundering, and in the midst of it one of the soldiers seized a scroll of the Torah and carried it out to the portico where a crowd of angry Jews was gathering below. Brandishing the scroll and hurling insults, he proceeded to tear it to pieces.

Soon after the Passover, when Cumanus had returned to Cæsarea, a delegation of elders from the afflicted village appeared before his tribunal chair and wailed that they could not go on living knowing that the affront to God that they had witnessed had not been avenged. Knowing that word of the incident was spreading throughout Judea — and sedition with it — the procurator ordered the offending soldier to appear before the Jewish envoys and had him beheaded on the spot. This quenched the flames for the moment, but not for long, as we shall see.

PAUL'S ZEAL for his second mission burned brighter than ever. As he set out with Silas on foot from Antioch in A.D. 49, it's likely that he had already determined to spread the gospel across Asia Minor, Achaia, Italy, and then to Rome itself. The first stop, however, was a very familiar one. Paul finally had a chance to spend some time in his native Tarsus, giving encouragement to the very first churches he had created and doubtless reacquainting himself with his family as well. Then, just as soon as the melting snows of spring would allow, he and his new companion from Jerusalem would make the climb through the beautiful but treacherous Cilician Gates and down into the high Anatolian plains of Galatia.

Traversing this narrow pass through the 4,000-foot-high Taurus Mountains was no routine feat for well-equipped armies, let alone two middle-aged hikers. The same steep rocky north-south wagon road, in some places no more than 30 feet wide, had been the only way for the Hittites to conquer Syria a thousand years before. Some 700 years later Alexander the Great had led 100,000 men through the same pass on their way to attacking the Persians. In a spring of melting snows, Paul and Silas would have been constantly wet and cold as they walked in shadows cast by the cliffs towering above them. Once they emerged onto the Anatolian plains, they still faced a 90-mile trek to their first destination in Pisidia.

Derbe again! How reassuring it must have been for Paul to be greeted so warmly by the Christians he had left behind just a year before in this small wayside. They, too, must have found their souls fortified when Paul and Silas, as would be their custom when reaching all the new churches of Asia Minor, read the letter of accommodation about circumcision and dietary rules that had been circulated by James the Just after the meeting of Christian elders in Jerusalem.

Then it was on to Lystra. In the same town where Paul had been stoned and left for dead, they now found a thriving Christian community. There they stayed in the home of a Jewish-Christian widow and must have been extremely impressed with her son, Timothy, because they decided to take him on the rest of their journey. The only problem was that the young man's father was Greek and hadn't circumcised his son. Paul insisted that it be done; and when Timothy agreed he performed the procedure himself as a Jewish rabbi.

Circumcised? Hadn't Paul campaigned arduously for the right *not* to circumcise Gentiles? True, but Paul was also practical. Timothy's late father was apparently well known enough as a Greek that having the lad at the apostles' side would have ruffled Jewish elders every time the missionaries appeared in a synagogue. Moreover, it may be that Timothy (who perhaps witnessed Paul's healing of the cripple the year before) himself insisted on circumcision to persuade Paul of his zeal for his missionary task ahead. Then one must also consider the nature of Paul himself. Having won the ideological struggle over circumcision, he could now afford to be magnanimous to the most stubborn of Jewish Christians.

The journey's next logical pathway would have been through Asia and on to the populous regional capital of Ephesus, but *Acts* says that the apostle found himself "forbidden by the Holy Spirit to speak the word in Asia." Some add that Paul had at one time suffered from malaria and was deterred by the prospect of being in that hot, coastal area during summertime.

Nor would the Spirit, Paul said, permit them to enter the cooler but more primitive and sparsely settled Bithynia on the Black Sea coast. Thus, they traveled on steadily westward towards Mysia until they reached the port city of Alexander Troas.

Many first century travelers knew the place well because it lay near the ancient city of Troy, whose ruins so many of them visited. It was in the agora of Troy that they would sit reciting Homer and his tales of the Trojan War. Founded by Alexander the Great, the walled city was given the added name Troas (for the large plain that led up from the sea) to distinguish it from the Alexandria in Egypt. The city also sat in the shadow of Mount Ida, whose northwestern spur runs almost to the coast.

There in Alexander Troas the three Christians would have found themselves in the midst of tourists and their guides as they left to spend the day in Troy or a night on the sacred mountain. On its peak, where Homer says Zeus sat watching the war's changing fortunes, stood an enormous 200-foot pine on which names of tourists had been carved for at least two centuries.

It was also at this gateway to Troy that Paul reported seeing a vision in a dream: "a man from Macedonia" stood in front of him beseeching him to "Come over to Macedonia and help us."

Paul had no doubts of his destination from then on. Macedonia, lying northwest across the Ægean Sea from Alexander Troas, was, of course, the home of the legendary Alexander and the hardy mountaineers who had conquered Greece before felling nearly every other empire to the east and south some three centuries beforehand. But in midsummer, Paul's impatience to get started may have been tested by the forces of nature. The *Meltemis*, fearsome hot winds from the north, were blowing as usual at this time and were not to be ignored by any ship captain contemplating a northwest passage. Their destination was Neapolis, a Macedonian port lying 100 miles straight into the daunting winds. It meant tacking among some offshore islands for 160 miles in all. It also meant waiting until the *Meltemis* eased off a bit.

It was probably at this point that the three Christian travelers linked up with a Macedonian physician named Luke. Alexander Troas was home to many Macedonians and a maritime crossroads for many more. Was Luke the Macedonian in Paul's vision? Did Paul, who suffered from his unspecified chronic malady, welcome Luke also because he could help sustain his health by medicines or massages? All that can be surmised is that Paul converted Luke in Alexander Troas and that he agreed to escort the missionaries to his native Macedonia. The reason for this conjecture is that Luke is the author of *Acts,* and it is from this point on that his report stops referring to the missionaries as "they" and begins writing of "we." The events also become more detailed, as if taken from a personal diary.

One can picture the ship passengers grumbling idly in a waterfront inn as they waited for the captain's decision to sail, then downing their last draughts and racing upstairs for their baggage once a messenger arrived with word that all was ready. The ship would then be towed out of the placid harbor by a longboat. Then it would soon be in the unruly open sea with passengers hunched over and holding fast to the tilted deck rails as the vessel hove up and down to the music of the *Meltemis* and sprayed their faces with salt water.

The captain would first head for the lee of Tenedos, a small island in which the Greek fleet once hid before surprising the Trojans with their invasion. From there it was on to the isle of Samothrace, where they most likely stopped to let some passengers off alongside its 5,000-foot mountain. For it would soon be August and Samothrace would again be host to the great festival of the Cabeiri, those mysterious fertility gods whose rites were secret to all but their initiates. Because seafarers also worshipped the Cabeiri as their protectors, the missionaries would have seen some of the sailors wearing purple sashes or amulets as their marks of initiation. And they probably found something else to do when the crew and many passengers kneeled in worship and burned incense in the Cabeiri shrine that was mounted on the ship's stern. Those who disembarked would journey to the deep valley where the Samothracian gods lived and where incense fumes rose in front of the stone phalli that were their symbols.

After spending the night moored in the mountain's shadow, the ship passed by the lovely isle of Thasos, which marked the northernmost extent of the Ægean and which was known for its marble, wine and nuts. Then it was on to the Macedonian coastline, with the sailors trimming the sail as gusts of wind came rolling off the nearby mountains. Soon the port of Neapolis was dead ahead, and directly south was the peak of Acte, which jutted into the sea and soared 6,000 feet.

The missionaries' destination was Philippi, eight miles from the port city and involving another steep climb. As the sweltering Neopolis receded behind them, they could see the foam of breaking waves below, and above, their first view of the ancient acropolis of Philippi with its fortified barracks. Founded nearly 400 years before by Philip of Macedon, Alexander's father, Philippi was certainly the regional capital and perhaps even "the first city of Macedonia," as its residents boasted. It was nearby that Anthony and Octavian had met Brutus and Cassius to avenge the murder of Julius Cæsar, and the event was commemorated by a large triumphal arch that adorned the city's main gate. It also explains the fortified barracks on the acropolis. Philippi's identity had been remade when Augustus chose it as a place to settle retired veterans and administer Roman provincial affairs. Roman in outlook and not too rooted in any provincial religions, Philippians were known for welcoming strangers and their willingness to hear new ideas.

Due to its different demographic complexion, Philippi had no synagogue. Since it took ten Jewish men — a *minyan* — to form a synagogue, one may assume there were not many Jews as well. Thus, the missionaries found themselves starting a prayer meeting of God-fearers by the side of the river Gangites. There, on the Sabbath, this small band of Jewish and Gentile converts would gather for the ritual washing of their hands before prayer and a reading of the Law and the prophets.

One of the members of this group was a widow named Lydia, who seems to have been a woman of some means. She came from the town of Thyatira, known for the quality of the purple dye it made from the murex shellfish. It was the most luxurious of dyes, being used in everything from priestly vestments to senatorial togas. Thanks perhaps to the liberal views of this city towards the role of women, Lydia seems to have been the owner of both a prosperous business and a large home.

She was also a devout God-fearer, perhaps from an association with the active Jewish community of her hometown. Certainly she must have been one of the first to receive Paul's message unconditionally, because soon after having been baptized with her whole household she came to the four missionaries and said: "If you have judged me to be faithful to the Lord, come to my house and stay."

Thus, Lydia's home may have become the first house church in Achaia. All indications are that it was growing and prospering when Paul again found himself in trouble with the authorities. But this time he certainly wasn't the instigator. One day he and his followers were going to their place of worship when they found themselves being followed by a slave girl, who kept chanting: "These men are servants of the Most High God, who proclaim to you the way of salvation."

Following the girl at some distance and urging her on were two men. Upon closer inspection, the missionaries determined that the men actually owned the seeress and made their living charging people for her prophecies. It soon became obvious that the girl's "keepers" had watched the Christians at worship and hoped that they would pay to hear some prophesies about their leaders.

For several days Paul said nothing as the girl dogged his footsteps, but enough was enough. Suddenly turning about-face, he addressed the spirit that ruled within the prophetess and commanded: "I charge you in the name of Jesus Christ to come out of her!"

"And it came out that very hour," Luke's diary recorded.

When Paul had walked on and the girl's owners finally recovered from the shock at what they'd witnessed, they realized that all they had left in place of their commercial asset was an ordinary housemaid. Now sputtering with anger, they rounded up a gang of sympathizers and went out to the riverside in search of the two foreign troublemakers. Later that day the local magistrates were already in the midst of hearing some routine cases in the city marketplace when suddenly there arrived a mob kicking and hitting a pair of strangers. "These men are Jews and they are disturbing the city," charged one of the slave owners. Amidst much shouting and confusion, no doubt too noisy for anyone to hear Paul and Silas claiming their Roman citizenship, the magistrates had the apostles stripped to the waist and gave orders to beat them with rods.

"And when they had inflicted many blows upon them," Luke reported, "they threw them into prison, charging the jailer to keep them safely." Taking this to mean that he might be flogged himself or even lose his life if they got away, the jailer put them in the most secure inner prison and fastened their feet in stocks.

This was one of the three times Paul wrote about having been beaten with rods. Delivered to a man who still might not have fully healed from the previous year's stoning in Lystra, the pain and damage were doubtless even more intense than the usual punishment. After being dragged to the jail in a senseless condition, then having to sit upright in the stocks when his body yearned to be stretched out and soothed must have been almost unbearable. Yet, *Acts* records that "about midnight Paul and Silas were praying and singing hymns to God, and the prisoners were listening to them..."

Being in a thickly walled stone building, they had not felt the first tremors. Singing, they would not have heard what had already reached the ears of cats, dogs and birds in Philippi. Then the first wave of the earthquake hit the city. Soon the vibrations were shaking the building every few seconds. Then the whole jail rocked. Wood-beamed doorways groaned and many bars securing the cell doors from the outside tumbled to the ground. In the innermost cell, the two prisoners even found that the bolts holding their common chain had pulled out of the wall.

The jailer just outside the cell had been sleeping; and when he scrambled to his feet with a start, all was dark. He must have assumed the noise and trembling were the result of a mass escape. The prisoners were still probably too stunned to move; but hearing only silence and knowing the penalty for an escape, the jailer drew his sword and shouted that he was about to kill himself. Then came a voice from out of the darkness: "Don't harm yourself, for we are all here!" It was Paul.

The jailer called out for lamps to be lit. Then he entered the cell, and trembling with fear, fell down before Paul and Silas and asked, "Men, what must I do to be saved?"

The poor shaken wretch associated the earthquake with divine powers of his prisoners, just as some in town would explain it by insisting that the sea god, Poseidon, who dwelled on the sea bottom near Macedonia, would sometimes shatter rocks with his trident just to remind men of his power. But Paul talked to him of another God instead. "Believe in the Lord Jesus, and you will be saved, you and your household," he said.

The Jailer then took Paul and Silas to his home in the middle of the night where he treated their wounds and gave them food. Then they preached the gospel to his family and baptized them all, probably with the same well water that was used to treat their sores. "And he rejoiced with all his household that he had believed in God," Luke wrote.

The next morning, as all of Philippi was staggering to its feet after the night's calamity, Lydia and other Christians probably went to the chief magistrates and told them they were about to be in big trouble for flogging and jailing two Roman citizens without trial. Paul and Silas apparently had been brought back to jail and bolted up again when some lictors arrived with an order. "The magistrates have sent us to let you go," they announced with official airs. "Now therefore come out and go in peace."

It would not be that easy. Paul, sensing he now had the upper hand, sent them back with a message of his own. "They have beaten us publicly, un-condemned men who are Roman citizens, and have thrown us into prison," he said. "And so now they cast us out secretly? No! Let them come them-selves and take us out."

The subdued magistrates soon came in person to apologize and to free them. But they also begged the missionaries to leave town quickly because their safety couldn't be guaranteed if the mob got stirred up again. So the two went back to Lydia's house and called in the small congregation for a final meeting. Some say that Luke stayed in his home city for a while to prac-tice medicine and help lead the small church Paul and he had founded.

Autumn was coming on quickly as Paul, Silas and Timothy set out for the southwest on the Via Egnatia for what would be a 100-mile trip. They passed through Amphidpolis, once a bone of contention between Athens and Sparta, then Apollonia on the waters of Lake Bolhe. There seems to have been little missionary activity along the way, for their destination was a city that could influence the whole region. Thessalonica, named for the daugh-ter of Philip, had become arguably the paramount city of Macedonia because the Via Egnatia crossed it and because it was the chief port for the north-ern inlets of the Ægean Sea. Southwest across its sheltered gulf rose the awe-inspiring peak of Mt. Olympus, nearly 10,000 feet high and covered with eternal snow and clouds. In that mist, as any Greek or Roman knew, were the palaces of the gods from which they maintained a dispassionate, bemused watch on the activities of the mortals below.

Thessalonica also had a large Jewish population, and Paul doubtless entered knowing that a familiar scene would probably be played out again.

Why did Paul seek out such large cities? Why did he not head for the countryside, where people tended to hold simpler values and not make weapons out of their wit and cynicism as they did in big cities? First, Paul felt the power of his message and his ability to deliver it would withstand a challenge by anyone. Second, he felt an urgency to preach the gospel to as many as he could in the shortest possible time. It would appear that Paul went to smaller places only when ill, injured or fatigued — as if he felt the need to reach out to at least *some* people even when in need of rest or recuperation. As his later letters indicated, Jesus had fulfilled all of the ancient prophecies and had risen from the dead. His second coming was imminent and everyone should be forewarned to live each day as if it were the last before the final judgment.

Indeed, Paul had not relaxed or modified his message in any way when he again approached a synagogue in Thessalonica and asked to speak. This time he found the congregation receptive, and for three consecutive Sabbaths, notes *Acts*, "he argued with them from the scriptures, explaining and proving that it was necessary for the Christ to suffer and to rise from the dead, and saying, 'This Jesus whom I proclaim to you is the Christ!'"

Some were persuaded and joined the missionaries immediately. They included "a great many of the devout Greeks and several of the leading women," wrote Luke. In the markets, Gentiles appeared receptive, too, although often not for the right reasons. That Thessalonica was a stronghold of Orphism serves to explain what could happen to Christian leaders in many cities with special cults. Orpheus, whose origins are shrouded in the distance of centuries, was the son of a Thracian king and one of the Muses. After sailing on the Argonaut he married the nymph Eurydice, who soon died from snakebite. Orpheus took a lyre to Hades and so enchanted the underworld gods with his music that they allowed Eurydice to return to the world above. The only condition imposed on Orpheus was that he not look back on his wife, who followed behind as they made their way up to the sunlight.

Naturally, he couldn't resist one look over his shoulder, so immediately Eurydice became a ghost and disappeared. Again devastated, Orpheus thereafter treated all women of Thrace with cruel contempt. Thus, at one of the Bacchanalian orgies held in Thrace, the women got their revenge: they tore Orpheus to pieces and flung them into the sea. Later the fragments were collected by the Muses and buried at the foot of Mt. Olympus.

Practitioners of Orphism had a mystical ceremony in which they ate raw flesh and drank blood to symbolize the tearing of the young man to pieces. Somehow all this evolved into a spring rite in which sin was expelled and the soul purified by the symbolic suffering and death of a godman. During the year, believers led an ascetic life, which included wearing white garments, abstaining from all animal foods and avoiding attendance at births and deaths.

One can see why neither Jewish customs nor the story of the resurrection would be strange or uncomfortable to such persons. But this would only have dismayed Paul and Silas. Against these traditions they had to preach that Christianity was more than a club created to ensure the salvation of members who have been admitted by secret rites. Yes, Orphism promised salvation, but it lacked any message of love and kindness towards one's neighbors. Only Christianity extended God's love and kindness to all.

And this takes us back to the synagogue where Paul was preaching. The four travelers had taken up residence in the nearby home of a man named Jason. Once again, the elders of a Jewish meetinghouse could not live with the concept of an invitation open to just anyone. The elders, "taking some of the wicked fellows of the rabble," as Luke says, "gathered a crowd, set the city in an uproar, and attacked the house of Jason, seeking to bring them out to the people. And when they could not find the four missionaries, they dragged Jason and some of the brethren before the city authorities, crying, 'These men who have turned the world upside down have come here, also, and Jason has received them. And they are acting against the decrees of Cæsar, saying that there is another king, this Jesus.'"

The rest isn't clear, but it seems that the authorities extracted some sort of stiff fine or security deposit from poor Jason that would be returned only if the strangers were compelled to leave town. Thus, in another nighttime exit, the young Christian community in Thessalonica bid Paul and Silas farewell on the Via Egnatia. Timothy stayed behind for several days to offer the new church what assistance he could.

Walking another 70 miles to the west, the missionaries reached Beroea, a much smaller place in the foothills of Mt. Olympus. Twenty miles upland from the sun-baked seacoast, it was cooled by winds and streams rushing down from the mountain. Beroea also seemed a more temperate place in which to introduce the Christian message because the members of its synagogue were known to be friendly and open-minded. As Luke, the travel diarist, puts it, "These Jews were more noble than those in Thessalonica, for they received the word with all eagerness, examining the scriptures daily to see if these things were so. Many of them therefore believed, [including] not a few Greek women of high standing as well as men."

Well, somebody from the Jewish congregation must have made a trip to Thessalonica. No doubt he went to the meetinghouse to worship. Perhaps after the service he was catching up on the news with some old friends and innocently mentioned the two visitors to his synagogue in Beroea and their compelling message. One can envision an elder overhearing and exclaiming, wide-eyed, "What? These same troublemakers who defiled our house of prayer are now polluting yours? Don't you understand that they preach the establishment of a new kingdom that flies in the face of both Roman and Mosaic Law? Don't you realize that these are the same kind of meddlers who got all Jews expelled from Rome? Is that what you want for the whole province of Achaia?"

After that, it was only a matter of time before the Jewish elders came to Beroea from Thessalonica and threatened to incite another mob scene. The only "victory" for the missionaries was that the indignant delegation seemed to be pacified by removing Paul alone. Silas and Timothy could remain to teach the new brethren for a while.

They conducted Paul down to the nearest seaport, and soon the apostle found himself on a ship for Athens. There is no indication that Paul had ever intended to invade this ancient citadel of philosophy and idol worship, but there he was, perhaps because it was the only place where ships from that small port were headed. Thus, he would have found himself on one of the combination sail-and-oared "coasters" that plied the strong tidal currents that surged in the narrow channel running between the long island of Euboea and the coast of Attica.

Being alone, and supposedly just waiting for Silas, Timothy and Luke to catch up with him, Paul had time on his hands to survey this dazzling city. Long past its political and military prime, Athens still remained the symbol of everything noble about Greece. It was also the place where the Roman elite went to polish their culture and to procure teachers, physicians, sculptors and musicians to grace their households.

As Paul strolled about Athens with its glittering acropolis 180 feet above, his dominant first impression may not have been the much-emulated, marbled public buildings, but the hundreds of idols and statues that lined street after colonnaded street. Yes, Paul had seen dozens in Tarsus and Antioch, but perhaps not so many varieties in one place. Here it was as if the sponsors of public idols strove to paint each one in the most vivid colors possible. Altars smoked with burning sacrifices, incense billowed out of temples, people stood with their backs turned on the street as they proffered some small gift to one of the many small shrines erected in almost every recess. Statues of naked women vied for attention with Priapic statues whose erect penises people stopped to rub for good luck or a laugh.

Silas or no Silas, Timothy or no Timothy, Paul couldn't stand watching all this wasted devotion and energy. "His spirit provoked," as Luke records, the apostle went to the synagogue on the Sabbath and argued "with the Jews and devout persons." At other times he was "in the market place every day with those who chanced to be there." Eventually, word of this man with a bold new message reached some leading educators, who invited him to the Areopagus to speak to a group of scholars and other luminaries.

This was no street corner lyceum. The Areopagus, not far from from the famed Parthenon on the Acropolis, was where major criminal cases are held. But when not so used it was constantly open for public debates and readings, for as Luke says, "all the Atheneans and the foreigners who lived there spent their time in nothing except telling or hearing something new."

An invitation was issued to Paul in that spirit and he quickly accepted. It's likely that Luke and the other missionaries had arrived in Athens by the time the apostle spoke, because the diary has captured only its most important passages:

> Men of Athens, I perceive that in every way you are very religious. For as I passed along and observed the objects of your worship, I found also an altar with the inscription, "To an unknown god." What therefore you worship as unknown, this I proclaim to you. The God who made the world and everything in it, being Lord of heaven and earth, does not live in shrines made by man, nor is he served by human hands, as though he needed anything, since he himself gives to all men life and breath and everything.
>
> And he made from one every nation of men to live on all the face of the earth, having determined allotted periods and the boundaries of their habitation, that they should seek God in the hope that they might feel after him and find him. Yet he is not far from each one of us, for "in him we live and move and have our being." Even some of your own poets have said, "for we are indeed his offspring."
>
> Being then God's offspring, we ought not to think that the

Deity is like gold or silver or stone, a representation by the
art and imagination of man. The times of ignorance God
overlooked. But now he commands all men everywhere to
repent, because he has fixed a day on which he will judge
the world in righteousness by a man whom he has appointed, and of this he has given assurance to all men by raising
him from the dead. [22]

It is safe to say that this unvarnished, blunt message was not met with
either the jubilation or intense questioning that had characterized audiences
in, say, Lystra and Philippi. One answer may be that while Athenians pro-
fessed their eagerness to hear new ideas, most already championed a religion or philosophy. Chief among those who held sway in Athens were the
Stoics and Epicureans. Stoics, their name derived from the very Painted Hall
in Athens (called Stoa), believed in virtue as man's highest calling. This is
achieved by performing one's duty according to rigid ethics — chief among
them absolute judgment, mastery over desire and control of soul over pain.

And what is the soul? There were many shades of Stoicism, but in general the soul was perceived as man's invisible, conscious self. Its true home
was somewhere in the cosmos, perhaps in the light of the sun or the silence
of the stars. A Stoic mustn't fear death because it is no more than an absorption
of the soul and its consciousness into the universe.

Describing Epicureanism is more difficult because the concept had been
twisted often since Epicurus came to Athens from his native Samos in 400
B.C. The highest good, he taught his followers, is happiness, which comes
by cultivating virtue. By the first century many had embellished these
tenets to the point of rationalizing that if happiness is indeed the desired end,
then it is perfectly proper to achieve it through such short cuts as an am-
phora of fine wine and heaps of succulent morsels.

Overlaid upon these barriers to Paul's message was one common to all
Athenian scholars. One might call it "polite indifference." If you view an orator's performance strictly as entertainment or gymnastics for the mind, you
aren't likely to bring a mob upon him as the offended Jewish elders did on
Paul. Thus, Luke states simply that "when they heard of the resurrection
of the dead, some mocked; but others said, 'We will hear you again about
this.'" And so, they just slipped away, no doubt chatting amicably in clusters about the next play or poetry reading. It was as if Paul had gone to the
arena prepared to fight a gladiator and instead found himself facing a
greased pig.

Some Athenians did thirst for more — including a member of the council that governed the Areopagus where Paul spoke — but there is no record of a church being established there during his visit. The missionaries soon departed, and their lack of success may not have filled them with confidence, because as they headed west for Corinth, a larger, tougher, bawdier commercial seaport, Paul described himself as approaching "with fear and trembling."

A.D. 51–53

NERO, BORN IN THE COASTAL RESORT TOWN of Antium nine months after Tiberius died, was now all of 13. He already bore the title, Prince of Youth, and the Senate had voted that he would become consul on his 19th birthday. Gifts were made to the Prætorians in Nero's name and at games held in the Circus he attracted much attention by wearing a robe usually seen only on a general or some other notable who had earned a triumph. Brittanicus was allowed to attend on that occasion, but only so that Agrippina could demonstrate an important contrast: Claudius' only natural son appeared in plain boy's clothing.

During these adolescent years Nero's life and hours were intertwined with a man who ostensibly bore the title of tutor, but who would soon become an unofficial regent and employ a steadying hand on Roman governmental affairs for the next dozen or so years. His name was Lucius Annæus Seneca, a Spaniard from Cordova who had become a leading Stoic philosopher, essayist, poet and playwright.

Many an eyebrow was raised at Agrippina's choice of Seneca. Then about 50, he had spent the last eight years living in Corsica — exiled by no less than Claudius for supposedly having an affair with Agrippina's youngest sister. What puzzles historians is that Seneca had been married and devoted to his wife Paulina all of his adult life.

Meanwhile, Agrippina, now known as the Augusta, continued to draw the palace reigns more tightly. Since the two co-commanders of the Prætorian Guard were holdovers from the Messalina years, she prevailed on Claudius to declare them a threat to the royal family and to replace them with a single prefect who would understand clearly to whom he owed his patronage. A veteran professional soldier, his name was Sextus Afranius Burrus, and he would soon join Seneca and the freedman Pallas as the troika who pulled Agrippina and the government. Narcissus remained attached to Claudius, but his one horse chariot was clearly losing the race.

Where was Claudius as his powers were being gnawed away? He continued to stay busy enough managing the grain supply, dedicating public works and settling tribal successorship disputes in places like Germany and Britain. Besides, one must remember that this was the same man who had to be dragged, trembling from behind a curtain to accept the throne. He had also fine-tuned his already keen sensitivity to conspiracy, so that he would have his private guard serve him in a host's home and even had them take pens from visitors who called on him. At the same time, his first instincts were not to challenge his wife and freedmen, but to accommodate what was going on around him.

Most of Agrippina's maneuverings were subtle but constant. In just one example, she arranged for Narcissus to head a project to commemorate the draining of the Fucine Lake. Work gangs were on the verge of completing an eleven-year tunneling project that was to drain this marshy body of water just north of Rome into the lower-lying Liris River so that many square miles of land would be available for crops. But just before the tunnel was breeched, Claudius saw an opportunity to stage some naval battles on a scale that would have impressed even the wastrel Gaius Caligula.

Narcissus was put in charge of building a ring of portable grandstands around the lake's perimeter. On the first night the stands were overflowing as two mock navies of several thousand condemned criminals, each side with six three-tiered rowing warships, clashed and fought until most were dead. The next day, when engineers told Claudius that the tunnel below the lake still wasn't dug through enough to drain, he decided on another evening's entertainment — a hand-to-hand infantry battle fought by gladiators on pontoons.

Again, most of Rome and its surrounding towns turned out for the spectacle. Claudius and Nero were in resplendent military garb. The grandstands were jammed and below them ringing the lakeshore were rafts holding stone throwers and catapults just in case any of the combatants might try to cheat the crowd of its entertainment by scrambling ashore.

Banqueting had just begun in the portable stands when the tunnel must have broken through from the sheer force of the water pressing above it. Like a bathtub whose plug was pulled, the water began to course towards the end of the lake where the tunnel had breeched. As it gathered momentum, the current swept along pontoons, grandstands, spectators, gladiators and everything else in its way.

Later, when officials began to tally up the considerable deaths and injuries, they looked for a scapegoat and Agrippina was quick to suggest one. Soon word spread that Narcissus, the man in charge of financing the project, had built cheap, rickety grandstands so he could pocket the difference and fatten his already considerable purse. Narcissus could do little but bite his tongue and hope that his days weren't numbered.

CUMANUS, THE NEW PROCURATOR of Judea, never quite had a chance to settle in or to get the knack of governing the Jews. Nor did they ever conduct "business" in the way he expected — especially when they set foot in Samaria.

As described before, Galileans, invariably the most exuberant or rebellious of festival attendees, always had to make their way southward to Jerusalem through the suspicious and often hostile region of Samaria. On one of these occasions, as they headed back after the Passover, a band of them arrived in a village called Ginæ, no doubt tired and thirsty and seeking service at some hostelry. The Galileans must have been too raucous or demanding, because they were refused. One can picture a tavern keeper facing a hot, thirsty, defiant gang of foreigners while his servant scurries out the back door to find some local young toughs to help defend the honor of Samaria. The result was an ugly skirmish that left several dead on both sides. Before long, Cumanus was confronted in Cæsarea by a delegation of Galilean elders and parents, all demanding that he avenge the deaths.

But it seems that their counterparts from Samaria had anticipated the appeal and had already plied the procurator with enough money to overlook the matter. When the exasperated Galilean elders returned home and reported that they were helpless to obtain retribution, their young hotheads became all the more inflamed. Declaring that anything was better than the "slavery" they were subjected to, they took their case to Eleazar, an infamous robber who lived with his brigands in the mountains. Off Eleazar and his new allies soon went, plundering many villages of Samaria in the name of revenge.

Now it was Cumanus' turn to fan the fires. Borrowing four regiments of footmen from Sebaste and arming many more Samaritans, he ordered the tribune Celer to lead them all against the Galileans. The Roman-Samaritan forces soon surprised Eleazer and his new recruits in the middle of some mischief. Many Galileans were killed, but many were also taken alive.

This settled nothing. For many weeks, armed bands of Galileans would strike into Samaria, pillaging and destroying. As they did, rival Samarian brigands would be doing exactly the same thing in Galilean towns. Soon there was talk of civil war. It was at that point that the leading families of Jerusalem took it upon themselves to douse the flames. They put on sackcloth, heaped ashes on their heads and approached their seditious countrymen with warnings that they would utterly subvert their entire country and its temple if they did not cast aside their weapons and return to calm.

The Galileans finally desisted and retreated to their local strongholds, but it was more like a temporary truce. Already, robbers and brigands crawled over the land as never before, and their favorite targets were Samaritans. No sooner had Cassius Longinus been recalled as governor of Syria when his replacement, Ummidius Quadratus, was confronted by a group of Samaritan leaders claiming that the same Galilean marauders had broken the truce. In fact, the Samaritans were downright insolent to Quadratus, charging that they would have settled the score swiftly if they didn't have to await permission from Roman rulers.

Quadratus, determined to make his new administration a fair one, decided to make his own investigation. After a trip to Samaria, he had all but convinced himself the Samaritans were the guilty instigators when he learned that Galilean adventurers again were out in the hillsides fomenting trouble. He ordered that all the Galileans that Cumanus had captured be crucified as a warning against further trouble. When even this didn't stop the bitter skirmishing, the new governor of Syria had the leading Samaritans, their Galilean counterparts, Cumanus the Roman procurator, his tribune Celer — and for good measure, the Jewish high priest — all sent off to Rome for trial by the emperor.

When the court date appointed them drew nigh, the palace freedmen became very concerned about the fate of Cumanus, whose appointment they had brought about. But here Claudius rose to the occasion. When the young Agrippa II, still being raised in the imperial household, beseeched him to hear the case personally, the emperor agreed. And despite the pressures of his own freedmen, the emperor ruled that the Samaritan delegation should be slain for bribing Cumanus and the procurator banished for accepting. The tribune Celer fared worse than all: he was brought back to Jerusalem and dragged by horses through the city to demonstrate that a just emperor had exacted retribution.

Yes, Claudius remained active in hearing judicial cases, but he still exercised little control of governmental appointments and administration. Proof enough of that was the next procurator of Judea. Felix was none other than the brother of the imperial financial secretary, Pallas, and Agrippina's closest confidant. Despite the example of Cumanus, Felix seems to have arrived in Cæsarea confident that he could do anything he wished to build up his political power and personal fortune.

Felix began with an "acquisition" that upset whatever equilibrium existed within the Jewish royal family. The young Herod Agrippa II had just shorn up his alliances with some surrounding city-states by marrying his two eligible sisters to two of their rulers. The youngest, Drusilla, was considered the fairest beauty in all Syria and with a modest demeanor that contrasted sharply with her outspoken older sister Bernice. Not long after Drusilla's presumably ideal marriage ceremony, Felix arrived on the scene and decided at once that he must have this particular woman as his wife. At first he showered her with promises of great wealth and happiness. When Drusilla refused, even feigning illness so as to avoid this unwanted suitor, Felix called upon a famous magician, who somehow cast a spell that made Drusilla annul her wedding and marry the procurator.

Transgressing the laws of her forefathers did not endear Drusilla to her sister Bernice, nor to their brother. But then, the older Bernice had begun living in incest with that same brother. Rather than presiding over one happy family, Agrippa II would soon arrive from Rome to govern a kingdom that was at odds with an aggressively ambitious Roman procurator for more reasons than ever.

PAUL WENT ON BY HIMSELF to Corinth, having sent Timothy and Silas back to Macedonia to buttress the young churches of Philippi and Thessalonica. If Paul went west by sea, it would have been but an easy day's sail from the Athenian port of Piræus across the Gulf of Corinth to its own port of Cenchreæ. Always in view toward him as he approached Corinth would be the 1,800-foot mountain known as The Arcocorinth and its citadel overlooking the whole region.

So short a distance, but what contrast from Athens! Although both were founded in ancient times, Corinth was not even a hundred years old when Paul arrived. The explanation: Corinth, the center of Greek resistance during the Roman Republic, was reduced to rubble at the same time Rome destroyed Carthage. Despoiled and desolate, its people having been sold into slavery and its treasures shipped off to Rome, it was not until 44 B.C. when Julius Cæsar decided to rebuild and resettle the city as the new capital of Achaia.

Given the city's natural location, it wasn't long before it became the commercial center as well. Set on the narrow isthmus, Corinth not only divided north and south Greece, it was also the closest city on the mainland to both the Ægean and Adriatic seas. Over the centuries sporadic attempts had been made to scour a coast-to-coast canal from the rocky isthmus, but they always faltered for lack of enough money and manpower. As it was, some ships were transported between the seas by a cumbersome series of rollers, which made for a fascinating tourist attraction in itself. Isthmus or no isthmus, Corinth remained a major naval center because the famous trireme, with its three tiers of oars, was invented and still built there.

Just as Corinth was a sailor's city, it was also the favorite destination of traders and tourists. There, both could find any goods by day, and after business hours, diversions that ran from the finest sporting facilities in Greece to old wine and young women. Indeed, a man on the prowl might find himself among a thousand available "priestesses" (actually slaves) atop the mountain at the flourishing temple of Aphrodite. As proof of its infamy, the Greek word *Korinthiazesthai* was a common slang word for fornication.

When it came to religion, this was no Athens with its many rituals and competing philosophies. In Paul's Corinth religion had already been captured by the commercial prophetess, the temple priest and the seller of amulets, trinkets and incense. But the striking exception, of course, was Judaism. There were many pious, hardworking Jews in Corinth who observed The Law, and, as ever, Paul made straight for them.

It was fortuitous for Paul that in his first days there he befriended Aquila and Priscilla while attending their synagogue. Aquila (and perhaps his wife as well) was a Jew from Pontus on the Black Sea. This tent and sail-making couple had most recently lived in Rome, from which they had been forced to move when the emperor banished all Jews. What a wonderful source of support they must have been to Paul. He arrived short on funds, required lodgings, needed a way to make a living and sought his first converts to Christianity. Aquila and Priscilla offered him a home and a place in their business. Perhaps they had already been baptized as Jewish Christians in Rome, because they quickly became the cornerstones of the first church in Corinth. And if Paul still lacked intimate knowledge of Jewish-Christian affairs in Rome, these new allies could certainly provide it.

Although Paul argued his case in the synagogues as usual, his stay in Corinth probably got off to a more successful start than elsewhere because he was also introduced to many people who belonged to the same trade guild as Aquila and Priscilla. Assuming that the tentmakers and leatherworkers of Corinth joined the same kind of clubs as they did in Rome, they probably also belonged to the Freemasons' lodge, which gave them opportunities to meet their fellow tradesmen on a social basis. It may even be that this became the basis for the first church of Corinth, just as Lydia's group of cloth-workers may have in Philippi. It's also likely that Aquila and Priscilla offered their home as the first Christian meeting place.

On the Sabbath, however, Paul could always be found in a synagogue, and not always the same one. According to Luke's account, the apostle first converted Crispus, the chief elder of one synagogue and all of his family. He then did the same later to one Sesthoges, who was also described as the "ruler" of a synagogue, and presumably a different one from Crispus.

The only thing that must have marred Paul's initial success in Corinth was his constant worry about the fate of young, fragile churches of Macedonia. After all, he hadn't spent much time at either one and was forced to depart suddenly, which is why he had sent Silas and Timothy back to them. Beyond his concerns for the churches themselves was the fact that his whole mission — his ability to spread the gospel all the way to Rome — would be severely impeded if the light dimmed in Macedonia. For Paul believed that the time left before the Messiah's return to judgment was growing short.

Then one day they were in front of him, Silas and Timothy reporting the joyous news that the churches in Philippi and Thessalonica had endured! They had personally experienced the same harsh ostracism that Jewish and Gentile Christians faced from the synagogue establishment. But their faith was strong and they had even grown in numbers.

The Macedonians missed Paul, and as evidence of their love and respect for him the churches had taken up a collection so that he could spend less time earning a living and more of it preaching the gospel in Corinth.

Now able to pay his own rent, Paul may have felt he had imposed long enough on Aquila and Priscilla. He now took a room in the house of one Titus Justus, who lived right next door to a synagogue that Paul often attended. Was this close proximity a recipe for trouble? On one hand, Paul's entire stay in Corinth lasted 18 months. Much of this time must have been spent living in the home of Titus, which indicates that Paul continued to have many more weeks of success in converting both synagogue members and Gentiles.

On the other hand, it may have been that very proximity and/or the growing number of conversions by Paul that disrupted the synagogue congregation and prompted the elders to try ousting Paul from Corinth altogether. Paul certainly saw it coming because he later recalled wrestling with his conscience one night when God spoke to him. "Do not be afraid," said the inner voice, "but speak and do not be silent, for I am with you and no man shall attack you to harm you, for I have many people in this city."

With that, Paul seemed to worry no more about the consequences of confronting the Jewish elders. One day when testifying in a synagogue that the Christ was Jesus, the members "opposed and reviled him," according to Luke. With that he "shook out his garments" and said to them, "Your blood be upon your heads! I am innocent. From now on I will go to the Gentiles."

This may have served as a rallying cry for the elders, because it was shortly thereafter that an embassy of leading Jews hauled Paul before the Roman proconsul in Corinth.

The man they found in the judgment seat deserves a proper introduction before we hear about the case before him. The proconsul (Achaia was administered by the Roman Senate rather than the emperor) was a man whose connections may have figured later in Paul's destiny. Spanish-born Junius Gallio was the brother of Seneca, Nero's increasingly influential tutor. Gallio, as erudite as his brother in Rome, had been proconsul but a few weeks when he sat in his judgment seat in the southern part of the immense open market square in Corinth. On these regularly appointed days anyone could come forth to lodge a complaint, and on this occasion Gallio faced a smoldering group of men in religious robes and long black beards. In their apparent custody was a small older man who certainly seemed like one of their own kind if only given the proper clothing.

After identifying his colleagues as the eminent leaders of several synagogues, the spokesman got down to business. "This man," he said, pointing to Paul, "is persuading men to worship God contrary to The Law (of Moses)."

Just then there was a hubbub as the spokesman tried to continue and the defiant Paul began to interrupt, but Gallio calmly raised his hand and shushed both parties. "If this were a matter of wrongdoing or a vicious crime, I should have reason to bear with you, O Jews," he said. "But since this is a matter of questions about words and names and your own law, I refuse to be the judge of these things."

Paul was let go and continued to preach in Corinth for some time thereafter. But he also had continuing responsibilities to the new churches in Macedonia and Asia Minor. In particular, Timothy and Silas had brought with them several questions that were being asked by the believers in Thessalonica. Although the concerns that reached Paul are not preserved, they seemed to have dwelled on when the end of time would come and how one should live in the meantime. Paul's reply, which is the earliest of his writings to the churches he established, begins with lavish expressions of his love for the Thessalonians, then attempts to answer their questions:

> ...For the Lord himself will descend from heaven with a cry of command, with the archangel's call, and with the sound of the trumpet of God. And the dead in Christ will rise first; then we who are alive, who are left, shall be caught up together with them in the clouds to meet the Lord in the air; and so we shall always be with the Lord. Therefore, comfort one another with these words.

> But as to the times and the seasons, brethren, you have no need to have anything written to you. For you yourselves know well that the day of the Lord will come like a thief in the night. When people say, "There is peace and security," then sudden destruction will come upon them as travail comes upon a woman with child, and there will be no escape. But you are not in the darkness, brethren, for that to surprise you like a thief. For you are all sons of light and sons of the day; we are not of the night or of darkness. So then let us not sleep, as others do, but let us keep awake and be sober. For those who sleep sleep at night, and those who get drunk get drunk at night. But since we belong to the day, let us be sober, and put on the breastplate of faith and love, and for a helmet the hope of salvation. For God has not destined us for wrath, but to obtain salvation through our Lord Jesus Christ, who died for us so that whether we wake or sleep we might live with him. Therefore, encourage one another and build one another up, just as you are doing.

> But we beseech you, brethren, to respect those who labor among you and are over you in the Lord and admonish you, and to esteem them very highly in love because of their

> work. Be at peace among yourselves. And we exhort you,
> brethren, to admonish the idle, encourage the faint-hearted,
> help the weak, be patient with them all. See that none of you
> repays evil for evil, but always seek to do good to one an-
> other and to all. Rejoice always, pray constantly, give
> thanks in all circumstances, for this is the will of God in
> Christ Jesus for you.[23]

This was not the letter of men trying to establish a new religion or a complex theology. Paul and Silas, and perhaps Timothy, made no effort to mask
their Jewish heritage. They simply believed that the promises of Judaism
had been fulfilled by Jesus, who had established a new covenant between
God and all of his children.

Paul now felt his stay in Corinth at an end. Again leaving Silas and Timothy behind to cultivate the seeds all three had planted in Macedonia,
Paul's destinations this time were Cæsarea and Antioch. His confidence in
the abilities of Silas and Timothy was illustrated by the fact that Aquila and
Priscilla packed up and left with him.

Luke writes that they stopped at the Corinthian seaport of Cenchreæ,
where Paul "cut his hair, for he had a vow." Most sea travelers to Cenchreæ
made it a point to stop at its temple of Poseidon and beseech the god for
good luck at sea. Since that would hardly be the case with Paul, the head
shaving may provide a clue as to his mysterious ailment. It was an ancient
custom among Jews who were seriously ill or distressed to shave their heads
and vow to go to the temple in Jerusalem. They would keep the shorn hair,
then have it ceremoniously burned at the temple altar. The marshy
Corinthian lowlands were especially known as a place where people
caught malaria, and it may be that Paul was afflicted. If so, he would have
had something in common with the proconsul Gallio, who came down with
malaria in Corinth and had to take an extended sea voyage in hopes of im-
proving his health.

From Cenchreæ, Paul, Aquila and Priscilla boarded a coaster headed across
the Ægean 250 miles due east to Ephesus, the largest city in the province
of Asia. There, *Acts* says that Paul "went into the synagogue and argued with
the Jews." They even asked him to stay on and preach again, but Paul declined. They were not the primary objective of his first visit to this busy commercial center. There were already a few Christians living in Ephesus and
Aquila and Priscilla would serve to prepare the way for Paul. Here they would
set up their tentmaking business, join the local trade guild, acquire ample
quarters and use it as perhaps the first Christian house church in Ephesus.

Ultimately, Ephesus would be the site of Paul's longest visit and largest Christian congregation — a sturdy bridge between the growing churches of Asia and Macedonia. But first he needed time to rest and gain new resources.

This meant returning to Cæsarea and Antioch. By now, it was mid-summer in A.D. 53, and instead of bounding into the salt spray kicked up by the northerly *Meltemis*, he could use the power of these ocean winds to shorten the 620-mile southeastern passage straight into the calm, man-made harbor of Cæsarea. By the time he returned, this second missionary journey had covered some 2,800 miles.

A.D. 54–55

NERO WAS NEARLY 17 BY NOW and was approaching his first anniversary as husband of Claudius' demure daughter, Octavia. The path to the throne paved by Agrippina was all but cleared, with just a few potholes in her way. Even Claudius himself did not seem to be one of them. Now 63, it was becoming difficult to attribute his tottering to physical infirmities or too much wine. Certainly no bold imperial edicts issued forth from him during this period.

Still, Agrippina fretted. Claudius had seemed equally benign and befuddled just before Messalina met her fate. And it was only recently that the emperor had been in his cups again muttering that it was his destiny first to endure his wives' misdeeds, and then to punish them.

So the Augusta decided to get on with her most dangerous design without further delay. Narcissus remained the old emperor's last armor — and vise versa. "Whether Britannicus or Nero comes to the throne, my destruction is inevitable," the aging secretary-general told his closest friends. "But Claudius has been so good to me that I would give my life to help him." Better that he had done nothing about Messalina and her "marriage" festival,

Narcissus lamented. "Once more there is unfaithfulness [because] Agrippina's lover is Pallas. *That* is the final proof that there is nothing she will not sacrifice to imperial ambition — neither decency nor honor nor chastity."

The freedman's anxieties soon eroded his health, the one thing his 400 million sesterces couldn't buy. Narcissus made a point of ruminating within earshot of the emperor and Agrippina about taking a long sojourn to the south, where he hoped the waters of a popular health spa in Campania might restore his strength. To his surprise, Agrippina obligingly pointed out that it would also be good for his gout, from which he suffered increasingly.

So off went Narcissus, and with him the emperor's hope for survival. Agrippina now sought expert advice on how to choose just the right poison. One with a sudden, dramatic effect would give her away. A gradual wasting potion might make Claudius, slipping into death, summon his son Brittanicus and restore his powers in a burst of tearful repentance. No, better to have a recipe that would create a physical disturbance — vomiting, fainting, whatever — where the victim would be carried from his couch with apparent food poisoning, then lapse into a deathly coma somewhere behind the scenes.

Agrippina's agents searched the records of criminal convictions and found the name of a woman, Locusta, who had recently been sentenced for poisoning. Pressed into imperial service, Locusta prepared a potion that was sprinkled on a particularly succulent mushroom. When it appeared on a tray with several untainted mushrooms, Agrippina was counting on the habit of everyone present to reserve the largest or most luscious morsel for the emperor.

With diners all helping themselves from the same plate, Claudius' food taster was caught off guard. The emperor reached out and down went the mushroom. Now Claudius had but one defense remaining: he was drunk. If there was an immediate effect upon him, his wife couldn't discern it. In time, the emperor staggered to his feet and lumbered off.

Agrippina waited in agony. Soon an attendant whispered in her ear that the emperor had evacuated his bowels — and apparently the poisoned mushroom in the process. Now the empress was beside herself. Had he realized? She waited, trying to make conversation and look composed. Then, a bearded man appeared in the back of the room and, with one arched eyebrow, gave her a look of reassurance.

Agrippina's bearded confederate was none other than Xenophon, the emperor's Greek physician, and no doubt already a much wealthier man for allowing a brief lapse in his devotion to the Hippocratic Oath. Xenophon soon confided to the empress that while pretending to help the discomfited Claudius to vomit, the physician had put a feather down his throat as he often did after one of the emperor's drinking bouts. But this time the feather was dipped in quick poison.

And so, on the night of October 12, the man who had never expected to be emperor but who managed to endure the office with reasonable aplomb, succumbed to unnatural causes after ruling Rome for 13 years and eight months.

The rest of Rome, however, would remain dumb until Agrippina was quite ready. The Senate was summoned and told that the emperor was seriously ill. Consuls and priests offered prayers for his safety. But upstairs in the palace the lifeless body of Claudius Tiberius Nero Germanicus Cæsar had already been wrapped in blankets and poultices.

Agrippina's whole being was now focused on negotiating that last remaining step. First she went to the room of Britannicus and held him in her heartbroken embrace as they prayed for his father's recovery. All the while, she had Prætorians positioned throughout the palace, with orders that Britannicus and his sister were to be detained in their rooms. Meanwhile, she issued periodic announcements as to the emperor's "condition" as she awaited word from her astrologers for the most propitious time to bring Nero onto the scene.

Finally at midday on October 13, A.D. 54, the palace gates were suddenly thrown open. Nero, attended by Guard Commander Burrus, approached the battalion that was on duty for the day. After the briefest of introductions from their commander, the new emperor was cheered, put into a litter and carried off to the Guards' camp. There, after reading a brief speech (written by Seneca) in which he promised them all gifts as generous as Claudius had bestowed 13 years before, Nero was hailed as Imperator. After that, Senate approval was a mere formality.

At his funeral Claudius was deified and praised for his religious reforms, his command of history and the like, but Roman writers say that one could hear muffled giggles and snickers throughout the ceremony. In just a short time, people were remembering Claudius more for his stammer of speech and lame leg, and Nero was given to calling mushrooms the "food of the gods." Why? "Because my father was made a god by eating one."

In the remainder of the year the Augusta was happy to rule in the name of a boy still preoccupied with teenage thoughts. Coins of the era show her large profile on one side and Nero's smaller one on the other. Nero often walked alongside as she was carried in her litter and when the Guard commander would ask the emperor the watchword of the day, it would often be "the best of mothers." Indeed, when the Senate met in the temple of Apollo on the Palatine, it found that carpenters had built a partition in the back of the hall so that Agrippina could stand behind a curtain unseen and listen.

But her zeal soon alarmed even her closest allies in the palace. After forcing the governor of Asia to commit suicide simply because he was a great-great grandson of Augustus (and a remote competitor to Nero), she tracked down the doddering Narcissus in Campania and finished him off as well. All these cruel deeds did was galvanize Seneca and the Guard prefect Burrus into an alliance to oppose her executions and blunt her growing administrative power.

If any one episode symbolized the turning of the tide, it may have been when an Armenian delegation was petitioning Nero and Agrippina entered the reception room. As she began walking up the center aisle to take her place on the dais with Nero, "everyone was stupefied," wrote Tacitus. Just then Seneca quickly whispered for the young emperor to descend and meet his mother before she got there. Then he made some excuse for them both to leave, added Tacitus, "so that the weakness in the empire should not be apparent to foreigners." From that point on, Seneca and Burrus managed to prevent Agrippina from conducting any public business.

Meanwhile, the young emperor was receiving a daily diet of instruction from Seneca on how to rule wisely. One can imagine him nodding and fidgeting as the tutor read solemnly from his own essay, *On Clemency:*

> In the breath of a prince there is life and death, and his sentence stands firm, right or wrong. If he is angry, nobody dares advise him. If he goes amiss, who shall call him into account? Now, for him who has so much potential mischief in his power and yet applies that power to the common good and comfort of the people...what can be a greater blessing to mankind than such a prince? Any man can kill another against the law, but only a prince can save him. So let him deal with his own subjects as he desires God should deal with him.[24]

Unfortunately. Nero cared not a fig for government. The immediate result was that Rome was governed efficiently and honestly by his mentors during these years. Meanwhile, his senior advisors reasoned that if their emperor thought only of race horses, slave girls and discovering how much he could drink, these were harmless enough diversions and would be outgrown soon enough.

In time, this policy began to work against everyone — mentors, mother and Nero himself. With no one to reprove his drinking and amours, the emperor began to conclude that his conduct was perfectly acceptable. When his elders urged restraint, Nero's young crowd of fast living chums would pander to him by asking, "Do you *fear* these people? You *submit* to them? Do you not realize that you are Cæsar and have all authority over *them?*"

Before long Nero's exploits had become a test of wills, as just one of many episodes illustrates. Nero, without consulting anyone, ordered that ten million sesterces be given to the man in charge of receiving petitions from all over the empire. This shocked his mother, and in an attempt to make him understand the value of money and rescind his reckless impulse, she had the sum in coins brought in and piled up before him.

As the heap mounted, Nero maintained a defiant sneer. "Double the amount!" he said. "I didn't realize I had given him so little."

A few weeks later Nero suddenly deposed Pallas from the position of financial secretary that had allowed him (along with being Agrippina's lover) to control most of the empire. Now the Augusta was in a rage, and this time she would let anyone within earshot know that Brittanicus was growing up (just going on 14, to be exact) and fully worthy of his father's throne — one held, she added, by an adopted intruder who used his office to maltreat his mother. Not even her own hand in poisoning Claudius was spared from her tirades. "I'll take Brittanicus to the Guard's camp," she would fume. "Let them listen when Germanicus' daughter is pitted against the men who now claim to rule the human race — old Burrus and that deportee (Seneca) with the professorial voice and fancy words."

Until then, Nero probably hadn't thought much about Brittanicus. But come to think of it, he was a mild, pleasant lad who inspired friendship and sympathy. Nero might have thought back to the previous winter's Saturnalia, when the young men of the palace had thrown dice to see who should be the mock king for the age-old festival. Nero had won and, after issuing some prankish orders to the rest, decided he'd embarrass Brittanicus by making him come to the middle of the room and sing a song.

The wine was flowing and the young pack was growing more boisterous, but silence quickly fell when this composed boy, who had yet to take part in a drinking bout, stood up and strode to the center. There he sang a poem about his feelings of loneliness at being separated from his father. When he was done, everyone had remained sadly silent.

Thereafter, the more Nero thought about Brittanicus, the more annoying he became. The more his mother used the boy as a threat, the more he began to think about summoning the same old woman his mother had recently pressed into imperial service.

Locusta.

Brittanicus, as did princely hostages from around the empire, customarily dined at a table together within earshot of the luxurious couches of their parents and mentors. A servant, however, was always at his side to taste his food. In this case the youth was handed a harmless drink. The taster did his part, but Brittanicus (as anticipated) found it too hot and sent it back. At that point another server in the hire of Nero added cold water containing Locusta's most powerful poison. With Brittanicus' first gulp his whole body convulsed and he instantly stopped breathing.

His companions jumped back from their seats in horror. Some panicked and fled, but others, more inured to high stakes palace politics, remained rooted in their seats looking to Nero. The emperor shrugged and remarked idly that epileptics often had seizures like this and that Brittanicus had been one since infancy. Carry him off, said Nero, and he'll soon regain consciousness. With that he returned to his dinner conversation.

Agrippina struggled to control her emotions, for she knew well that her last lever of control over her son had been removed. What shocked her more was that he had already learned to murder — and so coolly.

Octavia, seated beside her young husband, was a mask of stone, as if she had been trained by her father to hide all sorrow, affection and affliction.

If nothing else, the murder created a bond of sorts between two desperate women. Agrippina's first defense was to help build the retiring Octavia's status within the palace household. She also became more outwardly solicitous of anyone from tribunes of the Guard to leading patricians as if part of some embryonic but unarticulated plan to topple Nero. Whatever it was, all the whispered conversations were enough to alarm the young emperor.

Suddenly his mother found her military bodyguard withdrawn. Next, the Augusta (now in name only) was moved to smaller quarters and informed that she was no longer to hold morning receptions and evening soirees. Nero kept up the formality of calling on his mother from time to time, but he was always accompanied by bodyguards. And after a few words and a perfunctory embrace, he was gone.

As PAUL WAS SAILING to Cæsarea in late A.D. 53, Palestine was again being rallied by Rome to help provision an effort to resist another test of strength by Parthia. Hearing that Rome's new emperor was but a boy with no military experience or inclinations, the Parthians had again nibbled at the supposedly Romanized Armenia. Fortunately, Burrus and Seneca were up to the challenge, sending Rome's most experienced general, Cnæus Domitius Corbulo to Syria with unprecedented powers to stop them. Herod Agrippa II, now back in Jerusalem to rule at least a part of his father's kingdom, was ordered to raise an army — mostly from Galilee and Samaria — and join some other client kings for an all-out invasion of Parthia.

Such was the setting in late A.D. 53 when Paul sailed into Cæsarea upon his return from Greece. Few details are known of his visit. After going up to Jerusalem, sprawled on its 2,400 foot-high mount, he undoubtedly would have stopped often in Samaria and Phoenecia to re-energize the many Christian communities that now flourished along the Roman road. By winter the apostle would be in Antioch, from where he'd originally departed, to give an account of himself to the churches that had in part financed his second mission.

A long rest must have been on his mind, too, before setting out on his next mission to establish a bastion of Christianity in Ephesus that could equal the one at Antioch. But as a shepherd's flock increases, he can also expect that more sheep will wander off or fall to predators. So it was with the small, fragile churches of Galatia in the northeast corner of Asia Minor. Drawn mainly from the Jewish members of synagogues where Paul had preached in his first visits, these Jewish Christians were being swayed once again by the Pharisaic "circumcision party," which insisted that man was not freed from observance of the Law just because he believed Jesus to be the Messiah.

Paul had assumed that he had already surmounted this hurdle some 14 years before when the Christian elders met in Jerusalem. Now he was simply too weary of the whole business to resort again to friendly persuasion. In a letter to all the churches of Galatia, dictated to an amanuensis as he paced and gestured, Paul let his famous temper "out of the pen," as they say. After a few restrained words of greeting, Paul plunged right into his reason for writing:

> I am astonished that you are so quickly deserting him who called you in the grace of Christ and turning to a different gospel — not that there is a different gospel — but there are some who trouble you and want to pervert the gospel of Christ. But even if we, or an angel from heaven, should preach to you a gospel contrary to that which we have preached to you, let him be anathema.[25]

This is somewhat surprising, because the language Paul used implies no less than the curses that priests of so many mystery religions would (for the right fee) put on someone's intended victim. It conjures up the wax figurines into which people put the hair or nail cuttings of enemies, as well as the lead tablets on which they inscribed curses and buried in the ground in hopes it would endure "as long as lead," as the ancient saying goes. And for good measure, Paul added his wish "that those who are shaking your faith by insistence on circumcision would go all the way and mutilate [castrate] themselves as well!"

> O foolish Galatians! Who has bewitched you, before whose eyes Jesus Christ was publicly portrayed as crucified? Let me ask you only this: Did you receive the Spirit by works of the Law, or by hearing with faith? Are you so foolish? Having begun with the Spirit, are you now ending with the flesh? Did you experience so many things in vain? — if it really is in vain. Does he who supplies the Spirit to you and works miracles among you do so by works of the Law or by hearing with faith?
>
> Thus, Abraham "believed God, and it was reckoned to him as righteousness." So you see that it is men of faith who are the sons of Abraham. And the scripture, foreseeing that God would justify the Gentiles by faith, preached the gospel to Abraham, saying, "In thee shall all nations be blessed." So then, those who are men of faith are blessed with Abraham who had faith.[26]

Continued Paul: Mosaic Law, though of ancient derivation, was only meant to be subordinate and temporary, almost like the attendant who looked after the boy on his way to school and saw him safely into his teacher's hands. Thus, the Law has now guided man into the presence of his true teacher, Jesus Christ. In Christ, all are children of God through their faith.

The Galatians had joyfully accepted this new freedom when Paul first preached to them. Why, he asked, would they now want to turn back to such material matters as having to observe a rigid litany of rules about how they lived and dressed and ate? The men who have been undermining him in Galatia have their own ends in mind, said Paul. They mean to make the Galatians dependent on them for admission to the church. They want to claim as *their* prerogative the right to fix the price and terms of a person's salvation. If only Paul could see them in person and talk to them now!

In a short while, his anger spent, Paul became the loving shepherd again. Neither circumcision nor uncircumcision "is of any avail" in the eyes of God compared to "faith working through love."

> For the whole law is fulfilled in one word: "You shall love thy neighbor as yourself." But if you bite and devour one another, take heed that you are not consumed by one another.
>
> But I say, walk by the Spirit, and do not gratify the desires of the flesh. For the desires of the flesh are against the Spirit, and the desires of the Spirit are against the flesh. For these are opposed to each other to prevent you from doing what you would. But if you are led by the Spirit, you are not under the Law.
>
> Now the works of the flesh are plain: immorality, impurity, licentiousness, idolatry, sorcery, enmity, strife, jealousy, anger, selfishness, dissension, party spirit, envy, drunkenness, carousing and the like. I warn you, as I warned you before, that those who do such things shall not inherit the kingdom of God. But the fruits of the Spirit are love, joy, peace, patience, kindness, goodness, faithfulness, gentleness, self-control. Against such there is no law. And those who belong to Jesus Christ have crucified the flesh with its passions and desires.[27]

As soon as the next spring made the Cilician Gates passable, Paul was off again on the road to the churches of Galatia, Phrygia and Pisidia to restate this message himself with the same power and vigor he had used in the letter. Timothy and probably others must have been with him through the dangerous climb onto the Anatolian plain, but they probably went on to visit the churches of Greece. Paul's destination was Ephesus, and he entered it alone one autumn day for what would be a stay of some two years.

As Corinth was the hub of east-west communications for Greece, this city of 300,000 was the same for Asia Minor. Ephesus served the sea trade (by means of a narrow bay from the Ægean). Trade routes intersected there from all directions and it was the home of the Roman proconsul of Asia. But the city was known first as "the servant of the goddess." Tradition has it that over 700 years ago peasants saw a rock of some sort fall from the sky and land by a mountain stream that ran below a hill. They deemed it a sign from the fertility goddess and erected a small Achaic shrine over it. In time the modest shrine was replaced by successive temples. Earthquakes took their toll, but each rebuilt temple was more splendid than the one before. The one Paul encountered had taken over 100 years to build and was one of the Seven Wonders of the World. It measured 350 feet long by 180 feet wide, surrounded by Ionic pillars 60 feet high — many of them erected by Croesus, the wealthy king of Lydia before he was captured and enslaved by the invading Persian, Cyrus in 546 B.C.

The temple's object of veneration, however, had always been Artemis, or "Diana of the Ephesians." The first century version, embracing the features of the Egyptian goddess Isis as well, was the female embodiment of fecundity and the eternal rebirth of all living things. And so she was called The Mother of All Things. She had many breasts to embody her fertility. She bore the triple-tiered model of the temple on her head in the form of a crown to identify herself as the protectress of cities. A crescent on her forehead showed that she was also the moon goddess.

At first the city was built around the temple, where winemakers and tailors worked amidst its hubbub of eunuch priests, prostitute-priestesses and souvenir shops. But Ephesus had a chronic silting problem where the mouth of the Caystrus emptied into the bay, so that whenever an earthquake caused major damage (such as early in the reign of Tiberius), it was a good excuse to move the center of commerce nearer to the receding waterfront to the southwest. In Paul's day the famous temple was no less visited, but it sat apart from the central city on the eastern side of the Caystrus.

In the shadows of the great temple were many practitioners of magic and the occult. Ephesus was also known as "The Magic City," and therein flourished the followers of Dionysus, Isis and Cybele with their frenzied whirling and incoherent babbling in the grip of strong drugs or too much wine. In time, Paul would meet them all head-on, but at first he had to contend with a disturbing surprise.

As expected, Aquila and Priscilla were on hand to offer Paul shelter and their tentmaking shop should he need to support himself. As usual, the synagogue they attended had shown few signs of receptivity to The Way, but the couple had managed to preserve and nurture a core group of at least a dozen Christians. The surprise just mentioned was that not long before Paul's arrival, their synagogue at Ephesus had offered its rostrum to one Apollos, a Jew from Alexandria who preached a message that seemed more centered on John the Baptist than Jesus. Eloquent, persuasive and probably physically impressive as well, he came from a refined center of Jewish learning that had produced men like the historian Philo — in sharp contrast to the increasingly divisive and disruptive Jerusalem. With great fervor and effect, Apollos preached to the synagogue about repentance and of John's preparation of the one to come. And in John's name, he had baptized several people.

One night Aquila and Priscilla took Apollos home and patiently told him of the ministry of Jesus and all that had followed. To their relief, he accepted the gospel willingly. He left soon thereafter with their letter of introduction to the church at Corinth, and since then word had already come back that Apollos was not only becoming a formidable Christian preacher in Greece, but was also "powerfully confuting the Jews in public."

Paul was puzzled at first on hearing his friends' report. As various members of the small church came calling at the house of Aquila and Priscilla, Paul would interview them. "Did you receive the Holy Spirit when you declared your belief?" he would ask. "No," was the usual reply. "We never even heard there is a holy spirit."

"Well then, into what were you baptized?"

"Into John's baptism," they answered.

"John," said Paul, "baptized with the baptism of repentance, telling people to believe in the one who was to come after him — that is, Jesus."

Soon Paul gathered twelve of these church members together, took them down to the banks of the Caystrus, and baptized them in the name of Jesus. "And when Paul laid his hands on them," Luke reports, "the Holy Spirit came on them; and they spoke with tongues and prophesied."

Having reclaimed his small flock, Paul spent the next three months trying to increase it by preaching in the synagogue. Perhaps the influence and friendship of Aquila and Priscilla helped restrain the congregation from the uprising that usually confronted Paul after just a few weeks, but eventually too many were "stubborn" or "disbelieved," and some were "speaking evil of The Way before the congregation," *Acts* reports. " So Paul withdrew from the synagogue and instead found daily access to a lecture hall owned and/or used by a private teacher named Tyrannus.

Now this was an altogether different setting. If the small lyceum were just off the busy Street of Curettes, as archeologists say, it would be in the midst of shops and travelers. For some two years, Tyrannus would finish his classes by late morning and Paul would take over during the long afternoon siesta period, or from around eleven until four. At his feet would be some of his Christian disciples, but invited to join them would be anyone who wandered by and felt like dropping in — from nappers to curiosity seekers to serious scholars to drunken hecklers. But they were both Gentile and Jew, and before long "all the residents of Asia heard the word of the Lord," Luke's chronicle proclaims.

Part of the spreading word had to do with miracles. Or magic. In this "City of Magic" the two were bound to get mixed up in the minds of the people — with both good and bad results for Paul. Luke's narrative states that "God did extraordinary miracles by the hand of Paul" during this time — chiefly by healing the physically sick and casting evil spirits from the mentally afflicted. Paul won people to Christianity who had witnessed him healing. But as word spread, the apostle's true purpose was garbled. Soon people begged for bits of his clothing — perhaps a handkerchief or a rope he had used while tentmaking — because they, too, might have healing powers. And in this city of wizards, witches, seers, sorcerers, astrologers, diviners and palm readers word spread among those who hadn't even seen him that a man named Paul was performing a powerful brand of magic over at the Hall of Tyannus.

Some even tried to practice it in his name. At one point an itinerant "rabbi" named Sceva and his seven sons came to Ephesus. One can picture them as pseudo-mystics of some sort. They hawked their curative powers and sold papyri describing "secret" prescriptions for medicines in an Aramaic script that no one else could read. Walking about the streets to get the feel of the city, and seeing or hearing about Paul, they decided to incorporate the popular preacher's "Lord Jesus" in their mystic rites for curing a violent lunatic. No doubt after first pocketing a fee from the young man's family, Sceva the rabbi addressed the evil spirit inside him and said, "I command you in the name of Jesus, whom Paul preaches, to come out of him."

With that the evil spirit (perhaps the young man himself?) answered: "I know Jesus, and I know Paul. But who are *you*?" At that point, the story goes, the lunatic flew into a frenzy and began clawing at their clothes until the "healer" and all seven sons ran off yelping.

Paul knew that his healings came only to those who believed in the gospel. At the same time, his natural reaction was to lash out at all magicians in an attempt to clarify the difference between acts of the loving God and flimsy fakery. One can't prove that these charlatans at last grasped the gospel or that they were cowed by their awe of a more dominating power, but the fact is that there was a wave of repentance by astrologers and magicians throughout the city. "Many of those who were now believers came, confessing and divulging their practices," Luke reports. "And a number of those who practiced magic arts brought their books together and burned them in the sight of all; and they counted the value of them and found it came to 50,000 pieces of silver [probably drachmas]. So the word of the Lord grew and pre-vailed mightily."

Its impact, in fact, even reached the mighty temple of Artemis on the out-skirts of the city. Everyone from the shopkeepers in prime rental locations to the lone waif who proffered a cheap trinket in a tourist's path began to see their daily sales fall off. Yet the weather was fine and the city as crowd-ed as ever. What could be the reason? Without too much head scratching, they were able to pin the cause on the man preaching about Jesus down in some schoolmaster's assembly hall. But the people who became the most alarmed were the dozens of metalworkers and silversmiths who manu-factured the thousands of amulets, temple replicas and miniature Artemis statuettes that tourists bought to take back for their little household shrines.

Before long, one Demetrius, who seems to have headed up the silver-smith's guild, called a general meeting of his fellow tradesmen. "Men," he said, "you know that we get our incomes from this business. And you see and hear that not only at Ephesus but almost throughout Asia this Paul has persuaded and turned away a considerable company of people, saying that gods made with hands are not gods. And there is danger not only that this trade of ours may come into disrepute, but also that the temple of the great goddess Artemis may count for nothing, and that she, whom all Asia and the world worships, may even be deposed from her magnificence."

By the time the meeting had ended, the tradesmen had whipped them-selves into a lather, chanting "Great is Artemis of the Ephesians." Before long rumors were flying across town that these Christians, Jewish-Chris-tians or whatever they were had determined to take away the freedom of people to worship the gods of their choice. They might even try to bring down the temple itself!

The crowd had worked itself into a riled up mob that soon marched down through the center of town and massed at the main theater to demand that someone find a magistrate to try Paul on the spot. Paul probably would have welcomed the chance to address an entire theater of Ephesians, but friends were able to hide him from the angry guildsmen. However, the protesters did manage to get their hands on two of Paul's young Christian co-work-ers, Gaius and Aristarchus, and strong-armed them into the theater. Also dragged in was a man named Alexander, presumably the ruling elder of a synagogue and perhaps even a member of the metalworking guild.

While one of the guild chieftains scurried about to find an appropriate city official, the crowd continued to roil and boil in the theater. The gath-ering had now developed into a general display of trade guild strength. Some had brought the banners, drums and cymbals usually reserved for their official processions and now, to the beat of their thumping and clanging, the crowd chanted, "Great is Artemis of the Ephesians!" at the top of their lungs for over an hour. At last the Jew Alexander asked to speak, probably to tell the crowd that this had nothing to do with the Jews of Ephesus, but with some splinter sect led by a foreigner. But every time Alexander tried to speak he would be drowned out by the shouts of "Great is Artemis of Ephesus!"

At last onto the stage strode an official everyone seemed to recognize and respect. The chanting subsided as he raised his hand. "Men of Ephesus," he said in deep, soothing tones, "what man is there who does not know that the city of the Ephesians is temple keeper of the great Artemis and of the sacred stone that fell from the sky? Since these things cannot be contradicted, you ought to be quiet and do nothing rash. For you have brought these men here who are neither sacrilegious nor blasphemers of our goddess." If Demetrius and his craftsmen have a complaint against anyone, the courts are open, and there are proconsuls, he said. "For we are in danger of being charged with rioting today, there being no cause that we can give to justify this commotion."

The term "rioting" implied sedition, which might just send a company of sword-wielding Roman soldiers into the theater. In any case, the official dismissed the assembly and people departed orderly enough, no doubt to the relief of the trembling Gaius and Aristarchus.

All this happened in the midst of Paul's greatest success as a missionary. He clearly had many friends in Ephesus, no doubt some in official positions, and probably could have endured there if he had insisted upon it. But when his friends and followers strongly advised him to depart, the apostle did not refuse. For one thing, he had already made up his mind to go to Greece and take up a collection from the churches there for the impoverished and famine-afflicted Jewish Christians in Jerusalem. After delivering it personally, he was determined to go to Rome — and then on to Spain.

Paul had another reason for going to Greece as well. Throughout most of his stay in Ephesus, the joy he felt at spreading the gospel in the Asian capital had been offset by depressing news of dissension and even immorality among the churches he had founded in Corinth. Paul had even taken a brief side trip there from Ephesus at one point and found himself rudely treated. It hurt him deeply and was all the more troubling because in the organizational plan in his mind, Corinth was the Christian bastion in Greece. He could not hope to go on to Rome and Spain if this link in the chain of churches and communications that now stretched from Jerusalem to Antioch to Ephesus were not strong and healthy.

Early in A.D. 55 Paul had written a brief letter from Ephesus (which hasn't survived) that seems to have been a harsh admonition that idolatry, drunkenness and similar practices had no place in Christ's church. He was still awaiting a reply when some travelers from a church at the house of a woman named Chloe reported that the congregations in Corinth had begun breaking up into cliques. Some of it had to do with wealth and poverty. The meals following church services had dissolved into dinner parties which often found the well-to-do dining amidst plenty at one table while their less fortunate brethren made do with meager pickings at the next table.

Worse, said Chloe's messengers, were growing differences over who should lead the churches. Some members had been dazzled by the polished preaching style of the Alexandrian Apollos, who had been in their midst only recently. Because Peter was a known and revered name, some had decided that his ties to the original church in Jerusalem made him their logical spiritual leader. Others were calling themselves the Party of Christ because they would not be led by a flawed mortal. The memory of Paul and his place as their founder seemed to be receding in his absence. Why? Because their image of the apostle was not that of an imposing figure or spellbinding speaker. In fact, the more they thought about it, Paul's boldness as a leader stood out only in his letters. The man they remembered in person was, in fact, rather unimposing, and, to some, even disappointing.

This kind of turmoil occupied Paul constantly in Ephesus even as he spent mornings in the tentmaking shop of Aquila and Priscilla and afternoons in the Hall of Tyannus. Not long after the report from Chloe's church members, he was surprised when there suddenly appeared a three-man delegation claiming to represent all the churches of Corinth. (They might have found Paul lacking in charisma, but they certainly didn't hesitate to consult him with a long list of questions that were troubling them.) The questions ranged from how to conduct services to how to live amidst idol worship to whether they should settle their differences in civil law courts and thus accept the judgment of heathens. In addition to general questions like these, they cited issues involving specific members. One young man, for instance, had married his widowed stepmother. It seemed indecent. Was it?

Paul decided it was time to send the three men back with a letter covering all these subjects that could be read to all the house churches. So one day, as a hired scribe scrawled furiously, Paul paced back and forth dictating, his mind ablaze. He began by plunging into the subject of factions within the church.

...each one of you says, 'I belong to Paul,' or 'I belong to Apollos' or 'I belong to Cephas' [Peter] or 'I belong to Christ.' Is Christ divided? Was Paul crucified for you? Or were you baptized in the name of Paul? I am thankful that I baptized none of you [and here he mentions a few whom he actually did baptize]. For Christ did not send me to baptize, but to preach the gospel, and not with eloquent wisdom, lest the cross of Christ be emptied of its power.[28]

It is not words about the power of the cross that redeem men, but the power of God, Paul said.

For it is written, "I will destroy the wisdom of the wise, and the cleverness of the clever I will thwart."

Where is the wise man? Where is the scribe? Where is the debater of the age? Has not God made foolish the wisdom of the world? For since, in the wisdom of God, it pleased God through the folly of what we preach to save those who believe. For Jews demand signs and Greeks seek wisdom, but we preach Christ crucified, a stumbling block to the Jews and folly to the Gentiles. But to those who are called, both Jews and Greeks, Christ [is the] power of God and the wisdom of God. For the foolishness of God is wiser than men, and the weakness of God is stronger than men.[29]

Paul then turned to the unflattering remarks he had heard about his own lack of charisma as an orator and leader.

When I came to you, brethren, I did not come proclaiming to you the testimony of God in lofty words or wisdom. For I decided to know nothing among you except Jesus Christ and him crucified. And I was with you in weakness and in much fear and trembling; and my speech and my message were not in plausible words of wisdom, but in demonstration of the Spirit and power, that your faith might not rest in the wisdom of men but in the power of God.[30]

At the time he first came to Corinth, Paul added, the people were not yet spiritual people but men of the flesh — just "babes in Christ."

> I fed you with milk, not solid food, for you were not ready
> for it. And even yet you are not ready, for you are still of the
> flesh. For while there is jealousy and strife among you, are
> you not of the flesh and behaving like ordinary men? For
> when one says, "I belong to Paul," and another, "I belong to
> Apollos," are you not merely men?
>
> What then is Apollos? What is Paul? Servants through
> whom you believed, as the Lord assigned to each. I planted.
> Apollos watered, but God gave the growth.[31]

Next, Paul addressed the reports of immorality among specific people
in the church. The man who married his stepmother should be "removed
from among you." As for associating with immoral people, Paul reminded the Corinthians that his earlier letter of warnings was not directed just
at sinners from the outside, but churchgoers as well. For:

> ...you are not to associate with anyone who bears the name of
> brother if he is guilty of immorality or greed or is an idolater,
> reviler, drunkard or robber — not even to eat with such a one.
> For what have I to do with judging outsiders? Is it not those
> inside the church whom you are to judge? God judges those
> outside. Drive out the wicked person from among you.[32]

This led Paul to address the question of whether to take disputes among
the brethren to the civil law courts. The apostle's letter shows that he never
intended to impose new legislation on anyone or pose as a Moses-like law-
giver. Christianity was not a matter of rules and laws, much less subject to
those of nonbelievers.

> To have lawsuits at all with one another is a defeat for you.
> Why not rather suffer wrong? Why not rather be defraud-
> ed? But you yourselves even wrong and defraud, and that
> even with your own brethren.
>
> Do you not know that the unrighteous will not inherit the
> kingdom of God? Do not be deceived. Neither the immoral,
> nor idolaters, nor adulterers, nor homosexuals, nor thieves,
> nor the greedy, nor drunkards, nor revilers, nor robbers will
> inherit the kingdom of God. And such were some of you.

> But you were washed [with baptism.] You were sanctified.
> You were justified in the name of the Lord Jesus Christ and
> the Spirit of our God.[33]

Paul continued to address the specific list of questions brought to him. Should a man bother to marry given that the end of the world is at hand? It is better to remain single like himself, was the reply. But because of the temptation of the flesh, each man should have his own wife. And if only one spouse is a believer, let him not divorce, for that would make their children unclean, "but as it is they are holy."

Should a circumcised Christian attempt to remove the marks of it? "Let everyone lead the life which the Lord has assigned to him," Paul replied, because neither state "counts for anything [compared to] keeping the commandments of God." The same applies to slaves, he said. "Were you a slave when called [to Christ]? Never mind. But if you can gain your freedom, avail yourself of the opportunity. For he who was called in the Lord is a freedman of the Lord. Likewise, he who was free when called is a slave of Christ."

The purchase and consumption of meat that had been sacrificed to idols perplexed the house churches of Corinth. Paul took the occasion to transform a relatively simple question about food into an answer about one's duty to God. On one hand, Paul observed that eating meat sacrificed to idols did not matter in the sense that "We are no worse off [in the sight of God] if we do not eat and no better off if we do." On the other hand, "this liberty" to eat such foods could be "a stumbling block to the weak," he added.

> For if anyone sees you, a man of knowledge, at a table in an
> idol's temple, might he not be encouraged, if his conscience
> is weak, to eat food offered to idols? And so by your knowl-
> edge, this weak man is destroyed — the brother for whom
> Christ died. Thus, by sinning against your brethren and
> wounding their conscience when it is weak, you sin against
> Christ.[34]

The best exercise of a right is sometimes not to use it, Paul concluded. In his own case, his usefulness to the Holy Spirit had depended upon his decision to forego such inherent rights as having a home, wife, security, respect and peace. Instead, he had freely chosen homeless wandering, loneliness, peril and even shame.

Paul now turned to the many questions that had been asked about proper conduct in Christian worship. How should women dress? Paul's churches had already departed radically from Judaism in that women were warmly admitted as equals and served in every office. But when asked this specific question about dress, he reverted to his upbringing in the synagogue.

> Any man who prays or prophesies with his head covered dishonors his head, but any woman who prays or prophesies with her head unveiled dishonors her head [because] it is the same as if her head were shaven. For if a woman will not veil herself, then she should cut off her hair. But if it is disgraceful for a woman to be shorn or shaven, let her wear a veil.[35]

Even so, Paul did not attempt to issue an order regarding the obligations of women at worship. He appealed to each church's sense of propriety, adding that he was more interested in bringing people together than creating new divisions among them.

But he did express strong feelings about the Lord's Supper. This was in response to reports that the sacrament had degenerated into so many dinner parties of various cliques.

> When you meet together, it is not the Lord's Supper that you eat. For in eating, each one goes ahead with his own meal, and one is hungry and another is drunk. What! Do you not have houses to eat and drink in? Or do you despise the church of God and humiliate those who have nothing? What shall I say to you? Shall I commend you in this? No, I will not.

> For I received from the Lord what I also delivered to you, that the Lord Jesus on the night when he was betrayed took bread, and when he had given thanks, he broke it, and said, "This is my body which is for you. Do this is remembrance of me." For as often as you eat this bread and drink the cup, you proclaim the Lord's death until he comes. Whoever, therefore, eats the bread or drinks the cup of the Lord in an unworthy manner will be guilty of profaning the body and blood of the Lord.[36]

Church members also asked Paul about the practice of speaking in tongues during worship services. To many, this ability was a gift to be used. To some Christians it was all too reminiscent of the way the frenzied followers of Diogenes and other cult gods babbled in the streets at festival times. Others simply felt that it disrupted the service or showed disrespect to God.

Paul offered two replies on separate levels. In a practical sense, he said, those who speak in tongues possess a skill. Just as a body has many parts, the body of the church is served by apostles, prophets, healers, administrators, those who speak in tongues and those who interpret them. "I want you all to speak in tongues, but even more to prophesy," said Paul. But those who do should take care to be accompanied by someone who can interpret their meaning.

> If even lifeless instruments, such as the flute or the harp, do not give distinct notes, how will anyone know what is played? And if the bugle gives an indistinct sound, who will get ready for battle? So with yourselves; if you in tongue utter speech that is not intelligible, how will anyone know what is said?[37]

But Paul also saw the question about tongues as an avenue to instruct on a higher plane. Yes, speaking in tongues is one of the qualities that some Christians have, he said, but far more important than this are qualities that anyone can practice: faith, hope and love.

> If I speak in the tongues of men and of angels, but have not love, I am a noisy gong or a clanging cymbal. And if I have prophetic powers, and understand all mysteries and knowledge, and if I have all faith, so as to remove mountains, but have not love, I am nothing. If I give away all I have, and deliver my body to be burned, but have not love, I am nothing.[38]

Finally, Paul addressed the questions of death and the hereafter that had been posed. What happens when people die? Do they rise up in their present bodies? When will the end of the world come? But most of all, how could Paul himself be so sure that the resurrection actually happened? Reminding the Corinthians of the first sermons he had preached to them, Paul asked how they could now deny the salvation they had already received.

> For I delivered to you what I already received, that Christ

died for our sins in accordance with the scriptures, that he was buried, that he was raised on the third day in accordance with the scriptures, and that he appeared to Cephas [Peter], then to the twelve. Then he appeared to more than 500 brethren at one time, most of whom are still alive, though some have fallen asleep. Then he appeared to James, then to all the apostles. Last of all, as to one untimely born, he appeared to me. For I am the least of the apostles, because I persecuted the church of God…

[If] Christ is preached as raised from the dead, how can some of you say that there is no resurrection of the dead? But if there is no resurrection of the dead, then Christ has not been raised; if Christ has not been raised, then our preaching is in vain and your faith is in vain. We are even found to be misrepresenting God, because we testified of God that he raised Christ, whom he did not raise if it is true that the dead are not raised. If Christ had not been raised, your faith is futile and you are still in your sins. Then those who have fallen asleep in Christ have perished. If in this life we who are in Christ have only hope, we are of all men most to be pitied.[39]

Now Paul repeated some specific questions that had been raised about death and the hereafter. "How are the dead raised? With what kind of body do they come?"

You foolish men! What you sow does not come to life unless it dies. And what you sow is not the body which is to be, but a bare kernel, perhaps of wheat or some other grain. But God gives it a body as he has chosen, and to each kind of seed its own body. For not all flesh is alike, but there is one kind for men, another for animals, another for birds, and another for fish. There are celestial bodies and there are terrestrial bodies, but the glory of the celestial is one and the glory of the terrestrial is another. There is one glory for the sun and another glory for the moon and another glory of the stars, for star differs from star in glory.

So it is with resurrection of the dead, What is sown is per-

ishable, what is raised is imperishable. It is sown in dishonor; it is raised in glory. It is sown in weakness; it is
raised in power. It is sown a physical body, it is raised a
spiritual body…

Lo! I tell you a mystery. We shall not all sleep, but we shall
all be changed, in a moment, in a twinkling of an eye, at the
last trumpet. For the trumpet will sound, and the dead will
be raised imperishable, and we shall be changed. For this
perishable nature must put on the imperishable, and this
mortal nature must put on immortality.[40]

When this happens, Paul wrote:

"Death is swallowed up in victory.
"Oh death, where is thy victory?
"Oh death, where is thy sting?"

The sting of death is sin, and the power of sin is the law. But
thanks be to God, who gives us the victory through our
Lord Jesus Christ.

Therefore, my beloved brethren, be steadfast, immovable,
always abounding in the work of the Lord, knowing that in
the Lord your labor is not in vain.[41]

With this lengthy letter, signed after appending a closing paragraph in his
own hand, Paul hoped to bring reconciliation both among the Corinthians and between them and himself. In fact, just before the close he had expressed his hope of coming there the next spring after going first to the
churches of Macedonia. One of his purposes, he said, would be to take up
a collection that might ease the pangs of hunger that the Syrian crop fail-
ures had wrought among the Jewish-Christians in Jerusalem. So confident was he of the reconciliation that he urged the Corinthians to "put
something aside and store it up" each week "so that contributions need
not be made when I come."

But several days had passed and stretched into weeks, all without any
word from the Greek metropolis. Eventually, Paul learned to his shock
and amazement that the letter had struck the Corinthians as insulting.

Insulting? A letter about love, hope and salvation? How could this be?

Paul asked himself over and over. He felt the emptiness of a man whose family had been swallowed up in an earthquake.

Well, one can only assume that the Corinthians took umbrage, starting with Paul's first words. After all, he did call them "foolish" several times. He likened them to "babes in Christ." But it may also be that they simply saw too much in the letter that they considered unrealistic and too demanding of them when immorality flourished everywhere around their small band. Expel the wicked from their churches? Who would be the judge? Avoid civil law courts? How could they not defend their rights and property if falsely accused? How could anyone hope to attain the same standards of a man who had forsaken family and personal comfort to wander as a lonely and often unwelcome missionary? As if this weren't enough, Paul learned that some Corinthians were offended because he had accepted the Philippians' money for living expenses while at the same time refusing theirs!

At any rate, Paul was distraught enough to drop everything, swallow his pride, and take a ship to Corinth. But the first time he had tried a personal confrontation he had faced a sullen, icy group that simply didn't want to argue with him about anything. He returned to Ephesus dejected. In fact, he later described himself as being "so utterly, unbearably crushed that [I] despaired of life itself."

All this was roiling through Paul's mind in Ephesus that previous summer even as he preached sermons of hope to new converts, helped ban books on magic and stood up to the opposition of the trade guilds that served the temple of Artemis. Even as the pressure on him to leave the city mounted after the near riot of the guilds, (some have even alleged that he was detained there in prison for public safety reasons), Paul's greatest fear was not of mobs, but of being deserted by his churches in Corinth.

At last Paul decided to risk all, not on another strained visit, but on a single letter. His faithful assistant Titus would take it personally to Corinth and see that it was read to all the churches there. After giving Titus some lead time, Paul would journey 150 miles up the Asian coast to Alexander Troas. There, in the main port for tourists visiting the nearby ruins of Troy, Paul would wait until Titus returned with a report on his mission. If it were favorable, they would go on to both Macedonia and Corinth. If the cause were lost, Paul would visit the Phillipian and Thessalonian churches of Macedonia briefly, then set sail for Cæsarea.

As Paul paced and began to dictate his second letter to the Corinthians, his mood probably matched that of a father who was in the midst of losing a wayward son and had nothing left to lose by removing the shield from his most vulnerable emotions. It begins by appealing to them personally "by the meekness and gentleness of Christ" to consider his message. I don't wish to seem to be frightening you with letters, he says in reference to the previous one. In fact, Paul says he is well aware that people say behind his back, "His letters are weighty and strong, but his bodily presence is weak and speech of no account." But they may yet find out how bold he can be face to face!

I don't want to compare myself boastfully to others you hold in esteem, said Paul, but "we were the first to come all the way upon you with the gospel of Christ." One who works on behalf of the Lord should boast only of the Lord. But then, as if goading himself on, he asks that the Corinthians "bear with me in a little foolishness," for he feels that it was he who betrothed them as a bride to Christ and he worries that they have been deceived by those who preach a different gospel. Yes, perhaps his manner of speaking is unskilled, but "I am not in knowledge."

Were they upset because he had accepted no living expenses from them while he preached the gospel there? What a strange expression of envy! "When I was with you and in want," he pointed out, "I did not burden anyone, for my needs were supplied by the brethren who came from Macedonia." Moreover, children are not supposed to lay up money for their parents, but parents for children, and he is ready to give all of his personal capital for the churches of Corinth.

Not only would he continue not to burden them, but "as the truth of Christ is in me, I shall not be silenced in the regions of Achaia," Paul declared. Specifically, he would not be undermined by "false apostles, deceitful workmen disguising themselves as apostles of Christ."

Paul then asks the Corinthians not to think him foolish while he "boasts a little."

> For you gladly bear fools, being wise yourselves! For you bear it if a man makes slaves of you or preys upon you or takes advantage of you or puts on airs, or strikes you in the face.

> ...But whatever anyone dares to boast of — I am speaking like a fool — I also dare boast of that. Are they Hebrews? So am I. Are they Israelites? So am I. Are they descendants of Abraham? So am I. Are they servants of Christ? I am a better one (I am talking like a madman) — with far greater labors, far more imprisonments, with countless beatings, and often near death. Five times I have received at the hands of the

Jews the 40 lashes less one. Three times I have been beaten with rods. Once I was stoned. Three times I have been ship-wrecked; a night and a day I have been adrift at sea. On fre-quent journeys [I have been] in danger from rivers, danger from robbers, danger from my own people, danger from Gentiles, danger in the city, danger in the wilderness, dan-ger at sea, danger from false brethren, in toil and hardship through many a sleepless night, in hunger and thirst, often without food, in cold and exposure. And apart from other things, there is the daily pressure upon me of my anxiety for all the churches. Who is weak [that] I am not weak? Who is made to fall and I am not indignant?[42]

Paul takes his readers all the way back to the early days in Damascus when he was lowered in a basket to escape the local authorities. Then, again apologizing for boasting, he cites instances in which he received visions and revelations from God.

I know a man in Christ who 14 years ago was caught up to the third heaven — whether in the body or out of the body I do not know — God knows. And I know that the man who was caught up into Paradise — whether in the body or out of the body, God knows — and he heard things that cannot be told, which man may not utter. On behalf of this man I will boast, but on my own behalf I will not boast, except of my weaknesses.[43]

One of them, Paul adds, is that God, "to keep me at being too elated by the abundance of revelations," afflicted him with a "thorn" in the flesh.

Three times I besought the Lord about this, that it should leave me; but he said to me, "My grace is sufficient for you, for my power is made perfect in your weakness." I will all the more gladly boast of my weaknesses, that the power of Christ will rest upon me. For the sake of Christ then, I am content with weaknesses, insults, hardships, persecutions, and calamities. For when I am weak, then I am strong.[44]

Paul now declares that he is about to come to the Corinthians once again. There may be quarreling, jealousy, anger and the like, and he may have to mourn over those who have not repented of their sins, but he is coming nonetheless. And he warns the wayward that "I will not spare them — since you desire proof that Christ is speaking in me. He is not weak in dealing with you, but is powerful in you."

Paul's letter closes with prayers for love and peace, but he has clearly declared that he will make his stand in Corinth and not retreat.

It was now late summer when Paul said good-bye to Aquila, Priscilla and all the new Christians who now filled the Asian capital of Ephesus. Paul was still in such suspense at the outcome of this letter that he did not even plan any missionary work in Alexander Troas. Besides, the time there would be too short, with Titus meeting him almost upon his own arrival.

Troas was only two or three days by sea from the Corinthian port city of Cenchreæ. A week should have been enough for Titus to go from Cenchreæ to Corinth, deliver the letter, have it read to all the congregations and observe their reactions. But Paul waited a week in Cenchreæ and several more agonizing days with no sign of Titus. As each day of anguish ended, Paul could only conclude that he and his letter had been repudiated. Clearly, someone in Corinth must have had it in for him personally.

In time Paul gave up and took a ship across the Ægean to Philippi in Macedonia. He had been there only a few days, re-greeting his many church friends, when who should come striding up but a beaming, jubilant Titus. His effort had taken longer than expected, but the Christians of Corinth had accepted Paul's message! Unknown to Paul and Titus when they were in Ephesus, the churches in Corinth had fallen under the sway of someone (probably an elder whose name is not now known) who had fomented a revolt against the apostle. It took some personal preaching by Titus over several days, but the congregations had been persuaded to remove the ringleader and were now enthusiastically on Paul's side again. In fact, they were counting the days before he could be with him!

This must have marked the highest point in Paul's life and mission. One of his largest churches had nearly sunk back to the level of the many "religions" with their demonic idols, mercenary priesthoods and intoxicating rituals. But it had survived to live on a higher plane, and Paul could not wait to express his elation. He sat down quickly and wrote a fourth letter to the Corinthians that was intended to be comforting and healing.

He began by citing his own suspense and despair in Troas, but noting now that the effect was "to make us rely not on ourselves but on God, who raises the dead." And now that he has delivered Paul from "so deadly a peril," that "we have set our hope that he will deliver us again."

Paul acknowledges that perhaps his previous words had seemed harsh, but he points out, "I wrote you out of much affliction and anguish of the heart and with many tears, not to cause you pain but to let you know the abundant love that I have for you." The letter, added Paul, hadn't been written because the Corinthians had done wrong or because he had suffered wrong, but "in order that your zeal for us might be revealed to you in the sight of God."

As for the leader of the revolt against him, "the punishment by the majority is enough," and Paul now asks that they "turn to forgive and comfort him" lest he be "overwhelmed with excessive sorrow." He adds that "anyone whom you forgive, I also forgive."

Paul ends the letter by referring again to his most immediate purpose in visiting them: the collection of funds for the hard-pressed Christian church in Jerusalem. Even before he appears for a tearful reconciliation, he wants to have the matter of fund raising taken care of in advance. Besides, they wouldn't want to be outdone by the Macedonians, would they?

> ...for I know your readiness, of which I boast about you to the people of Macedonia, saying that Achaia [the province] has been ready since last year; and your zeal has stirred up most of them. But I am sending the brethren [Titus and two companions] so that our boasting about you may not prove vain in this case, so that you may be ready as I said you would be.[45]

Why did Paul attach so much importance to collecting money (and probably food staples) for their brethren nearly 900 miles away? The first and most practical reason was that the Jerusalem Christians were in genuine need. Just as in the times of Pontius Pilate, the Jewish temple priesthood had to contend with an oppressive procurator (Felix), a violent Zealot group, rebellious native Syrians, the stealthy Sicarii, a plague of wild-eyed religious reformers and a new king (Agrippa II) of unproven allegiances. The very existence of the temple itself could be threatened, and the ruling Sadducees could not even be sure of where the challenge might come. And, as before, when similar conditions existed, the high priest would look nervously at the newly emerging Christians. At the very least, he would see that they were shown no favors and certainly no distributions of alms from the Chamber of Secrets.

The collection was also seen by Paul as a way to remind the Gentile churches of their Judeo-Christian heritage in Jerusalem. To the Judeans, it would provide reassurance that they were venerated. And if in the process they also came to appreciate the fact that Paul had founded more churches among the Gentiles than any of the Jewish-Christian apostles, then so be it.

Finally, Paul was looking well beyond a visit to Jerusalem. His mind was already on Rome and beyond. Although the apostle did not say so directly in his letters, he certainly knew that the Christian church in Rome was built principally on its ties to the Jewish-Christian community in Jerusalem. Visiting the Roman Christians would certainly be less difficult if he arrived with the blessing of the church they looked to first for guidance. Perhaps taking the collection personally to Jerusalem could help. So might a vow to bow to Jewish customs while in Jerusalem. For as Paul had said in that emotional letter to the Corinthians,

> ...whatever anyone dares to boast of...I also dare to boast of that.
> Are they Hebrews? So am I.
> Are they Israelites? So am I.
> Are they descendants of Abraham? So am I.
> Are they servants of Christ? I am a better one...[46]

A.D. 56–59

NERO TURNED 19 IN A.D. 56 and now spent less of his time in tutoring. Seneca was spending more of his governing Rome, which may have functioned more smoothly in this brief span than at any time since Augustus. But the emperor, seeming to show interest only in the display of pomp at ceremonies requiring an imperial presence, reserved his most ardent energies for living the life of an obscenely rich youth whose appetites were restricted neither by a distant mother nor preoccupied freedmen.

The man-child's misadventures became more excessive and turbulent with each passing day, as if the only lesson the debaucheries of Gaius had taught Nero was a competitive drive to exceed them. All this was kept from public view until the restless young emperor, having no restraints upon him inside the palace, began rampaging the streets of Rome at night with a gang of young rowdies. As soon as darkness fell he would slip on a wig or slave's dress and go out to the taverns with his friends. After tearing up a public house or getting tossed out by the unsuspecting keeper, the aroused pack would prowl the darkened streets, breaking shop windows, grabbing whatever merchandise they wished and then auctioning it off to strangers on the street. Then they would go off and lay in wait to stab some innocent stroller to death and cast his body into the sewers.

Before long the desire for greater and more dangerous thrills led Nero and his band to scale walls and rob homes and have their way with the women they found inside. But they weren't always successful. In one instance a newly appointed junior senator, Julius Montanus, ran into his dark atrium one night to find a stocky masked intruder smothering his wife in a groping embrace. The masked man wheeled on him with a blow to the head, but Montanus bulled him to the ground and fought for his life. The young senator-to-be had grabbed the man's hair with one hand and was bashing his head with his other fist when he felt the hair strangely slipping from his grasp. Just then some more hooligans rushed in and pried their confederate loose. They were carrying him off when they crossed a patch of lamplight and Montanus realized that the man had been wearing a wig, and that it was askew across his face.

Could it be *him*?

The more the dazed Montanus recovered and recalled that frenzied night, the less he could deny the fact that he had been wrestling in mortal combat with the emperor of the Roman Empire. He waited in agony for a word, a reprisal — anything — from the palace on Palatine Hill. The irony is that Nero thought himself unrecognized. Indeed, no one at all heard much from the emperor for the next several days because he was laying low with two black eyes and several bruises.

But Montanus knew only his own private anguish. At last, unable to endure the suspense, he sent Nero a note apologizing for his unintended attack on the royal personage. "So," fumed the emperor after reading it, "he knew that he was striking Nero!" A message was sent back to the young patrician. A few days later, Montanus, who had not even begun to serve his first day in the Senate, paid for his slur by committing suicide.

Before long word of the emperor and his midnight marauders was soon all over Rome, and, as Tacitus reports, it "came to resemble a conquered city."

Before long, the end of the night no longer brought down the curtain on the emperor's excesses. Nero's true identity was now public and he displayed it all day long. As the writer Suetonius scolds:

> He prolonged his revels from midday to midnight, often
> livening himself by a warm plunge, or, if it were summer,
> into water cooled by snow. Sometimes, too, he closed the
> Naumachia [the huge enclosed basin, used for mock naval
> battles] and banqueted there in public, or in the Campus

Martius, or in the Circus Maximus, waited on by harlots and dancing girls from all over the city. When he drifted down the Tiber to Ostia or sailed about the gulf of Baiæ, booths were set up at intervals along the banks and shores, fitted out as brothels and eating-houses, before which were matrons who played the part of bawds and hostesses, soliciting him from every side to come ashore.[47]

Yet, buried thinly beneath this beastly nature was an ego that fancied itself an artist and athlete, be they as poet, singer, actor, lyre-player wrestler or chariot driver. Of these, what seemed to enchant the emperor most was the sound of his voice. He had now begun voice and acting lessons. The reason why he now delivered all judicial opinions only in writing was not so much a desire to craft them carefully, but not to strain a voice that his courtiers told him had "magical qualities."

Indeed, a friend or servant might find the emperor lying on his back holding a leaden plate to his chest as he breathed deep to strengthen his lungs. He would also purge himself with a syringe, deny himself all foods said to injure the voice and induce vomiting should he eat them. Although his voice hadn't reached booming proportions, he soon longed deeply to appear on stage. Intimate friends quickly came to recognize what he had in mind when he often quoted the Greek proverb, "Hidden music counts for nothing."

Nero's ardor was just as great when it came to chariot races and games in the Circus. At the beginning of his reign, callers might find their adolescent emperor playing with ivory chariots on a board as they addressed him. So passionate was his enthusiasm for the races that one of his first acts as emperor was to increase the prizes and number of events. It soon became common for drivers to race all day long and into the night. And Nero became such a devotee of the Green team that he allowed his Prætorians to be used as laborers in expanding its stables.

Being a spectator was agony to Nero. He wanted to be a driver. Yet, no emperor had ever allowed himself to appear as one in public. Seneca and Burrus tried at first to compromise: they rebuilt an enclosure in the Vatican valley, across the Tiber, northwest of the city, that the young Gaius Caligula had used to accommodate his yen for chariot driving. There, in this replica of the Circus Maximus (but hardly its seating capacity), the young man could drive his horses away from the public eye. But before long Nero, of course, had happily invited his crowd of young dandies to observe him in the stands and certainly didn't shoo away the admiring commoners who scaled the walls of the circus and applauded wildly when they saw who was plying one of their favorite pastimes. It wasn't long before Nero treated slaves and a few friends to a private performance in the empty Circus Maximus, with a freedman dropping the napkin in the starting position usually occupied by the magistrates of Rome.

Clearly all this pent-up ambition had to have an outlet. Nero may not have officially debuted in public as a singer or driver, but his dress and manner already shouted otherwise. His hair was often done in rising waves from front to top as were the most dashing charioteers. Just as frequently he would be in Greek clothing, or a "pseudo-Greek" concoction consisting of a flowered mini-tunic with a frilly muslin collar. If ostensibly dressing "Roman," it might be with an amply flowing toga below the waist and a tunic above it, adorned by a garish scarf around the neck. Whatever Nero's dress of the day, his appearance and speech invariably signaled that he was more preoccupied with the theatrical and equestrian arts than the governance of 60 million subjects.

Seneca and Burrus have been accused of nurturing this bent. After all, say their critics, the emperor's mental absence from important affairs prolonged their own influence and wealth (Seneca was on his way to building a fortune of 600 million sesterces despite his essays extolling the simple life). Perhaps, but it also rekindled the fire in Nero's mother. Agrippina, though reduced to the status of dowager-in-waiting, began using her all-too-brief audiences to carp at her son for his foppish ways.

Nero had three other women competing for his attentions as well. The least of them was his meek wife, Octavia, whom the court had come to regard as somewhat akin to a piece of palace furniture. The second was Acte, the lovely ex-slave who often occupied the emperor's chambers. The third and newest in Nero's life was Poppæa Sabina. Born of an illustrious family, Poppæa was considered the most beautiful woman of her day — and in possession of a clever and shrewd mind to go along with it. Her father's only mistake had been to support the hated Sejanus during the reign of Tiberius. But despite the public ridicule that followed, the family remained one of the wealthiest in Rome. Outwardly, Poppæa seemed respectable and reserved — almost mysterious. Inwardly, she never stopped scheming to use her beauty to climb the ladder of political power.

Poppæa was already married to a knight and the mother of an infant son when she succumbed to the wily charms of one Marcus Salvius Otho. One of Rome's most extravagant dandies, Otho was also one of Nero's closest chums in everything from tavern tripping to street crime. Just how close they were became evident when Otho persuaded Poppæa (or she him) to divorce her husband and marry him. Before long Otho was praising her charms and graces to anyone within earshot. Sometimes he would even leave the emperor's dinner table early because his wife's charms were simply too irresistible.

One should not share such thoughts with an emperor, because before long Otho had been prevailed upon to share his treasure with his royal friend. Soon Poppæa would be seeing less of Otho and more of Nero. And all the while she played her new lover like one of his lyres. First she was flirtatious, pretending that only his dashing demeanor had made her succumb. But after she had snared her prize she became distant and haughty. "Now *there* is a man of character," she would say of her husband, "whereas you, Nero, are kept down because you keep a mistress [Acte] who is but a servant. What a dreary, menial association!"

As the besmitten Nero reached out for ways to keep Poppæa, Otho receded from the emperor's company. Then one day a palace freedman informed Otho that he had been named governor of Lusitania in western Spain. He soon departed without his wife (but would, as if to avenge the insult, return one day as emperor).

Poppæa was now left with all her bets placed on one man. Although Nero showered her with gifts that exceeded anything her own wealth had ever provided, Poppæa managed to display a permanent pout. As she saw it, her prospects of marrying the emperor were thwarted, not by Octavia's barely perceptible presence, but because she was stoutly defended by the emperor's mother. So Nero became subject to a constant stream of nagging. He was under his "guardian's thumb," Poppæa would whine. He was master of neither himself nor the empire. "Otherwise, why the postponement of our marriage?" she would ask. "I suppose my looks and glorious ancestors aren't enough. Or do you distrust my ability to bear children? Or is it the sincerity of my love?

"No," she would wail as skillfully manufactured tears began to flow," I think you are afraid that, if we are married, I might tell you frankly how the Senate is downtrodden and the public enraged by your mother's arrogance and greed. If Agrippina can only tolerate daughters-in-law who hate her son, let me be Otho's wife again! Oh to go anywhere in the world where I can merely *hear* about the emperor's humiliation rather than witness it here! How can you tolerate this danger we live in?"

In the porous palace of Nero, word of these performances naturally reached Agrippina as soon as they happened. She saw the verbal assaults as aimed not directly at herself, but at Octavia. Although shy, bewildered and no match for the clever Poppæa, the emperor's wife-in-name-only was Agrippina's only remaining means to obtain imperial power.

With one exception. Agrippina was still one of the most comely women in Rome. She had often used Cupid's arrow as efficaciously as a commander uses a brigade of archers. She used her sexual weapons in her struggle back into Roman society after an impoverished exile by Caligula. She had used them to mesmerize and marry Claudius. She had used them to make Pallas an ally and the richest freedman in Rome. She tried them — and perhaps succeeded — on Seneca when she needed his influence. Now they were needed again — in this case to win influence over another emperor.

Her son.

THE JUDEA THAT PAUL returned to in A.D. 56 had been ruled for four years by the procurator Felix. And now his position was more precarious than ever. His appointment under Claudius had come through the influence of his brother, Pallas, the emperor's financial secretary. But Pallas had just "retired" one step short of being accused of financial malfeasance and Felix found his protective shield suddenly removed. He might have had an ally in the young Jewish king Herod Agrippa II if it weren't for the fact that he had married Agrippa's sister and she couldn't stand the sight of the king's consort-in-incest, her older sister Bernice. Against all these distractions, the procurator had to go about controlling the combustible Jews and Greeks, line his pockets inconspicuously and avoid any episode that would cause notice by Neronian courtiers who would like the slightest excuse to apply for such a plum procuratorship.

Felix, however, was neither delicate nor diplomatic. Jerusalem had again become a boiling cauldron, and the procurator drew most of the blame for it. One might think that with a Jewish wife he would have gained some empathy for people and insight as to their customs. Instead, he is described by the historian Josephus as a man who "practiced every kind of cruelty and lust," one who "wielded the power of a king with all the instincts of a slave."

In his early years as procurator, Felix had concentrated on rooting out brigands in the name of assuring public safety. But always more took their place, and the reason why their numbers seemed endless is that what Rome defined as "robbers" included political rebels as well. For many years before, both Jerusalem and the Galilee region had their share of "Zealots," although never in enough numbers to be considered sects as had the Pharisees, Sadducees and Essenes. Who was a Zealot? Typically, he was an impatient, risk-taking young man who saw Rome as an excessive tax levier and oppressor of Jewish customs and pride. And he was ready to forego family life and live apart in the hills, associating even with cave-dwelling pirates if the end result was the same — disruption of civil authority and eventual expulsion of Rome from the region.

And so, when an armed "prophet" from Egypt arrived in Judea and called for a religious revolt, he attracted some 30,000 followers in short order. There is no record of his name, but Josephus says the prophet-warrior led his rag-tag troops some five furlongs away from Jerusalem to the Mount of Olives, which overlooks one of its walls. He promised them that at his command the city walls would fall down and that he would then lead them through the breech and on to victory over the small Roman garrison that happened to be guarding the Fortress of Antonia at the time. Before he had a chance to make good on his promise, Felix rode out from Cæsarea with a great number of horsemen. Splintering and splattering the poorly armed commoners in all directions, his men cut down 400 of them and took another 200 as prisoners. The ringleader got away, but in his retreat he raced through neighboring villages, exhorting the people to take up arms against Rome. When virtually all refused, their homes were plundered and burned. Then the band of survivors took up camp in the surrounding wilderness where they fomented trouble for many months to come.

Meanwhile, in Jerusalem, some Zealots for liberty decided that stealth would serve them better than open rebellion — a course that proved far worse to Roman and Jewish leaders alike. For it was at this time that Jerusalem became infested with the more menacing and undetectable Sicarii.

Anyone in the temple vicinity might suddenly encounter the Sicarii — perhaps a pilgrim on his way to deliver the temple tax from a far-off synagogue or maybe a Syrian merchant coming to buy hides from a temple official. Suppose that it's on the eve of a festival and the streets are full of loud noises and fast-moving strangers. Suddenly the victim would see the flash of a short blade in a glint of light and feel a sliver of steel slice into his midriff. As the blood began to spurt, he would look for just a split second into the burning eyes of a young man whose face is hidden in the folds of a robe.

Such were the Sicarii (the name taken from the short, upturned Roman sword, the *Sicæ*). A political movement? Nothing that well articulated. An emerging religious sect? No, because few of its "practitioners" ever met in one place or long enough to forge a philosophy. Rather, carrying a concealed dagger and puncturing a target in a crowd at lightning speed was a quick and efficient way that the wronged or downtrodden or impatient — but invariably infuriated — young rebel could exact a stealthy revenge upon whomever he deemed to be his oppressor.

The first notable to be slain by Sicarii was Jonathan, the high priest. After his death many were stabbed near the temple every day. However, the impact was worse than the actual number of deaths that resulted because people feared to walk the streets and viewed anyone who approached with great suspicion. Moreover, the stealthy manner in which such deaths were afflicted sowed the seeds of fear and suspicion into organizations that were once seen as pillars of their community, including the temple priesthood itself.

Jewish turmoil was both a bane and a blessing to a procurator. Yes, conflict was incessant and one never knew what hour of the day or night troops might have to be deployed in the name of peacekeeping. But this constant agitation among factions also meant that one or the other was willing to pay to have the trouble settled (in its favor, of course) by a prestigious and impartial third party. The thorniest problems came when *both* factions paid for the procurator's skillful mediation services and both expected to prevail.

Such was the case in the very city that housed the Roman government in Judea. Cæsarea made a compact center stage to demonstrate the age-old animosities that separated Jews and their Hellenistic neighbors (quite apart of anything to do with Roman oppression). Jews there claimed pre-eminence because over a hundred years before, Herod the Great had built a city of marble from a crude village with a makeshift harbor. True enough, the local Hellenes admitted, but Cæsarea was once called Strato's Tower (for an ancient lighthouse that stood on the shore) and at the time there was not a single Jewish inhabitant.

As reported earlier, in A.D. 44 riots had broken out in Cæsarea immediately following the death of King Herod Agrippa I. Since then, the two factions had managed to confine their old animosities to taunting one another on the streets or contesting in games of strength at festivals. But in the months preceding Paul's visit, the enmity had erupted in episodes of rock throwing that left several people seriously injured.

The Jews were generally more populous and wealthy and invariably managed to keep the upper hand, but the great majority of troops under Felix' command were Syrian Gentiles from Cæsarea and nearby Sebaste. As would later be alleged, the Syrians "counseled" with Felix and fattened his purse as a token of thanks. The next time a gang of Jewish rowdies started tossing rocks, Felix marched his troops in their midst and ordered them to stop. When a few bricks came flying in his direction, he hotly commanded the soldiers to slay several, then go looting through several Jewish homes. It stopped only after a hastily assembled group of more moderate and mature Jewish leaders went out and mollified Felix with pleas and presents.

That was supposed to be the end of it, but the more hot-tempered Jewish youths weren't about to give up the cause on orders of a few soft old men.

They took to the streets, caves and roadsides, vowing to wipe out the Syrian population of Cæsarea if they had to. And soon the silent steel of the Sicarii penetrated the Roman military capital as it had Jerusalem.

As THE YEAR A.D. 56 began and brought Paul's three-month stay in Corinth to a close, his reconciliation with the churches there was so complete that he could turn to writing the longest and perhaps most important letter of his missionary life. It was addressed to the Christian churches in Rome, and it was an attempt to introduce himself properly into their presence when he arrived sometime in the following year.

> For God is my witness, whom I serve with my spirit in the gospel of his Son, that without ceasing I mention you always in my prayers, asking that somehow by God's will I may now at last succeed in coming to you. For I long to see you, that I may impart to you some spiritual gift to strengthen you, that is that we may be mutually encouraged by each other's faith, both yours and mine. I want you to know, brethren, that I have often intended to come to you (but thus far have been prevented) in order that I may reap some harvest among you as well as among the rest of the Gentiles. I am under obligation both to Greeks and to barbarians, both to the wise and the foolish: so I am eager to preach the gospel to you who are in Rome.[48]

First, however, came the already-delayed voyage back to Jerusalem. Paul saw it as a much needed time of reconciliation and renewal before going on to Rome and Spain. Indeed, as the delegation of churchmen prepared to sail from the Corinthian port of Cenchreæ, a deaconess named Phoebe was already departing for Rome from the port that faced the other side of the isthmus. In her baggage was the letter Paul had written to the Christians there.

If Paul faced his newest journey with a peaceful resolve, his feelings certainly weren't shared by his fellow travelers nor by the churches they were leaving behind. Just as Paul and his churchmen were about to sail from Cenchreæ they had discovered a planned attempt on Paul's life by the Jewish elders of Corinth. If Jews could become so riled in an otherwise peaceful city, how might the temple leaders react in a Jewish city constantly wracked with outer conflict and internal division? Disciples on both sides of the Ægean were saddened on a personal level as well. Paul was already showing the signs of old age. If he were truly headed for Rome and beyond, chances were they would never see him again.

Paul would not be deterred, however. He directed the other delegates to sail across the Bay of Samathrace for their planned destination of Troas. Then he, Luke and probably Timothy booked a hasty passage on another ship headed up the coast to Macedonia. Paul's breach with the Corinthian churches had already caused him to miss his goal of reaching Jerusalem by the Passover on April 7. Now he was determined to arrive in time for the Festival of Pentecost, which followed a few weeks later.

After a five-day absence, Paul and Luke reunited in Alexander Troas with their fellow delegates. Including the apostle, who may have personally represented the churches in Corinth, there were nine in all, drawn from three of the four Roman provinces in the area. There was Sopater from Macedonia and Aristarchus and Secundus of Thessalonica; Gaius represented Derbe and the hard-working Timothy his hometown of Lystra. From the many churches up and down the coast of Asia came Tychicus and Trophimus. In addition, it's logical to assume that Luke, the diarist, also served as delegate from his native Philippi.

Why so many to bring a gift? Their numbers would serve to ward off robbers in a dangerous land. But the size of a visiting delegation also added to its respect, and Jerusalem was a city accustomed to receiving many groups of luminaries who came to pay the temple tribute. Equally important is that these were the leaders of their respective churches. They had worked hard to raise the money and had wanted to travel as pilgrims to the birthplace of The Way. And they all wanted to cling to Paul for as long as they could.

The nine men stayed in Troas a week as they made preparations for passage to Cæsarea. They also worked to bolster the small Christian church there. Luke records that on their last night there, a Saturday, Paul spoke at a communal fellowship meal being held in one of the three-story tenements that clustered around the small harbor. In fact, Paul, being Paul, was still speaking at midnight. A young man named Eutychus, who had perched on one of the broad, open windowsills, fell asleep, rolled right off his ledge and plunged into the courtyard three stories below.

When they heard the sickening thud, everyone rushed down and those first to Eutychus declared him dead. But Paul wasn't far behind. He wrapped the lad in his arms and reassured everyone that he was still breathing. Paul revived him, and as soon as Eutychus had been carried off to his home to recover, Paul went back upstairs, finished his sermon and led everyone in the Lord's Supper.

As dawn broke, Paul was still sitting in the upstairs room talking to a few members of the Troas church when his companions came for him to board their ship for its first stop, Assos. But no, Paul couldn't tear himself away just yet. A few months before he had visited Troas all too briefly on his way to reconcile with the Corinthian church, and now he wanted to make up for lost time. Despite having no sleep, this tireless missionary had decided he would stay with the Troans a while longer. He'd then walk the 25 miles to Assos and meet his shipmates there.

When they finally sailed off with Paul, it was 35 miles south to Mitylene on the island of Lesbos, then 60 miles to Chios, 70 to Samos and another 30 or so to Miletus, each leg involving an overnight as the local crews loaded and unloaded their cargo. Miletus was a formidable city in itself despite being overshadowed by Ephesus. Blessed with four harbors and rolling pastures, it was a place where herders of sheep met and bargained with wool craftsmen. Miletus was also a city of culture and of many philosophers. But its importance to Paul at the time was that it lay just 20 miles from Ephesus. Paul wanted to visit his churches again but probably risked danger if he were seen there by anyone connected with the Temple of Artemis. Besides, if he had scarcely been able to tear himself away from a few churchmen in Troas, he might be smothered in the embrace of the many in Ephesus and never make it in time for the Pentecost Festival.

So Paul sent a message asking the leading Ephesian Christians to meet him in Miletus. If this was a man who was physically unimpressive or lacked oratory skills, one would scarcely know it, for the Ephesian elders came in haste at the chance to see him.

Perhaps it was on the long walk from Troas to Assos when he realized that his arrival in Jerusalem would produce confrontation rather than reconciliation, because the Paul who spoke to his friends at the harbor in Miletus was more somber than the one who had sailed from Macedonia. The apostle began by recounting how he had faced hardships and heartaches in preaching the gospel in the provinces.

> And now, behold. I am going to Jerusalem, bound in the Spirit, not knowing what shall befall me there; except that the Holy Spirit testifies to me in every city that imprisonment and afflictions await me. But I do not account my life of any value nor as precious to myself, if only I may accomplish my course and the ministry that I received from the Lord Jesus, to testify the gospel of the grace of God.

And, now, behold, I know that all you among whom I have gone about preaching the kingdom will see my face no more. Therefore I testify to you this day that I am innocent of the blood of all, for I did not shrink from declaring to you the whole counsel of God. Take heed to yourselves and to all the flock, in which the Holy Spirit has made you guardians, to feed the church of the Lord which he obtained with his own blood.

I know that after my departure fierce wolves will come in among you, not sparing the flock; and from among your own selves will arise men speaking perverse things to draw the disciples after them. Therefore be alert, remembering that for three years I did not cease night or day to admonish everyone with tears.

And now I commend you to God and to the word of his grace, which is able to build you up and to give you the inheritance among all those who are sanctified. I coveted no one's silver or gold or apparel. You yourselves know that these hands have ministered to my necessities, and to those who were with me. In all things I have shown you that by so toiling one must help the weak, remembering the words of the Lord Jesus that "It is more blessed to give than to receive."[49]

With that it was time to go aboard ship. Paul then knelt and prayed with the Ephesians. Everyone was in tears, Luke writes, "because of the words he had spoken and [because] they should see his face no more."

From Miletus it was a day-long 80-mile run south to Cos by the crisp northerlies of spring, then a pass by Rhodes, with the parts of the earthquake-toppled Colossus of Rhodes still strewn about the harbor. The pilgrims now headed west to Patara in Lycia near the southwestern corner of Asia Minor, and a major center of the cult of Apollo.

There they transferred to a large cargo ship headed for Phoenecia.

This time they were in for a four-day, 400-mile open sea voyage. One can imagine schools of leaping dolphins leading the ship as it plunged into the deep blue waters. Their midpoint would have been Cyprus, where, passing the capital of Paphos on their left, with its gleaming temple of Aphrodite, Paul doubtless wondered if the proconsul Sergius Paulus had remained a Christian.

After another day's run, they could sight the busy harbor of Tyre, one of the original Phoenician cities. Tyre was a major cargo loading port for the western provinces, and the churchmen stayed seven days there. Just as the stop in Miletus had brought out the elders from Ephesus, word of Paul's landing in Tyre drew a flock of Christians from all around. The meeting was all the more emotional because these locals confirmed that Judea was in turmoil and begged Paul not to go. When Paul and his company insisted they must head on south, their new friends escorted them out of town and to the docks, praying and weeping all the way.

After a single overnight in Ptolemais and another outpouring of Christians to greet them, the delegation again boarded ship for a final 35-mile run and put in at the exquisite marble-covered harbor of Cæsarea. Paul's companions were already on edge at being in a strange new land, and now they could also sense the grim tension of its residents as well. Jew and Hellene had clashed often in the streets and their tempers were now held in check only by the fact that Cæsarea was policed by far more Roman troops than anywhere in Judea. Yet, neither side was at all mollified at having been under the capricious thumb of Felix, the Roman procurator, for seven tumultuous years.

Paul's party, however, slipped into the market throngs with no apparent incident. There they were hosted by none other than Philip, the same member of Stephen's original seven who had established many of the Hellenistic churches that now flourished up and down the Judean-Phoenician seacoast. Philip had settled in Cæsarea with his four unmarried daughters, all of whom were credited with the gift of prophesy. The newcomers must have gained new reassurance and strength as Philip told them of seeing firsthand the resurrected Jesus.

During their stay with Philip the delegates were surprised when a well-known Christian prophet asked to see them. His name was Agabus, and he had just come down from Jerusalem. His objective (had he been sent by the Jewish Christians there?) was to see Paul. After the briefest of greetings, Agabus grabbed the belt from Paul's outer cloak and proceeded to tie his own hands and feet with it in the fashion of the old Hebrew prophets.

"Thus says the Holy Spirit," he declared. "This is how the Jews at Jerusalem will bind the man who owns this girdle and deliver him into the hands of the Gentiles."

Agabus had so frightened everyone that for the first time members of Paul's own delegation broke down in tears, urging him as well not to go.

"What are you doing, crying and breaking my heart like this?" Paul answered. Their concern touched him deeply, but he was also piqued because it was as if they still didn't comprehend his mission. "I am ready not only to be imprisoned, but even to die at Jerusalem for the name of the Lord Jesus," he declared.

And what about the gifts that dozens of churches had collected? No, he could not be dissuaded now. And so, the delegates showed their own resolve by joining him to the man. In fact, so did several Christians from Cæsarea. After staying overnight in Joppa in the home of a Christian from Cyprus, the Cæsarean Christians turned back and the nine envoys faced the last 20 miles alone.

As they approached the walls of the Holy City, most of Paul's companions were no doubt awed by the glistening of the temple bronze and the stout city walls that Herod and his successors had put up to defy all threats of invasion. For Paul, this was his fifth visit and his first in eight years. Only at this point does *Acts* inform us that Paul had a married sister living in Jerusalem — and nothing more.

Luke writes that the Jewish-Christian brethren "received us gladly" upon their arrival. Perhaps Paul arranged to stay that night in the home of his sister. But a longer reunion could wait, because on the very next day Paul had arranged a meeting with James and all the Jewish-Christian Elders. There he introduced his associates and made a formal presentation of the funds that had been raised, which were gratefully received. Encouraged to bring the elders up to date, Paul gave an impressive account of his missionary work in Antioch and the western provinces. James, in turn, gave his own progress report, pointing with equal pride to the many churches that had sprung up throughout Judea, Samaria and Galilee. No doubt he took pains to point out that it was only after much pain and turmoil that the Jewish-Christians had been able to achieve a tacit co-existence with the temple authorities.

And so, it was only a matter of time before the conversation turned to the one fear that James and his elders had about Paul's visit — that it might, as before, result in disrupting this fragile accord. James and his disciples were grateful for the gift but worried as to whether it implied an obligation they couldn't honor. After skirting diplomatically about the issue, one of the elders advanced an idea. "You see, brother, how many thousands among the Jews here have believed [in Jesus]," he said. "They are all zealous for the Law, and they have been told that you teach all the Jews who are among the Gentiles to forsake Moses, telling them not to circumcise their children or observe the customs. What then is to be done?"

He answered his own question: "We now have four men among us who have vowed to undergo the Jewish purification ceremony. Why not join them? Purify yourself as well and pay their expenses. That way all will know that what they have been told about you is untrue and that you are in observance of the Law."

Well, Paul had never *rejected* Jewish customs for those who wished to observe them (*"Are they Hebrews, so am I! Are they Israelites, so am I!"*). The commitment meant abstaining from wine for seven days, shaving his head, burning his shorn hair on the altar and offering a formal sacrifice to mark the end of the period. The referred-to "expenses" entailed buying five lambs and ten pigeons for the final sacrifice. Paul was determined to hold together the Jewish and Gentile components of Christianity. He had no doubt been purified before and doing so again was a small price to pay for peace.

For six days Paul, with shaven head, appeared in the temple with his fellow initiates without incident.

On the final day his luck ran out. Some Jewish pilgrims from Ephesus happened to see Paul in the temple. "Look over there! Isn't that fellow the same rabble rouser who tried to lead the synagogue astray in Ephesus?" Indeed, this was the same man they had seen earlier in the market walking with Trophimus, a fellow Ephesian they knew to be a leading Gentile Christian. What was going on here? Had this Paul shaved that Gentile's head and smuggled him into the temple for some sacrilegious purpose?

The Ephesian Jews didn't wait to ask questions. They rushed up to Paul and tried to grab him while the apostle recoiled. "Men of Israel, Help!" they called out to the crowd. "This man is teaching people everywhere against the Law and this place. He has also brought Greeks into the temple and he has defiled this holy place!"

It was only a matter of seconds before their shouts had flashed from the Court of the Gentiles to the streets below. A few moments later Roman sentries overlooking the temple courtyards from the walls of the adjacent Fortress of Antonia puzzled as they saw a mob of angry men surging from the spacious Court of the Gentiles towards the inner precincts. A short, balding man was being held against a wall and the others were rushing toward him as if to tear him limb from limb.

Well, moments like this were why the Romans maintained extra riot control details during festivals. A hundred men strained to push the massive temple gates shut as quickly as possible and a riot squad led by a tribune named Claudius Lysias descended the long stairs from their barracks into the Court of the Gentiles. Petrified by the sight of armed soldiers brandishing swords and pushing them away with heavy shields, the Ephesian Jews melted away, leaving a bloodied and tattered Paul trembling in their midst.

"Arrest this man," the tribune commanded, and Paul was quickly bound in chains. Almost as an afterthought the officer turned to the crowd and asked what it was his new prisoner had done. But the uproar was so deafening that he couldn't make any sense of the men shouting and shaking their fists. Actually, Lysias later said he thought Paul might have been the so-called Egyptian prophet who had led 4,000 men into the wilderness several months before. But all he knew for sure at the time was that his men had better pick up their prisoner like a sack of figs and haul him up the steps to the Fortress Antonia before the crowd regained its bluster and over-whelmed them all.

When they had reached the steps Paul turned to the tribune. "May I say something to you," he asked in Greek.

"You know Greek?" replied the surprised Lysias. "Are you not the Egyptian who stirred up that revolt recently?"

His prisoner answered: "I am a Jew from Tarsus in Cilicia — a citizen of no mean city. I beg you, let me speak to the people."

The tribune shrugged and ordered Paul set upright. Maybe he would learn at last what this was all about. Paul climbed several steps so that he looked out on the men in the courtyard. And when he motioned with his hand, there was a great hush. Speaking in Hebrew, Paul began to tell them the story of his life: how he had been raised in Tarsus, was taught Jewish Law at the feet of the great Gamaliel, and had come to persecute the fol-lowers of the crucified Jesus. He told of his role in the persecution of Stephen and his encounter with the voice of Jesus on the road to Damas-cus. Paul then began to explain how Jesus was God's own son and how the Holy Spirit had sent him to the Gentiles.

But this crowd wasn't in the mood to stand in the hot sun and hear a long story in the first place, and now they began to add up the obvi-ous: this polluter of the Law was also proclaiming a new Messiah and promoting him to Gentiles as well. Soon the muttering had changed to shouts of derision. "Away with this fellow," one voice called out. "He shouldn't be allowed to live!" Others began echoing the cry until soon they were waving their garments in the air and kicking up dust as a sym-bol of rejection.

Before the scene got any uglier, the tribune hastened Paul up to the fortress barracks overlooking the temple. When the heavy door had been shut and secured, Lysias ordered that Paul be examined by the usual scourging to find out why he had agitated such a large crowd. They had stripped his already-bloody clothes to his scarred waist and tied him up with thongs when Paul looked up at a centurion standing by.

"Is it lawful for you to scourge a man who is a Roman citizen, and un-condemned?" he asked.

When the tribune heard it he walked over and squared himself before Paul. *"You're* a Roman citizen?" he asked.

"Yes."

"My citizenship cost me a lot of money," the tribune mused to no one in particular.

"But I was *born* a citizen," Paul replied.

So Lysias dismissed the soldiers who had been waiting to examine Paul by flogging. The prisoner was unbound but detained for the night. By the next morning Lysias had determined the real reason for all the commotion. He had Paul taken to the meeting place of the Jewish Sanhedrin, which gathered in a large, long hall off the Court of the Israelis in the temple. There, Paul found himself confronting a mixture of Sadducees, who included virtually all of the leading priests, and the Pharisees, who made up the remainder. By this time, all had been able to inquire about Paul and form some impressions. Some older members by then would have remembered him as the hot-headed young temple official who had gone off to bring back members of the fledgling Way and wound up joining them. He had since corrupted perhaps hundreds of Jews by imploring them to abandon the Law and follow a false messiah. Had he himself begun eating "the other thing" and ignoring the Sabbath? Was he himself even still a Jew? If not, what was he doing in the temple attempting to undergo the purification ceremony? And who were those other shaved heads with him?

The tribune Lysias ordered Paul to rise and explain himself to the body. The meeting did not begin well. "Brethren," Paul began as an introduction, "I have lived before God in all good conscience before this day."

No sooner had these opening words passed when an imposing fellow shouted "Blasphemy!" and ordered the man nearest Paul to strike him in the mouth.

Stunned, Paul shot back at the leader: "You whitewashed wall [referring to what Jews used to cover privies and mud sheds]. "Are you sitting to judge me according to the Law, and yet contrary to the Law you order me struck?"

Someone whispered to Paul that the council was accustomed to being addressed as "Elders of Israel" and that the man he had just insulted was the high priest Ananias. "Would you revile God's high priest?" another member asked aloud.

Paul became somewhat contrite, but without changing the salutation. "I did not know, brethren, that he is the high priest," he said. "For it is written, 'You shall not speak evil of a ruler of your people.'"

But Paul could see how on edge his judges were, and at this point he resorted to a tactic that was somewhat diversionary and certainly divisive. It was easy to spot the Pharisees in the room with their amulets, tassels and long robes. Realizing that they were as numerous as the Sadducees, he said: "Brethren, I am a Pharisee, a son of Pharisees. It is with respect to the hope and the resurrection of the dead that I am on trial here!"

This was like driving an ax into a piece of firewood, because the Sadducees believed that death is death and Pharisees believed that the dead rise to become spirits. In an instant the members were arguing among themselves. One of the Pharisees managed to quiet things down long enough to say, "We find nothing wrong in this man! So what if a spirit or an angel spoke to him?"

With that the room again was full of shouting, jostling and even beard pulling. Lysias the tribune watched from a respectful distance at first; but now fearful that some of them might turn on Paul, he shouted towards the entrance for some of his men to rush in and take the prisoner away.

So it was back to the barracks again while Lysias pondered what to do. After all, he was only the commander of a thousand men. This was beginning to look like a matter for higher authorities.

Paul pondered his fate as well. And Luke was to write later that during the night "The Lord stood by him and said, 'Take courage, for as you have testified about me at Jerusalem, so you must bear witness also at Rome.'"

But that same night Paul's fate was also being discussed by another group. *Acts* doesn't indicate whether the instigators were members of the Sanhedrin itself or some of the crowd that had attacked Paul in the temple courtyard two days before. In any event, about 40 revengeful men took an oath not to eat or drink until they killed Paul. It's quite likely that they were part of the small temple security force or that the Sanhedrin had at its disposal a clandestine band of zealous youths who could be counted on to "take care of " certain temple business that the Romans wouldn't sanction. The irony is that Paul himself may well have belonged to a similar group long before when called upon to root out a new upstart movement called The Way. In any event, the council sent a representative to the barracks the next morning to tell the tribune that the elders of Israel were prepared to resume hearing Paul's case in an orderly fashion later that same day.

But the real plan was to seize and kill him before he ever reached the council room.

During the same morning, the sister whose name no one seems to recall, and whom Paul had not seen for at least eight years before his recent arrival, intervened to save his life. Somehow she caught wind of the plot, and sometime during the interim before Paul was to be escorted out from the barracks, she ordered her young son to hasten there and warn his uncle.

Before long the tribune Lysias was confronted by one of his centurions who had a local boy in tow. "Paul the prisoner asked me to bring this young man to you, as he has something to say."

The tribune took the lad by the hand into an unoccupied room and asked him, "What is it you have to tell me?"

"The Jews have agreed to ask you to bring Paul to the council today, as though they were going to inquire somewhat more closely about him," said the boy anxiously. "But do not yield to them, for more than 40 of them lie in ambush, bound by a vow not to eat nor drink until they have killed him."

None of this surprised Lysias. He thanked the boy and sent him home after promising to tell no one. Then he calmly called in two of his centurions and said: "At the third hour of the night I want 200 soldiers with 70 horsemen and 200 spearmen prepared to go as far as Cæsarea. I also want mounts for Paul to ride. And I want him brought safely to Felix, the governor."

Then Lysias sat down and wrote a letter to Felix describing the situation. Before signing off, he added his own opinion: "I found that he was accused about questions of their law, but charged with nothing deserving death or imprisonment. And when it was disclosed to me that there would be a plot against the man, I sent him to you at once, ordering his accusers also to state before you what they have against him."

Paul and his escort departed in the dead of night. The size of the guard sent to arm one politically unimportant pauper gives an indication of two things: how dangerous it was to be outside the walls of Jerusalem and how much this "Gentile" brand of Christianity agitated the Jews in their heartland. About 30 miles north and presumably out of danger from any followers from Jerusalem, the soldiers turned back and left the horsemen to deliver Paul to Felix.

With the prisoner safely standing before him in silence, Felix read the letter from Lysias and asked Paul what province he came from. When Paul told him Cilicia, Felix promised to hear his case "when your accusers arrive." Meanwhile, he was to be kept in the maximum security dungeon of Herod's castle.

The accusers did not disappoint. The Sanhedrin must have obtained a lawyer and set off for Cæsarea with all haste, because five days later Felix was seated in his judgment seat with Paul standing at one side and a delegation of distinguished Jewish elders on the other. Speaking for the latter was one Tertullus, a lawyer who was trained in Roman rhetoric and more apt to sway a Roman procurator.

Tertullus, after praising the "most excellent Felix" for the "peace" and "reforms" he had bestowed on the Jews, asked for his help in punishing the "pestilent fellow" before them. Paul was cited as a "ringleader of the sect of the Nazarenes" and "an agitator among all the Jews throughout the world." He had even tried to profane the temple before he was seized.

Here is Luke's summary of what Paul said in turn:

> As you may ascertain, it was not more than 12 days since I went up to worship at Jerusalem; and they did not find me disputing with anyone or stirring up a crowd either in the temple or the synagogues or in the city. Neither can they prove to you what they now bring against me.
>
> But this I admit to you: that according to the Way, which they call a sect, I worship the God of our fathers, believing everything laid down by or written by the prophets, having a hope in God which these themselves accept, that there will be a resurrection of both the just and the unjust. So I always take pains to have a clear conscience toward God and toward men.
>
> Now after some years I came to bring my nation alms and offerings. As I was doing this, they found me purified in the temple, without any crowd or tumult. But some Jews from Asia — they ought to be here before you to make this accusation if they have anything against me. Or else let these men themselves say what wrongdoing they found when I stood before the council except this one thing which I cried out while standing among them, "With respect to the resurrection of the dead I am on trial before you this day."[50]

The Jews pressed for a decision, but Felix put them off. "When Lysias the tribune comes down, I will decide your case," he said, dismissing them. He then ordered that Paul be kept in minimal custody, with rights to be visited by his friends and have food brought to him. This was a blessing because Luke and the others had also come down from Jerusalem, the latter probably beginning to wonder when they would be able to make their way back to their homes in the provinces.

Lysias later came and added his first-hand account of what happened, but Felix continued to postpone a decision. Several days later Felix' Jewish wife Drusilla joined him and together they dabbled at more interrogations without giving indication of when they might decide the case. Eventually autumn turned, the north winds began to blow and Paul's church friends from the provinces — his constant source of moral support — simply had to take the last sailing ships available. Finally there was just Luke, Timothy and certainly the comfort of Cesarean Christians like Philip and his daughters.

From time to time Felix would summon Paul, have a pleasant enough conversation, then return him to his quarters. Why? Although Felix was not about to release an innocent man to the Jews, he was probably hoping that Paul's churches might raise a purse for his freedom just as they had for their needy brethren in Jerusalem. But Paul also knew that if simply discharged alone into the streets of Judea, the Jews would kill him.

Felix had his own case to consider. The same Jewish elders were petitioning Rome to recall Felix on charges of orchestrating the Jewish-Syrian riots in Cæsarea. Releasing Paul would only inflame them.

Thus, Felix would toy with the imprisoned Paul for two years until he himself was forced to go to Rome.

Paul no doubt felt the confinement of his mission more acutely than even his spare, stonewalled quarters in the dungeon Herod the Great had built in Cæsarea. During that agonizing time he concluded that the only way out — to survive and continue his mission's fulfillment — was to be "freed" from Cæsarea, yet "forced" to go to Rome.

SINCE EARLY ADULTHOOD Nero had yet another concubine who closely resembled Agrippina, all of which could prompt him to joke to friends that he was having intercourse with his "mother." Now, Agrippina, donning the garb of a seductress, decided to make it authentic. In the months that followed, the two were seen everywhere together, often in a litter trading embraces and lover's kisses. Tacitus writes that it became Agrippina's habit to wait until midday, "the time when food and drink were beginning to raise Nero's temperature." Then "she would appear before her inebriated son all decked out and ready for incest."

Seneca and Burrus weren't pleased with the intensity of Poppæa's campaign for wedlock, but they were even more alarmed by Agrippina's behavior. Intermediaries were enlisted to warn the young emperor. Did he know that his mother was boasting publicly of her intimacy with her son? Had he considered that the army would never tolerate a monarch guilty of incest?

Poppæa was hardly deaf to these reports as well and used them as an opportunity for her to goad the emperor to stand up like a man. Did this not prove that it was time to get rid of Agrippina? If so, why not play upon this new-found intimacy and trust to find a way to take her off?

As luck would have it for both parties, Agrippina had already laid plans to visit her country mansions in Tusculum and Antium, and a relieved Nero saw her off eagerly with fond farewell kisses as she departed. Meanwhile, he resolved to use the interim to find a way to do the deed. He was stumped, however, because Agrippina was far too experienced in removing enemies to be duped by poison or ambush. At last, a novel idea was advanced by Anicetus, a freedman who now commanded the naval fleet at Misenum. Anicetus had been Nero's original boyhood tutor until displaced by Seneca and he had always loathed Agrippina.

His idea was absolutely bizarre. Anicetus said that he had once seen a ship in a stage play that had been built to break apart during a mock storm. He suggested that a ship could be constructed with a section in the center — right above the sleeping cabin — that could break loose at sea and either crush or drown the occupants. After all, he said, who would think to blame a human conspiracy for the wiles of wind and water?

The plan seemed almost laughable at first, but Nero found his mind wandering back to it often. After all, the sea would be a natural ally because the emperor traditionally presided over festival of Minerva at Baiæ near the naval fleet on the Bay of Naples. This year the week long festivities would begin on March 19.

When Nero issued his mother a flowery invitation to join him there, it was warmly reciprocated. Upon her arrival in Baiæ, Nero met his mother on shore and welcomed her with outstretched hands and embraces. He then conducted her to Bauli, a sumptuous family villa that overlooked the shore near Cape Misenum across the beautiful blue bay from Baiæ. Misenum was home of the western Roman naval fleet. And as the ships in the harbor nearest the villa swayed silently in the windless, starry night, one — a smaller barge with ornamental carvings on the bow — stood out as exquisite compared to the more lumbering, utilitarian warships alongside it. Upon learning that the smart new vessel was hers, Agrippina took it as a supreme compliment because she had been accustomed to traveling in the unadorned warships.

Once she arrived at the emperor's residence, she was constantly the object of Nero's lavish attentions. Sitting next to her son in the place of honor, they reclined for many languid hours talking of their lives together and the times to come. When he finally saw her off in the harbor, he gazed into her eyes and clung to her under the full moon. Then he kissed her breasts and she departed up the gangplank.

The sea, however, wasn't an assassin's ally at all. The water was still and the skies ablaze with stars. Agrippina boarded her special ship, accompanied only by two close friends, and went into her well-appointed quarters astern near the tiller. One of her attendants, Crepereius Gallus, stood not far from the tiller talking happily about her mistress' restored luminance. The other, Acerronia, bent over the Augusta, massaging her feet as Agrippina reclined on a couch.

Once the ship had glided to a midway point in the bay, the captain gave a silent signal. Suddenly an onslaught of heavy lead weights, that had been secretly suspended above the flimsy cabin ceiling, came crashing in on the three women. Crepereius was brained by falling ceiling beams and died instantly. Agrippina and Acerronia were saved because the beams were stopped by the back of the couch on which the Augusta reclined.

The ship was supposed to sink as well, but seemed to refuse. The problem for sailors in on the plot was that they were outnumbered by those who weren't. When the plotters tried throwing their weight to one side in order to capsize the ship, the others naturally rushed to the other side to prevent it. Still, the ship began slipping gently below the water line. When Acerronia found herself thrashing about in the bay, she cried out (probably assuming that Agrippina was near her in the dark) "Help! Save the emperor's mother!" With that two of the conspirators rushed over and struck her dead with poles and oars. But Agrippina had managed to muffle her terror, just as when she had seen Brittanicus poisoned in front of her eyes. Although she had lost the use of one shoulder where a falling object had struck her, Agrippina managed to swim sidestroke in the still bay until she came to some moored fishing boats. From there she was taken to her villa on Cape Misenum.

Back in her bed at last, the exhausted Agrippina finally had time to reflect on what had happened. She didn't need to be convinced that the ship had been rigged to collapse at sea. But examining her remaining strengths and routes of escape, Agrippina concluded that she had only one: to profess ignorance of the whole matter. So she dispatched her household overseer, Agerinus, to inform her son that, by divine mercy and his lucky star she had survived a serious accident. The messenger was also instructed to insist that Nero should not take the trouble to visit her because what she needed now was plenty of rest.

Nero, meanwhile, had been half-crazed with anguish as he paced alone awaiting the outcome. When finally informed that the whole affair had been bungled, he concluded that its instigator would be all too obvious to Agrippina. "She may arm her slaves," he fretted to attendants. "She may even whip up the army or gain access to the Senate and accuse me of wounding her and killing her friends. What can I do to save myself?"

Whenever the young emperor was unable to solve a problem, his path inevitably led to Seneca and Burrus. It's doubtful that either was in on the plot; but both were awakened in their suites and brought to their distraught ruler. For a long time they heard the light-haired, red-bearded youth's ruminations in silence, neither one wanting to commit to a course that might bring himself down as well. Finally, they must have been convinced that matters were coming to a head so fast that it was now a matter of Nero striking before Agrippina did. Seneca ended the suspense by turning to Burrus and asking if the Prætorian Guard could be ordered to kill her. Burrus replied that the Guard was devoted to the whole imperial house and to the memory of Agrippina's father Germanicus. He doubted seriously that it would commit violence against his offspring.

By this time the three had been joined by Anicetus, the fleet commander. He spoke up at that point and said that because the whole scheme had been his to begin with, it was his obligation to see it through. The two imperial advisors nodded with great relief. Then Nero, mustering his last ounce of pluck, cried out, "This is the first day of my reign!" He ordered Anicetus to go quickly, shouting after him to "Take men who obey orders!"

Just minutes after Anicetus and his men had departed, in rushed Agrippina's messenger to assure that she was well and loyal to her son. Her response to the calamity was so different from what Nero had anticipated that he was momentarily struck dumb. But realizing that his own "delegation" was so irretrievably committed, he perceived an advantage at the same time. The emperor quickly reached for a sword lying on a nearby table, dropped it at the freedman's feet, and shouted to his guards that he had just thwarted an attempt on his life. "Arrest and bind this man!" he called out. Already his mind was manufacturing the story that his mother's agent had plotted against his life and that she had committed suicide out of shame.

Meanwhile, word of Agrippina's shipboard disaster had spread all around the towns that stretched along the Bay of Misenum. Not knowing what had become of her party, people ran out onto the beach or climbed aboard fishing boats and drifted about in the calm waters in search of survivors. The whole shore echoed with prayers, wails and the din of ignorant inquiries and speculative answers.

When news came that Agrippina was safe, one could hear a chorus of rejoicing ripple along the beaches as word spread from group to group. But then just as quickly, menacing bands of soldiers broke through the crowds and ordered them home. The reason is that the fate of Agrippina — great granddaughter of Augustus, daughter of Germanicus, wife of Claudius, mother of Nero — had already been sealed. Anicetus, accompanied only by a naval captain and lieutenant, had wasted no time in brushing past the servants in her villa on Cape Misenum. Barging into her bedroom, lit only with a single flickering lamp, the three marines found Agrippina alone with a maid.

Soon even the maid melted into the darkness.

"Are you leaving me, too?" Agrippina shouted in scorn from her bed.

She turned next to the three shadows in the doorway. "If you have come to visit me," she called out, "you can report that I am better. But if you are assassins, I know my son is not responsible."

Perhaps ten years before, when Agrippina had asked her astrologers about Nero, they had answered that he would become emperor but kill his mother. At the time she was in the midst of risking all to marry Claudius and advance her son above Brittanicus. "Let them kill me, provided that he becomes emperor!" she had answered defiantly.

Now the assailants closed around Agrippina's bed in silence. First the captain hit her over the head with a truncheon. Then, just as the lieutenant was drawing his sword to finish her off, she threw aside her blanket and exposed her abdomen. "Strike here," she cried out, "for this is what bore Nero!"

But the three naval officers were not as deft with swords as Prætorians. It took many thrusts and twists before Agrippina finally expired in a blood-soaked pile of pillows and bedsheets.

For the next week or so, the emperor remained at Baiæ in a very convincing state of numbness. His genuine state of speechless shock displayed both an outward sign of grief and an inward state of disbelief that so daring a deed had actually been done. And he anguished over how it would be received. Would the armies of Germany revolt on learning the fate of the great commander Germanicus' daughter? Would the Senate believe the ship "accident?" Would it tolerate a divorce of the deified Claudius' daughter Octavia after it had barely stifled its rage at the poisoning of his son Brittanicus?

Nero had taken no chances on a funeral in which throngs of mourners might erupt into an angry mob. Agrippina, her body reclining on a couch, was quickly cremated in back of the mansion in which she had died. In the first days afterward, Nero remained distracted and distraught. At night he claimed to see his mother's ghost, along with the whips and blazing torches of the Furies. By day he was driven nearly mad by the martial trumpets that signaled the official mourning by wailing constantly from towns around the bay. But as days passed, no reaction at all had come from Germany or from Rome. Hope and confidence slowly returned to the emperor, beginning, perhaps, when Burrus prevailed

on the colonels and captains of the Guard to come to him with con-
gratulatory handclasps for having escaped from the menace of his mother's evil conspiracies. Nero's friends crowded into the temples to offer
thanks for his deliverance, and soon, sacrifices were being offered by town
magistrates throughout Campania.

Meanwhile, a letter written by Seneca for the emperor had gone to the
Senate explaining what had happened. A confidant of Agrippina had been
caught with a sword with which he had intended to murder the emperor
in his very bedchamber. Once discovered, Agrippina had acknowledged her
guilt by taking her own life.

But she was guilty of other crimes as well, the letter continued. She had
been responsible for most of the scandals and murders during the latter years
of Claudius. And as Nero had tried to assume his destiny, she had wanted to be co-ruler — to receive oaths of allegiance from the Guard and to
subject the Senate to the same humiliation. She had opposed gratuities to
soldiers and civilians alike. She had even tried to break into the Senate house
and deliver verdicts to foreign envoys. "I can hardly believe that I am safe
from her now," the emperor's letter continued. "Nor do I derive any pleasure from the fact."

The Senate obligingly expressed its relief and made appropriate shows
of jubilation at the emperor's newly gained safety. Still, Nero worried on.
Would the *people* of Rome welcome him back? Nero was encouraged to see
for himself, so he did, with a long train of sycophants preceding him and
exhorting crowds along the way. When the emperor would gaze from his
carriage along the road he saw families lining the streets, some sitting in tiers
of wooden parade seats as though attending a triumph. And as he entered
Rome he was greeted by senators, their wives and children lined up along
the carriage path according to sex and age. Puffed with pride, Nero could
barely keep the grim look of mourning as he proceeded to the temple of
Jupiter Capitoline and paid his vows to the god.

The truth, Nero was beginning to grasp at last, is whatever an emperor
proclaims it to be.

And where was Poppæa? "How quickly will Octavia be divorced and
ourselves wed?" she must have been asking already. But one can also
imagine Burrus and Seneca imploring the emperor to make her bide her time.
After all, they would say, the Senate was not likely to see Octavia, the
daughter of a deified emperor, pushed aside so quickly. Besides, Nero himself had come to realize that the Senate's acquiescence to "the deed" was
in fact begrudging at best. No one believed that Agrippina would have sent
a single elderly ex-slave, brandishing a large sword, past a platoon of

Guards and into the emperor's bedroom. At best they blamed the concoction on Seneca.

If the emperor needed other evidence that not all the applause was sincere upon his return, he could have donned one of his wigs at night and slunk into the streets. There he would realize that not all of Agrippina's statues had been thrown down and crushed. One of them, for instance, had been rescued and propped on a wall with garment thrown over it so as to make the head appear veiled. Around the neck had been affixed an inscription: "I am abashed and thou art unashamed."

Someone else had hung a leather bag from one of Nero's statues as if to remind him that the penalty for parricide was to be sewn up in it with a cock, an ape or wild dog and thrown into the Tiber to drown.

In the Forum, someone had left a baby boy to which was fastened a tag saying: "I will not rear you up, lest you slay your mother."

In latrines and on walls everywhere, a prowling Nero could have found newly scrawled graffiti, such as this:

> Orestes and Alemeon, both their mothers slew,
> What Nero does is therefore nothing new.

Or this one:

> Sprung from Æneas, pious, wise and great,
> Who says our Nero is degenerate?
> Safe through the flames one bore his sire. The other,
> To save himself, took off his loving mother.[51]

If an emperor could do anything he wanted, why was it so difficult for a 22-year-old man in the fullness of his artistic powers to break tradition and appear on the Roman stage like a common performer? Nero's answer: create a situation in which it would not be shockingly uncommon to see members of high-born families singing, dancing and reciting poetry in public. This would explain why Rome erupted in a profusion of games and theatrical spectacles soon after Nero's return. It began when the emperor prevailed on certain impoverished members of the ancient nobility to perform in the public theater. It didn't matter so much what they did, but that they were seen — all in exchange for sizable fees that allowed them to maintain their lavish styles of living.

At about the same time, he proclaimed the Youth Games, or Neronian Games, which were held ostensibly to mark the first ceremonial shaving of the imperial beard. For several days, in as many as six theaters at once, eminent men and women were pressed into joining professional players. Some performed in the hunting theater, others in the Circus or in a stage orchestra. It was not uncommon to see patrician men playing parts with effeminate gestures and songs while their women danced in indecent dress. Some played the flute and danced in pantomimes or drove horses. Others who were too old or ill to do anything else were compelled to sing in choruses.

Goading them all on with lavish prizes was the young man in the royal box. Performers were given horses, slaves, gold, silver and all manner of costly jewelry as prizes. During a performance the emperor would often turn to the crowd and throw tiny brightly covered balls into their outstretched hands. Those who seized the little balls would return them for the expensive prize described inside.

On the final night of the Neronian Games, the big moment came. The crowd quieted quickly when they first glimpsed Cæsar striding upon the stage wearing the garb of a lyre player. "My lords," he intoned, "of your kindness give me ear." Awkwardly, and very nervously, he sang and played a piece called "Attis" and then "The Bacchantes," neither of which was familiar to the audience because they had been written by the emperor himself. Beside him stood Burrus and Seneca, prompting him like schoolmasters at a child's recital.

According to most accounts, the emperor wasn't such a bad poet, but his voice was weak and husky, so that nervous giggles and guffaws began to spread from row to row. Unknown to those in the forward seats was the fact that the rear tiers had been commandeered by an army — literally. To support his debut, Burrus had mustered a few hundred Prætorians in civilian garb. Before long, at every pause in the performance they would unleash a storm of applause while menacing all around them to join in. By the time the songs had ended there were shouts of "Glorious Cæsar! Our Apollo! Our Augustus! None surpasses thee, O Cæsar."

But this was just the half of the emperor's newfound independence. At just about the same time Nero was inaugurating the Youth Games, he directed the erection of a new neighborhood of taverns and portable cabanas for assignations in the grove of trees that had been planted around the lake that Augustus had constructed to display naval games. The whole complex catered to every form of vice imaginable. And for those who might be shy or hesitant, Nero's agents were on hand distributing free coins to help start off their evening.

People of every station were goaded into going to the lakeside festivities. But those who were sensible — perhaps magistrates and ministers by day — were both amazed and depressed at the extent of the money being spent. They grieved because they feared it would bankrupt the country and compel Nero to embark on confiscations and other evil deeds in order to continue at this pace.

They should have been even more worried about what it cost to keep Poppæa pacified. For example, the mules that drew her carriage were each shorn with gilded shoes that probably cost 400,000 sesterces per animal. It is also said that Nero kept for her a stable of some 500 asses. Those that had foaled were milked daily so that Poppæa might bathe in their milk to preserve the loveliness of her skin.

A.D.
60–61

THE EMPEROR WAS IN HIS GLORY. He fished with a golden net, never wore the same garment twice and played at dice for 400,000 sesterces a point. He proclaimed a new series of Greek-style stage competitions, and their focal point was a lavish new public bath, gymnasium and school of music built in the shadow of the Pantheon. At its dedication the emperor won the first prize for lyre playing (no one else challenged him). Then, wearing the garb of the music guild, he proudly entered the gymnasium to witness his name being enrolled on a scroll honoring contest winners.

Naturally, all this took a severe toll on the 2.2 billion sesterces treasury surplus that Claudius had built up. And so did two costly military excursions during this period. One was in Britannia, where at least 50,000 Roman settlers and soldiers had been massacred by tribesmen in a frenzied rebellion against high taxes and seizure of their ancestral lands. A heroic force of just 10,000 well-disciplined Roman soldiers eventually reclaimed Britannia by slashing its way through an opposing force of no less than 150,000 Britons, but the financial cost of victory was probably more than could ever be recouped in reparations from the shaggy islanders and their meager, depleted economy.

The second military excursion fit into the same category of being politically necessary but economically unrewarding. Large but bleak Armenia had been for centuries the symbol of Roman-Parthian hegemony. Whoever could claim rulership over Armenia and get away with it was generally deemed to be the dominant power. In A.D. 60 Parthia was engaged in fending off some rivals on its eastern borders and Rome saw an opening to put its own man on the throne of Armenia. Its most famous general, Cnæus Domitius Corbulo, was ordered to invade the hilly, windswept land and install as its king an Armenian prince who had grown soft and effeminate while lounging in Rome as a palace hostage and courtier of Nero. Corbulo did so just in time to learn he'd been made governor of Syria. So he returned to Antioch leaving in Armenia a new king he knew was not physically or military prepared to withstand the reaction of the Parthians once they learned about it.

The combination of Nero's personal extravagancies and the military's unforeseen needs caused an embarrassing currency devaluation — the first in imperial times. The *denarius,* for example, was lowered to 90 percent of its silver content. The *as,* which had been set at a half-ounce of copper 147 years before, was now chopped to a quarter-ounce. The immediate result was that people paid more in real terms for merchandise, but relatively less to their creditors.

But of all the events of this two-year period, probably none created more anguish in Rome itself than the murder of Lucius Pedanius Secundus. Pedanius was the prefect of Rome (the equivalent of a city manager) and was generally respected for the way he administered its 16 precincts. Thus, people were shocked to learn that Pedanius was murdered in bed by one of his slaves. One story was that he had set a price on the man's freedom but had refused to make good on the bargain. Another version is that the two were in competition for a lover.

Whatever the cause, what consumed public debate was an ancient law stating that when a man is slain by his slave, all other slaves in the same household must be killed in return. Pedanius had 400 — an awesome retribution for even the sternest of slave owners.

Soon a large, riotous crowd of protesters had gathered and converged on the Senate house as a debate ensued on whether to amend or rescind the old law. The most powerful speech for the opponents of leniency was made by Gaius Cassius Longinus, the same senator who had once governed the Jews of Syria. Stating that he had never before opposed relaxation of other ancient laws, he could not help but do so in this case.

A man who has held the consulship has been deliberately murdered by a slave in his own home. None of his fellow slaves prevented or betrayed the murder...

Pretend, if you like, that we are deciding a policy for the first time. Do you believe that a slave can have planned to kill his master without letting fall a single rash or menacing word? Or even if we assume he kept his secret — and obtained a weapon unnoticed — could he have passed the watch, opened a bedroom door, carried in a light and committed the murder without anyone knowing? There are many advance notifications of crimes. If slaves give them away, we can live securely. Or if we must die, we can at least be sure the guilty will be punished...

Our ancestors distrusted their slaves. Yet slaves were then born on the same estates, in the same houses, as their masters, who had treated them kindly from birth. But nowadays our huge households are international. They include every alien religion, or none at all. The only way to keep down this scum is by intimidation.

Innocent people will die, you say. Yes, and when in a defeated army every tenth man is flogged to death, the brave have to draw lots with the others.[52]

As Cassius spoke, the crowds milled outside, shouting for mercy to be shown the many women and children, if nothing else. Yet, not one senator dared to speak or vote against Cassius. When the crowd began to pick up stones and bar the order from being carried out, Nero ordered troops to line the entire route by which the 400 slaves would be taken to their execution. That night the order was carried out to the last woman and child.

THE USUAL TENSIONS in Judea were aggravated at this time by its unsettled role in the Roman-Parthian battle of attrition for Armenia. Had Corbulo's perfunctory excursion actually subdued the wretched place or would the Syrian governor soon be conscripting Samaritan and Galilean boys as front-line sacrifices to Parthian bowmen in an all-out war? Would Syrian corn and wheat supplies be carried off as army provisions, leaving famine and inflation in Jerusalem? Would the garrison at Cæsarea be depleted for the big war, leaving the rest at risk to police their tempestuous Jewish and Syrian townsmen?

But what among these could match the inner turmoil going on within the apostle Paul after two years in a Cæsarean jail? Was his mission doomed to dissipate in the dark emptiness of captivity?

Moreover, Felix the procurator had been recalled to Rome and Christians wondered what to make of it. As reported earlier, the leading Jews of Cæsarea had petitioned the emperor to censure the procurator for helping Syrians in town raid their homes and loot their property the previous year. The evidence against Felix was strong. Moreover, the Jews were probably able to win a nod of favor from Poppæa, who was known to have been attracted to the Jewish religion, as were several women among the nobility. Indeed, Felix was quietly replaced and sent into obscurity.

Mid-summer saw the arrival of a new procurator. Porcius Festus seemed to be more eager to ease Jewish-Hellene tensions if for no other reason that they eroded the strength and stability of a province that was essential to containing Parthia. After just three days inspecting his new quarters at Cæsarea, Festus hastened on to Jerusalem to see how he might improve relations with the temple authorities.

One of the many causes of instability in Jerusalem arose from the fact that the position of high priest had changed hands among so many quarreling factions. Ironically, there had been fewer changeovers before the reign of Herod Agrippa I when the Romans had asserted control of appointments. Now, in the past ten years under the auspices of Agrippa II there had been six different high priests. This not only encouraged factionalism, but created situations where new high priests were constantly testing the limits of their authority under Rome.

Well, the elders certainly weren't going to ask that Romans rather than Jews appoint high priests, but they could ask for help in stopping the spread of splinter groups.

After all, murder of the high priest Jonathan by the Sicarii had never been avenged. How could one be sure it hadn't been committed by an overzealous Christian — maybe even by one of Paul's Gentile converts? Festus, they said, could help restore stability by having the prisoner Paul sent up from Cæsarea so that they could judge him properly.

Festus had already heard about the failed ambush of Paul and feared another attempt on the road to Jerusalem. No, he said, "Paul is being kept in Cæsarea. Let the men of authority among you go down there with me. If there is anything wrong about the man, let them accuse him."

Festus returned in around ten days, and another deputation of Jewish elders was not far behind. The very next day Festus was in his judgment seat, with the accusing advocate on one side and the chained prisoner on the other. But to the procurator's surprise, no new evidence was introduced to substantiate the charge of defiling the temple. The advocate did enter a new accusation: that in championing a messiah, Paul had challenged the emperor's authority, but even this seemed like an afterthought. As far as Festus could make out, the Jews were arguing that the sage Jesus, who died some thirty years before, was indeed dead, while Paul was arguing that he was alive.

Paul rose to his own defense. "Neither against the laws of the Jews nor against the temple, nor against Cæsar have I offended at all," he said.

But Festus, still hopeful of doing the Jews a favor, asked Paul: "Do you wish to go up to Jerusalem, and there be tried on these charges before me?"

Said Paul: "I am standing before Cæsar's tribunal, where I ought to be tried. To the Jews I have done no wrong, as you know very well. If then I am a wrongdoer and have committed anything for which I deserve to die, I do not seek to escape death. But if there is nothing in their charges against me, no one can give me up to them. I appeal to Cæsar."

Festus recessed briefly and gathered his councilors about him. One can imaging them whispering: "Procurator, if he is freed now, the elders will hate you, and may even find a way to kill him. If you go to all the trouble of trying him in Jerusalem and then finding him not guilty, even greater passions will be inflamed and many more could be killed."

Festus returned to his judgment chair and addressed Paul. "You have appealed to Cæsar, and to Cæsar you will go."

Going to Cæsar invariably meant having an armed escort, so Paul must have felt great relief on many fronts. The endless dark days in a dank jail would soon be behind him. He would be under protection from temple vigilantes. He would be free to continue his mission in the capital of the empire.

If Paul found his "trial" in Cæsarea so brief and undramatic after so many months of preparation, he would soon have another opportunity. Although Rome governed lower Judea directly, Agrippa II remained king of a region stretching north from the Lake of Gennesaret (Galilee). Paying a welcome visit to the new procurator was just as important to him as it had been to the temple authorities, so Agrippa and his queen arrived in Cæsarea just a few days after Paul's hearing had concluded.

For Agrippa, now 32, it was more than just a protocol visit. The king had stayed aloof from the previous procurator because Felix was married to his younger sister Drusilla.

Since Agrippa was in charge of naming high priests, Festus wanted all the information he could get about affairs within the temple hierarchy. But he would also welcome the king and queen's insights on another matter. The procurator was in the process of writing a letter to the emperor's petitions secretary about a prisoner named Paul. Perhaps the two might help him frame the charges to be presented at trial.

"Why, yes," said Agrippa, "I would like to hear the man myself."

"Then tomorrow you shall hear him," said Festus.

The next day Paul might have been taken aback when he was led from the dinginess of his cell to the large assembly hall full of glitterati. Therein had gathered Agrippa, the bejeweled Bernice, their entire entourage and all the notables of Cæsarea. Paul might also have spotted a few Christians, among them the faithful Luke.

Festus stood along with the chained and tattered man before him. "King Agrippa and all who are present," he said, "you see this man about whom the whole Jewish people petitioned me, both at Jerusalem and here, shouting that he ought not to live any longer. But I found that he had done nothing definite to write my lord about him. Therefore I have brought him before you, and especially before you, King Agrippa, that after we have examined him, I may have something to write. For it seems to me unreasonable, in sending a prisoner, not to indicate the charges against him."

One senses that Paul instantly recognized the setting to be something akin to what he expected when he addressed the emperor himself in Rome. It would not only be a defense, but also a chance to tame the lion as well. Extending his hand in a slow sweeping gesture, Paul began by saying how much he welcomed the king's presence "because you are especially familiar with all customs and controversies among the Jews." Stating that his own history and "manner of life" is "known by all Jews," and that he, a Pharisee, was on trial for none other than believing the messianic promise that God had long made to the twelve tribes of Israel. For,

> Why is it thought incredible by any of you that God raises the dead?
>
> I myself [in his youth] was convinced that I ought to do many things in opposing the name of Jesus of Nazareth. And I did so in Jerusalem. I not only shut up many of the saints in prison, by authority from the chief priests, but when they were put to death I cast my vote against them. And I punished them often in all the synagogues and tried

to make them blaspheme. And in raging fury against them, I persecuted them even to foreign cities.

Thus I journeyed to Damascus with the authority and commission of the chief priests. At midday, O king, I saw on the way a light from heaven, brighter than the sun, shining around me and those who journeyed with me. And when we had all fallen to the ground, I heard a voice saying to me in the Hebrew language, "Saul, Saul, why do you persecute me....?"

And I said: "Who are you, lord?" And the Lord said, "I am Jesus whom you are persecuting. But rise and stand upon your feet; for I have appeared to you for this purpose, to appoint you to serve and bear witness to the things in which you have seen me and those in which I will appear to you, delivering you from the people and from the Gentiles to whom I send you, to open their eyes, that they may turn the darkness into light and from the power of Satan to God, that they may receive forgiveness of sins and a place among those who are sanctified by faith in me."[53]

"And it is for this reason that the Jews seized me in the temple and tried to kill me," said Paul. "To this day I have had no help but what comes from God. And so I stand here testifying both to small and great, saying nothing but what the prophets and Moses said would come to pass: that the Christ must suffer, and that by being the first to rise from the dead he would proclaim light both to the people and to the Gentiles."

Festus interrupted. "Paul, Paul, you are mad," he sighed loudly. "Your great learning is making you mad."

"I am not mad, most excellent Festus," Paul retorted. "I am speaking the sober truth. For the king knows about these things, and to him I speak freely; for I am persuaded that none of these things has escaped his notice, for this was not done in a corner. King Agrippa, do you believe the prophets? I know that you believe."

Agrippa laughed nervously. He could see where this might lead. "You think to make me a Christian in such a short time?"

"Whether short or long," answered Paul, "I would to God that not only you but also all who hear me this day might become such as I am — except for these chains."

Doubtless Paul had planned a longer expository, but suddenly Agrippa and Bernice rose, which meant that their entire retinue did as well. And as Agrippa strode off into a corridor with Festus, the procurator could be heard saying, "This man is doing nothing to deserve death or punishment. He could have been set free had he not appealed to Cæsar."

This was the last public interrogation Paul would have to face in Cæsarea. By now it was late September in A.D. 60 and the northwest winds were already swirling. While they brought relief from the sweltering nights in the fortress dungeon, the winds were also signaling the last days in which passenger ships could sail north and west. Indeed, the Romans were busy trying to locate a merchantman bound for Italy that also had enough capacity left to accommodate a centurion, a few of his soldiers, Paul and several other prisoners. Paul had also received permission to be accompanied by Luke and the tireless Aristarchus, who had helped bring the church collection from Macedonia, and who had refused to return as long as Paul was imprisoned.

Open seas shipping in the Mediterranean generally ceased for the winter around mid-November. It was now mid-October and the delay, I suspect, may have been caused by the inability to find a cargo ship owner who was willing to risk a round trip voyage that late. Finally, the best that the procurator's agents were able to find was a ship returning to its home port of Adramyttium, which lay a little southeast of Alexander Troas in Asia. Once the party from Cæsarea arrived there they would have to find another boat for Italy.

The man in charge of the prisoners was a centurion named Julius. That he was a decent fellow was demonstrated the first night when the ship pulled into Sidon, some 50 miles to the north. There, Julius allowed Paul and his companions to go ashore and greet a group of Christians who had caught wind of his arrival.

From Sidon they lumbered north against difficult crosswinds, passing to the east of Cyprus, then hugged the coast of Cilicia and Pamphylia before reaching the Lycian post of Myra in south central Asia Minor. Myra, being a major destination between Alexandria and Syria, had in its harbor a large grain ship from Alexandria. Usually, the owner of a leviathan like this was content to make one round trip per sailing season, but this ambitious merchant may have been trying to squeeze out one last run and take advantage of the higher prices fetched in the midst of winter. In any case, the ship was headed directly to Italy, and Julius the centurion decided to gamble that this would be the last time he would have to bother transferring such a large and cumbersome party.

So off they sailed, 276 passengers and a heavy load of wheat, combating a stiff northwesterly wind and waves that kept the giant ship rolling. For awhile they were able to reduce the headwinds by hugging the southern coast of Crete; but at the midway point of the island, just off the city of Lasea, the coastline angled to the northwest and the winds came howling in again. At that point the captain managed to maneuver the big vessel into a small harbor called Fair Havens.

Paul had already known high seas and shipwreck. Now he sought out the owner and captain. "Sirs," he said," I perceive that the voyage will be with injury and much loss, not only of the cargo and the ship, but of our lives."

Doubtless the word of this experienced traveler carried some weight, but the captain and owner worried that trying to winter in this particular harbor would also be dangerous. Besides, the winds had now abated some, so they set off hoping to reach Phoenix, some 60 miles further west along the shore of Crete. The harbor there faced the southeast, the most sheltered direction from the winter winds. It meant lying over for perhaps four months and incurring some unplanned expenses, but at least they'd arrive intact the next spring.

For several hours the ship even enjoyed a gentle southerly wind. But no sooner had it turned the corner of Cape Matala, the sharpest promontory on the Cretan coast, when it was slammed on the starboard side by a violent northeaster that swept down from the mountains. The unrelenting winds blew the huge ship out to sea. The captain tried desperately to slow its course by turning the bow into the wind, but to no avail. It even took hours to bring up the small harbor rowboat that had been towed behind the stern.

Their fear now was in being blown *too* quickly across the Mediterranean and crashing into any number of rocky outcrops that dotted their path. So the captain lowered the sail and let the ship drift. When the winds were just as severe the next day, the crew began dumping cargo overboard. The third day they cast out all the ship's tackle they could spare to further lighten their weight.

Now came a barrage of rain as well. A storm of such breadth lashed away at them that the passengers saw neither sun nor moon for days. After more than a week the galley fire had been doused and the bread was soggy, but most of the bedraggled passengers had ceased to care about eating anyway. They had all but given up hope of being saved from the raging seas.

It was about this time that the oldest of the prisoners began to assume a greater role in the ship's destiny. Paul, says Luke, sternly reminded the captain and owner that they should have listened to him on Crete. But having said that, Paul began going around urging everyone to take heart. "There will be no loss of life among you, but only of the ship," he assured. "For this very night there stood by me an angel of the God to whom I belong and whom I worship, and he said, 'Do not be afraid, Paul, You must stand before Cæsar. And lo, God has granted this to you and all those who sail with you.' So take heart, men, for I have faith in God that it will be exactly as I have been told. But we shall have to run onto some island" [in order to be rescued].

The storm had now shown them nothing but high winds and gray skies for 14 days. They had been drifting in what they thought to be the widest, deepest part of the Mediterranean. But some of the sailors began to sense that they were approaching land, so they took out their remaining lead-weighted line and began taking soundings. One hundred twenty feet quickly became 90 — then less. Fearing they would smash into rocky shoals in the darkness, the crew quickly cast four anchors from the stern. Then they counted the hours and minutes to daylight as the waves beat against the stern.

At one point Paul noticed some sailors quietly lowering the longboat. As they started to creep aboard, they explained that they were about lay out anchors from the bow. But Paul was sure this was but a ruse for them to escape from the ship and imperil everyone else. Not only were the passengers seasick and weak, they would hardly know how to handle a ship in fair weather, much less a storm. Paul quickly sought out Julius. "Unless these men stay in the ship," he warned, "you cannot be saved." The centurion ordered them out of the boat; then he commanded his soldiers to cut away the ropes of the small boat and let it go.

As lighter skies signaled the coming of dawn, Paul was up and about, urging people to eat. "It will give you strength," he said, "since not a hair is to perish from the head of any of you." And as he urged them, he also took bread and offered thanks to God. And after they had all eaten, they further lightened the ship by throwing overboard all of the remaining wheat.

Daylight revealed a small bay not too far from where they'd anchored. Luckily, it also had a sand beach. The captain ordered the foresail raised. Then he had the anchors cast off in hopes of being able to run the ship up on the beach. But about halfway into the bay the ship ran into a shoal or reef and the bowsprit stuck fast in it. Water began to rush over the tilted bow. Surf waves crashed against the stern and its timbers began to break up. The soldiers dragged up the prisoners and drew their swords, preparing to kill them lest they escape. But Julius the centurion had come to see how important Paul was to their survival. He couldn't spare Paul and kill the rest, even if the escape of any of them meant his own death. Julius shouted at his men to sheath their swords. He ordered everyone on deck who could swim to jump overboard and make for the beach. When they were clear of the ship, he handed the others planks and pieces of the ship, then lowered them down so that they could float their way to shore.

The first gasping, salt-stained survivors to the beach found a crowd of local people had already gathered there in the rain and wind. Some islanders helped eke out their existence by selling shipwrecked survivors into slavery. But these natives, almost all simple fishermen, "showed us unusual kindness," wrote Luke, "for they kindled a fire and welcomed us all."

Paul and his shipmates quickly learned that they had drifted some 600 miles west from Crete. They had washed up on Melita (Malta), an island 50 miles south of Sicily and part of the province by that name. The reason why it was given the Greek name for "honey" was for the fine nectar that swarms of black bees made from the many herbs growing on its rocky slopes.

Paul made an impression on the islanders from his first moments on their soil. He had gathered a bundle of sticks and was putting them on the fire when a viper jumped out (probably from the sudden heat) and fastened itself on Paul's hand. The natives gasped, because their superstitions deemed it a sign that the stranger must be a murderer. Even though he had escaped death in the sea, the gods must have chosen the viper to exact their justice. But Paul simply shook the snake into the fire. And after not swelling up or falling down dead, as they swore he would, the people changed their minds and decided he must be a god himself.

As soon as he could, Julius the centurion marched his charges some six miles into the interior to the chief town, also named Melita. Although they were officially confined to some sort of government facility, Paul and his companions seem to have had considerable freedom (Julius may have reasoned that an island 18 miles long is enough protection against escape during winter). On one occasion during the mild winter, Luke reports that they spent three days as the guest of Publius, the island's chief magistrate.

"It happened that the father of Publius lay sick with fever and dysentery," Luke noted. "Paul visited him and prayed. And putting his hands on him, he healed him. And when this had taken place, the rest of the people on the island with diseases also came and were cured," says Luke, whose own medical skills must have helped as well.

During those quiet winter months, Paul would finally have had some moments alone to plan what he would say to the authorities in Rome and how he would go about contacting the Christian and Jewish communities. But what he would tell both Christian and Jew had not changed from what he had already said in the letter he had sent from Corinth two years before. The lengthy, powerful *Letter to the Romans*, which several first century churches copied and used in their services, embodied the length and breadth of his beliefs after nearly 30 years of proclaiming the gospel.

God, Paul had written the Romans, has always revealed himself to man through his external creations and wonders. An upright life can come only through reconciliation with God. But that reconciliation had been made difficult in a world that had become brutal, treacherous and malicious. Those who made it so were without excuse,

> ...for although they knew God, they did not honor him as God or give thanks to him, but they became futile in their thinking and their senseless minds were darkened. Claiming to be wise, they became fools, and exchanged the glory of the immortal God for images resembling mortal men or animals or reptiles.
>
> Therefore, God gave them up in the lusts of their hearts to impurity, and to the dishonoring of their bodies among themselves, because they exchanged the truth about God for a lie and worshipped and served the creature rather than the Creator, who is blessed forever! Amen.[54]

The Jewish world was guilty in its own way, Paul wrote. It was obstinate, smug and impenitent, relying on observance of its special laws and condemning the rest of mankind as sinners — even when the accusers themselves were breaking the Law.

> What then? Are we Jews any better off? No, not at all, for I have already charged that all men, both Jews and Greeks, are under the power of sin...[55]

Thus, Jews and Greeks are both in dire need of righteousness and without the visible means of attaining it.

> But now the righteousness of God has been manifested apart from law, although the law and the prophets bear witness to it: the righteousness of God through faith in Jesus Christ for all who believe. For there is no distinction; since all have sinned and fall short of the glory of God, they are

justified by his grace as a gift, through the redemption which is in Christ Jesus, whom God has put forward as an expiation by his blood, to be received by faith. This was to show God's righteousness, because in his divine forbearance he had passed over former sins; it was to prove at the present time that he himself is righteous and that he justifies him who has faith in Jesus.[56]

It is only through our faith and God's grace that we become reconciled, Paul continued.

Since we are justified by faith, we have peace with God through our Lord Jesus Christ. Through him we have obtained access to this grace in which we stand, and we rejoice in our sufferings, knowing that suffering produces endurance, and endurance produces character, and character produces hope, and hope does not disappoint us, because God's love has been poured into our hearts through the Holy Spirit which has been given to us.[57]

Does this reconciliation mean that we can continue to live in sin?

By no means! How can we who died to sin still live in it? Do you not know that all of us who have been baptized into Christ Jesus were baptized into his death? We were buried therefore with him by baptism into death, so that as Christ was raised from the dead by the glory of the Father, we too might walk in newness of life.

For if we have been united with him in a death like his, we shall certainly be reunited with him in a resurrection like his. We know that our old self was crucified with him so that the sinful body might be destroyed, and we might no longer be enslaved to sin...

Let not sin therefore reign in your mortal bodies, to make you obey its passions. Do not yield your members to sin as instruments of wickedness, but yield yourselves to God as men who have been brought from death to life, and your members to God as instruments of righteousness. For sin

will have no dominion over you, since you are not under
law but under grace.[58]

If God is for us, who is against us? Paul asked the Romans in his letter. If
he gave up his own son for us all, will he not also give us all things with him?

No, in all these things we are more than conquerors through
him who loved us. For I am sure that neither death, nor life,
nor angels, nor principalities, nor things present, nor things
to come, nor powers, nor height, nor depth, nor anything
else in all creation, will be able to separate us from the love
of God in Christ Jesus our Lord.[59]

Within three months, Paul, Luke and Aristarchus had also established
a small Christian community in Melita. Now it was the first week of March
and the first southerly winds had made all of the stranded travelers eager
to go. Fortunately, another Alexandrian cargo ship had been wintering in
the same harbor. Its name was *The Twin Brothers* (meaning the gods Castor and Pollux), and their carved likeliness jutted from under the bowsprit.
The day before it set sail, the new Christians of Melita came down to the dock
with many gifts and "put on board whatever we needed," Luke reported.

Soon the winds had become favorable. After about 75 miles, *The Twin
Brothers* put in at the Greek-Silician city of Syracuse for three days. Another 75 miles further north, they called at Rhegium at the tip of the Italian boot.
From there more favorable southerly winds drove them 220 miles in two
days to the Bay of Naples. Since Puteoli was the port for all Alexandrian grain
ships, one can picture *The Twin Brothers* gliding slowly through the blue waters as it passed the ruins of Tiberius' villa atop Capri and approached the
promontory of Misenum where Agrippina breathed her last. One might even
imagine Seneca, sitting on the balcony of his villa at Neapolis, glimpsing *The
Twin Brothers* writing of his delight at watching the sun glisten off the
grain ships that sail in from Alexandria.

It must have been an equal delight for Paul to learn that there were Christians in Puteoli. As Julius busied himself housing his soldiers and charges,
Paul and his friends were given permission to stay in the homes of local Christians. During the week they remained in Puteoli, one of the two younger
men probably hastened to Rome with news of the apostle's arrival. Later,
as Julius and his party traveled north to Rome on the Appian Way, they were
still some 40 miles from the city at the Market of Appius when they were
hailed by a group of Christians. Walking out to greet Paul involved a two-

day journey, no less, for people who had to leave their jobs as servants and tradesmen. Then, when still 33 miles from Rome at a place called The Three Taverns, their ranks were swelled as another group of Christians greeted them. More came as they entered the outskirts of the city and walked by the towering tombs of patricians and generals that lined the ancient street.

Among those who met him, Paul must have been most gratified to greet a young man who had come all the way from Philippi in Macedonia. His name was Epaphroditus. Luke, you will recall, was an elder of the church in Philippi. When he had written home that Paul would soon sail from Cæsarea, the faithful churchmen in Philippi had resolved not only to send money for his needs, but also to assign him a volunteer who could serve as his go-between with the churches while in confinement. Epaphroditus, as he had lingered over the winter in a strange and bewildering city, must have wondered if the man he was supposed to meet had vanished into thin air. Now they were walking side by side trading the news of many months.

On that day, Paul must have even forgotten that he was a prisoner about to be tried for his life. As Luke reported, "He thanked God and took courage."

A.D. 62–63

THE EMPEROR OF ROME was now 25 and the unchallenged master of his realm. To be seen listening to the advice of a boyhood tutor or the chidings of an aging soldier was not only unseemly, but perhaps even subject to dangerous misinterpretation by foreign ambassadors or their kings. Yes, men like Seneca and Burrus kept a storehouse of administrative detail in their heads, and allowing them to conduct affairs did leave an artist with more time to refine his skills, but sometimes their mien was simply too heavy to tolerate.

In any event, Burrus was looking like death warmed over. For over a year the Prætorian prefect had complained of a lump in his throat and now he was barely able to force down food. Soon his tumor got the best of him, but Nero may have had a hand in it. Tacitus says that the emperor brought his own doctor to Burrus' bedside and insisted that his throat be painted with a wondrous new balm, which was, of course, a poison.

Memories of Sejanus were revived in the person of Ofonius Tigellinus, who succeeded Burrus as prefect of the Prætorian Guard. Tigellinus got the promotion because he was both a companion in Nero's youthful debaucheries and because he pandered to the emperor's every whim. "I have no divided allegiance like Burrus," he would assure the emperor often. "My only thought is your safety."

Seneca, without the careful delineation of power that he had honed with Burrus over several years, soon found the ship of state being rowed to confusing cadences. Lest the lesson of Burrus be lost on him, word soon spread that the emperor's Guardsmen had murdered the financial secretary, Pallas, not long after retiring to his country estates. The only explanation: imperial finances were deteriorating rapidly and the old man's 400 million sesterces were simply too irresistible.

Pallas' wealth was probably matched by that of Seneca. Moreover, the latter had been under constant attack, both by envious patricians (his gardens were said to outdo the emperor's for splendor) and by debtors who were squeezed by his steep interest rates. There was also constant carping about how the learned tutor slurred his pompous protégé behind his back. "He openly disparages the emperor's amusements, underestimates him as a charioteer and makes fun of his singing," they would hiss. Or, one might hear: "How long must merit at Rome wait to be conferred by Seneca's word alone? Nero is a boy no longer and ought to discharge his tutor!"

By this time Seneca was not spending much time in Nero's company anyway. One day he requested an audience during the emperor's morning reception. It was quickly granted. As dozens of courtiers strained to hear, Seneca approached the throne and begged his master to release him after 14 years of service so that he could return to a quiet, simpler life of repose and study. He expressed gratitude for all the riches and estates showered on him by the emperor, but pleaded that he was too old to bear the burden of maintaining them. If only the emperor would take them back — minus a sumptuous villa or three — he, Seneca would consider his life fulfilled to be able to return to the pursuit of simple Stoic virtues.

The emperor appeared to be surprised at the request. "My first debt to you is that I am able to make an impromptu reply to your premeditated speech," he said. "For it was you who taught me to improvise as well as to make prepared orations.

"If my life had been warlike, you, too, would have fought for me. But instead you gave what our situation demanded — wisdom, advice, philosophy — to support me as a boy and youth. Your gifts to me will endure as long as life itself. My gifts to you may seem expensive, but many people far less deserving than you have had more. I omit, from shame, to mention certain ex-slaves who flaunt greater wealth. I am even ashamed that you, my dearest friend, are not the richest of all men."

It seemed at first that Nero was not about to let Seneca go. "My reign is only beginning," he said at one point, and "you are still vigorous and fit for state affairs and their rewards." Besides, he said, "If you return my gifts and desert your emperor, it is not your unpretentiousness and desire for retirement that will be on everyone's lips, but *my* meanness and *your* dread of my brutality."

But all these well-rehearsed, flowery protestations were apparently for the court's consumption. Having said them, Nero sighed theatrically and assumed a sad pose. "Well then, my old friend, if youth's slippery paths lead me astray, be at hand to call me back!" Then he embraced and kissed Seneca. The tutor expressed his gratitude and departed.

Seneca soon resigned himself to losing the argument about giving up the excess trappings of wealth. But as soon as he could he ceased holding receptions, dismissed his entourage and retreated to his country villas to devote the rest of his life to writing and studying. Invitations to visit Rome were met with regrets that his health would not permit it. The real reason was that Seneca had witnessed what had befallen others who had been in the effusive public embrace of the emperor. Now he, too, knew the constant wariness that comes with the knowledge that excessive flattery was often followed by treachery.

The time that Nero had once spent with men like Burrus, Pallas and Seneca was now filled by the omnipresence of Tigellinus. Thus, it should be no surprise that in no more time that it had taken Sejanus to inflame the fears of Tiberius, Tigellinus was soon whispering to Nero about this and that threat to his safety. And the more Rome's financial condition deteriorated, the more ways were found to condemn wealthy nobles so that their estates could be consumed in the furnace of Nero's greed.

Perhaps the most prominent of these purges involved Rubellius Plantus. Two years earlier, this mild-mannered, politically inactive patrician was ordered to take his family and live in the province of Asia on the western Ægean. The reason was that he was a distant offspring of Augustus and might be a possible rallying point for Nero's opponents.

But distance wasn't enough for Tigellinus. Soon he fomented rumors that Asia was already proclaiming Plautus emperor. Why, Plautus had even gone to Corbulo in Syria and the governor's mighty armies would soon be marching on Rome to claim the throne.

In the midst of all this rubbish — or because of it — Tigellinus dispatched a cohort of Guardsmen to Asia. Plautus, although warned by friends and urged to take up arms, chose instead to continue his unadorned life uninterrupted.When the squad of killers arrived at his home, they found him stripped for exercise. And there he was slain as he was. When the victim's head was brought to Nero, the emperor looked it over and said to himself: "Nero, how could such a long-nosed man have frightened you?"

The last vestige of Nero's former life was now the girl he had married at age 16. Octavia, quiet and shy, certainly had no powerful defenders — only that the daughter of Claudius led a chaste life and was adored by the public. Nero's escape route consisted of writing a letter to the Senate, which had just dutifully expressed great joy at his having managed to escape from the Plautus menace in Asia. In a rambling discourse about his solicitude for the national interests, he deemed it important to have an heir. Alas, his wife was barren. Hence, unless the conscript fathers disapproved, he was planning to divorce her.

Well of course they didn't disapprove. But just as word got out on the streets that Octavia was divorced and on her way to Campania under military guard, not an hour passed before statues of the emperor were toppling all over town to protest the fate of their beloved Octavia. In another few hours an angry mob had overwhelmed guards at the palace and invaded the living quarters, knocking over more statues and destroying drapes and furniture. Only after reinforcements were rushed in from the Prætorian barracks was the crowd driven back outside with clubs and swords.

Nero was so shocked at the display that he sent word that he would remarry Octavia if that is what would please Rome. With that the protesters overturned Poppæa's statues and carried Octavia's about on their shoulders, setting them about in various temples and forums. Even the emperor was acclaimed again.

But not by Poppæa. The empress-in-waiting was as furious at Nero as with the display of mass violence. She chose to convince him with tears, however. Falling at his feet, she cried: "Now that things have reached this sorry state, it is not marriage I'm fighting for, but my life. It's in danger every day from Octavia's dependents and slaves! They pretend to be the people of Rome! They commit outrages in peacetime that could hardly happen even in war! Their real target is the emperor — and all they lack at this point is a leader. If these disorders continue, one will surely be found. Octavia may be in Campania, but even her distant nod causes riots!

"What have I done wrong?" wailed Poppæa. "Whom have I injured? Is all this because I am going to give an authentic heir to the house of the Cæsars? Would Rome prefer an Egyptian flute-player's child? If you think it best, take back your empress voluntarily — don't be *coerced* into doing so. Otherwise, protect yourself! Punish severely. Because once the mob loses hope of keeping Nero through Octavia, it will find her another husband."

Torn between Poppæa's entreaties and his fear of the mob, Nero thought he could pacify both if only there were better *reasons* for disowning Octavia. The emperor found his mind wandering back to Misenum and Anicetus, the inventive fleet commander who had seen to his mother's unfortunate mishap.

This time no violence would be needed, no collapsing boat, no swords. All Anicetus would have to do is confess adultery with Octavia. Great rewards would be his — and an agreed-upon place of retirement free of all worries.

The alternative, of course, would be death.

Before long, Anicetus appeared before a "council of state," which had been assembled from among various senators and friends of Nero. There, Anicetus made a brief, dramatic confession of a scandalous affair with Octavia, then slipped away to a new villa in Sardinia (where it's said he lived out a long and serene life). Nero published an edict reporting to the people that Octavia had tried to win over the fleet by seducing its commander. For this she had been confined on the island of Pandateria.

No one could stop Nero, but no exiled woman ever received more sympathy or prayers from the Roman people. They had lamented the banishment of the elder Agrippina by Tiberius and that of Julia Livilla by Claudius, but both had been mature women with at least some happy memories to look back on. Octavia was barely 20. She had seen her father and brother poisoned. No sooner had she been married than she had been discarded by her husband, first for a slave, then for a scheming shrew who strutted about the palace and bathed in mule's milk.

Octavia had been on her island no more than a few days when the dreaded order came for her to die. She protested that she was no longer Nero's wife, but his sister. She asked for Nero's mercy. The response was to have her bound tightly, then open her veins.

However, her terror retarded the flow of blood and made the messy process take too long for the soldiers. So Octavia was carried into a hot vapor bath where, after a few minutes she suffocated. Then her head was cut off and taken to Rome for Poppæa to inspect.

Poppæa and Nero were soon married, and less than a year later there were wild cheers to the announcement that she had borne the emperor a daughter. Rome erupted in maudlin celebration. Mother and daughter were given the name Augusta. Thanksgivings were offered to the gods. A new Temple of Fertility was commissioned. Golden statues of the Two Fortunes of Antium (Nero's birthplace) were to be placed on the throne of Capitoline Jupiter.

In less than four months the baby was dead. Now came yet more inventive forms of sycophancy. The infant was declared a goddess and voted a shrine and a place on the gods' ceremonial couch.

Both events, however, had helped dim the public memory of Octavia. But just about this time she came creeping back into Rome's collective conscience.

Someone — a very skilled writer — had authored a play entitled *Octavia*. And now secret copies were making their way around Rome's finest homes.

The writer obviously knew the characters intimately. What made reading the play so deliciously dangerous was knowing that the author was surely aware that to be identified meant certain death, for every word in it rang out with loathsome rebuke to Nero and Poppæa. In one scene, for example, the emperor has just ordered a Prætorian Guardsman to bring him the decapitated head of Plautus. His tutor, Seneca, begs him one last time to temper his greed and violence for the good of mankind.

Guard:	It shall be done without delay. I'll to the camp myself.
Seneca:	Is that just treatment for one so near to you?
Nero:	Let him be just who has no need to fear.
Seneca:	The best antidote to fear is clemency.
Nero:	A king's best work is to put enemies down.
Seneca:	Good fathers of the state preserve their sons.
Nero:	Soft-hearted graybeards should be teaching children.
Seneca:	Headstrong young men should be sent to school.
Nero:	Young men are old enough to know their minds.
Seneca:	May yours ever be pleasing to the gods.
Nero:	I, who make gods, would be a fool to fear them.
Seneca:	The more your power, the greater your fear should be.
Nero:	I, thanks to Fortune, may do anything.
Seneca:	Fortune is fickle. Never trust her favors.
Nero:	A man's a fool who does not know his strength.
Seneca:	Justice, not strength, is what a good man knows.
Nero:	Men spurn humility.
Seneca:	They stamp on tyrants.
Nero:	Steel is the emperor's guard.
Seneca:	Trust is better.[60]

The more a Roman pored over *Octavia*, the more he would have to conclude that only one man could have written it. And only one man would have had the courage to risk his life for the chance to warn the emperor one last time where he was headed.

It was Seneca himself.

In Syria the long burden of supporting the Roman governmental and military machinery began to prove too much for the farmers and tradesmen who staggered beneath it. Adding to the continuing draught conditions and high taxes was the fact that the long-threatened military confrontation between Rome and Parthia finally erupted — not once, but twice in these two years. And yes, the object of all this squandering of resources was the very same bleak, mountainous land of Armenia that lay northeast of the Syrian border.

In A.D. 60 Corbulo, the governor-general of Syria, had escorted a Romanized Cappadocian émigré prince to the Euphrates River and sent him off in his bid to become Nero's client king in Armenia. But this proved a greater insult than could be endured by the Parthian king Vologeses I. When the two forces reached a standoff in Armenia, Nero's advisors decided to teach the Parthians a lesson by sending another general, Pætus, eastward with yet another excursion requiring, of course, men and provisions from the fragile Syrian-Judean economy.

But Pætus proved to have more ambition than common sense. In his haste to assail the Armenian capital of Tigranocerta, he outran his food supplies, had to dig out a makeshift winter camp far from his military objective and nearly froze his men to death in one of the coldest winters the region had ever seen. Only by the clemency of Vologeses (who actually had another rebellion to put down on his eastern border) were the desperate, hungry Romans allowed to break camp and stagger back through Syria.

The emperor and his men had seen enough of Pætus, and their angry response was to vest Corbulo himself with the sweeping military powers the Senate had granted Pompey a hundred years before when he subdued the very eastern provinces they were now defending. Syrian-based legions had long been known for their ease of life, for dodging guard duty and letting their armor rust. Corbulo had made his reputation in Germany with a no-nonsense, spit-and-polish dictatorship, and now he superimposed it on the Syrian legions with endless drilling and marching. As for provisions, Corbulo redoubled his efforts to collect enough wheat, corn and dried meat from the villages of Palestine to assure troops would never again have to worry about starving in their camps.

As spring approached, the Parthian Vologeses was grooming his troops for an ambitious two-front attack — one in Armenia and the other a march west across the Euphrates River and straight into the Syrian heartland of Judea. But he changed his mind when spies returned with reports that the Romans had reached an awesome state of readiness. First, they had erected fortified towers all along the Euphrates crossing points so that invaders could expect a hailstorm of darts from archers and boulders from catapults. Secondly, small Roman detachments had darted out on the military roads that would carry the Parthians westward and filled all their water oases with sand.

So instead of an invasion, Vologeses decided he would rather continue being Rome's client king, especially because it would, as ever, be in name only. In an elaborate ceremony arranged on the site of Pætus' unlucky winter camp, Corbulo agreed that Vologeses' brother Tiridates would become king of Armenia. In exchange, Tiridates knelt before a statue of Nero in a makeshift rostrum (supplied by no less than the Jewish King Herod Agrippa II) and promised to travel to Rome shortly to perform the same homage.

The position of the Jewish temple leadership in Jerusalem was no less stressful than that of Syrian farmers and merchants. The primary mission of the high priest was to preserve the temple as a worldwide center of Jewish worship — one that would be open and ready to accept the constant influx of pilgrims as well as delegations bringing the annual temple taxes that had been collected from hundreds of village synagogues throughout the Roman and Parthian empires. It also meant conveying the illusion of political solidarity with Rome all while keeping the temple treasury safe from the rapacious appetites of Roman generals and administrators. All this was difficult indeed for a people who were not officially a nation and had no military defense of their own.

The above explains why, in these years, the fragile détente between the Jewish Christians and the temple authorities began to fray. Paul's arrest in the temple and his "escape" to Rome had certainly put his sponsors, the Jerusalem Christians, under hostile scrutiny. Now two things happened that the Christians could not withstand. First, Festus died unexpectedly, leaving Judea temporarily without a procurator. Then Herod Agrippa saw fit to depose the high priest. His successor was Ananus, whose father had held the same position when Jesus was tried and crucified. But whereas the father was known as a "fortunate man" who had served long "with dignity," the son was described (by Josephus) as "a bold man in his temper and very rigid." Unlike the Pharisees, who were known as rather gentle judges, Ananus was, the historian Josephus adds, "also of a sect of the Sadducees who are very rigid in judging offenders."

In his first few days in office Ananus decided it was time to confront — and even eliminate if necessary — the leader of the Jerusalem Christians. That this man was James the Just, the brother of Jesus, was both ironic and ignorant on his part, for it would be difficult to find a more pious Jew. As Josephus described him,

He drank no wine or intoxicating liquor and ate no animal food. No razor came near his head. He did not smear himself with oil and took no baths. He alone was permitted to enter the Holy Place, for his garments were not of wool but of linen. He used to enter the Sanctuary alone, and was often found on his knees beseeching forgiveness for the people, so that his knees grew hard like a camel's from his continually bending them in worship of God and beseeching forgiveness for the people. Because of his unsurpassable righteousness he was called the Righteous...and "Bulwark of the People"...[61]

If the temple authorities were looking for evidence of James' sedition, it could not be found in his preachings or writings. Indeed, because James did not travel to the Jewish Christian churches as Paul did among the Gentiles, one of his sermons was transcribed around this time and circulated widely among them. His writings on living the proper Christian life drew deeply from prophets, psalms and proverbs of ancient Jewry. Would any devout Pharisee quarrel with the following?

Cleanse your hands, you sinners, and purify your hearts, you double-minded. Be afflicted and mourn and weep. Let your laughter be turned to sorrow and your joy to gloom. Humble yourself before God and he will exalt you.[62]

Or might the prophet Jeremiah have said these words?

Come now, you rich; weep and wail at the miseries which are coming upon you. Your wealth is rotten and your garments are food for moths. Your gold and silver are corroded clean through with rust; and their rust is proof of how worthless they are. It is a rust which will eat into your very flesh like fire.[63]

If he had inquired, the high priest Ananus would even have learned that James believed more in the traditional Jewish definition of salvation than did Paul. Whereas Paul preached that salvation was available to all through God's grace if they but believed, James preached:

What does it profit, my brethren, if a man says he has faith but has not works? Can his faith save him? If a brother or sister is ill-clad and in lack of daily food, and one of you says to them, "Go in peace! Be warmed and filled!" without giving them the things needed for the body, what does it profit? So, faith by itself, if it has no works, is dead.

But someone may well say, "Have you faith?" My answer is, "I have works. Show me your faith apart from your works, and I will show you my faith by means of my works." You say that you believe that there is one God; you do well. Even the demons also believe — and shudder. Do you want to be shown, you foolish fellow, that faith without works is barren? Was not Abraham our father justified by works when he offered his son Isaac upon the altar? You see that faith was active along with his works, and faith was completed by works, and the scripture was fulfilled which says, "Abraham believed in God, and it was reckoned to him as righteousness, for he was called the friend of God." You see that a man is justified by works and not by faith alone.[64]

In fairness to James and Paul, their views on salvation didn't contrast as sharply as the above would seem to indicate. When Paul preached that salvation was an unearned gift of God, he said often that if a person sheds his slavery to sin though God' grace, his subsequent acts and deeds can do no other but to reflect his new devotion to Jesus.

For we are his workmanship, created in Christ Jesus for good works, which God prepared beforehand, that we should walk in them.[65]

Either view, however, would probably not have assuaged Ananus. What made the new high priest foment was the repeated references in James' sermons to the end of the world and the day of judgment.

Make firm your hearts for the coming of the Lord is at hand. Brothers, do not complain against each other, that you may not be judged. Behold, the judge stands at the door![66]

Just who was this "judge at the door?" As always, the message led to Jesus, and that is what Ananus found so intolerable. And he had any number of reasons for acting at this time. Putting up with an unpredictable splinter sect was a luxury at a time when the Parthians might come thundering down on the temple at any time. But of even more immediate concern was that Passover was again approaching. More Jewish Christians than ever would be pouring into Jerusalem and one heard talk of organized pro-Jesus demonstrations.

Now James himself was hardly a brigand or renegade, but sometimes movements grow beyond the ability of their leaders to control them. This was on the mind of Ananus when he summoned the Sanhedrin into session at the beginning of the Passover festival. The decision was to invite James to an overtly friendly "consultation." When the Christian leader appeared before the council, Ananus told him in essence: "Many people have come to believe that Jesus was the Messiah and many have done so because of you. Would you, the brother of Jesus, be good enough to acquaint these people with the facts about Jesus so that they are disabused of this notion? We vouch that you are a righteous man and that everyone will accept what you say. So please mount the temple parapet, where you can be easily seen, where your words will be audible to all, and make it clear to the crowd that they must not go astray as regards Jesus."

Soon thereafter the elderly James found himself being half led, half pushed up the long stairs to one of the stone porticos that overlooked the teeming, pushing Passover throng in the courtyard below. When the criers had shouted for attention and the crowd quieted down, Ananus announced his purpose. Turning to James, he said: "Righteous one, whose word we are all obliged to accept, the people are going astray after Jesus, who was crucified. So, tell us, what is meant when you tell people about 'the door of Jesus'?'"

James took a deep breath and replied as loudly as he could: "Why do you question me about the Son of Man? I tell you, he is sitting in heaven at the right hand of the Great Power, and he will come on the clouds of heaven!"

These words generated a great uproar in the crowd below, and shouts of "Hosanna to the Son of David" went up. The elders realized that they had miscalculated, so they did what they had agreed on in such a case. Suddenly the crowd saw James being lifted up by several men and hurled to the stone pavement in the midst of their feet. Although he was elderly and frail, James did not die from the initial fall. He struggled to his knees as if trying to pray and said,

> "I beseech thee, Lord God and Father, forgive them for they
> know not what they are doing." While they pelted him with
> stones, one of the descendants of… the priestly family to

which Jeremiah the prophet bore witness, called out "Stop! What are you doing? The Righteous One is praying for you!" Then one of them, a fuller, took the club which he used to beat out the clothes, and brought it down on the head of the Righteous One. Such was his martyrdom...[67]

Ananus certainly hadn't acted with unanimous support. Many leading citizens were outraged. Herod Agrippa soon received letters protesting that the high priest had no such right. Another letter went by sea to Alexandria, where the new Roman procurator, Albinus, was preparing to make his way north to take up residence. Upon arriving in Cæsarea, Albinus sent off an angry letter saying that Ananus had no right either to convene the Sanhedrin or put men to death without his approval. The king, probably after consulting Albinus, withdrew the high priesthood from Ananus after he had been in office only three months.

Might Albinus have brought a higher ethical standard to the procuratorship? On the contrary, he helped sow the seeds of Jerusalem's destruction because he actually made private agreements among the leaders of robbers and of merchants who charged scandalous prices in a period of shortages. Thus, nothing was stolen or sold but what Albinus did not receive a portion of the proceeds. And when thieves were put in jail, their relatives could buy their way out for a price.

Now the procurator did, in a misguided effort, make attempts to snuff out the Sicarii. The daggermen were everywhere in Jerusalem during the Passover festival and many had been thrown in jail awaiting trial. But during the height of the festival, the Sicarii had also kidnapped Eleazer, chief scribe to the temple. They sent the high priest a message that they would return the scribe if he would persuade Albinus to free ten Sicarii who had already been arrested for murder. Albinus, who regularly received lavish gifts from the temple authorities, agreed to do so for, presumably, yet another payment. But the effect was calamitous, for the Sicarii now contrived to kidnap all the temple executives they could catch in hopes that the authorities would release even more of their confederates from jail. Soon, as Josephus reports, "as they had again become no small number; they grew bold and were a great affliction to the whole country."

Albinus' stay lasted only two years. When he learned that Gessius Florus was coming to succeed him, he sought to "settle accounts" as follows. He took all the imprisoned murderers and others whom he deemed serious offenders and had them all put to death at once. All those who remained in jail for robbery and lesser crimes he dismissed if they would pay him money. After a suitable interval, he simply emptied the prisons of all who remained — namely, the deranged and destitute.

Now we must add another dash of poison. Albinus' departure just happened to coincide with the completion of the temple construction, more than 80 years after Herod the Great began it. The celebrations were muted by the fact that 18,000 temple workers now had no wages. They might risk traveling 100 miles north to work on the new city of Neronia. Or if they were lucky they might be one of the relatively few chosen for a make-work project to begin paving parts of Jerusalem with white stone slabs.

But most were left to fend for themselves. They roamed the cities and countryside, joined by the aimless convicts Albinus had freed. All of southern Syria was rife with unemployment, hunger and crime. And whether one was a beggar or brigand might depend on what day it was.

IF JULIUS THE CENTURION needed any further proof that this Paul was a special person, it became evident enough when dozens of Christians turned out on the Appian Way to escort him into Rome. Indeed, the "prisoner" seemed to be celebrating a triumph rather than going to trial. Thus, when Julius turned over Paul to the governor of the Foreign Camp, located on the fringe of the Prætorian Guard grounds just outside the city's northeastern walls, it must have been accompanied by a glowing report of his conduct and a warm parting embrace. This explains why Paul was eventually given the right to live in his own rented apartment with only a single guard to remind anyone who cared that there dwelled therein a person under house arrest.

Only Paul's heritage and unswerving missionary habit would explain why, when still surrounded by Christian well-wishers, he would excuse himself so that he could call together the Jewish elders of Rome. There, still bound to his lone soldier by a single long chain, he asked them for an opportunity to explain his mission. "It is for this reason I have asked to see you and speak with you, since it is because of the hope of Israel that I am bound with this chain," Paul told them.

The elders must have seemed puzzled at first. "We have received no letter from Judea about you," they said, "and none of the brethren coming here has reported or spoken any evil about you. But we would like to hear what your views are, for we do know much about this sect, yet know that it is disparaged everywhere."

Paul, the prisoner, could not preach in the synagogue as he was accustomed. Rather, the elders did him the courtesy of calling "in great numbers" at his own lodgings.

There they listened literally all day long as Paul explained his life and why he was now a "slave" of Jesus, the risen Messiah.

Some of the elders were convinced, but as usual the great majority were not. And it was at that point that Paul despaired of further arguments and hurled a charge that had so often riled synagogue congregations. "The Holy Spirit," he said, "was right in saying to your fathers through Isaiah the prophet":

> Go to the people and say, You shall indeed hear but never understand, and you shall indeed see but never perceive. For this people's heart has grown dull, and their ears are heavy of hearing, and their eyes they have closed; lest they should perceive with their eyes and hear with their ears, and understand with their heart, and turn to me to heal them.[68]

Finally the elders rose to depart. But Paul could not resist one more statement that surely cut their bonds forever. "Let it be known to you then that this salvation of God has been sent to the Gentiles," he said. "They will listen."

It was as if he and Barnabas were again shaking the dust off their feet at the Jewish elders of Pisidian Antioch so many years ago.

If Paul had any further contact with the Jewish community after that, there is no record of it. There is abundant evidence that he taught Roman Gentile Christians while also keeping up a busy correspondence with the churches abroad. Paul's letters during his early months in Rome show every indication of a highly active — even exuberant — apostle. With him all the way from Jerusalem and the shipwreck were Luke and Timothy. Aristarchus and Tychicus, who had been at Paul's side during his arrest in Jerusalem before having to sail home, seem to have re-joined him in Rome as quickly as possible. Others who served the mission operating out of Paul's guarded apartment were Epaphroditus (his new assistant from Philippi), one Jesus (called Justus), Demas of Thessalonica, a runaway slave named Onesimus and Mark (the same cousin of Barnabas who had accompanied Paul on his first missionary trip in Cyprus).

Probably the first letter Paul dictated upon his arrival was to the church of Philippi that had so generously provided him with a rented apartment, a stipend and the services of Epaphroditus. That this freed him to preach was clear enough in his effusive letter to the Philippians. "I want you to know," he wrote,

that what has happened to me has really served to advance
the gospel, so that it has become known throughout the
whole Prætorian Guard and to all the rest that my imprisonment is for Christ. And most of the brethren have been made
confident in the Lord because of my imprisonment, and are
much more bold to speak the word of God without fear.[69]

Paul's message to the Philippians on living a Christian life was doubtless the same that he preached to the Romans who came to visit his apartment at this time.

...let your manner of life be worthy of the gospel of Christ so
that whether I come and see you or am absent, I may hear of
you that you stand firm in one spirit, with one mind striving
side by side for the faith of the gospel.

...Do nothing from selfishness or conceit, but in humility
count others better than yourselves. Let each of you look
not only to his own interests, but also to the interests of others. Have this mind among yourselves, which you have in
Christ Jesus, who, though he was in the form of God, did
not count equality with God a thing to be grasped, but emptied himself, taking the form of a servant, being born in the
likeness of men.

...Do all things without grumbling and questioning, that you
may be blameless and innocent, children of God without
blemish in the midst of a crooked and perverse generation,
among whom you shine as lights in the world, holding fast
the word of life, so that in the day of Christ I may be proud
that I did not run in vain or labor in vain. [70]

And despite his chains and years of false imprisonment, Paul showed
no rebelliousness at any government, nor did he urge his fellow Christians
in any such direction.

Let every person be subject to the governing authorities.
For there is no authority except from God, and those that
exist have been instituted by God. Therefore, he who resists
the authorities resists what God has appointed, and those

who resist will incur judgment. For rulers are not a terror to good conduct, but to bad. Would you have no fear of him who is in authority? Then do what is good and you will receive his approval, for he is God's servant for your good... [71]

Pay taxes that are due and honor to whom it is due, Paul continued. And observe the Ten Commandments. "Love does no wrong to a neighbor; therefore love is the fulfilling of all the law."

Paul was also kept busy mediating specific problems that arose among the Gentile churches abroad. For instance, The Christians of Colossæ, some 130 miles east of Ephesus, had sent their chief elder, Epaphras, all the way to Rome to seek Paul's counsel about a problem they faced. It is a special tribute to Paul to note that he had not even founded this Gentile church. Along with churches in Hierapolis and Laodicea that lay along the valley of the Lycus River, it had been founded by those who had first heard Paul in Ephesus.

What drove Epaphras across the Adriatic to see Paul was a religious dispute that had split the church at Colossæ. Some of its members were well educated Greeks who held the view that there was a vast gulf between God in his goodness and man, with his physical limitations. But by leading lives of self-denial, reflection and other virtues, man could, they believed, rise at last to complete fellowship with God. These people accepted the gospel because they saw Jesus as one of the intermediaries of higher learning who could help them on their journey to God's embrace. In time, these church members, with their fasts, vigils and holy days, began to deem themselves a higher class of Christians. They had also begun to lay down regulations as to food, drink and other aspects of daily living, so that one of their best-known slogans was "Touch not. Taste not. Handle not." What these people seemed to disdain most about Christianity was its very simplicity.

Paul's worst fear — and here it had tracked him down in Rome — was that the Gentile churches he had worked so hard to open to all classes and callings might be captured by a new sort of stifling, exacting, Pharisaic rule makers. And in his letter to the Colossians he rose to the challenge. Jesus, he wrote, was *not* one of several intermediaries to God, but the embodiment of God and all his wisdom. In Jesus, he said, *all* fullness dwells.

He is the image of the invisible God, begotten before all creation, because by him all things were created, in heaven and upon earth, the things which are visible and the things which are invisible, whether thrones or lordships or powers or authorities. All things were created through him and for him. He is before all things and in him all things cohere. He is the head of the body, that is, of the church. He is the beginning, the firstborn from the dead, that he might be supreme in all things. For in him, God in all his fullness was pleased to take up his abode, and through him to reconcile all things to himself, when he had made peace through the blood of the cross.[72]

The questions brought to Paul in Rome weren't always of cosmic consequences, but his answers sometimes were. Another case confronting the apostle involved one of his co-workers. Onesimus was a slave who had run away from his home in Laodicea. His master was a Christian named Philemon. Paul had become greatly attached to the youth and took a strong interest in his future. But he also knew that there could be no future or security for a runaway, so he convinced Onesimus to go back and start life anew.

But convincing Philemon was another matter. Even the most lenient of masters usually believed in the sternest of measures against a runaway lest others be tempted to do the same. Paul himself risked censure in appealing to Philemon. He wrote a carefully worded letter asking him to receive the young man kindly — not as a slave but as a brother Christian. If Onesimus had stolen anything from Philemon, Paul promised to make restitution himself. Paul makes it clear that he could — and would prefer to — retain the young man in Rome, for his present position as a prisoner and possible martyr for the faith has enhanced his authority in the eyes of believers. But he would rather have Onesimus voluntarily pardoned and sent back to Rome so he could continue to serve him in Philemon's place.

Finally, Paul further made sure that Philemon alone would not to be the sole judge of the matter. He addressed the letter to his wife and the church elders as well. He even referred to Onesimus warmly in his letter to the Colossians, whose church was only eleven miles east of Laodicea.

After several busy weeks in Rome, it was time to send out some of his closest workers with the letters to the Philippians, Colossians and Philemon (and the church of Laodicea) and another letter to the churches of Ephesus. Tychicus, Paul's fellow envoy to the Jewish Christians in Jerusalem, would take the slave Onesimus and go to Laodicea, then journey another eleven miles east to Colossæ. The letter to the churches of Philippi would be delivered, much to their surprise, by Epaphroditus, the same lad they had only recently sent to see to Paul's personal needs.

What happened is that Epaphroditus had fallen seriously ill during Paul's first weeks in Rome, probably a victim of one of its periodic flu epidemics. Although in danger of dying, he had managed to pull through, and now Paul thought it best that he be sent home to recover fully. At the same time, he wanted to spare Epaphroditus the awkwardness of being accosted on the streets of Philippi and asked why he wasn't at Paul's side. Thus, the apostle went on at great lengths to explain how hard the young man had worked for him — even risking his life in the process. "But God had mercy on him," Paul wrote, "and not only on him but on me, lest I have sorrow upon sorrow. I am the more eager to send him, therefore, that you may rejoice at seeing him again, and that I may be less anxious."

Paul resumes his good cheer in the closing, extending greetings from "all the saints" [Christians] in Rome — especially those of Cæsar's household."

The latter reference raises an intriguing question. In addition to ministering to the Christians of Rome, did Paul attempt to win over the leaders of Roman society? One can certainly assume that the centurion Julius and the other guards probably told all their fellow soldiers and tavern chums about their harrowing shipwreck on Malta and how the Christian prisoner from Cæsarea had bolstered their courage. But there is an important distinction here: this is not the same as Paul reaching out to show Roman nobles The Way.

Did he? Paul's confinement would have made it difficult. Great men did not enjoy being jostled in crowded, smelly streets just so they could sit in the cramped dwellings of the humble and learn at their feet. That's why they held morning receptions in their own perfumed atria. Nonetheless, it would be logical to assume that Paul tried. There is an exchange of letters supposedly between Paul and Seneca that are definitely of antiquity but disputed as to their authenticity. The 14 letters (actually more like memos or messages) show that the apostle contacted Seneca and that the emperor's "tutor" (more like his chief of staff) responded favorably. The shortcoming here is that the correspondence lacks substance — most of it merely reflecting Paul's attempts to arrange meetings with Seneca and the latter's thanks for Paul's having enclosed a book or a writing of some sort. The letters further fail to confirm whether any such meetings actually took place.

Still, the hypothesis is logical — even compelling. After all, did not Paul seize the chance to appear before everyone from the proconsuls Paulus in Cyprus and Gallio in Corinth to the procurator Festus and king Herod Agrippa in Cæsarea? Was he not unfailingly confident that he could somehow un-

lock the hardest of hearts with the gospel? Why did he see Rome as the culmination of his mission? Was it not as much to confront the highest imperial officials as it was to comfort Roman Christians? Such logic points to the
likelihood that in Seneca, Paul saw a sensitive and sympathetic philosopher,
a tutor who might read his works to a receptive young emperor, and a powerful official who might also help Paul secure a hearing before Nero himself rather than some obscure prætor in his stead.

The letters that purport to be from Seneca seem a curious mixture of polite encouragement and evasive procrastination. However, it is equally
likely that Paul's appeals for a dialogue came just as Seneca's star was descending. The Roman knew, perhaps unlike Paul, that the emperor had long
since shut out all formal tutoring and that a rising artist and charioteer had
scant time to hear an old man expound for hours on the immortality of a
Jewish prophet and his new sect.

And what of Paul's impending trial? The wait was agonizing. True, Roman
law prohibited any citizen from being held without trial for more than two
years. But the mechanism at the time for appealing such injustices was either deficient or dependent on the lubrication of bribes to make the gears of
justice turn. And Paul's case may well have been complicated by the shipwreck on Malta. One can imagine Luke or Timothy sitting on a hard bench
for two hours in the office of the secretariat for foreign affairs for the fif-
teenth time, only to be reminded by a sleepy bureaucrat that Paul's papers
had been lost at sea and that officials in Cæsarea had not yet supplied him
with copies. After all, Festus had died and the new procurator may have
had only rudimentary information about Paul's case.

As his confinement neared the two-year mark, Paul seems to have become resolved to enduring his fate, be it as a martyr for the faith or as an
acquitted missionary ready to launch a new chapter in his life as he embarked
on the road to Spain. In any event, Paul wrote the church at Philippi that
he hoped to have the courage "to honor Christ in my body," whether in life
or death.

> Yet which I shall choose I cannot tell, I am hard pressed be-
> tween the two. My desire is to depart and be with Christ, for
> that is far better. But to remain in the flesh is more necessary
> on your account. Convinced of this, I know that I shall re-
> main and continue with you all, for your progress and joy in
> the faith, so that in me you may have ample cause to glory
> in Christ Jesus because of my coming to you again.[73]

One wonders how Paul greeted the news that James the Just had been martyred in Jerusalem and the Jewish Christian church decimated. Had Paul's well-meant collection for the church been a mistake? Was he in some indirect way responsible? Would the church of Peter and James endure?

A.D. 64–65

SO GLORIOUSLY HAD NERO'S ARTISTRY bloomed — which his courtiers vied to verify — that it was really more than the rough-edged Latins of Rome were able to appreciate. No, only the ears of Greeks were so fine-tuned, so the emperor spent the spring of A.D. 64 in Neapolis and the other ethnic Greek cities on the Campanian coast singing and playing his lyre night after night before audiences that appeared truly enraptured (as stern guardsmen lined the rear aisles).

The more applause Nero heard, the more encouraged he was to dream more grandly. The emperor, still only 27 but now in the tenth year of his reign, began planning a Grand Tour of Greece. He would go to Olympia, Corinth and wherever its fabled Olympic Games were being held, and compete himself for their glorious prizes.

Back in Rome to lay plans for his departure, Nero amused himself in May and June with a series of feasts in public places. For example, at the artificial lake Augustus had built for naval games, the emperor would let the water in and out on successive days, depending on whether he was sponsoring a wild beast hunt, a sea fight or gladiatorial combat. Then the lake was flooded once more for a floating banquet. To bring this about, Tigellinus and his Prætorians floated dozens of great wooden casks, which were used by ships and taverns to store wine. On top of these they fastened planks. Over these were thrown purple rugs and soft cushions. Thus, while the floating platforms were pulled about by rowed vessels with gold and ivory fittings, Nero, Tigellinus and their royal party languished in the summer night as they gazed out from their barge on a torch-lit lakeside, rung with taverns and brothels. Cascading across were the sounds of singing and shouting. Naked prostitutes swayed and gestured from the shoreline. Revelers, as Tacitus reports, would

> ...enter the brothels and without hindrance have intercourse with any of the women who were seated there, among whom were the most beautiful and distinguished in the city, both slaves and free, courtesans and virgins and married women; and these were not merely of the common people, but also of the very noblest families, both girls and grown women. Every man had the privilege of enjoying whichever one he wished, as the women were not allowed to refuse anyone.

> Consequently, indiscriminate rabble as the throng was, they not only drank greedily but also wantoned riotously. And now a slave would debauch his mistress in the presence of his master, and now a gladiator would debauch a girl of noble family before the eyes of her father. The pushing and fighting and general uproar that took place, both on the part of those who were actually going in and on the part of those who were standing round outside, were disgraceful. Many men met their death in these encounters, and many women, too, some of the latter being suffocated and some being seized and carried off.[74]

Should anyone of the times doubt that Nero had become thoroughly degenerate, it would have become clear a few days later when the emperor went through a formal wedding ceremony with one of a gang of male perverts called Pythagoras. In the presence of witnesses, the emperor put on the bridal veil, gave a dowry, was married and performed in the nuptial bed with his new "mate" as the "wedding" party looked on.

Rome's revelries came to an abrupt halt in July. For on the nineteenth day of that month, the entire city was swept up in a fire that raged for six days and proved to be the worst in its history. The fire, they say, started in the Circus Maximus where it adjoins the Palatine and Cælian hills. It broke out in shops selling oil and other inflammable goods. Fanned by a high wind, the conflagration quickly swept the whole length of the Circus. After rampaging over level spaces, it quickly climbed the hills and whirled through the public shrines and homes of the wealthy. Then it returned below, devouring its way through the narrow winding streets of the Subura and surrounding neighborhoods where it seemed almost to be chasing the helpless people as they fled screaming in its path.

When it finally burned itself out (for it was beyond the ability of its residents to extinguish it) the fire had consumed all but four of Rome's 14 precincts. Three precincts were leveled to the ground. The calamity had no parallel since the destruction of Rome by the Gaul invasions, which had begun exactly on the same date 418 years before. Gone were most of Palatine Hill, the Theater of Taurus and most of the Circus Maximus. Tragically gone forever were many ancient temples and monuments dating back to the Gallic and Punic wars. But even these losses could not equal what was lost in so many homes of nobles: Greek artistic masterpieces, statues of ancestors and the authentic records of family genealogies.

The fire was so devastating that those who remained alive were said to worry more about whether the city itself would survive than about their own possessions. By the sixth day, some survivors were already camped out in temples and public monuments, where they clung to their few remaining possessions. Others hovered about the city walls or in surrounding fields.

So, who started it? Nero, of course, seems to be everyone's nominee, and circumstantial evidence would indicate that it certainly furthered his home-building ambitions. One reason why the state treasury reserves were disappearing so rapidly was that the emperor was in the process of building a massive new palace. To explain just how enormous it was to be, picture the valley of the Forum as roughly an ellipse stretching from east to west. Its temples and public buildings were situated in the western half, with the eastern part a jumble of warehouses, market buildings and the polygot neighborhood known as the Subura. Overlooking the Forum and Subura along the southern length of the ellipse was the Palatine Hill with its patrician palaces. Nero had been building a complex, called the Domus Transitoria, on the eastern part of Palatine Hill. If he could acquire and raze several hundred acres of the jumbled Subura — he may even have thought of it as slum clearance — Nero could then construct a vast estate in the center of the empire's largest city that would be much larger than the Forum itself.

Thus, in one version of the fire's beginning, Nero sent Prætorians in plain clothes all over the city one night lighting torches to homes and warehouses. People who ran from one neighborhood to help friends in other areas would have to scurry back because they learned their own homes were now burning. Soon there were reports that fire-fighting companies would not act unless paid outrageous fees. When the panicked home dwellers ran to the aqueducts with their own empty pails, they found only trickles and spurts of water because the homes of the rich had siphoned off so much of the flow. Then came the plundering of burning homes by soldiers and others who were supposedly sent to help.

And watching all this from a porch atop his palace on the Palatine — so the story goes — was the emperor himself. He was dressed in the Greek lyre player's garb and could be heard singing a song he had written himself entitled "The Capture of Troy."

The other version says that this is but fancy embroidery. Nero at the time was just returning to the city after visiting his seaside ancestral home of Antium (modern Anzio), some 25 miles to the southwest. He reached the walls just as the fire was beginning to engulf his still-unfinished Domus Transitoria on the Palatine. Yes, he strummed his lyre on his palace portico, as he helplessly and sadly watched the flames ravage the Palatine with the palaces of his Julio-Claudian ancestors.

Whatever the cause, the aftermath produced the only good or compassionate deeds of Nero's reign. He threw open the Field of Mars as well as his own gardens for relief of the homeless. Some were allowed to live in its public buildings and for others he built temporary accommodations. Food was brought from Ostia and the price of corn was slashed sharply. Nero then began clearing housing sites at his own expense before turning them over to their owners. His engineers directed that rubble be collected and heaved into empty corn ships returning down the Tiber and then dumped into the marshes around Ostia.

In truth, the fire caused some good because it prompted many meetings that led to improvements in city planning and regulations for better public safety. Streets were made broader and straighter. Heights of houses were limited and each was to be equipped with firefighting equipment. No two dwellings could have a common wall. Moreover, a fixed portion of every building had to be fireproof stone. Public aqueducts were posted with guards to prevent illegal tapping for private uses.

Still, Nero never escaped the gossip and derision of Romans that he had been directly responsible for the fire. The prominence and propriety given to the renewed construction of his new palace was a daily reminder. Some half-joked that it was so large it would probably stretch all the way to the ancient Etruscan city of Veii some twelve miles outside the city walls. Thus, this graffiti about town:

> All Rome's become one house. To Veii fly,
> Unless it stretch to Veii, bye and bye.

One could also read this on walls:

> While Nero sweetly struck his lyre
> Apollo strung his bow.
> Our prince is now the god of fire,
> The other god our foe.[75]

Many priestly supplications were made to various gods and oracles to ascertain the cause or the divine reason behind the fire. The Sibylline books were consulted and prayers addressed to Vulcan, Ceres, Juno and other gods. Ritual banquets and cleansing rites were held. But nothing seemed to dull the enmity people felt toward Nero. It was perhaps as long as a year after the fire that he tried to put an end to the persistent suspicions about his own motives. Then the emperor retaliated by revealing that the real cause of the fire had been the mysterious Christians. He even referred to them as a "deadly superstition."

Why Christians? Why not blame it on a group of Egyptian astrologers or a gang of unemployed actors or even saboteurs from some hostile foreign power? The best answer is why *not* Christians? They were a growing group and one that, like the Jews, remained apart from the rest of society. Their seemingly secret religious practices made ignorant outsiders uneasy and gave rise to rumors that they practiced cannibalism in some macabre ritual dictated by their founder that involved drinking blood and eating a body. This same foreign sect was hated in some families because it had pitted husband against wife, son against father and slave against master.

After the fire had subsided, many a Roman would swear he had heard a Christian leader predict a day in which the world would be dissolved by flames. And — worst of all for the Christians — what a strange coincidence it was that the fire had spared all of Trastevere, which lies west of the Tiber, and much of the Aventine Hill, which lies just across from it. How interesting that these were the very places that contained most of the Christian population! And how strange that when one walked these streets one could sense a marked indifference to the civil mourning that all other Romans were displaying at the loss of so many sacred temples and venerated shrines.

It isn't clear how many arrests were made at this time (for thousands more would be held and tried in the next two years). But it was enough at the time to make the emperor's point. When hunting games were given in the theater, it was thought clever to wrap Christians in hides and make them quarry along with the wild animals. It was also at this time that Christians and other condemned persons were first used to dramatize scenes in stage tragedies. Thus, real "actors" played Hercules being burned on a mount or Adonis being torn to pieces by wild boars or when Icarus being thrown down from the heavens.

The emperor himself seemed to enjoy being in the midst of it. The Circus Maximus was still too charred for public use, so Nero increasingly opened his own private circus and surrounding gardens that lay west of the Tiber some four miles from his palace on the Palatine. In both the circus and the gardens Nero reminded one and all who had started the fire. Christians were swabbed with pitch, fastened to poles, and made into human torches to help light the gardens at night or be displayed as exhibits in the circus. And in both cases, the emperor was often present, mingling with the crowd in the gardens or driving about the circus dressed as a charioteer.

But the spectacle soon sickened even the most hostile Roman. As Tacticus observed: "Despite their guilt as Christians and the ruthless punishment it deserved, the victims were pitied. For it was felt they were being sacrificed to one man's brutality rather than to the national interest."

With the capital of the empire nearly gutted and its emperor continuing to put his own rebuilding priorities above the common good, one can easily see why the Roman world was now ransacked for funds. It began in Rome itself, where temples were emptied of their treasuries and the gold that had been dedicated for triumphs and vows. Provinces were ruined — the privileged and poor alike. Not only were the treasuries of foreign temples scoured, but their statues taken as well. Yet, still unmolested was the enormously wealthy temple in Jerusalem.

Within Italy the frantic imperial search for money meant uncovering more suspected plots, which of course brought about more forced suicides and confiscations of estates. But the law itself became more onerous as well. Nero, for instance, caused the Senate to amend a statute that required one-half of a freedman's estate to go directly to the emperor. The amount now became five-sixths if the deceased bore the name of any family of which Nero was "connected" — a term that could be stretched to include almost any family. Yet it hardly mattered, for the same new law stipulated that in the case of a deceased who was "ungrateful" (did not bequeath the emperor five-sixths) his *entire* estate would go to the state treasury. There were penalties as well for any lawyer who had helped to write such a will.

Well, as with Caligula, it was only a matter of time before the collective disgust and exasperation that festered within the silent majority began to burst open. In the winter of A.D. 65 — some six months after the fire — a plot to dispose of Nero began to coalesce.

Within a few days the number of participants had swelled to over 50 — including nobles, Prætorians, possibly Seneca himself and even a poet bent on revenge for being forbidden to vie with Nero in competition. All were united by their hatred of the emperor and saw as a noble successor one Gaius Calpurnius Piso, a consul-designate from a venerable and illustrious family.

The only problem with a cabal of that size is that someone was bound to give it away. The deed was to be done as Nero inaugurated a day of games as part of the annual festival to the goddess Ceres. Plautius Lateranus, a large, athletic senator, was to approach the emperor in his box and kneel as if he were to begin a petition for help. As he lowered himself he would grab the emperor in a wrestling hold as others rushed in with concealed daggers to take off Nero, as the Romans would put it.

The day before the games began, a household servant of a senator named Flavius Scævinus thought it odd that his master was sharpening an ornamental dagger that had been a family heirloom for decades. The same day Scævinus asked him to prepare some bandages. After observing his master frowning in whispered conversations with visitors all day, the servant decided to head for Nero's palace to see if he could trade some suspicious information for a handsome reward.

Within three hours Scævinus was standing before Nero and Tigellinus, haughtily calling his turncoat servant a well-known rascal and liar. But then the slave suggested that one of the men in hushed conversation with the senator the previous day be brought in and questioned separately. When the two versions of the meeting failed to match, both senators were marched off to be tortured. The second senator opened up before Tigellinus' men laid a hand on him.

Within a day the Prætorian camp was full of conspirators in chains. Plautius Lateranus was hurried off to execution without even having a chance to bid his wife and children farewell. Piso opened his veins as he saw Prætorians approaching his home, but not before larding his will with repulsive flattery of Nero in hopes of earning his wife clemency. Meanwhile, Nero was wild with fear, not knowing how many were in on the plot. His personal guard was redoubled and all Rome was put in custody, with armed soldiers patrolling the city walls and public squares.

Soon Nero's fears reached beyond the conspirators to all possible suspects. Was his retired tutor Seneca a conspirator? It seems that Piso had once sent a messenger to Seneca asking for his support, but the emissary had returned with only a vague comment that he was too ill and wished Piso well. But no matter: it was time to free the emperor of those who shared memories of unhappy events (such as the murder of Agrippina).

One evening Seneca and his wife Pauline were dining with two guests at their villa some four miles from Rome when the property was suddenly surrounded by Prætorian troops. A nervous tribune appeared at the door and said that the emperor wanted to know if it was true that Seneca had wished the Pisan conspiracy well. Seneca replied evenly that he had refused to let Piso call on him "on grounds of health and love of quiet." He added that Nero of all people should know that Seneca always gave him "more frankness than servility."

The tribune departed, but in a few hours the troops were back on Seneca's doorstep again. The tribune had conferred with Nero and Poppæa and it was clear that no reply Seneca could have made would have sufficed. This time the tribune had a junior officer face the old man with the emperor's fateful orders.

Seneca's wife and guests began to weep. Seneca calmly asked if he could make some amendments to his will. He could not, said the officer. Then, would there be time to have his book collection removed to a safe place? "Not possible," said the soldier.

Seneca turned to the others behind him and said, "Being forbidden to show my gratitude for your friendship, I leave you my one remaining possession and my best: the pattern of my life. If you remember it, your devoted friendship will be rewarded by a reputation for virtuous accomplishments."

As Seneca's stricken guests looked on, the old scholar climbed into a warm bath, opened his veins and stoically bid them be of courage. Were they really unaware that Nero was cruel? After murdering his mother and brother, was it not only natural for him to kill his tutor as well? After playfully sprinkling some wine on his servants as his "libation to Jupiter," Seneca lost consciousness. He was finally carried to a steam room, where he suffocated to death.

Dozens more died in the aftermath. Annæus Junius Gallio (the same proconsul who had heard Paul's case in Corinth), was denounced as a public enemy simply because he was Seneca's brother. Perhaps the most irrational of all the charges came against Junius Torquatus, a distant descendant of Augustus. Because Torquatus had squandered his wealth foolishly, said Nero's prosecutor, it followed that he must be covetous of the goods of others. And if he was covetous, this must surely imperil the one who possessed the greatest wealth of all.

All went to their fates meekly except for one battle-toughened colonel who told the emperor he admitted his guilt and "gloried" in it. When pressed by Nero as to why he would violate his oath to protect the emperor, his exact words were these: "Because I detested you. I was as loyal as any of your soldiers as long as you deserved affection. I began detesting you when you murdered your mother and wife and became an actor, charioteer and arsonist!" Except for Seneca, perhaps, Nero had never been spoken to in this way, and the words were a shock to his ears.

As the next summer approached, Rome was still a junkyard of charred, skeletal buildings, stacks of bricks and roof tiles piled beside rebuilding sites, families making do in public parks full of makeshift tents and a nobility wracked by purges, taxes and corruption. On top of this, the fire had been followed by a full-blown plague that struck down people of all classes. No miasma was discernible in the air or water, yet houses were full of corpses, the streets clogged with never ending funeral processions and the skyline broken by spires of black smoke curling up from burning pyres.

But somehow the city managed to assume a festive mask for visitors as the second series of Neronian Games opened. Knowing that the emperor was now determined to appear on stage anywhere he chose, the Senate politely tried to avoid scandal by offering him, in advance, the first prize for song and a special crown for his "eloquence" (even though it wasn't an official category of competition). But Nero declared there was no need for favoritism. He would compete on equal terms and rely on the conscience of the judges to award him his just due.

First, he recited a poem on stage. But when the crowd shouted that he should display "all his accomplishments" (their exact words), Nero made a second appearance as a lyre player, throughout which he was the soul of propriety. So that he would not lose points from the judges, he used only his robe to wipe away perspiration while performing. He allowed no moisture from his mouth or nose to be visible. At the conclusion, he awaited the judges' verdict on bended knee and with a gesture of humility to the audience. As he knelt, the theater crowd cheered in measured, rhythmical cadences.

The emperor may have been a national disgrace to the Senate (and to visitors from foreign lands), but the Roman rabble seemed to love the show they were getting. Those who didn't follow the clapping rhythm in fashion were often cuffed by the Guardsmen who roamed the theater aisles.

It was not long after the Games that Nero's wife died. Poppæa was said to have prayed often that she might die before she passed her prime, and Nero accommodated her. Poppæa was pregnant, and it seems that one night her husband came home drunk and probably foul-tempered. Soon afterward he either kicked his wife in the stomach or jumped on it with enough force to kill her.

Now his disconsolation was overflowing. Rather than having Poppæa cremated in the Roman fashion, Nero had her body stuffed with spices and embalmed in the manner of foreign potentates. Then she was placed in the Mausoleum of Augustus where her widower could visit her.

Nero missed Poppæa so greatly after her death that upon learning of a woman who resembled her he sent for her and kept her among his concubines along with the one who looked like his late mother.

WHAT OF THE ROMAN CHRISTIANS at this time? Just how many were arrested after the fire and how many died in Nero's gardens? Did Christians continue to meet in their house churches? Did they continue coming to Paul? Did Paul comfort the flock and confront the authorities?

The information available today about these two years is sparse — and for quite logical reasons. The Great Fire was devastating beyond anything that great cities like Corinth or Antioch ever experienced in their long histories. Thousands died in the blaze itself and just as many perished in the plague that followed. Jails and dungeons were no less afflicted, and records of prisoners and trials went up in flames in equal proportion to sacred scrolls and family heirlooms. The fact that predominately Christian neighborhoods were among the least touched does not mean that some Christians did not suffer loss of life and property. Moreover, Christians were made to suffer an especially inhumane persecution directed only at them. But even those who escaped that hideous display now lived amidst a wave of treason trials and property confiscations. Everyone in Rome cowered under a cloud of suspicion as informers cupped their ears to even the most innocent of conversations in hopes it would yield them a percentage of some victim's estate.

Those who were snared in this madness were jailed and/or sent off as slaves to construct a 160-mile canal that would allow a delusional monarch to be rowed from Rome to Misenum rather than brought by carriage. Is it then any wonder that most Christians had either vanished in the chaos or wished to behave as though they had?

This climate may be why many Christians started frequenting the catacombs, that growing labyrinth of underground necropoli that were being bored through the travertine rock on the city's southern outskirts.

Yet, there was still another devastating turn of events for Christians at this time. Until the Great Fire, they were little understood by the authorities and simply regarded as a sect of Judaism. This meant that it was one of the *religiones licitæ* and thus to be officially tolerated. When Nero singled out Christians as the sole cause of the fire, Christians by fiat became *religiones illicitæ* — one of the few superstitions or cults banned by the state for its seditious or sinister practices. Officially, Christians were to be as loathed as, say, the Celtic Druids, with their witches and gory human sacrifices. Legally, it meant that Paul, for example, could no longer defend himself by proving that he had broken no Roman laws. Now, if an advocate could only prove that the defendant was a Christian, it would be sufficient to justify punishment.

There is no record of any official decree declaring Christianity *religione illicitæ* and ordering a formal persecution. But the stigma was nearly the same. If the governor of a province happened to despise Christians, he would have little trouble in depriving them of life and property, just as the police in a Roman precinct might be easily prevailed upon to arrest a Christian on some complaint of his neighbors.

Paul continued to exist amidst this peril and confusion. No writer of the time says that he perished in the fire or the plague that followed. Some say that he was acquitted of his charges — or was simply released after being confined for two years without trial — and went on to visit the churches in Asia or Achaia. Perhaps so, but the very tenacious oral tradition in Rome is that Paul remained there for all or most of the time following his first arrival from Malta.

This view would seem to be supported by a letter that Paul wrote to Timothy who had probably returned to his home in Lystra by then. For the first time in any of Paul's letters from Rome, this one is filled with the grim air of approaching finality. "At my first defense, no one took my part," he writes. "But the Lord stood by me and gave me the strength to proclaim the word fully, that all the Gentiles might hear it. So I was rescued from the lion's mouth."

But now the others had gone: Demas having forsaken him for "the present world" and gone back to Thessalonica, but others like Crescens, Titus and Tychicus because Paul himself sent them back to the churches on various missions. Only Luke remains with him. And now, he tells, Timothy,

> ...I am already on the point of being sacrificed. The time of my departure has come. I have fought the good fight. I have finished the race. I have kept the faith. Henceforth there is laid up for me a crown of righteousness, which the Lord, the righteous judge, will award to me on that Day — and not only to me but also to all who have loved his appearing.[76]

Paul devotes most of the letter to expressing his love for Timothy, whom he regards as a son, and to the need for holding steadfast to the mission being entrusted to him.

> You then, my son, be strong in the grace that is in Christ Jesus. And what you have heard from me before many witnesses, entrust to faithful men who will be able to teach others also. Take your share of suffering as a good soldier of Jesus Christ.[77]

Paul exhorts Timothy not to become entangled in "stupid, senseless controversies" over points of theology because "it will lead people into more and more ungodliness, and their talk will eat its way like gangrene." Finally, he urges Timothy to learn from the suffering that Paul himself endured during their times together in places like Antioch, Iconium and Lystra, "yet from which the Lord rescued me." Indeed, he adds,

> ...all who desire to live a godly life in Christ Jesus will be persecuted, while evil men and impostors will go on from bad to worse, deceivers and deceived. But as for you, continue in what you have learned and have firmly believed, knowing from whom you learned it and how from childhood you have been acquainted with the sacred writings which are able to instruct you for salvation through faith in Christ Jesus.

> ...I charge you in the presence of God and Christ Jesus who is to judge the living and the dead, and by his appearing and his kingdom: preach the word; be urgent in season and out of season. Convince, rebuke and exhort. Be unfailing in pa-

> tience and in teaching. For the time is coming when people
> will not endure sound teaching, but having itching ears
> they will accumulate for themselves teachers who suit their
> own likings, and will turn away from listening to the truth
> and wander into myths. As for you, always be steady. En-
> dure suffering. Do the work of an evangelist. Fulfill your
> ministry.[78]

Again, the tradition and the letter to Timothy indicate that Paul continued to live under custody in Rome during this two-year period. Had he been
condemned and in jail, conditions would have been so severe that having
access to a transcriber like Luke, or even his own writing instruments,
would be very unlikely. Rather, Paul's reference to having endured a "first
defense" may have been a preliminary hearing — perhaps a perfunctory proceeding so that the prætor's office could say that Paul's case had been
heard more or less within the two-year limit on holding an accused without trial. But the fact that the apostle was not acquitted is obvious from his
continued confinement in chains. And the likelihood that he did not expect
imminent resolution of his fate is indicated by the fact that he ends the letter by asking Timothy to come to Rome "soon" and bring him some books
and parchments he had left behind on this earlier travels.

No, Paul did not die in the first persecutions after the fire. To be dispatched so quickly was probably the lot of slaves and foreigners. Because Paul was a Roman citizen, and because his case was already lodged
somewhere in the bureaucracy, his life was prolonged by the confusion and
delay that followed the fire.

At some point during this time, the apostle Peter arrived in Rome. As pre-
viously asserted, he had probably visited the city earlier. But this time he
was resolved to stay and to stand by the Christians of Rome in their hour
of need. He would not deny Jesus this time, even if it cost him his life.

COMPARED TO THE NEW PROCURATOR of Judea, who arrived at the beginning of this period, the corrupt Albinus had been "a most excellent man,"
the Jews would joke ruefully. For while his predecessor had made his bar-
gains with thieves in private, Gessius Florus was as open as he was
pompous. "It was as though he had been sent as an executioner to punish
condemned malefactors," the historian Josephus wrote. "Nor could anyone
outdo him in disguising the truth, nor contrive more subtle ways of deceit."
Whereas Albinus had ruined individual men, Florus despoiled whole cities

and ruined entire toparchies to the extent that a great many Jews of prominence now fled their own country and took up residence in foreign lands.

During all this, Cestius Gallus, now the governor of Syria, never saw fit to send an embassy to investigate the claims of Florus' cruelty. In fact, when Cestius came down to the Passover in April of A.D. 65 and stayed in Herod's palace, an enormous throng flocked into the public square outside and implored the governor to grant them relief from the miseries brought on by Florus. But as the two Romans stood side by side on the portico above the street, Florus could be seen laughing as Cestius pointed out something in the crowd as if enjoying a private joke. When Cestius finally quieted the throng below, he assured them jovially that he would see to it that Florus treated them "in a more gentle manner." The next day he set off for Antioch.

Everyone assumed that Florus would mend many of his ways for fear that a delegation would be sent to Cæsar accusing him. But Florus must have reasoned in a different way. If he could incite a rebellion among the Jews and bring in Roman troops to smother it, his own evil deeds would be overlooked in the process.

Yet another episode in Cæsarea can serve to illustrate how Florus' mind worked. At about the time he came to take up residence there, the city's Hellenistic population had at long last gotten the upper hand over their Jewish neighbors. They accomplished this, not by battle, but simply by successfully petitioning the emperor to be allowed to take over control of the municipal government.

The two contentious cultures of Cæsarea were ready for any spark that would set their passions ablaze again. The kindling was one of the major synagogues in town, which happened to adjoin an empty plot owned by a Greek. The Jewish congregation was already crowded and wanted to expand their facilities. They had already offered the landowner many times the property's fair value, but he, in what could only be a deliberate affront to the Jews, began erecting some stores and workshops on the land. As the walls began to go up, it was obvious that the Greek owner had designed them in a way that could only be interpreted as an affront to this neighbors. The walls left such a narrow passage — or what was more an alleyway — between the shops and the synagogue that the Jews arriving on the Sabbath would scarcely be able elbow their way to and from the synagogue's main entrance.

In a few days a group of incensed young Jews served notice they were going to tear down the project. But when Florus got wind of it and threatened them against using force, the synagogue elders stepped in to avoid trouble. With an offer of eight talents, they persuaded the procurator to halt the work. But Florus, once accepting the money, left for a trip to Sebaste, which was about eight miles away. He hadn't "stopped" the project, he said. He merely meant that the Jews were free to try whatever solution they wanted while he was gone.

On the next Sabbath as the first of the Jewish worshipers wound through the ugly, narrow passageway that now constituted the only path to their synagogue, they encountered a Greek Cæsarean on the portico outside the main door. The Greek was hunched over an earthen pot that he had placed upside down before the doorway. On this makeshift "altar" he was butchering a small bird. The Jews quickly recognized this as the sacrificial rite for cleansing a leper — meaning by this sign that the Jews were a leprous people and should be quarantined.

As usual, the young men among the Jews wanted to tear the Hellene to shreds as well as any other Greek who showed his face. The older men struggled to restrain them. Meanwhile, the Greek prankster had several friends hiding nearby, waiting for the Jews to strike the first blow. Hearing angry shouts and not being able to see what was happening to their friend, the gang of young Greeks burst out of hiding and once again, clubs and fists were flailing in all directions. When a small group of Roman soldiers tried to break up the melee, they were simply swallowed up in it.

When the Jewish elders realized that the melee was beginning to threaten the synagogue itself, they grabbed the Torah and other sacred books from the Ark inside and fled to the outskirts of the city. After sequestering the books in another building not far from Sebaste, they continued on to that city in a desperate search for Florus. Finally locating him as the guest in the home of a prominent citizen, the Jews found themselves in the company of a man not at all happy to be aroused from his leisure. However, the desperate elders pressed their case. Couldn't his excellency do something to punish the mischievous Greeks for polluting their meetinghouse? Especially in light of the eight talents they had already given him?

But Florus responded only with more cruel contempt. He cut off the pleas of the elders and ordered them arrested on charges of violating Roman law by taking the sacred books out of Cæsarea without official permission.

Such was the justice of Florus. Later, as he turned his attentions to a far greater source of ill gain — the temple treasury in Jerusalem — he would touch off an uprising that did not stop until the entire Jewish nation had spent its people and wealth in a frenzied, suicidal struggle to disgorge the Roman oppressor.

A.D. 66-67

AS THE YEAR BEGAN, the emperor would remark that he, at long last, was beginning to feel as though he were being "housed as a human being." His new palace, now called The Golden House, had, by having first priority on all men and materials during the post-fire restoration, reached a state of completion sufficient to accommodate the imperial court.

It was never to be fully furnished during his lifetime, but Nero could already claim that it was the largest dwelling ever built. Nor did any "home" ever occupy so much land within a large city. At long last the Domus Transitorium (the palace on the Palatine that Nero had been building before the fire) and the new structure begun after the fire were now connected as a contiguous property that replaced hundreds of common dwellings and dominated the world's greatest city.

Within the more than 300 acres that Nero had seized out of the fire-ravaged north and central section of the city were grounds containing an artificial lake sculpted in the shape of the Mediterranean graced with clusters of miniature buildings representing the major port cities along the great sea.

Situated about this centerpiece was a mixture of woods, tilled fields, pastures and vineyards, through which roamed both wild and domestic animals.

Also roaming through this tract was the Golden House itself with its long winding colonnades. One entered a vestibule high enough to contain a colossal statue of the emperor 120 feet high. In the rest of the house, all surfaces were overlain with gold and adorned with jewels and mother-of-pearl. Some dining rooms had ceilings of ivory whose individual panels could be opened so that pipes could send out sprays of perfume or showers of flower petals on the guests below. The main banquet hall was circular and constantly revolved day and night like the heavens. The combined effect of gold, ivory and marble gave a sunny glow, which accounts for the name, "Golden House." But the name was also chosen by Nero to symbolize the introduction of a new golden era for Rome, led by an emperor more splendid than any who had gone before him.

Fortunately, Rome now had at least one showplace at a time when the streets were otherwise a jumble of piled up roof tiles and half-restored temples. This was important, because the imperial court had already known for a few months that the Parthian Tiridates, younger brother of King Vologeses, was headed for Rome with a royal entourage to pay Nero the obeisance that conditioned his return to the throne of Armenia. Could the capital of the civilized world expect to provide anything less than a splendorous reception to the brother of its second most powerful monarch?

Indeed, when Tiridates finally showed in Rome, it was with 3,000 horsemen and an entourage that seemed to contain most of Parthia's royalty and possessions. Even as dawn broke the Forum was already so crowded that one could not even see the rooftops for the people sitting on them. When Tiridates climbed the rostrum to do obeisance to the emperor, sitting in his chair of state and wearing triumphal dress, such a great roar went up that the Parthian actually jumped back in fright. But he quickly recovered and said what all Rome wanted to hear: "I have come to thee, my god, to worship thee as I do Mithras. The destiny thou spinnest for me shall be mine, for thou art my fortune and my fate."

In exchange for his brief inconvenience, Tiridates was presented with the diadem of Armenia. He also got permission to rebuild its war-torn capital of Artaxata, a "loan" of many Roman artisans to help him do so and gifts worth some 200 million sesterces.

Nero gained one thing that was dearest to him: peace of mind that his greatest rival wouldn't menace Syria and other eastern border states while he took time off to tour Greece and establish himself as the greatest artist and athlete in all history. From that point on, the emperor's activities were focused on two tasks: outfitting a suitably impressive cavalcade and assuring that absolutely no threats to the throne remained in Italy while he was gone.

The train of wagons that lumbered from Rome in September A.D. 66 might have been enough to conquer Greece again had they been military. Instead they carried lyres and plectra, masks and buskins. Once away from Rome, Nero dressed more as he thought a Greek and a performing artist should be seen. He let his hair grow long and hang down his neck, but in front his blond hair was arranged in tiers of curls. By day he might be seen in a short, flowered, ungirdled tunic adorned with a muslin neck-cloth. Dinner often saw him wearing the kind of bright-colored silk gown that a man would sport in Rome only during the Saturnalia or some equally frivolous occasion.

Because Nero also knew the Greeks to be more "reasonable" about sexual practices than the suffocating patricians of Rome, he was eager to oblige on that front as well. Wherever he went, his "Sabina" was now at his side. Sabina, as most Romans knew by then, was an adolescent boy named Sporus who caught Nero's eye because he resembled the late, lamented Poppæa Sabina, whom the emperor had managed to kill by kicking her in the stomach while pregnant. Because he looked so much like her, Sporus was made a eunuch and now traveled with his own entourage and wardrobe wagons. Not long after their arrival Nero and Sporus were solemnly married in a lavish ceremony in which the bride was given away by Tigellinus. Greek cities everywhere held celebrations to mark the marriage, uttering prayers for the union that even included one that healthy children might be born to them.

From then on Nero had two constant bedfellows at once: the pervert Pythagoras, whom he had "married" during the Neronian games, and Sporus, whom courtiers now addressed as "Queen" or "Lady Sporus."

Once he arrived in Corinth, the emperor took care of one more "security" issue before plunging into the arts. He first ordered the commanders of Upper and Lower Germany to commit suicide, which these two powerful generals did without a peep. He then ordered the great Corbulo to report to his party in Greece. Corbulo came promptly, probably assuming that he was about to be put in charge of the Syrian legions again in order to put down the increasingly rebellious Jews. Instead, Corbulo was told to end his life. "I deserved it!" the general muttered to his friends — meaning that had he known the emperor's intent, he could have commandeered the powerful legions of Syria and destroyed Nero almost unopposed.

Meanwhile, when Nero and Tigellinus had left Rome, they put in charge a freedman, Helius, with orders to eradicate any sign of trouble with no less finality than his master would have displayed in person. As the historian Dio Cassius put it:

> Thus, the Roman Empire was at that time a slave to two emperors at once, Nero and Helius. And I am unable to say which was the worse. The only point of difference was that the descendant of Augustus was emulating lyre players and tragedians, whereas the ex-slave of Claudius was emulating the Cæsars.[79]

ALL ACROSS THE EMPIRE people were now subdued for Nero's triumphant tour — all except the Jews, who yearned for a peace that Florus wouldn't allow. Just as Nero was traveling to Greece, the procurator of Judea and a well-armed cohort arrived in Jerusalem to announce that he wanted 17 talents from the temple treasury (presumably to help toward the rebuilding of fire-torn Rome). Immediately people came running from all directions, begging him to honor the sanctity of the temple. At the same time, young and bitter men began weaving through the crowd about Florus with a large basket, loudly asking for "alms" so that the procurator would be sated and go away.

This was all the provocation required. Florus unleashed his well-armed men on the Upper Marketplace, looting homes and killing anyone they could find inside. By day's end the arm-weary Romans had crucified, stabbed and otherwise murdered more than 3,500 Jews — including some leading citizens who bore the title of Roman knight.

The next day people were out in the streets wailing over their dead when they spotted still more Roman horsemen riding up from the hills below. Priests rent their garments, gathered the city leaders and ran several furlongs outside the city walls to greet the troops with promises of peace and goodwill towards Rome. But once again, a few hotheads couldn't resist snickering and shouting insults from behind. This time the tribune in command ordered a cavalry charge; and as the panicked crowd ran headlong for protection inside the city walls, the Romans trampled or clubbed to death nearly as many as they had killed the day before.

Florus and most of his troops departed at once for Cæsarea, but this only made matters worse because they left but a small garrison to protect the city from further uprising. Perhaps this, too, was part of the procurator's scheme, because he knew that both the Roman soldiers and Jewish elders were at risk from a growing mob of Zealots and Sicarii who threatened to seize the temple and declare all-out war on Rome. At first the outcome teetered. Florus had sent a letter to Cestius, the governor of Syria, accusing the Jews of insurrection, and the elders of Jerusalem had responded with their own letter of rebuttal. Cestius sent a personal emissary to investigate. He was joined by Herod Agrippa II, who came down from his northern kingdom of Gaulanitus-Trachonitis and delivered an impassioned appeal to a throng of thousands not to defy a power that had conquered everyone from the wild Germans to the warmongering descendants of Alexander the Great.

Shortly after his departure, Agrippa sent 3,000 horsemen to help keep the peace in Jerusalem, but even they weren't enough to cool the flames of hatred burning against Rome. Nor the rivalries starting to build within various resistance groups. In the first overt action, Manahem, already infamous as a brigand in Galilee, took a mob south to the fortress of Masada, overpowered its small Roman garrison and returned wearing armor that Herod the Great had stored up for meeting threats from Parthia and its clients. When Manahem killed the high priest and began scheming to get himself crowned king of Judea, he was murdered by an equally large group of Zealots.

Led by Eleazar, son of the assassinated high priest, the Zealots proved no less bloodthirsty than Manahem and his cutthroats. At the time, the few remaining Roman soldiers were holed up in the Tower of Mariamme, the strongest fortification in the Palace of Herod. When Metilius, the ranking Roman officer, learned that Manahem was dead, he sent the new rebel leader a message offering to give up his arms if his small detachment could go back to Cæsarea unharmed. The Zealots sent a delegation of four men, who pledged the security of their right hands.

When the fatigued and hungry soldiers filed out of the fortress and piled up their weapons, the surrounding crowd of Zealots and their supporters recognized the faces of individuals who had broken in to this or that house and slain a family member in the streets just days before. It was too much. Suddenly a yell went up from the Zealots and they swarmed over the dazed Romans with their swords. All except Metilius were cut down within two minutes. The commanding officer was spared only after promising that he would turn Jew and become circumcised.

All this left the moderate Jewish leaders with a profound sense of dread: they lamented the chaos now pervading their city and they knew what would happen to other Jewish communities when word of the massacre spread. In fact, it had already begun, ironically, at roughly the same hour on the same day. At Cæsarea, in about one hour's time, some 20,000 Jews were slaughtered and the city all but emptied of its Jewish inhabitants. This could only have happened on direct orders of Florus, perhaps based upon the report of a hard-riding reconnaissance officer from Jerusalem.

Now the cycle of revenge and retribution spun out of control. When news spread of the massacre at Cæsarea, Jews in cities where they dominated the population rose up and killed their Syrian neighbors. Soon every city in Syria was divided into two armies. Yet, the dividing lines weren't always simple. In some cases, Jewish merchants and religious leaders would side with the Syrians because they feared the ferocity and plunder of the Jewish rebels. And everywhere greed undergirded everything as homes and temples were pillaged for their riches.

Of the turmoils that erupted in virtually every Jewish community, the most tragic was again in Egyptian Alexandria with its half million Jews. At one point the Hellenist leaders called a meeting of their people in a theater to discuss sending an embassy beseeching Nero to rescind the rights of equality that Claudius had given the Jews there over 20 years before. When the Jews heard about it, and several of their boldest barged into the theater to harass the Greeks, the prefect Alexander arrived urging them to be quiet so as not to provoke the two Roman legions that were stationed outside the city. But some of the hotter Jewish youths made such sport of the governor's pleas that he became convinced they wouldn't subside unless they were taught a lesson. Coincidentally, the two regular legions had been joined by some 5,000 other Roman troops who had arrived at their camp from Libya for some sort of military exercises. Alexander ordered them all to set upon the Delta, where most of the Jewish quarter sprawled, and kill and plunder as they saw fit. When some Jews gathered arms and rushed out at them, the ferocity of the soldiers only increased. They did not stop until more than 50,000 Jews lay dead in heaps.

In Antioch, the Syrian governor Cestius added up the stream of arriving dispatches and concluded that Jews everywhere were up in arms. Taking nearly two legions and joined along the way by the loyal King Agrippa and his men, the Roman army marched through Galilee and Samaria, destroying whole cities in their path. When they reached Jerusalem, they pitched camp at Gabao, about six miles from the city walls. It was now August during the Feast of Tabernacles and Jerusalem was already crowded with pilgrims. It was the Sabbath day, and Cestius had hoped to strike when all were in some pious, passive state, but the tremendous shouts going up within the city walls showed him that the rage of the Jews had overcome their desire for religious rites. Few in the crowd had any military training, nor had anyone organized them into brigades. Yet, their frenzy simply propelled them out of the city gates with such force that they actually pierced the ranks of the Romans and slaughtered many. The invincible Romans scattered in all directions, and when the Jews counted the dead bodies left behind, they numbered 515. The Jews themselves counted their losses at 22. Most of them withdrew back into the city, but some bands chased the Romans, who were making for their camp, and captured many of the animals that carried their weapons of war.

For once it was the Romans who were in real danger, because in addition to facing the walled bastion that was Jerusalem, they had all around them Jewish refugees and robbers camped about on mountainsides and poised for action. King Agrippa took all this into account and persuaded Cestius that now might be a good time to send the Jews an embassy.

The governor's message complimented them for their show of strength and said there was now an opportunity to admit the Romans into Jerusalem if each side guaranteed the other's safety. For Cestius was prepared to offer his right hand and a guarantee of forgiveness if they would but lay down their arms. Behind this was King Agrippa's conviction that the more sober elements of the Jews would sue for peace and thus split from the militant seditionists.

But both sides miscalculated. Agrippa proved wrong because the envoys had no sooner been admitted into Jerusalem than they were pounced on and killed before saying a word. This, the seditionists had done to guarantee that no Jew would be tempted to cease fighting in return for his security. Yet the rebel leaders were not prepared for the wrath that erupted from the rest of the populace. Obviously, the mass of ordinary tradesmen and townsfolk hoped privately that the Romans would have been able to arrange a settlement that would end the killing. Now, in a rage, they rose up and chased the seditionists into the inner city, where they barricaded themselves inside the temple.

Cestius, unaware of it, bided his time for another three days, using it in part to ride into neighboring villages and seize their corn. Then as the month turned to September, the governor moved his men to within a furlong or two of the city and set camp on Mount Scopus, which overlooked the king's palace and almost the whole city besides. Then, after using his siege engines to set parts of the city aflame with fiery missiles, he marched his troops inside the outer city walls and pitched camp against the royal palace. The Jews expected Cestius to begin an immediate assault on the temple walls, but again he halted and waited.

When the remaining priests and elders saw the Romans wavering, they sent word that they were ready to open the temple gates if Cestius would again guarantee peace. But while the governor wondered aloud if this was more treachery, the rebel leaders found out what was afoot and hurled one of the leading citizens from the temple wall in a show of defiance. Then, as Cestius watched, they heaved large rocks at the already lifeless body.

After this, Cestius spent five days trying to besiege the temple. Thousands of fiery darts were flung over the walls. More than once the Romans used their famed tortoise shell tactic (called a Testudo) in which some men stood in a cluster with shields raised while others dug to undermine the base of the city walls. They tried scaling the walls as well, but each time they were beaten back with considerable casualties.

Perhaps with a little longer siege, Jerusalem would have fallen. It is also alleged that Cestius still did not realize how many people on the ramparts were praying that he would succeed and offer them a chance to repent (when their own leaders would not do the same). But one day Cestius unceremoniously ordered his troops to pull camp and leave. The task at hand was simply too risky.

Yet, the governor could not even look forward to an orderly departure. The more emboldened of the rebels poured out of the city and harassed the Romans' rear, stealing their baggage and animals. And whenever the weary soldiers crossed narrow valleys they were pelted with stones and darts from hundreds of taunting Jews on the hillsides. Cestius managed to return to his original camp at Gabao, six miles from the city. There they stayed for two nights, but the crowds of Jewish harassers were growing so large around them as to begin resembling an army. The governor, realizing that to camp there any longer was a danger, ordered his pack animals all killed except for those that carried darts. Then he ordered his men to close ranks, carry only their weapons and march rapidly to the town of Bethoron, another 14 miles to the northwest on the way to Cæsarea.

The hostile crowds pressed on them from the moment they broke camp. Every time the Roman columns had to file through narrow passes, they lost more men and horses. Although it was relatively easy to lead a horse up a slope, the troops were now descending rapidly; and as their assailants shouted from above and stones came crashing down on them, horses often tumbled down — sometimes with the men who were holding their reins. Moreover, parts of columns were now attacked and killed as they wound through the passes, unable at times to see the soldiers in front of them. All of this increased the sense of confinement and pending doom.

That night after the weary, unnerved Romans tried to camp in the hills of Bethoron, Cestius realized his situation was desperate, for the marauding Jews had filled all the hilltops around them, waiting for daylight. Quietly, he selected 400 of his best soldiers and placed them at the strongest of his fortifications at the makeshift camp. They were ordered to place their flags all about the camp so that when the Jews saw them fluttering in the dawn's light they would assume that the entire army was still there. Then Cestius took the rest of the forces with him and set out on a silent march hoping to get at least four miles away and down into the safer coastal plain before they were noticed.

By dawn the next day, when the Jews awoke and realized what had happened, they quickly rushed the 400 defenders and easily wiped them out. After trying in vain to catch the fleeing Cestius, the Jewish troops — if the rebels could now be called an organized fighting force — spent the day retracing the Roman route of the previous day and retrieving a wealth of discarded siege engines, carts, animals, and supplies along the way. They also took toll of the Roman dead, which were 5,300 footmen and 380 horsemen.

The Jewish victory occurred on October 23, A.D. 66, in the 12th year of Nero. It also marked their military apex in a war that would grind them down for six more years.

Back in Antioch, Cestius sent an appeal to Nero in Achaia that he was in great distress and needed a larger army to put down the Jews. And he blamed Florus for causing all his woes.

There was no Corbulo to call on for heroics — Nero had seen to that. Instead the command went to a career soldier who was as squatty, rough-hewn and prone to earthy jokes as Corbulo had been tall, regal and aloof. Raised in a nondescript village in the Sabine country, the new commander had begun his military career in Thrace as a tribune of the troops and had risen on the strength of his practical soldiering skills to command legions in Germany and Britain under Claudius. His name was Titus Flavius Vespasian. He was already about 60 and, some said, his best campaigns were behind him. Perhaps so, answered Vespasian's defenders, but he came with a rare and valuable resource — a son, Titus, whose military skills were as respected as his loyalty to his father. Vespasian had a second, younger son as well, whom we will meet soon enough.

IN THE SUMMER OF A.D. 67, there were no emergencies of governance to distract the emperor on his triumphant tour through Greece. Only one battle was being fought at the time, and it was not in Jerusalem. Rather, Jewish-Roman hostilities were centered for the moment on Jotapata, a walled city of some 40,000 about 70 miles due north of Jerusalem.

All this was as expected by the Jews. In the winter of A.D. 67 they had known that the new Roman commander, Vespasian, would march east from the Syrian legionary headquarters at Antioch, then down through Galilee and Samaria, attempting to lay waste everything in his path toward Jerusalem and its temple of treasures. In the winter and spring months before the expected storm the Jewish leadership had chosen governors-general to conscript and arm troops in each of seven geographic regions.

The first region to feel the Roman onslaught would be Galilee, and thanks to the most extensive history ever written of ancient Israel, we know a great deal about the summer of A.D. 67. The author of that history was none other than Josephus, the same young priest who was picked to head the resistance effort in Galilee. Since he becomes a major player in his own history, he deserves a full introduction at this point.

By his own immodest account, Josephus was destined for a priestly life almost from birth. He was born in Jerusalem, the son of a leading priest and the latest in a long line of priestly families under the Hasmonean kings. At age 16 he immersed himself, successively, in the lives and learning of Judaism's three major schools of thought: the Pharisees, Sadducees and Essenes. But during that same period he began attaching himself increasingly to one Bannus, a monk-philosopher who lived in the Judean desert and wore clothes of bark and leaves and ate only vegetation. But by age 19, Josephus was back in Jerusalem and beginning his public career as a priest.

His most formative experience came at age 26 when he was named as part of an embassy that the Jewish elders sent to Rome. The purpose was to help plead the case of some men, whom Josephus describes as pious æsthetic priests, whom the procurator Felix had sent off in chains to be judged before the emperor. No, it had nothing to do with Paul, but Josephus did encounter another trial very much in common with the apostle. Midway in the open sea, the immense grain ship that bore them was swamped in a mighty storm. Writes Josephus:

> We that were in it, being about 600 in number, swam for our lives all the night. Upon the first appearance of the day, and upon our sight of a ship of Cyrene, I and some others, 80 in all — for God's providence prevented the rest — were taken up in the other ship.

> And when I had thus escaped and had come to...Puteoli, I became acquainted with Aliturius, an actor of plays, much beloved by Nero, and a Jew by birth. Through his interest I be-

came known to Poppæa, Cæsar's wife, and took care as soon
as possible, to entreat her to procure that the priests might be
set at liberty. And when, besides this favor, I had obtained
many presents from Poppæa, I returned home again.[80]

Josephus adds that his greatest impression from the long journey was
that of Rome's insurmountable power. Acknowledging that talk of revolt
was already in the air in Jerusalem, he took pains to persuade his countrymen "that they were inferior to the Romans not only in martial skill,
but also in good fortune," and that to rebel rashly would "bring on the dangers of the most terrible mischiefs upon their country, upon their families
and upon themselves."

How much of this was brilliant foresight, or simply for the consumption
of his Roman patron when he wrote his history some 20 years later one can't
say; but within six years Josephus, despite his continued misgivings, had
emerged as one of the seven makeshift generals chosen to withstand the coming Roman storm. At the age of 33 Josephus had despotic powers over a dominion that covered over 600 square miles and contained perhaps 600,000
persons. From his explanation, one might fancy Galilee to be one of the more
desirable places on earth in peacetime,

> ...for the soil is universally rich and fruitful, and full of the
> plantations of trees of all sorts, inasmuch that it invites even
> the most slothful to take pains in its cultivation, by its fruit-
> fulness. Accordingly, it is all cultivated by its inhabitants
> and no part of it lies idle. Moreover, the cities here are very
> thick, and the very villages there are everywhere so full of
> people, by the richness of their soil, that the very least of
> them contain about 15,000 inhabitants.[81]

When Josephus first entered Galilee, his primary concern was to win over
the area's leaders. So he chose 70 of the most prudent men (as had Moses)
to hear all cases involving life or death, then seven judges in each city to hear
lesser individual disputes. Josephus himself focused on building walls
around the 15 largest cities and raising an army that would grow to 60,000
footmen, several hundred horsemen, 4,500 mercenaries and his own personal guard of 600.

These tasks proved relatively easy compared to finding serviceable
weapons and cooperative troops. The Romans' core strength was discipline,
Josephus would lecture anyone within earshot; and his own rag-tag units

were not only untrained, they were quick to argue with each other and even their superiors. Added to the young general's challenge was the fact that some cities resisted his leadership and put forth their own candidates. And some gangs of brigands still roamed the countryside, constituting armed forces that might or might not decide to attach themselves to the Jewish defense effort.

One of these thorns in Josephus' side was one John of Gischala, a man he describes as a "knavish and cunning" vagabond. When Josephus arrived in Galilee, John was known only as a marauder who led a gang of about 400 men in a life of plundering Romans, Jews and Syrians alike. But John, it seems, had greater leadership ambitions. Displaying a sizable cache of money, he persuaded the young general that he would use it to rebuild the walls of his native Gischala if he were made commander of the forces there.

Once established in Gischala, John had a shrewd scheme that went beyond rebuilding walls. Since the area was a major producer of olive oil for export, he sent agents throughout the Jewish cities of Syria persuading citizens that they should buy only oil produced by Jews and not of foreigners. Thus he was able to sell oil at twice the price that Jews had paid before, and in the process garnered an immense sum of money. This he used to persuade leading citizens of Galilee that they should overthrow Josephus and install him as governor-general. He also increased the intensity of robberies in the countryside, then went about campaigning among the populace with promises that the plundering would end if only he were put in charge!

At the same time, John spread rumors that Josephus was in collusion with the Romans. Whether by design or not, one of the travelers who passed under the noses of John's highwaymen one day was Ptolemy, the chief steward of Herod Agrippa and Bernice. By the time the robbers had relieved Ptolemy and his entourage of their baggage train, they had found themselves with some six hundred pieces of gold, several silver cups and place settings, and an untold number of royal garments. The booty was so great that the brigands reconsidered what might be their fate if King Agrippa set his soldiers upon them, and so they decided to seek out Josephus and deliver the goods to him.

They found the general staying in the town of Taricheæ as he supervised fortification of its walls. The governor duly scolded them for their treachery, and having other duties to attend to just then, left the royal plunder with the leading elder of Taricheæ for safekeeping until it could be sent back to the king.

Well, the robbers, still smarting from their unwelcome reception by Josephus, began spreading word in neighboring towns that the governor himself had betrayed the Jewish cause by returning to the allies of Rome a wealth of property that could have been converted to instruments of war. All night long the clamor spread, so that by the next morning, thousands of armed men converged on the hippodrome at Tarichææ, chanting that Josephus the traitor be displaced at once. Others demanded that he be burned, and before long the riled-up mob left the hippodrome and jostled its way to the house where Josephus was staying — still asleep, as a matter of fact. When the shouting of the approaching mob reached the ears of Josephus' personal guardsmen, all melted away in fear except for four, who awakened the young governor.

By the time the crowd appeared in the street in front of Josephus' house, they were startled when the governor himself jumped out at them from the front door. His clothes were rent and ashes were sprinkled on his head. His hands were behind him and his sword was hanging around his neck.

After recovering from their shock, some of the more zealous among them began to reproach Josephus. Those who thought his government too taxing shouted for him to produce the king's riches so they could share them. Others demanded he confess that he was in league with the Romans, for they assumed that his pitiable dress meant that he was ready to confess to everything and throw himself on their mercy. .

But Jospehus' humble posture was merely the cutting edge of a stratagem, which was to set his critics arguing amongst themselves. When he raised his hands for silence, they assumed he was ready to confess all. But when he had their attention, he said: "I neither intended to send this money back to Agrippa nor to gain it myself. For I never did esteem one who is your enemy to be your friend. No, people of Tarichææ, I saw that your city stood in greater need than others for fortifications and that you needed money to build a wall. I was also afraid that people of other cities should lay a plot to seize upon these spoils. So therefore, I intended to retain this money so that I might build you a wall.

"But if this does not please you," added Josephus, "I will produce for you what was brought me and leave you to plunder it."

As he expected, the people of Tarichææ loudly commended him, while those who had run down from Tiberias and other surrounding cities began to call him harsh names, for they would rather take home some loot than build walls for Tarichææ. Soon the two groups had begun quarreling, and Josephus decided to employ a second "stratagem," as he described his brainstorms. He climbed atop the roof of his host's house, and again signaling to them, said, "You shout in such a confused noise that I cannot tell what it is you want of me. If you would but elect a few of your number to represent you, they may come into the house and talk with me about it."

When the elected delegates appeared on the portico, Josephus bid them enter with a bow and ushered them into the most private part of the house, whereupon he closed the door so that no one might hear what went on. What the delegates found were the four guards who had remained loyal to their governor. The guards set upon them with whips and scourged them so severely that "even their inner parts were raw and bloody."

Meanwhile, the remaining crowd had relaxed its ire, assuming that negotiations were underway with regard to disposition of the king's property. Suddenly the doors were thrown open and the "ambassadors" were flung out upon the crowd in such a bloody state that everyone threw down their arms and ran away in terror.

Such was the ingenuity of Josephus. He seems also to have had that "good fortune" he attributed to the Romans, because his thwarting of the designs of John had a rippling effect. Leaders of other cities who had been threatened by the robber-merchant of Gischala to the point of overturning the Jerusalem-appointed government now rushed to the governor's support. Josephus took advantage of the changing tide to declare that all those who did not renounce John within five days would have their homes and families burned. Thus, 3,000 of John's followers left him immediately and deposited their arms with Josephus.

Ready or not, the Romans were marching in the late spring of A.D. 67. Vespasian, ever practical and patient, would have preferred more time to organize, but with reports that Jewish troops were sallying out of Jerusalem and inflicting casualties in isolated Roman outposts, his movements took on a new urgency. First, he dispatched his son Titus to Alexandria to march back with the illustrious fifth and tenth legions. Vespasian would march the 15th legion from Antioch. Attached to the 15th were 18 cohorts — five from the camp at Cæsarea and others from various Roman garrisons — and typically with a thousand or so footmen each. Now add to these the auxiliaries of archers, horsemen and footmen from several client kings. When all these converged with the forces of Titus at Ptolemais on the Syrian coast, the fighting men numbered some 60,000 in all. This still didn't count vast numbers of servants, who remained by their masters in battle and were often adept with weapons as well.

Thus, one can scarcely imagine the seditionist cause in Galilee brimming with confidence when it became known that Vespasian himself was on his way from Ptolemais. As soon as the seemingly endless train of men, horses and siege engines could be seen winding through the mountains and passes, many Galileans were overcome with fear and fled into the fields and mountains. In fact, when the general came to Gadara, the first city in his path, "he found it destitute of any men grown up and fit for war."

Poor Gadara. Vespasian, ordinarily a good-natured man with a quick wit, was grimly determined that the first city he encountered would be made to pay for the slaughter of the Roman garrison in Jerusalem and the humiliating retreat of Cestius to Cæsarea. His men slew every woman and child in Gadara. Then they set fire to it and all the surrounding villages. As horrifying as this scorched earth policy might have struck a Jew, to Vespasian it was a logical, even defensive, tactic to employ when one's army is in a strange land and always vulnerable to being surrounded and cut off from its supply lines.

Jotapata, however, was no Gadara. As Vespasian's troops wound upwards through the surrounding hills, the general's intelligence reports had identified it as Galilee's most populous, strongly fortified city. If he could demolish Jotapata with one bold stroke, he reasoned, the region's lesser cities might just dissolve in fear like Gadara.

The Romans had delayed their march to Jotapata for some four days while their engineers planed off the top of a steep road that made it difficult to transport such a large train of men, carriages and animals. The roadwork was still in progress on May 21 when Josephus hastened from Tiberias to Jotapata. Although their leader's arrival raised the spirits of the defenders there, it had the same effect on Vespasian as well. When told that Josephus, the general of all Galilee, was now in the city he planned to assault, the Roman counted it a blessing and ordered his battle preparations hastened. In fact, he had auxiliaries march immediately to the city and surround it lest his good fortune be thwarted by Josephus' escape.

Within two days Vespasian's army had set up camp within a mile of Jotapata and was ready for battle after a well-rested night. Until then the Jews inside had been too petrified to venture outside the walls, even for firewood. Now, as they saw the Romans methodically begin preparations for a siege, they realized that they could either die from fright or die bravely in battle. Suddenly the gates opened and erupted with a ferocious charge of Jewish footmen. The Romans, recalled Josephus, "had skill as well as strength; the other had only courage, which armed them and made them fight furiously."

The hand-to-hand combat lasted all day and ended only when darkness made it impossible to see one's foe. By Josephus' count, the Jews had killed 13 Romans and "wounded a great many." The Jews suffered 17 dead and more than 600 wounded.

The same desperate scene went on for four more days as well until both sides stopped due to sheer exhaustion. It was at this point that Vespasian decided to return to his original plan: the slow, systematic siege.

Jotapata was built on a steep precipice that surrounded it on three sides. Only at the north side did the mountain descend more gradually toward a plain. This side Josephus had encompassed with a high wall. Vespasian met with his counselors and resolved to raise a bank against the north wall. So they had cut down all the trees on the mountains adjoining the city and collected a vast amount of stones as well. Then, covering the soldiers with a shield against the darts that were constantly hurled from above, they began piling up the debris alongside the wall. At the same time, they kept the Jews all along the ramparts busy dodging the rocks and fiery missiles that were being hurled inside by no fewer than 160 Roman siege engines.

But this was not a one-sided affair. By night, small raiding parties would sneak out from the city to burn the timbers that supported the makeshift siege tower or to pull down the large iron-plated roofs that shielded the workers. Meanwhile, Jewish workmen were building the north wall still higher. To protect them against Roman darts, they stretched the thick hides of newly killed oxen between upright pikes. Thus, as the Romans raised their tower, the walls of Jotapata became higher by 35 feet.

All this caused Vespasian to summon his counselors again. This time the Romans agreed that while they could probably take the city by armed force, they could do so with greater certainty if they simply waited until starvation weakened the defenders. So they simply ceased the fighting and waited in silence, hoping that the number of deserters would increase as well.

Inside, the defenders took stock. Corn they had aplenty, but water was another matter. The city lacked a spring-fed fountain, relying traditionally on rainwater. And the approaching summer was the season with the least of it. They decided to ration water, but in time the stark reality that a man could have only so much per day to slake his thirst made him think all the more about it. The Romans knew of their plight, and would taunt those on the ramparts by lining up at their water carriers and making a show of draining their canteens.

But Josephus was not to be outdone by games of the mind. One morning the Romans squinted up at the battlements and saw that the Jews had flung garments along the ramparts for as far as the eye could see. The clothes were hung out as on laundry day, all dripping with much of the precious water they had left.

After this taunt the Romans resumed their attack — and the Jews welcomed it. For as Josephus explained, "As they despaired of either themselves or their city being able to escape, they preferred death in battle before one by hunger and thirst."

Soon Josephus perceived that the city couldn't hold out much longer. He faced an excruciating dilemma. Meeting with the city elders, he said that there was little else he personally could do to improve their lot. But if he could escape, he could rally other cities in Galilee to come to their rescue and defeat the Romans. This reasoning may have been sound, but it only fanned the feelings of despair. As Josephus' own diaries state (with himself described in the third person):

> Yet this plea did not move the people, but inflamed them to hang about him. Accordingly, both the children and the old men, and the women with their infants, came mourning to him and fell down before him. And all of them caught hold of his feet, and held him fast, and besought him, with great lamentations, that he would take his share with them in their fortune. And I think they did this, not that they envied his deliverance, but that they hoped for their own; for they could not think they should suffer any great misfortune provided that Josephus would but stay with them.[82]

Josephus says that he was touched by these entreaties, but that he knew, too, that if he tried to escape, his own people would probably arrest or kill him. So he announced to the Jews of Jotapata, "Now is the time to begin to fight in earnest, when there is no hope of deliverance left." And to show them what he meant, Josephus himself led a party of raiders that rushed out from the main gate and ran to the edge of the Roman camp where they pulled down several tents and set fire to other parts. From that day forward the daring and bravery of the Jews was relentless. They learned that when they made these disruptive raids, the Romans, laden with their heavy armor, couldn't pursue them very far.

But so mighty was Rome that even passion could be manipulated to the conqueror's advantage. Vespasian calmly rebuffed the angry cries of his troops for revenge. "Nothing is more courageous than despair," he counseled. And when the Jews saw that their plan failed, it would be like a fire being quenched for lack of more fuel. Instead, Vespasian chose to wear down and decimate the raiders by having Arabian archers and Syrian slingers prick them with a hail of missiles from a safe distance.

When the general's earthen bank had advanced against the walls to his liking, he gave the defenders their first look at a battering ram. As thick and long as the mast of a ship, the instrument was carved like the head of a ram and capped with a thick head of iron. Above the ram, which swung from leather straps, was a roof covered with animal hides, so that the men who swung it back and forth were protected from the hail of darts and rocks from above.

The ram was now fixed in place. From its very first stroke, as Josephus reports, "the wall was shaken, and a terrible clamor was raised by the people within the city, as if they were already taken."

The ingenious Josephus countered this by having the people fill large sacks of chaff. These they lowered down the wall by ropes to the place where the ram was battering back and forth. Thus, every time the ram struck, its impact was muffled by the overstuffed sacks and the damage greatly minimized.

But then the Romans countered. They invented a long contrivance on poles on whose ends they fastened knives. Now they could jab the pole at the ropes that held the sacks of chaff and cut them down.

Thus, the ram continued with its former efficiency, and soon the extended wall that Josephus' men had hastily built could be seen to ripple with each blow as it prepared to give way. So the Jews resolved to make what was perhaps their boldest sally ever. They rushed out in the dead of night with fire, bitumen and pitch. When they broke through the few guards around the battering ram, they smeared it with pitch and set it afire. Now as it began to burn through, a strong and brave youth hoisted a huge stone atop the north wall. Then he climbed along side it and stood in full view. Several Roman darts struck him at once, but he managed to push the boulder down directly on the fiery ram, breaking it in two. Then, as he was about to die from his wounds, the youth hurled himself on top of the ram's head.

But now it was the Romans' turn for a rally. When Vespasian had left camp to investigate the ruckus at the walls, a dart hit him in the heel. It had been flung from some distance and lacked enough force to penetrate deeply. But soldiers saw their commander fall. They saw his blood on the ground beside him, and word spread that he was seriously wounded or even dead. Now Roman discipline was abandoned to Roman rage as soldiers clamored for a full-scale assault. Far worse for the Jews inside the walls was that another battering ram was soon wheeled into the place of the burned one, and once again the sickening sounds of impending doom reverberated throughout Jotapata. Moreover, the Romans took the largest of their siege engines and trained them en masse against the same crumbling wall. Before long the huge stones that they hurled had carried off pinnacles of walls and broken off the corners of the towers. As Josephus adds:

One may learn the force of the engines by what happened

this very night; for as one of those who stood around Josephus was near the wall, his head was carried away by such a stone so that his skull was flung as far as three furlongs. And in the daytime, a woman who was with child had her belly so violently struck, as she had just come out of her house, that the infant was carried to a distance of half a furlong, so great was the force of the engine. The noise of the instruments themselves was very terrible...as was the noise of bodies when they were dashed against the wall.[83]

The defenders fought on through the night, the streets now running with blood from bodies that were being piled up all around. The noise from the missiles and the battering ram made everyone all the more wretched because the mountains behind them would send back an echo with each blow. The cries of the stricken and their mourners would resound with an eerie echo as well.

Then, just around daybreak, the north wall began crumbling from the ram's hundreds of blows. Vespasian's first action was to place a ring of horsemen and archers around the walls so that there would be no escaping once the city was taken. Next, the veteran general ordered his bravest horsemen to get off their mounts, to don heavy armor and stand with poles and ladders at the base of the embankment where the wall had been breached. His best footmen were then brought into position to be ready to ascend the ladders and hurl themselves into the opening where the upper part of the wall had fallen in. Also brought into position were hundreds of archers, who would keep the defenders pinned down with a hail of darts.

As Josephus saw these preparations unfolding below him, he ordered that all the women be shut up in their houses (not just for the personal safety, but because he didn't want the resolve of his men weakened by female wailings of despair when they saw the Roman onslaught). Calling his men together, the Jewish governor-general told them to cover their ears as soon as the Roman trumpeters gave the signal to charge, for neither did he want them to quake at the terrible roar that would go up from the invaders. And he told the men to kneel down and cover themselves with their shields when the Romans first charged. For this would allow them protection until the first wave of arrows was expended. Then, only when they saw the Romans beginning to lay their instruments for ascending the walls, they should then rise up and in one ferocious rage rush into a life or death battle with the enemy.

Soon the trumpets blew, and Josephus' men did just as they were told. After a rain of darts so thick that they seemed to block the light, the defenders rushed out and began to topple the first of the ladders that had been placed against the wall. The combat went on for a few hours, but the Jews at last began to sag because the Romans had the luxury of suspending their assault so they could replace tired men with fresh ones. They also climbed with shields braced together, as though it were a wall of steel advancing at the Jews.

It seemed that the Romans would finally break through, but at that point Josephus had one more "stratagem" to employ. He gave orders to pour scalding oil down on those who were still on the ladders. The Jews had boiled a great quantity of it, and when it was still hissing from the heat of the fire, they poured it over the walls. Now the Romans screamed and tumbled down, one on top of another, in horrible pain. Being encased in helmets and heavy breastplates, the boiling, unctuous fat trickled through their bodies from head to foot, causing them to writhe on the ground in unbearable agony.

Next, Josephus' men poured boiling fenugreek (an oriental herb used in making curry) upon the boards of the Roman ladders. The means of ascent now became so slippery that the men furthest along the ladders fell upon those beneath them. Others plunged into the earthen embankment below, where many were killed by arrows from Jewish archers on the ramparts above.

The Romans were furious and clamored for more Jewish blood, but Vespasian prudently called off the assault for the day, for evening was already coming on. The Jews had suffered only six killed, although some 300 were wounded.

They now had some time to catch their breath, but not for a good reason. Vespasian had decided on a new tactic: raising the earthen banks still higher. He also began erecting three towers, each 50 feet high, and with iron plates on all sides. Once put into place atop the banks, the towers would actually look down inside the walls of Jotapata and allow archers and slingers inside them to bombard the defenders continually.

This is exactly what happened. But it was not by a mighty Roman onslaught that Jotapata was finally taken, but by thieves who crept in during the still of night. For it was approaching the 47th day of the siege when a deserter came to Vespasian and told him that the people of the city were much less numerous and more exhausted than he had assumed. The deserter said that even the guards at a particular watchtower by the breached wall were so fatigued that they usually lapsed into sleep sometime after midnight. If the Romans used stealth, he said, they could kill the watchmen in their sleep and take the city before the rest of the people awoke the next morning.

The Roman commander hesitated, fearing a trick. So far the Jews of Jotapata had been unfailingly loyal to one another. Vespasian remembered one man in particular who had been captured and tortured by fire in hopes of getting some insights into Josephus' defenses and tactics. The man had never uttered a word of betrayal. And even when the Romans crucified him in front of the wall, he had died in silence with a smile on his lips.

But then the general thought again. How much could he lose by investigating the theory? So he ordered that the deserter be kept in custody, then killed if his advice proved to be a sham.

Late the same night a small band of elite Roman troops quietly dropped down on the city from the towers that had just been erected on the earthen bank. Titus, ever the most daring and valiant of the Roman commanders, was first over the wall, followed by two of his best tribunes and some members of the 15th legion. They found the watchmen sleeping, as predicted, and quickly cut their throats. Now they entered the city stealthily, creeping through dark, narrow streets all the way to the citadel, which was in the most elevated part of the city. Now they waited until most of the Roman army slipped over the wall in the still darkness and hastened on cat feet to meet them.

By dawn the Romans had already made progress downhill, entering homes quietly and butchering people in their sleep. Even when they aroused whole neighborhoods and encountered resistance, people elsewhere in the city still failed to understand what was happening inside their walls. As the sun rose and the families of Jotapata would ordinarily stretch themselves on their rooftops and start baking bread, they faced an armed and angry Roman mob, chasing down helpless victims in narrow streets, for the Romans were incensed at those who had poured out the hot oil and the wild-eyed raiders who had rushed out to ambush them their camp. When the elders and guardsmen around Josephus grouped together briefly, the discussion was not how to defend themselves, but of how to escape and/or when to kill themselves. Some did so on the spot.

That day, on June 16, the Romans killed everyone they could find in the town — about 40,000 in all. Vespasian also resolved to destroy everything in Jotapata and level the fortifications. But before doing so the Romans spent the next two days methodically searching for anyone who might still be hiding in basements and cisterns — or even in the piles of dead bodies that lay rotting all around in the blistering heat. Most of all, they wanted Josephus. He held the key to the subjugation of all Galilee. Where was he?

In the midst of the final slaughter, the young governor-general was, he writes, "assisted by a certain supernatural providence." He, along with about 40 of the city's leaders, had descended into a deep pit in a quiet part of the city. Off to the side of it was a large den that was hidden to anyone above ground. Quite conveniently, Josephus reports, the den was already equipped "with provisions enough to satisfy them for not a few days."

Two days passed. Late each night Josephus would clamber up the sides and look about for some way of escaping, but all avenues were tightly guarded by the Romans. On the third day Josephus was betrayed by a woman who was interrogated by the Romans (further evidence that many of Jotapata's elite had taken care to provide themselves a place of refuge). Vespasian immediately dispatched two tribunes, who called down into the pit for Josephus to come out. They promised their right hands as security if he did so.

But Josephus couldn't be persuaded, knowing that Vespasian must be well aware of how the rebels of Jerusalem had treated a Roman embassy after promising their safety. This time the Romans lowered into the pit a single tribune named Nicanor, whom Josephus had known and respected in the days before the rebellion. Nicanor talked in a mild and gentle tone, reminding Josephus that Romans had a tradition of showing respect and hospitality to foes whose courage they admired. He vowed solemnly that Vespasian wanted to see Josephus — not to punish him, but to preserve a man of such courage. Vespasian, he said, would never pretend friendship and display perfidy.

At this point, Josephus (always appearing to be the detached historian in his writings) says he began to recall many dreams and prophecies that had come to him at night and wondered if God were beckoning him to some purpose that he should follow.

> Now Josephus was able to give shrewd conjectures about the interpretation of such dreams as have been ambiguously delivered by God. Moreover, he was not unacquainted with the prophecies contained in the sacred books, being a priest himself.

So he put up a secret prayer to God:

> Since it pleaseth thee, who has created the Jewish nation, to depress the same; and since all good fortune has gone over to the Romans, and since thou hast made a choice of this soul of mine to foretell what is to come to pass hereafter, I willingly give them my hands and am content to live. And I state openly that I do not go over to the Romans as a deserter of the Jews, but as a minister from thee.[84]

So Josephus announced he would accept Nicanor's invitation. Now it was his own confederates with whom he had to contend. They were incensed to a man. "Josephus," one of them thundered, "are you so fond of life that you accept slavery? Yes, the Romans may have good fortune, but it is up to us to take care that the glory of our forefathers not be tarnished."

Another drew his sword and made ready to hand it to Josephus. "We will lend you our right hand and our sword," he said. "And if you will die willingly, you will die as a general of the Jews. But if you die unwillingly, it will be as a traitor to them." And with that several of them thrust their swords at him in a show of what would happen if he tried to abscond in Nicanor's company.

A tense silence ensued, and the next words they heard from Josephus were not those of their governor-general, but those of a philosopher-priest prepared to deliver a formal oration. Could anyone pretend that he was not the same courageous warrior he had been a few days ago? Yes, it is brave to die in war. But how courageous would it to be to die at one's own hand when one's conquerors stand ready to spare him? "If they would spare their enemy, how much more ought we to have mercy upon ourselves!"

Indeed, said Josephus the philosopher, if a person is a coward who will not die when he is obliged to, is it not an equal coward who will die when he is *not* obliged to? It is a most unmanly act to kill oneself just as would be a ship's captain who would deliberately sink his own vessel because he feared a storm.

And now from Josephus the priest:

> Self-murder is a crime most remote from the common nature of all animals, and an instance of impiety against God our creator.

> Do you not think that God is very angry when a man does injury to what he hath bestowed on him? For from him it is that we have received our being, and we ought to leave it to his disposal to take that being away from us.[85]

When his colleagues would still have none of it, Josephus became the advocate and defender of Roman law. "Our law," he argued, "justly ordains that slaves who run away from their masters should be punished, even though the masters they run away from may have been wicked. So, shall we endeavor to run away from God, who is the best of all masters, and not think ourselves guilty of impiety?"

No, concluded Josephus the priest. If one has a mind to die, "it is good to die by the hand of those who have conquered us. Should the Romans prove treacherous with their offer, I shall die cheerfully and carry away with me the sense of their perfidiousness as a consolation greater than victory itself."

A remarkable extemporaneous dissertation for one trapped in a cave by allies and foes alike. But the Jewish leaders finally had enough of words and rushed at him from all angles with drawn swords. All were committed to die and they were infuriated that their own general would delay it any longer. "However, in this extreme distress, he was not destitute of his usual sagacity," Josephus the historian writes of Josephus the general. "Trusting himself to the providence of God, he put his life at risk" as follows:

"Men," he cried out, "since you have resolved to die, let us commit our mutual deaths to determination by lot. He to whom the lot falls first, let him be killed by whom has the second lot so that fortune will make its progress through us all. This way, no one will perish by his own hand; for it would be unfair to the rest if somebody should repent and save himself."

The proposal seemed just. They drew lots, Josephus included. As the Roman tribune Nicanor watched from the entrance to the den, the man who drew the first lot, bared his neck to the next, and so forth, each supposing that their general would be one of the next to die with them. The rest Josephus reports in his own words:

> Yet was he and another left to last, whether we may say it happened so by chance or whether by the providence of God. And as he was very desirous neither to be condemned by the lot, nor — if he had been left to the last — to imbrue his right hand in the blood of his countrymen, he persuaded the man who was next to last to entrust his fidelity to him, and to live as well as himself.[86]

Josephus never says what happened to the man who was next. But Josephus himself was then led by Nicanor through the Roman camp as crowds of soldiers strained to get a look at the Jewish general who had bedeviled them for more than two months. Now, as the haggard Josephus stood in the tent of Vespasian, a throng of soldiers outside clamored for his immediate execution. But inside the tent, Titus delivered an ardent appeal to his father, citing Josephus' bravery, and now, his almost regal calm under such adversity. Vespasian replied simply that the governor of Galilee would be bound and held under close guard until such time as he could be sent to Nero for disposal.

Josephus had been silent until this time. Now he spoke up firmly. He said that he had something important to say to the Roman general that was for his ears alone.

Vespasian hesitated suspiciously, then ordered all senior staff officers except Titus and two commanders to withdraw from the tent.

The remaining men sat quietly and curiously facing their captive. "Vespasian," said Josephus without a trace of supplication, "do you think no more than that you have taken Josephus captive? In truth, I come to you as a messenger of greater tidings.

"You intend to send me to Nero? Why? Thou, O Vespasian, will be Cæsar and emperor. And so, too, will thy son.

"Bind me now still faster," said Josephus, "but keep me for thyself, For thou, O Cæsar, are not only lord over me, but will be over the land and the sea and all mankind. And for saying such things, I certainly deserve to be kept in closer custody in order to be all the more severely punished should I prove rash in stating that all this has been prophesied to me by God."

Well, Vespasian was outwardly a modest and uncomplicated man, even given to jokes at his own expense. Perhaps he felt awkward at hearing these words in the presence of others, but deep inside he had already felt that God had inexplicably destined him to become emperor even though he was content with a general's life. So he had Josephus imprisoned, yet began making discreet inquiries as to the accuracy of the young general's previous predictions. For instance, Josephus was known to have told intimates that Jotapata would fall on the 47th day of the siege and that he would be taken alive. Vespasian heard all this and began to believe that Josephus, albeit a strange messenger to him from a Jewish God, had been correct in foretelling his own future. So, while he kept Josephus under close watch, he gave him gifts of clothing and jewelry and "treated him in a very obliging manner" with "Titus joining his interest in the honors that were done him."

IN JUNE OF A.D. 67, Nero's repression and the humid, languid summer found Rome in an equally torpid mood. With much of officialdom in Greece with Nero, those who weren't seemed relieved to escape to their country villas. But for everyone who remained, fear and suspicion were as stifling as the heat. And the more that news of Jewish-Roman warfare filtered back to Rome, the more the Jewish tanners and traders that worked along the banks of the Tiber in the shadow of Capitoline Hill were ostracized or bullied. And a Jewish-Christian would fare scarcely better, even though most were taking pains to explain that they were something quite apart.

Peter at this time may already have been in Rome for several months. He had probably been driven out of Jerusalem five years before when James was murdered, then spent the remaining years among the churches of Antioch and eastern Asia Minor. Roman tradition is that he brought his wife and at least one daughter, Petronilla, to the city with him. Indeed, many women in the second and third centuries were named Petronilla and the Catacomb of Domitilla in Rome contains frescoes and carvings honoring the daughter of Peter. The Catholic tradition is that Petronilla was paralytic and that one day as Peter was healing others in public, the crowd urged him to heal his daughter as well. He is said to have obliged, but only temporarily, because he believed her paralysis gave her strength "for the salvation of her soul." [87]

Peter himself is said to have been sponsored or housed by a senator named Pudente as he preached largely in a precinct of the Subura by the same name. The apostle reportedly baptized the family of Pudente, and the names of the senator's daughters, Prudentia and Praxedes, have been handed down through the centuries. Indeed, Pudente is said to have made his home into a Christian place of worship, and the oral tradition is anchored in a basilica of St. Pudentiana, still located at the foot of Esquiline Hill in the former Subura.[88]

By now Peter was determined to lead and comfort the Christians there, both Jewish and Gentile, no matter what the cost to himself. He was now well over 60 years, yet apparently still retained his full head of hair and rough, muscular features. This conjecture is based only on the fact that the frescoes in the Christian catacombs and mausoleums are remarkably consistent despite the often-crude talents of their artists. Peter is seen as a stocky, muscular man with thick curly hair and beard. Paul is invariably portrayed as slight and somewhat stooped, with balding head, thin face and long straight beard.

Might the absence of Nero have given Peter or Paul a freer hand to spread the gospel in Rome? This is doubtful because it also meant that there would now be no restraints on the corrupt freedman Helius, who remained behind as de facto emperor. Unlike Nero, whose passion for arts and athletics left him scant time for governance, Helius' sole charge was to keep order in his master's absence.

Equally bad, the same *religiones illicitæ* that now marked Christians in Rome would soon be exported abroad. Indeed, as local authorities tried to anticipate threats to the emperor's safety and pleasure that might flare up within their borders, Christians could expect to be rounded up with all other suspected seditionists and criminal elements, then used as animal bait in the games or herded off to haul pots of earth in some public works project.

Exactly this was beginning to happen when Peter decided to interrupt his preaching and write a letter to the churches of Asia Minor. No doubt his Greek was adequate for conversation, but not for writing. Yet, the letter received by the churches of Asia Minor was in perfect Greek. Why? Because Peter arrived in Rome accompanied by a man who was both a Roman citizen and facile writer in Greek. He was none other than Silvanus, the man known also as Silas (the shortened version of the same name) who, some 25 years before, had undertaken the first missionary journey to Asia Minor with Paul after Barnabas had decided to go his separate way. It would also be Silvanus, who knew both apostles so well, who would deliver Peter's letter to the churches they had founded in Pontus, Galatia, Cappadocia, Asia and Bithynia.

Peter urged them to hold to their faith despite impending personal peril. By God's great mercy, he wrote,

> ...we have been born anew to a living hope through the resurrection of Jesus Christ from the dead, and to an inheritance which is imperishable, undefiled and unfading, kept in heaven for you, who by God's power are guarded through faith for a salvation ready to be revealed in the last time. In this you rejoice, though now for a little while you may have to suffer various trials, so that the genuineness of your faith, more precious than gold...may redound to praise and glory and honor in the revelation of Jesus Christ.[89]

As God loves you, love one another, Peter urged.

> You know that you were ransomed from the futile ways you inherited from your fathers, not with perishable things but with the precious blood of Christ, like that of a lamb without blemish or spot. He was destined before the foundation of the world but was made manifest at the end of the times for your sake. Through him you have confidence in God, who raised him from the dead and gave him glory so that your faith and hope are in God.

> Having purified your souls by your obedience to the truth

for a sincere love of the brethren, love one another earnestly from the heart. You have been born anew, not of perishable seed but of imperishable, through the living and abiding word of God. For "All flesh is like grass and all its glory is like the flower of grass. The grass withers, and the flower falls, but the word of the Lord abides forever."[90]

Peter admonished the Christians of Asia Minor to abstain from the passions that "wage war" in their souls to retaliate against ruthless reprisals.

Maintain good conduct among the Gentiles, so that in case they speak against you as wrongdoers, they may see your good deeds and glorify God on the day of visitation.

Be subject for the Lord's sake to every human institution, whether it be to the emperor as supreme or to governors sent by him to punish those who do wrong and praise those who do right. For it is God's will that by doing right you should put to silence the ignorance of foolish men. Live as free men, but without using your freedom as a pretext for evil, but live as servants of God. Honor all men. Love the brotherhood. Fear God. Honor the emperor.[91]

Again, Peter urges the churches to stand fast in the midst of their coming ordeal.

The end of things is at hand: therefore keep sane and sober for your prayers. Above all, hold unfailing your love for one another, since love covers a multitude of sins. Practice hospitality ungrudgingly to one another. As each has received a gift, employ it for one another, as good stewards of God's varied grace...

Beloved, do not be surprised at the fiery ordeal which comes upon you to prove you, as though something strange is happening to you. But rejoice so far as you share Christ's sufferings, that you may rejoice and be glad when his glory is revealed. If you are reproached for the name of Christ, you are blessed, because the spirit of glory and of God rests upon you. But let none of you suffer as a murderer or a thief

or wrongdoer or a mischief maker. Yet, if one suffers as a
Christian, let him not be ashamed, but under that name let
him glorify God. For the time has come for judgment to
begin with the household of God. And if it begins with us,
what will be the end of those who do not obey the gospel of
God?[92]

This was the last written communication from Peter. Most likely he had
been under surveillance by agents of Helius for most of his stay in Rome
— especially because he was linked to a senator. Having jotted down
enough for an advocate to justify five minutes before a bored judge, they
could have seized Peter on the street at any time and carted him off to jail
with no notice whatever.

Why Peter? Probably because Helius needed a continuous supply of real
and potential troublemakers to fuel the prosecutorial furnace and demonstrate his diligence to a nervous emperor. Indeed, Helius had already begun
inventing charges so wild as to cause head scratching among the most dutiful of his lackey-advocates.

Just one example of this farcicality is how Helius used Nero's absence
to take off one of Rome's foremost senators, Sulpicius Camerinus, together with his grown son. The charge was that his family name had included
the name of Pythicus, which it had received as an honor for oratory in some
Greek games perhaps centuries before. Continuing to use this name, it was
now charged, showed irreverence for the title, Pythicus, which was awarded to Nero for some of his artistic victories in Pythia.

When the senators and knights weren't being picked apart, Helius swat-
ted at philosophers and out-of-favor religious orders to keep up his pace.

And this brings us back to Peter.

How ironic it was that only a minute's walk from where the Via Sacra
ended at the door of Rome's most venerated institutions, the Senate house,
squatted a small, mean, stone building that seems oddly misplaced on
such a splendid street, for it deserved to be hidden in the shadows of
Rome's history. But the Mamertine Prison was nonetheless a Roman tradition
in its own right. It was erected many centuries beforehand as a fortification
around a large cistern, which probably lay atop one of Rome's many underground streams or natural springs. Thus, the walls of its soot-colored
travertine rock are round (the present tense used here because it can still be
visited today). Inside the outer parts of the building, which served as barracks for guards, the walls of the old cistern measure perhaps no more than
30 feet in diameter.

Long ago the deep cistern was partially filled in to build a small prison with two tiers. The top was a crude foyer and guard station. The bottom layer was more like a grotto, with no more than six or seven feet from floor to rocky ceiling. All that separated the two levels was a small stairway and a bored hole in the top floor perhaps three feet in diameter.

In the early days of the Republic the building, known then as the Tullianum, was not so much a prison (for Rome kept no long-term prisoners), as an execution place. Some enemies of the state — often defeated but defiant foreign rulers — were simply cast into the hole and into utter darkness until they succumbed to starvation, fetid air and loss of hope.

The Tullianum was also the place where condemned men were held briefly before execution. Perhaps once or twice a year before a triumph or certain festival, the public might see the ugly wooden doors creak open long enough to admit a few dozen brawny bare-chested slaves who had been marched there from the public slave barracks north of the old city walls. The men would enter the hole by means of the narrow, slippery stairs. Then the victims would be pushed down one at a time — always foreigners at first, for it was unlawful then to kill a Roman inside the pomerium, or sacred boundary of the city. As the victim gagged in the foul darkness and struggled to collect his wits, the burly executioners would rush out from the blackness, grab their prey and hold him fast while one of them wrapped his hands around the man's neck and snapped it in two.

Their assignment now completed in the slippery dank cistern, the slave crew would simply leave the dead to rot away, perhaps to have their remains pushed out into the underground sewer system several months later when the next group arrived to do its duty. In subsequent years, even prominent Romans occasionally perished in a similar manner. For instance, Cicero is revered as a lawyer and orator. Yet, when serving as consul 113 years before Nero he sent the rival senator Cataline and several co-conspirators to the same grim place to be strangled in exactly the way just described.

The Tullianum languished as but an embarrassing historical memento for many years after it became more common to house prisoners in another, larger building, the Lautimæ, that sat alongside it at the foot of Capitoline Hill. But by Nero's time the ugly little coop, now known more commonly as the Mamertine, was in use again as a holding place for prisoners from the overcrowded Lautimæ. Those not yet destined for execution were housed in the small upper room, which had a window opening to the neighboring guards' quarters.

The tradition is strong that agents of Helius watched and recorded

Peter's preachings and miracles of healing from the time he first performed them in the public squares of the Subura. If this led to any formal charges, they have never been discovered, but Helius could have picked from any number of possibilities. Peter could have been cited for teaching philosophy publicly, for being a leader of a *religiones illicitæ* or for being a dangerous Jewish rabble-rouser during a time when the Jews of Rome were trying desperately to be inconspicuous.

In any case, the tradition among Catholics in Rome today is very strong that Peter simply disappeared from view one day and was taken to the Mamertine prison. Whether he stayed in this horrid place for days or weeks is impossible to say. However, oral traditions of events within those walls have been alive in Rome ever since the first century and they have been reflected in narrative carvings on sarcophagi. Also lending credence are frescoes in the Roman catacombs dated back to the fourth century (and no earlier due to the more rapid erosion of the soft, damp tufa stone on which they were carved).

First, it is said that the prisoners in the Mamertine were parched for thirst, and that Peter touched a rod to a place in the old cistern wall, causing a spring to gush forth. The plausibility of this story is enhanced by the fact that the Mamertine itself was a cistern built on or near an underground stream.

The second account is that Peter preached the gospel and made believers of two of his guards, then baptized them with water from the same underground spring. We know their names as Processus and Martinianus, and that they were entombed on the Via Aurelia after dying much later, and that Christians venerated their tombs from the beginning.

Thirdly, a story that must be accepted or rejected on faith because one cannot imagine how there could have been witnesses to verify it. Peter's guards, it is said, were prepared for him to leave the Mamertine free. "Nero is in Greece and has forgotten all about you," they reportedly told him. So, late one night after leading a liturgy, Peter strode out the dingy prison doorway and made for the city walls. Perhaps at first he thought himself directed by the Holy Spirit, as he had that night more than 30 years before when he was arrested for preaching in the temple at Jerusalem. But as Peter was about to pass through the gate of the city, he saw Christ coming towards him.

Peter fell down in astonishment and asked: "Lord, where are you going?"
Jesus replied: "I am going to be crucified once again."
Then Peter repeated himself: "Lord, you will be crucified *again?*"
And Christ replied: "Yes, I will be crucified again."
"Then, Lord," answered Peter, "I am returning to follow you."

No sooner had Peter turned around than Jesus vanished. After weeping and collecting his thoughts, Peter understood that the words were meant for his own martyrdom, that the Lord would suffer with him as he would for all those who lived and died in his name. And so, Peter, bursting with new strength, returned to the prison glorifying God and singing praises to the risen Christ.

It is also a strong tradition that on June 29 — the day officially marked by Christians beginning in the third century — that Peter was taken from the Mamertine. He was probably bound, pushed onto a mule-driven cart and hauled northward on the road that borders the Tiber. After a mile or so the grim cavalcade would cross the Neronian bridge from the 14th district of Rome and proceed along the Aurelian consular road into the Vatican area.

No one knows where the name "Vatican" comes from. For centuries it was simply an outlying suburb full of marshes, vineyards and banks of clay that were used for brick manufacturing. It was there that the mother of Caligula built large gardens, and where the young emperor began building the private racetrack that came to be known as the Circus of Caligula and Nero. Official games now took up some 80 days per year, and with the Circus Maximus still undergoing reconstruction, the Vatican Circus was now their focal point. And the condemned people in the cart would be needed to enliven the spectacle.

The Circus, by the way, was an exact replica of the one in the city center: 590 meters long and 95 wide. At its center or spina was a huge Egyptian obelisk that Caligula had loaded onto the world's largest cargo ship, sent to Ostia, dragged some 20 miles by teams of oxen, then set upright in his private circus. And it seems to be there, at the base of the giant obelisk, that Peter was taken to be crucified. It is said that Peter asked only one thing of his executioners: "I beg you crucify me in this way — head down — and no other way." And he explained that he was not worthy to be executed as had his lord and master.

His request would have been gladly granted, for executing a prisoner upside down would only add to the theatrics of the spectacle. As any first century Roman knew, criminals or conquered peoples were crucified in a variety of positions so as to demonstrate to the living populace the many ways that rebels can pay for abusing the government of Rome.

So Peter suffered as had his Lord, hanging naked on the cross, his heels and hands nailed. Finally, if the guards were in a merciful mood, one of them might crush the victim's thighs with a few mighty hammer blows. Now with no means of support, the body would thrust forward and suffocate because the lungs had no means of taking in air.

It's doubtful that many Christians were there to see Peter die. Chances are it was only Romans who witnessed their fellow humans writhing on crosses as a diversion to the main spectacle of races and animal hunts.

Many of the early Christian sarcophagi and frescoes depict Peter and Paul facing death together in Rome. But oral traditions do not, and it is more likely that all these sculptures and paintings simply reflect an understandable desire to associate the deceased with both apostles.

Paul indeed was caught in the same wave of repression unleashed by Nero's nervous custodians of Rome, but again it is the oral tradition that seems more logical. That is, the apostle, now in his mid-sixties, was probably seized where soldiers would know where to find him — the same apartment he rented under house arrest from the day he arrived in Rome.

The Catholic tradition is that Paul was led south, beyond the sacred pomerium (the boundaries within which no foreigner might be buried) on the road to Ostia. Three miles further, just before reaching the village of Ardea, stood a lovely grove of Eucalyptus trees. There in a small clearing stood a beheading block that was to be the last destination of Paul, the tireless traveler for the cause of Christ.

There is no record of what happened, but we do know from his own letters that Paul remained fettered to a soldier for at least two years of confinement in Rome. Soldiers changed guard three times a day and they took on different assignments. This strongly suggests that many military men came in close contact with him and that at least some listened as he dictated letters and preached to the faithful who came to his apartment. And this, more than anything, would justify his claim that there were Christians even in the very household of Cæsar. Thus, it is not at all difficult to imagine the apostle's last minutes. He would be comforting a young man who was probably tearful and trembling as he unsheathed his sword and struggled to carry out his orders. And as his neck was being stretched out on the block, Paul would be reminding the soldier that he, too, could know the grace of Jesus Christ if he would but ask for it.

A.D. 68–69

By January a.d. 68 Nero had been absent from Rome longer than any other emperor save Tiberius. But it had been a glorious 16 months and well worth the cost of the crackdown on potential troublemakers at home, for the Grand Tour had seen a flowering of his talents and the culmination of his destiny. The emperor had led his bulky entourage wherever games were held (save Athens and Sparta, which soothsayers had cautioned him against visiting). By November the emperor had won 1,808 prizes in athletic and dramatic contests. The judges had acclaimed him Pythian Victor, Olympian Victor, Universal Victor, Victor of the Grand Tour and so on.

Sometimes it required ingenuity — and sometimes even a spell of temporary blindness — for the judges to figure how to award the first prize to Nero. On one occasion during the Olympic Games, the emperor was driving a team of ten horses when he was knocked out of his chariot. His servants rushed from the sidelines, pushed him back into it and handed him the reins, but he was too dazed to continue. Nonetheless, the judges awarded him first prize (perhaps on grounds that he would have won had not some flaw in the track caused his fall). In any case, the judges' decision proved prudent because the grateful emperor gave them a million sesterces.

All those about him were constantly sunny in the presence of such a winner — especially the senators who attended him. Nero, like Caligula, hated the Senate as an institution and enjoyed using its members in servile roles. His freedmen constantly scrutinized their faces, gestures and shouts at the games for any sign that they were not blissfully happy to be in the emperor's company. Thus, they were usually to be seen listening reverently to his performances and leading the wild applause as he accepted his prize.

But the private thoughts of most Romans were quite otherwise. Dio Cassius, writing years later, offered this assessment:

> How could one endure...an emperor, an Augustus, named on the program among the contestants, training his voice, practicing various songs, wearing long hair on his head while the chin was smooth-shaven, throwing a toga over his shoulder in the races, walking about with one or two attendants, looking askance at his opponents, and constantly uttering taunting remarks at them, standing in dread of the directors of the games...and lavishing money on them all secretly to avoid being brought to book and scourged?
>
> And all this he did, though by winning the contests of the lyre players and tragedians and heralds he would make certain his defeat in the contest of the Cæsars. What harsher proscription could there ever be...what stranger victory than one for which he received the crown of the wild olive, hay, parsley or pine and lost the political crown? Yet, why should one lament these acts of his, seeing that he also elevated himself on high-soled buskins only to fall from the throne, and in putting on a mask threw off the dignity of his sovereignty to beg in the guise of a runaway slave, to be led about as a blind man, to be heavy with child, to be in labor, to be a madman or to wander as an outcast...?
>
> The masks that he wore were sometimes made to resemble the characters he was portraying and sometimes bore his own likeness. But the women's masks were all fashioned after the features of Sabina [Poppæa] so that, although dead, she might still take part in the spectacle. All the situa-

tions that ordinary actors simulate in their acting he, too, would portray in speech or action or in submitting to the action of others.[93]

Greek audiences also appeared happy and grateful, for they often received lavish gifts. But the truth is that the Greeks themselves were fleeced to pay for the performances and gifts. As in Italy, Nero commanded the survivors of executed freedmen to leave him half their property. Later he took away the entire estates of those who were executed and banished all their children with a single decree. Executions became so common that Dio Cassius describes "dispatch bearers hurrying back and forth [from the camp of Nero and Tigellinus to various guardsmen] bearing no other communications than 'Put this man to death' or 'So and so is dead...'"

Yet, after draining off so much of their money and chopping down their leading men, Nero still found a way to evoke applause as the Grand Tour wound down. On November 28 of A.D. 67, in an oration delivered in the stadium at Corinth, he suddenly declared all of Greece free of Roman taxation.

> It is an unexpected gift, Hellenes...which I grant you, one so great that you were incapable of requesting it. All Hellenes who inhabit Achæa and the land until now called the Peloponnese receive...exemption from tribute, which not even in your most fortunate days did you all enjoy, for you were subjects either of foreigners or of one another.

> Would that I were making this gift while Hellas was still at its height, so that more people might enjoy this boon! For this, indeed, I have a grudge against time, for squandering in advance the fullness of my boon. Yet even now it is not out of pity but out of good will that I bestow this benefaction upon you, requiring your gods, whose care for me both on land and sea I have never found to fail, for affording me an opportunity to bestow so great a benefaction.

> For to cities other rulers, too, have granted freedom, but Nero alone to an entire province![94]

Perhaps the emperor knew by then that his tour would soon end. Helius had been writing him urgent letters begging him to return to an increasingly restless Rome. In early December, Helius underscored the urgency of his plea by sailing to Greece in the fastest ship available and personally begging the emperor to return to save his throne. It was not so much that Rome itself was in an uproar, but the provinces were a different matter. Britain and the two Germanys were rife with angry outbreaks. And rumors were incessant that the commanders of several legionary forces were nervous that they might be the next to follow Corbulo and the German commanders to their deaths. And what about Vespasian with all those legions in Syria? He was being heard from all too little.

Nero seemed quite unperturbed about all this. Yet, winter was at hand and the number of games had dwindled. Perhaps it would be convenient, after all, to display his crowns to the people at home and treat them again to the talents that won so many laurels for Rome.

The return of Nero in March, A.D. 68 was a theatrical event worthy of a conqueror's most lavish triumph. In a revival of an ancient tradition in which the Greeks honored the winners of their games, a portion of the city wall was torn down and a section of the gates broken in. First to march through the breach were men bearing the crowns won by the emperor. Then came those bearing on the end of spears wooden panels upon which were inscribed the name of the games, the nature of each contest and a statement that it was won by Nero Cæsar, "first among Romans from the beginning of the world." Next came the emperor himself, riding in the carriage Cæsar Augustus had used for triumphs and clad in gold-spangled purple vestment. His head was crowned with a garland of wild olive and his hand held the Pythian laurel. The imperial train, comprised of the soldiers and senators who had been to Greece, passed through the Circus and the Forum, then ascended to the temple of Jupiter Capitoline. From there it proceeded east to the Golden House.

The city was all decked out with garlands, ablaze with lights and reeking with incense. And throughout the procession, the senators led an unending chorus that shouted "Hail, Olympian Victor! Hail Pythian Victor! Augustus! Augustus! Hail to Nero, our Hercules! Hail to Nero, our Apollo! The only Victor of the Grand Tour, the only one from the beginning of time! Blessed are they that hear thee!"

When he had finished these ceremonies, Nero announced a series of horse races, and all of his crowns for chariot racing that he had won in Greece were then carried back to the Circus in the Vatican and placed around the obelisk that stood at its center.

Once the festivities had ended, Nero and his courtiers went down to

Neapolis to spend the rest of the spring. As always, it was *so* much more Hellene than Rome and far more in tune with his artistry.

But those in the other provinces increasingly were not. At just about the same time that the royal entourage was winding its way to Neapolis, Gaius Julius Vindex, the governor of Gaul, decided that he had had enough of an emperor who pranced about in high heels and gave birth to babies on stage. Vindex was a Gaul from Acquitania, descended from a long line of royalty and a father who had become a Roman senator. He was powerful in body, of shrewd intelligence and had a burning desire to lead his people in a great undertaking.

Vindex called together the leaders of the Gauls and delivered a long and detailed tirade against Nero — the first such public utterance anyone could remember. Nero must fall, he charged, "because he has despoiled the whole Roman world, because he has destroyed the flower of their Senate, because he debauched and then killed his mother and now does not even preserve the semblance of sovereignty." Said Vindex:

> Many murders, robberies and outrages, it is true, have often been committed by others. But as far as the other deeds committed by Nero, how could one find words fittingly to describe them?

> I have seen this man — if man he is who has married Sporus and been given in marriage to Pythagoras — in the circle of the theater, sometimes holding the lyre and dressed in loose tunic and buskins, and again wearing high-soled shoes and mask.

> I have seen him in chains, hustled about as a miscreant, heavy with child, eye in the travail of childbirth — in short imitating all the situations of mythology by what he said and did.

> Will anyone, then, style such a person emperor and the Augustus? Never! Let no one abuse these sacred titles. They were held by Augustus and Claudius, whereas this fellow might most properly be termed Thyestes, Oedipus, Alemeon or Orestes, for these are the characters he represents on the stage. Therefore, I urge you to rise against him...and liberate the entire world![95]

Vindex finished to lusty shouts of approval. What made his words so refreshing and appealing was that he did not seek any office for himself. Rather, he proposed the name of Servius Sulpicius Galba, a distinguished Roman patrician who was then serving as governor of Spain.

As Galba was contemplating the meaning of all this, Nero himself received a dispatch about Vindex in Neapolis just as the royal party was finishing lunch while at the same time watching a wrestling match. The emperor showed no visible reaction to its contents. In fact, he left his couch and vied with one of the contestants so that he could try out a new wrestling hold.

The next day Nero wrote the Senate, apologizing for not coming to Rome. He had a sore throat and needed to devote some care to his voice because he had been hoping to go there and sing for them. Besides, he had important business to tend to in Neapolis. He had just overseen the erection of a lavish shrine to the memory of Poppæa Sabina and must now plunge himself into the dedication ceremonies.

As for Vindex, Nero actually seemed rather pleased at the news. He had increasingly viewed the ambitious Gaul as an irritant and now at last had a solid reason to order his disappearance and seize his property in the bargain. After sending orders to Rufus, the governor of Germany, to go to Gaul and remove the troublemaker, the emperor returned to more important pastimes.

Rufus, it turned out, held the emperor in the same esteem as Vindex. After all, his able predecessor had been ordered to fall on his sword simply because he had proven inconveniently competent at his post. But what happened next between two men of similar purpose is one of the great tragedies of Roman military history. Rufus brought his forces to the city of Vesontio in Gaul as if ready to besiege it. Vindex marshaled reinforcements and marched toward the city to help the defenders. Both generals sent messages back and forth inquiring as to each other's intentions. Then finally they held a personal meeting at which they realized that both loathed the emperor.

Now the bizarre happened. Vindex ordered his officers to continue marching the army to Vesontio at a leisurely pace. There, the two forces would link up in what would be the first opposition army to Nero.

But for some unexplained reason, no notice was sent to the Roman forces that were now encamped about the city. When the Romans saw the Gauls approaching directly at them, they grabbed their swords and shields and rushed out to battle. The confused Gauls were hacked down by the hundreds before they could regroup and try to make sense of what had happened. Vindex was so grief-stricken at the fate of his men that he committed suicide as a sacrifice to them.

297

Rufus was of a similar mind, but now his own troops demanded that he take up Vindex' cause. Rufus might have done so, because he was a large, energetic man and witnessed his men throwing down statues of Nero and hailing him by the titles of Cæsar and Augustus. But he steadfastly told them that it was up to the people and Senate of Rome. And it may have been just as well, because on April 2 Galba in Spain declared himself emperor and sent an appeal east for support from the armies of Britain, Germany and Gaul. Within a few weeks he received it.

When word reached Nero of Rufus' "treason" in Gaul, eight days passed before he gave the Senate any reply or direction. All that anyone could tell was that the emperor was still thinking grandly, because he talked of embarking on a Grand Military Tour in which he would journey to Syria, the Caucuses and Alexandria to show that he was mightier than even Alexander the Great.

When Nero finally did journey to Rome, he neither addressed the Senate nor issued any orders for combating his foes in the provinces. Indeed, when a delegation of anxious senators finally called at the Golden House, the emperor spent the allotted time showing them some new, unusual water organs and prattling about how he would soon demonstrate them in the theater.

When Rome and Nero learned that Galba had agreed to lead the rebels and was preparing to march toward Italy, he fainted dead away and spent the next 24 hours senseless in bed. In the ensuing days Nero's mindset would range from ignoring everything one day to conjuring up wild plots on another. Among the latter, which were all thankfully abandoned, were massacring all men in the city of Gallic birth, poisoning the entire Senate at a banquet and setting fire to the city after first letting all the wild beasts loose.

But all this aimless writhing only fueled the seething resentment against him. If any one event made the public spill into the streets, it may have been the arrival of a large Egyptian grain ship at Ostia. Rome was in the throes of a severe corn shortage, and when news traveled that a great cargo ship was on the horizon, spirits rose. But they sank even lower when the ship tied up in the harbor: its entire supply consisted of sand for the court wrestling arena and other bric-a-brac for the Golden House.

The unrest now turned to open taunts and jeers. On one statue of Nero someone hung a sign in Greek that said: "Now you have a *real* contest and you must at last lose."

To the neck of another statue a sack was tied, inscribed with the words: "I have done what I could, but you have earned this sack."

And this graffiti on a wall: "By your singing you have stirred up even the Gauls."

On June 8, A.D. 68 the emperor was at dinner when he received word that virtually all the armies to the north and west were in revolt. He tore the dispatches to pieces, upended the table in a fit of rage and dashed to the ground his two favorite drinking cups, which were carved with scenes from Homer's poems. He lurched outside and went into the adjoining gardens where he exhorted the tribunes and centurions of the Guard to prepare to take him to Ostia. Then he ordered some trusted freedmen to rush there in advance and prepare a fleet for him. But most of them gave evasive responses as they melted away into the darkness, and one even shouted a line from Vergil's *Æneid* over his shoulder:"*Is it, then, such a dreadful thing to die?*"

Now the emperor was left with his wine and a few servants. He mumbled and his mind wandered. He talked in one minute of going to Parthia as a supplicant to the king. The next minute it would be about entreating the Senate to give him the prefecture of Egypt. Or maybe if he went to the Senate with a heartfelt apology, it would simply allow him to go peacefully to Egypt, where he could earn his living as a lyre player. Soon Nero's senses had drained away with all the wine he had drunk and his servants convinced him to go to bed and make his plan on the morrow. Before he was led to his bedchamber, Nero took care to take a small box of poison that had been prepared by Locusta, the same old alchemist who had served to take off Brittanicus and other imperial nuisances over the years.

While the emperor had fretted in his cups, the consuls of Rome had received the same dispatches from the provinces. The solidarity shown by the provincial legions had finally stiffened the Senate's spine enough to gather in special session that night and declare Galba emperor. The Prætorian Guard was persuaded as well. Eventually, the Roman people would be going wild with delight, many even wearing liberty caps to signify that they had been set free from slavery. But not that night, because they weren't sure where the deposed emperor was or what he might be planning.

When Nero awoke the next morning, the potion he had placed on the bedside table was gone. So were all the servants and guardsmen. After wandering the cavernous corridors alone for several minutes, he finally found himself with just three loyal subjects. They were Phaon, one of his freedmen, Epaphroditus, his private secretary, and Sporus, his adolescent eunuch and "wife."

Their only course now was for Nero to retire to Phaon's own villa in the northern suburbs near the fourth milestone. But as the road led out near the

Prætorian camp, Nero needed to travel in disguise. Barefooted and in his tunic, he put on a faded cloak, covered his face with a handkerchief and mounted a worn-out horse. A nasty late spring squall was beginning to kick up, which would keep most people off the streets. But Nero shuddered as they passed by the Prætorian camp and heard a shout go up for Galba. And then they heard someone inside the wall say, "Is there any news about Nero?"

It was raining hard now. The four wet stragglers had passed the camp and had just turned a corner when Nero's horse started at the smell of a corpse lying on the road. As Nero steadied himself by gripping the bridle with both hands, his face was exposed and a man on the roadside recognized him instantly. The observer was a retired Prætorian guardsman, and as he saw the rider's face, his hand went up with an automatic reflex to salute the emperor.

Now the party couldn't be sure if or when pursuers might be on their trail. Their pace quickened. As they turned into a by-path leading to Phaon's villa in the early morning, they dismounted and set the horses loose. Nero, told to sneak in so that slaves and servants wouldn't notice, made his way amid some thick bushes and brambles that lined the back wall of the house. Nero had great difficulty negotiating the prickly thicket until someone threw down a cloak over the bushes so he could tread on it.

Phaon urged him to go crouch inside a nearby pit that had been used to dig sand, but Nero refused to "hide underground," as he put it, while he was still alive. So, while the others tried to clear the way for him to enter the house without being detected, Nero sat in the bushes, picking the thorns and twigs from his torn cloak. Adjacent to the bushes was a small fishpond of green slimy water, into which he dipped his hand for a drink. "This is Nero's distilled water," he muttered, referring to how his drinking water was always boiled first, then cooled with ice.

Still signaling for quiet, Phaon opened the back door and told Nero to crawl on all fours into the hallway, and then into the first vacant room. There a cloak had been placed over an old saggy couch, and Nero slumped on it bemoaning his fate. "What an artist the world is losing," he wept and wailed repeatedly.

It was now obvious that there would be no further plan, no retaliation, no escape. Nero's companions could talk only of the indignities that would be visited on his body if he did not take steps quickly to prevent them. Refusing some coarse bread that was offered him, Nero asked his companions to dig a grave, collect any marble that could be found for a marker, bring some water for washing his body and wood for a fire to burn it.

His decision was reinforced shortly thereafter when one of Phaon's couriers brought a letter from the Senate. It announced that Nero had been pronounced a public enemy and was now being sought so that he could be punished in the "ancient tradition."

It meant that the convicted criminal was stripped naked, fastened by the neck to a forked stake and then beaten to death with rods.

Nero sobbed softly. He picked up two daggers he had brought with him and pressed their points to his chest. Then he put them down, pleading that the fated hour had not yet come. Rather, he turned to the boy Sporus and begged him to begin a widow's wailing. Then, changing his mind again, he beseeched anyone from his party to help him take his life at once. Now he reproached himself for his cowardice. "To live despoiled, disgraced," be mumbled, "does not become Nero, does not become him. One should be resolute at such times. Come now, rouse thyself."

What did rouse him finally was the sound of horsemen who had come with orders to take him alive. "Ah, the trampling of swift-footed studs in my ear," he said, quoting *The Iliad* in a quavering voice. Then he drove a dagger into his throat. Epaphroditus quickly reached over and closed his hand over Nero's to give the blow added force.

He was all but gone when a centurion rushed in. The guardsman placed a cloth to the wound as if to be aiding him, but Nero merely gasped, "Too late." He died with his eyes so set and staring that all who saw him shuddered with horror.

Nero's death came on June 9, A.D. 68. He had lived 30 years and five months, of which he ruled the world for 13 years and 10 months.

Thus, so pathetically ended the Age of Augustus with the last of his descendants.

WHEN JOSEPHUS WAS LATER to reflect upon the sea of Gennesaret (Galilee) before the Jewish wars, he wrote of how it had been "blessed by the Creator."

> Its waters are sweet, and very agreeable for drinking, for they are finer than the thick waters of other fens. The lake is also pure, and on every side ends directly at the shores and at the sand. It is also of a temperate nature when you draw it up, and of a more gentle nature than river or fountain water, and yet always cooler than what one would expect in so diffuse a place as this.

And as for the surrounding countryside:

> Its soil is so fruitful that all sorts of trees can grow upon
> it...for the temper of the air is so well mixed that it agrees
> very well with those several sorts, particularly walnuts,
> which require the coldest air, flourish there in vast plenty.
> There are palm trees also, which grow best in hot air. Fig
> trees also and olives grow near them, which yet require an
> air that is more temperate. One may well call this place the
> ambition of nature, where it forces those plants that are nat-
> urally enemies to one another to agree together.[96]

This scenery would change abruptly to one of complete devastation in
A.D. 68 as the army of Vespasian continued its slow march south to Jerusalem.
After the destruction of Jotapata, the general might well have sped directly to the center of Jewish life just 90 or so miles away. That he waited nearly a year was due in part to the general being a deliberate tactician who wished
to systematically eliminate all remaining impediments to the Roman advance
on all sides of Jerusalem, no matter how trivial. But weighing equally in favor
of deliberation was intelligence indicating that the defenders of Jerusalem
would use the time to exhaust themselves in a convulsion of rivalry and
treachery. For each time the Romans would encircle and wipe out a Jewish
settlement, a knot of the most zealous — often the most well armed — defenders would somehow escape and work their way back to Jerusalem. Some
were patriots. Some were the worst sort of criminals. And inevitably when
these young, hate-filled firebrands arrived, they only made the mix of personalities and factions within the holy city of Jerusalem all the more combustible in the days before taking its final stand against the Roman oppressor.

So it was in early A.D. 68 when into the gates of the capital came John of
Gischala and his band of brigands. When the city of Gischala was about to
be taken by Titus, the long-time enemy of Josephus and some 2,000 followers
had abandoned their women and children and fled to Jerusalem. But rather
than entering with their tails between their legs, they were greeted as heroes as they rode through the city gates. People inside crowded around them,
eager for reports on the war in Galilee. John dwelt not on defeats and es-
capes, however. He proclaimed that his men had come to strengthen the defense of Jerusalem, because this, after all, was the best place in which to defeat the Romans. He reported the Roman condition as weak and predicted
that many more contingents from Galilee would soon arrive to bolster
Jerusalem for its final victory. After all, if the Romans had struggled so mightily in taking smaller towns like Jotapata and Gischala, how could they
hope to surmount the most formidable walls in the world?

Almost at the very time John entered Jerusalem, Titus and Vespasian changed tactics, sending word to the remaining towns that they would offer sanctuary for surrender. This invariably forced the issue in each city, causing most people to flock to the Romans for protection and the diehard rebels to head for Jerusalem. Yet, the results were what neither the defectors of Galilee nor defenders in Jerusalem expected. By this I mean, first, that the Galileans who surrendered were simply left to roam and forage. The Romans did nothing for them while at the same time laying first claim on all available food supplies. This forced people to coalesce in roving roadside gangs that robbed and plundered anyone in their path. When these grew to such size to attract reprisals by Roman garrisons, the most desperate of the gang leaders fled to Jerusalem for protection. So now the capital was teeming, not with the valiant heroes John had promised the populace, but with the worst elements from all over Judea and Galilee. And once they were inside the walls of Jerusalem, these disheveled and disorganized bands not only helped themselves to supplies that were needed for the war effort, but "omitted no kind of barbarity," writes Josephus.

> For they did not measure their courage by their rapines and plunderings only, but proceeded as far as murdering men. And this not in the night time or privately...but they did it openly in the day time, and began with the most eminent men of the city.

> This caused a terrible consternation among the people, and everyone contented himself with taking care of his own safety, as they would do if the city had been taken in war.[97]

The most rapacious of all the troublemakers were the Zealots, still led by the defiant Eleazar, who had seized control of the temple the year before and stunned the priesthood by decreeing that sacrifices by "foreigners" were forbidden. The new temple guardians arrested some of the city's leading men, including one who had been in charge of the public treasury. Worried that the populace would soon form a mob and demand their release, a dozen or so leading Zealots stole into the prison and cut the throats of their victims. Then they went about the city announcing that the dead elders had been caught in a conspiracy to surrender to the Romans.

When no one revolted, the Zealots decided they would make their seizure of the temple official by appointing their own ruling priests. Disregarding the families who had supplied high priests for generations, they gave offices to what Josephus calls "certain unknown and ignoble persons...that they might have their assistance in their wicked undertakings."

Indeed, they even cast lots for the position of high priest. The "winner" was a bumpkin named Phannias, who came from a tiny backwater village. Until he saw his mates casting lots and asked to get in on the fun, Phannias had not even known what a high priest was. Now, as the lucky winner, he was outfitted with the sacred garments as though the chief actor in a comedy. Soon "High Priest" Phannias had gotten into the spirit of the day, strutting about the inner temple courtyards giving orders with a grave face as his companions guffawed and swilled wine from sacred vessels. The same crew ate off ritualistic plates and threw them in a corner when they were dirty.

Some people could bear this no more and decided that they cared no longer about the risks of speaking out because life in these conditions was not worth living. One was Ananus, the same high priest who had ordered the murder of James, the brother of Jesus, and now a high priest with no temple and only the vestiges of his personal prestige. One day Ananus could be seen going among the crowds in the marketplaces, reproaching the people for their sloth in doing nothing against the Zealots. It was obvious that Ananus no longer cared whether he was observed or not. Soon he was surrounded by a large, curious crowd that clearly wanted to hear more. Ananus obliged by mounting some steps and announcing to them that he despaired of living.

> For to what purpose is there to live among a people so insensitive to their calamities and [who have] no notion remaining of any remedy for the miseries that are upon them? For when you are seized upon, you bear it! And when you are beaten you are silent! And when the people are murdered, nobody dares so much as to even groan openly! O bitter tyranny that we are under!
>
> But why do I complain of tyrants? Was it not you, in your sufferance of them, who have nourished them? Was it not you who overlooked those who first of all got together? For they were then but a few, and by your silence have grown to be many.[98]

Romans, lamented Ananus, had at least traditionally respected ancient Jewish customs by keeping their distance from the inner temple precincts.

But those who now occupied them "walk about in the midst of the holy places at the very time their hands are still warm with the slaughter of their own countrymen." How ironic, he said with scorn to the murmuring crowd, that "one may soon find the Romans to be the supporters of our laws and those among ourselves the subverters of them!"

With exhortations like these, Ananus gradually was able to rouse the ordinary people to rise up against the Zealots. They weren't skilled in warfare, but they outnumbered the temple captors by far, and it was the sheer size and frenzy of this makeshift army that was able to storm inside the temple and force the Zealots from the large Court of Gentiles into the walled inner-precincts. Having done that, Ananus chose a continuous, rotating guard of 6,000 volunteers to keep the Zealots penned in their now-smaller temple quarters as they planned their next move.

Ever since his arrival, John of Gischala had been waiting for the chance to thrust himself into the leadership of Jerusalem. But because John was patient and Vespasian was still nowhere in sight, he began by appearing as an interested and helpful participant in the meetings of Ananus and his advisors. John knew that he and his men from Gischala were not powerful enough alone to wrest control from the Zealots, so he plotted to rise within their leadership by plying them with useful information known only to him. Thus, in the evenings after Ananus and his advisors had gone home, John would sneak past the guards who watched the temple walls and report what he had heard to the waiting Zealots. Meanwhile, he cultivated the greatest of friendships and trust with Ananus himself.

Soon afterward, John embarked on his next ploy. He went to the Zealots and told them he had just returned from a meeting in which Ananus and the city leaders had agreed to send Vespasian a message to the effect that, if he would come quickly, they would open the gates to him. He said that Ananus, as self-appointed high priest, had proclaimed the following day a religious fast, meaning that people would come to the temple on the pretext of prayer and then take it by storm once inside.

Ananus, of course, had said none of this, but the frightened Zealots were now asking their new confidant what to do. John's answer was that they needed help from a foreign army. But with Vespasian coming so soon, the reinforcements would have to be already nearby. Who else but the neighboring Idumeans? They were practically Jews anyway, having once spawned none other than Herod the Great. Probably *not* mentioned was that these were the same neighbors who had opened their country to the Babylonians 600 years before so that they could rush in after them and plunder the stricken Jews. But all that was forgotten as the Zealots quickly drafted a letter appealing for help. Ananus, they charged, was about to hand over the metropolis to Vespasian and only a few brave patriots stood ready to defend it.

One can guess that the Arabs quickly realized that they had three interesting options. If they entered Jerusalem and didn't like what they found, they could raid the wealthiest Jewish homes and depart with whatever they could cart off. They could also wait until the Romans came, have a hand in forcing defeat from within, and gain reward from Vespasian. Or, if the flattering letter was correct and the addition of the noble and valiant Idumean forces made the Jews the stronger force, they'd get their reward from the victorious Jews.

Whatever their frame of mind, the appeal was enough to rally Idumean warriors in a mad rush to arms as if, says Josephus, "they were going to a feast." Soon 20,000 Idumean warriors — much to the astonishment of Ananus — were thronging outside the gates of Jerusalem, demanding to be let in.

What to do? Ananus had his senior-most priest call down from the ramparts. "It is true that many troubles indeed have fallen upon this city," he said, "yet none of them has given me more cause to wonder at her fortune as right now, when you have come to assist wicked men who each deserve a thousand deaths. They are murderers and robbers who have profaned this most sacred temple and who are right now getting drunk in the sanctuary and expending the spoils of those whom they have slaughtered upon their insatiable bellies. When the men of this city look down on you with your finest armament," shouted the priest, "what can we call this procedure of yours but the sport of fortune?" The people, he added, were ready to invite the Idumeans to send in an inspection team and assess the situation for itself. Meanwhile, "do not wonder why the gates are shut against you while you bear so many arms."

Crowds are seldom in a mood to assimilate intricate reason, and this one paid scant attention to Ananus' spokesman. All the Idumeans knew was that they had dropped what they were doing and rushed to Jerusalem — and for what? To be left outside the walls with no food or warmth as night came on?

It's true that the Idumeans hadn't come prepared to camp outside the walls, and to make their mood even uglier, a storm began to rage as night fell. It struck, wrote Josephus,

> ... with the utmost violence, and very strong winds, with the
> largest showers of rain, with continued lightning, terrible

thundering and amazing concussions and bellowings of the earth that it was as if it were an earthquake. These things were a manifest indication that some destruction was coming upon men, when the system of the world was put in this disorder, and anyone would guess that these wonders foreshadowed some grand calamities that were coming.99

As the Idumeans shivered beneath their makeshift roofs of locked shields, the inventive Zealots inside the temple devised a way to use the noise of nature to good advantage. Amidst the loud thunder they overpowered the few guards who had huddled about outside and darted off in the night shadows to the main city gate. There, as expected, they also found people shut tight in their houses and the watchtower guards in disarray from the storm. The Zealots had brought saws from their armory, and in the darkness they began to cut the bars of the gate. By this time the Idumeans were lined up ready, one by one, to squeeze through the small opening made by the saws.

Once the angry Arabs streamed inside, they were ready to chop everyone in the city to bits. But cooler heads prevailed for the moment. The Zealots persuaded them to congregate in the upper city where they attacked the remaining guards and set up their own watch over the temple. Now, after resting briefly and no doubt helping themselves to the Zealots' storehouse of temple wine, they burst forth in a wild frenzy of hate.

By then some of the people had realized that a hostile force was in their midst and began rushing out of their houses as well. Many, assuming that they had only the Zealots to contend with, fought back boldly and defiantly. But at the sight of so many irate Idumean troops as well, they were soon overwhelmed.

> The Zealots also joined in the shouts raised by the Idumeans. And the storm itself rendered their cry more terrible, Nor did the Idumeans spare anybody, for as they are naturally a most barbarous and bloody nation, and had been distressed by the tempest, they made use of their weapons against those who had shut the gates against them and acted in the same manner as to those that supplicated for their lives as to those who had fought them. Now there was neither any place for flight nor any hope of preservation, but as they were driven one upon another in heaps, so they were slain.100

As the first daylight appeared, some 8,500 bodies were counted in the outer temple alone. Yet the Idumeans were still not satiated. They now plundered homes and butchered everyone inside. Among them were Ananus and the leading priests, who were first upbraided for their discourtesy in not opening the gates. The killers, said Josephus, proceeded to cast away dead bodies without burial. "I should not be mistaken," he added, "if I said that the death of Ananus was the beginning of the destruction of the city, the overthrow of her wall, and the ruin of her affairs."

A new type of governance now began in Jerusalem. The bloodletting went on to the extent that 12,000 more were killed. Many of the leading citizens were arrested and invited to go over to the Zealots and Idumeans, but all refused. Their stubbornness "brought upon them terrible torments," writes Josephus, "for they were so scourged and tortured that at last they considered it a favor to be slain."

Eventually the new rulers grew arm-weary from all the killing or perhaps decided that merely bringing about the death of men wasn't enough. If they could hold "tribunals" and judge the accused guilty of various crimes, they could gain legal authority to divide up the property of the "traitors" as well. To give this show some legitimacy, they called together 70 ordinary citizens to serve as judges, assuming all the time that these frightened wretches would be cowed into voting as their new masters wanted.

Now came a series of rump trials, among them the case of one Zacharias, who was one of the richest and most respected men in Jerusalem. The charges were that he had been part of the plot to betray the city to Vespasian. There was no proof that Zacharias was part of any such doings, but the defendant could see that anything he could say mattered naught and that his life wasn't worth a mina (the smallest Jewish coin). So Zacharias stood up, waved off the accusation with a few words of bitter sarcasm and launched instead into a fierce, biting indictment of his accusers. He recited all the Jewish laws they had broken and the low state to which they had brought the great city.

Now the Zealots were in turmoil. They had their hands on the hilts of their swords and would have run him through right there were it not for the fact that they had determined to make a show of impartiality. They decided to calm down and wait for the jury of 70 to convene in private and return with a "suitable" verdict.

After a considerable time, the 70 judges filed back into the large courtroom and with solemn, ashen faces announced that Zacharias was acquitted. They had chosen to die rather than have his death on their consciences.

The Zealots sat in silent disbelief for a few eerie moments. Then, without a sound two of their boldest members rushed at Zacharias from their benches with drawn swords and hacked him down as he stood in proud defiance. Other Zealots were ready to deliver the same fate to the 70 judges, but the leaders decided to herd them out of the building while beating them with the flat parts of their swords. Then they were kicked down the court steps and sent stumbling into the crowd milling outside as messengers to the rest that they were no better than naughty slaves.

Some Idumean leaders had seen all this. In fact, after several days in the city, their commanders began to realize that their first perceptions of the situation in Jerusalem simply had not been accurate. They had watched the Zealot leaders get sloppy drunk and brag about all the tricks they had played on the rest of the citizenry. They observed the tortures and sham trials. They had failed to see any evidence that anyone had offered to hand Vespasian the city. Moreover, the Romans were reported to be still many miles away and showing no signs of preparing to march. So, one day the Idumeans surprised the Zealots by announcing that they were leaving. And perhaps because they felt guilt at the disaster they had helped bring about, the Idumeans bulled their way into the prisons and led their 2,000 occupants outside the gates under their protection as the Zealots looked on helplessly.

And what of the Zealots now? Initially, the people grew somewhat bolder, as if testing their outnumbered overlords. But the Zealot leaders quickly adopted an even more insolent attitude. Their Arab rescuers of several days ago were now depicted as witless barbarians who had only hindered the Jewish cause. Before others could regroup, the Zealots had resumed their trials, with even more speedy convictions of those who headed the most illustrious and wealthy families who still remained.

Vespasian's camp was not oblivious to all this, for his intelligence scouts slipped in among the departing Idumeans and got an earful. The general's advisors unanimously urged that they march quickly and descend upon the Jews lest they might reunite again. But the ever-practical Vespasian opposed them all. If the Romans began the siege just then, he said, the Jews would indeed unite just as they feared. But if the Romans continued to tarry, they could count on having fewer enemies. After all, the Jews were not then engaged in making armor, building walls or recruiting auxiliaries. Rather, they were in the process of destroying themselves with their own hands.

The general then turned to his younger, ambitious aides. "If any one of you imagines that the glory of a victory gained without fighting is insipid," he said, "let him know that a glorious success, quietly obtained, is more profitable than the dangers of battle. For we ought to esteem those who succeed through temperance no less glorious than those who have gained great reputation by their actions in war."

Indeed, every day a greater number of Jews managed to escape the walls of Jerusalem. How could this be, you may wonder, when the Zealots guarded the gates and killed those who challenged them? It was so because by now the Zealots had deduced that to harbor traitors in their midst would only detract from their defenses. It would be better to let such people purchase their freedom for a steep price. Thus, rich people who were willing to forfeit everything they possessed were allowed to leave, while the poor were slain if they tried to escape.

At about this time John of Gischala had finished his "preparations." With his own band of men from Gischala and all the former Zealots he had won over by perfidy, he appeared before the decimated Zealot leaders and proclaimed himself leader of Jerusalem. Actually, John had been thinking in grander terms than the cutthroats and highwaymen he sought to replace. John proclaimed a new Jewish monarchy with himself as king.

WITH PETER AND PAUL GONE, there was every reason to believe that the Christians might either be stamped out or dissolve of their own accord. Certainly it was not a year in which one could expect Christian boldness. To proclaim the Way in Judea was to risk being seen as an impediment to the Zealot cause against the Romans. In the rest of Syria a Christian message would likely be brushed aside by Hellenes who were trying their utmost to display oneness with their Roman governors. Greece and Asia were still in a torpor after Nero's Grand Tour, and as far as most people understood, Christianity was still a banned religion. In Rome, even the death of Nero brought only a brief sigh of relief. Who could know what the rigidly aristocratic and traditional Galba thought about Christians and the recent persecutions?

Some Christian house churches continued to meet in Rome, but only those that were small and/or cohesive enough to trust each member completely. Increasingly, many Christians found it safer to meet and pray together inside the labyrinth of underground necropoli that had only recently begun to be carved out of the soft tufa rock underlying the open land that lay just outside the city walls.

These underground tunnels did not originate because of any special Christian causes, but simply because no Roman could legally inter their dead inside the city walls and because land around the perimeter was becoming too expensive for individual families. Thus, enterprising landowners began hiring the guild of fusatores (excavators) to create more affordable space underground.

When first begun, the underground necropoli were called "coemeteria," or sleeping places. But after a large excavation along the Appian Way was dubbed the "Catacombs," all others have been since referred to by the same generic name. At the end of Nero's time, these labyrinths probably extended no more than two miles. Over centuries the many networks of tunnels would extend some 360 miles in all.

Entering a catacomb usually began simply by walking into a hillside and then descending gradually. One always took an oil lamp, but during the daytime they were also illuminated by weak shafts of light from bores that the fusatores created to remove rubble to the ground level.

Once the eyes were accustomed to the dark, one's most powerful impression might have been what a cosmopolitan place Rome was. Along the great highways were tombs of Roman patrician families, but along these narrow corridors one found the graves of tanners and traders and bakers and seamen from every place in the world. Most of the bodies were deposited in rectangular niches and then covered over with marble or terra cotta slabs giving the deceased's name. But there were also whole chambers, or cryptia, decorated with stuccoes or expressive paintings in richly contrasting colors and lit (during family visits) with large candelabra. The artistry could never be called exquisite because those who labored in the catacombs faced certain handicaps. The light was poor, of course, and the rock porous, meaning that it didn't resist dampness well nor permit precise carving. It also tolerated only one coating (usually of lime and volcanic dust). But mostly it is obvious that very few of the living had had funds with which to hire a trained artist. They made do with their own funereal art.

It would not be difficult to pick out the Christian tombs because the headstones almost always contained recognizable symbols, carved crudely by the hands of loved ones. As with early Christian graves elsewhere, the ones in Rome employ such symbols as a fish (Christ), ship's anchor (salvation), the lamb (also salvation), the peacock (immortality), the fish and basket of loaves (for the Lord's Supper) and the dove (the soul). One could find crude frescoes of Peter and Paul, but more often the symbol of the sword was used to mean Paul (by his beheading) while Peter was revered by a cock (referring to the time when he wept bitterly as he heard the cock crow to begin the day of Jesus' crucifixion).

All these subterranean activities didn't mean that Christians were wholly secretive or cowardly. While it is true that few would dare, for example, to preach in a marketplace or even volunteer one's name to a stranger, the faith burned brightly in the souls of hundreds and many found ways to keep their light from being buried under a bushel. One such illustration was the way in which the graves of Peter and Paul came to be established and venerated.

No one knows who came forth to take responsibility for the burial of Peter's body — might it have been the senator Pudente? — only that it had taken a special act of courage in the midst of Nero's wave of repression in Rome. One can assert with much more confidence where Peter was entombed: just across the street from the circus in which he was crucified. In the Trionfale section of the Vatican, the Circus of Caligula and Nero spread out along the bottom of a hillside. Neither emperor ever finished the racetrack in marble, and its base of travertine and upper story of wood projected a gray gloominess, with its Egyptian obelisk peering out atop the walls.

The Circus was situated from west to east. Running the length of its northern side were the basalt paving stones of the Via Cornelia. Across the road the hillside began its gradual rise, with a large stairway leading to another road at the top. It was at the foot of this once-unused hillside that one could find a growing necropolis in the late first century. Most of the graves were simple and poor, with no markers. But what would strike an unknowing visitor as strange at first glance is that several of the monuments and graves seemed to be clustered around — and on the hillside above — a slightly larger grave. In front, at street level, was a low wall not quite hip high. In the middle was a simple unmarked grave covered by terra cotta tiles. In the back was a red plaster wall.

So far the above could have referred to a million unmarked graves in Italy. This one was distinctive, however, because the back wall was covered with graffiti: Christian symbols, greetings from visitors in many languages and invocations to Peter. Running the length of the low wall in front was a narrow drainage ditch to prevent rainwater from rushing down the hill and flooding the area. In the ditch people from all nations tossed coins and notes of prayer.

Was this the grave of Peter? Christians of the period certainly thought so and no one has ever proven or even plausibly claimed that he was buried elsewhere. Any lingering doubts have been allayed by further excavations beneath the Vatican Basilica (see author's epilogue).

The resting place of the apostle Paul is no less the subject of strong oral tradition, but not as easy to confirm scientifically. South of the city proper, where the Tiber swings southeast and practically meets the road to Ostia, there had already existed a large necropolis that served the polyglot of foreign-born families who occupied the Trastevere neighborhood across the river. It is along an unpretentious side path in that necropolis, lined with the tombs of pagans and Christians alike, where the oral tradition places the simple grave of Paul. It was said to be covered with a thin marble slab through which are bored two square openings and one round hole of different dimensions.

The openings allowed pilgrims to lower objects of devotion, such as thuribles of frankincense or pieces of cloth, so as to be blessed by touching the holy tomb below. Atop the marble slab was an inscription that appeared as if it might have been scrawled in haste by someone who did not want to remain for long under the watch of Roman soldiers standing nearby. The inscription says simply in Latin,

PAULO

APOSTOLOMART[YRI]

AFTER 14 OPPRESSIVE YEARS under Nero, the people of Rome desperately needed time for repose. Instead, they were to see a succession of bloody internal struggles that brought four emperors in less than two years and nearly toppled the empire Cæsar Augustus had bequeathed just 55 years before.

In theory, Servius Galba was just the man to usher in a new era. A wealthy widower who had held the governorship of Spain just prior to Nero's downfall, this rigid aristocrat was steeped in patrician tradition to the point of clinging to the largely outmoded custom of requiring that his entire household staff line up first to bid him good morning and again to say good night. After serving many commands with distinction, Galba at 70 had no other ambition than to restore integrity to Rome's sacred institutions and — above all — to free the monarchy from the tyranny of the Prætorian Guard.

But almost as soon as Galba and his military support entered Rome in August A.D. 68, the impression he made on the common people could seen by the snide graffiti on walls everywhere. Jokesters had much to pick from. Galba had a beaked nose and a permanent scowl. One side of him seemed to sag from an old war wound and he had to be helped in and out of his ceremonial armor. Romans also learned that the new emperor's austerity was a two-edged sword. He'd refused any bonuses to the provincial armies that had first declared for him. When the Prætorians wanted a little something for welcoming him in town, he told them "I am accustomed to levy soldiers, not to buy them." When a cohort of marines flocked to the palace to protest his refusal to include them on the regular army's payroll, the new emperor had cavalry units charge through them until they scattered in fear.

The penury wasn't just confined to the military. One of Galba's first acts was to give the Senate an itemized account showing that Nero had bestowed some 2.2 billion sesterces of public funds on various cronies, mistresses, chariot drivers and the like. He now decreed that the recipients each must return 90 percent and commissioned 50 knights to go about collecting it. Since nearly all the recipients were wastrels in the first place, one can imagine the turmoil that erupted in trying to reclaim the money.

But Galba's worst shortcoming was that he was old and had no heir. This kept several possible pretenders on the alert, the most decisive of which was 37-year-old Marcus Salvius Otho. This is the same Otho who had been married to Poppæa Sabina until Nero snatched her away and sent him to govern Lusitania. Since Lusitania fell within the domain of the governor of Spain, Otho had served well under Galba and felt he should have been handed the choicest of positions. He was not, simply because Galba knew what a carouser and spendthrift he'd been while growing up at Nero's side. But when the ambitious Otho went to the Prætorian Guard commanders and promised that he would be a much more generous emperor, it was only a matter of days before Galba's reign came to an end.

On January 15, A.D. 69, Prætorians surrounded a defenseless Galba in the Forum, toppled his litter and surrounded the old man as he struggled to his knees. Galba sputtered that he'd grant them their accursed bonuses if that's what they had come about, but it was too late. They swiftly hacked him to pieces and carried off his severed limbs as personal trophies. They knew that by then the new emperor Otho was already inside the Prætorian barracks doling out sizeable bonuses.

As if to validate Galba's judgment, Otho began his reign by appropriating 50 million sesterces to finish work on the Golden House. Nero's statues reappeared in the city and the boy-eunuch Sporus found himself brought back as an imperial playmate.

But Otho was to last even less than Galba. Almost as soon as Otho seized the throne he faced armed opposition from another contender from the provincial legions. The day Galba had marched into Rome, the legions of Upper and Lower Germany were no less expecting of bonuses than were the Prætorian guardsmen. When told the old man had refused them as well, the legionaries looked about for a new champion and quickly found one in a Roman political hack who had just been named their commander.

This lazy, good-natured, gluttonous lout was Aulus Vitellius, whose only attribute seems to be that he came from an illustrious family. His father was Lucius Vitellius — the same venerable senator who was once crony of Tiberius, governor of Syria and chief sycophant to Gaius, Claudius and Nero. The younger Vitellius had dabbled at various public positions but was never considered a military man. The most common explanation of how he got to rule Germany springs from the fact that both Vitellius and the consul Titus Vinius were big supporters of the Blue faction at the races. Vitellius, badly in debt, begged Vinius to ask Galba for the rich governorship of Lower Germany. Galba was receptive on grounds that such an indolent fellow would be least likely to rebel against him. "No men are less to be feared than those who think of nothing but eating," reasoned the emperor. "Perhaps Vitellius' bottomless gullet can be filled by the resources of the province." Indeed, gluttony was his most outstanding trait. By now a jowly, overstuffed 54, Vitellius usually began his first banquet at noon, was woozy and wobbly by mid-afternoon, then took a long nap so that he'd be alert enough to repeat the sequence the same evening.

As for his military prowess, a contemporary writes, "He was ignorant of soldiering, incapable of forethought, knew nothing of marching order or scouting, or how far operations should be pressed forward or protracted. He always had to ask someone else."

Yet, his was an army that seemed happy to run itself in his name, thanks to two ambitious generals. Fabius Valens was an older career soldier who had been raised in poverty and who now was developing a taste for the finer things that could be gained either by bribing or plundering the towns along his marches. His counterpart was Alienus Cæcina, a handsome, statuesque youth who easily inspired admiration among his men. Once, in his first command, Cæcina had been convicted of misappropriating public funds. He had insisted all along that it had been done on Galba's orders. Now he was eager to erase the black mark from the public's memory and Galba from his.

Within just two weeks Valens could claim 40,000 men in Lower Germany and Cæcina another 30,000 in Upper Germany. But this was just the core. Both were reinforced by German auxiliaries, and the strategy was for Cæcina to take his men direct to alpine Italy via the Pennine Pass while Valens was to wind south through Gaul, winning the province to his side — or destroying it.

During March and April the rival troops of Vitellius and Otho would trample and churn up the northern half of Italy. As soon as the Vitellian legions of Germany and Gaul marched off towards Rome, their thinly defended camps were challenged and sometimes overrun by the tribes of Germany. As Vitellians marched through Italian towns they seized crops and animals, ransomed homes for cash and plundered if no bribes were forthcoming. When the rivals finally converged and clashed along the Po River, Romans charged against fellow Romans they had served with in other campaigns. And soldiers on both sides showed scant respect or trust for their officers, whom they suspected of hoarding the plunder from conquered towns. As for the goals of the emperor and his rival, the only difference to the common soldier is which one might host the most lavish banquet in the Golden House.

It finally came to an end April 16 near a little village along the Po named Bedriacum. After one of the bloodiest free-for-alls in Roman history, Otho, in perhaps the only noble act of his career, decided his outnumbered troops had been put through enough. He committed suicide in his tent after bidding his officers to go and make peace with their countrymen.

The rehabilitation of Italy now depended on a new emperor exercising decisive authority. Instead, it was another three months before Vitellius and his ungainly caravan would appear within sight of Rome. Victorious generals had to be feted and Roman visitors had to be escorted through the now famous battlefield of Bedriacum. As Tacitus described it,

> Forty days after the battle, it was a disgusting and horrible sight: mangled bodies, mutilated limbs, rotting carcasses of men and horses, the ground foul with clotted blood. Trees and crops all trampled down: the countryside a miserable waste. No less heartless was the stretch of road which the people of Cremona had strewn with laurel-leaves and roses, erecting altars [to Vitellius] and sacrificing victims as if in honor of an oriental despot.[101]

The victorious army's return was also slowed by its own pillaging and the need to stop gangs of abandoned Othonians from doing even more. Italy, which had already been exhausted from provisioning the war, was now picked clean of whatever people had left. And the people themselves joined in, some of them buying uniforms from soldiers so they could charge off and settle old scores with enemies and rival towns.

A final reason for the slow march to Rome was Vitellius himself. As one wag explained, "This was because he couldn't advance a step without first eating everything in his path. Rome and Italy were scoured for dainties to tickle his palate and leading provincials were ruined by having to provide for the feasts."

It was finally July 15 when Vitellius approached the gates of the Eternal City to take his place in the pantheon with the likes of Julius Cæsar and Octavian Augustus. However, having collected a gaggle of 60,000 troops, servants, friends, entertainers, prostitutes and other camp followers, he decided to pause at the seventh milestone long enough to spruce up so that he would arrive in the splendor that Romans expected. Thus, while Vitellius changed into a toga, all around was a cacophony of snack and souvenir sellers, men urinating along the roadside and harlots beckoning from carriages.

The jumble was worsened when city notables arrived with their welcoming retinues, followed by relatives of soldiers picking their way through the mass in search of this or that cohort. Then came the cutpurses and pranksters, including a band of street lads who would sneak up behind a soldier and cut away his sword belt. Then one of their chums would run up and ask, "Hey, soldier, have you got your sword on?" After one too many guffaws from the crowd, some soldiers decided this was hardly the triumph they expected. Swords came out and people were killed, including a father who had come out to greet his long-absent son.

Only then did the mob quiet down and again lumber forward for its triumph in Rome. The enormous parade ended with Vitellius giving a grandiloquent eulogy to himself in which he extolled his industry and self-discipline. The unknowing crowd applauded wildly.

In the weeks that followed, the new emperor spent his days languishing in the Curia, where he seemed to tolerate debate as long as it was confined to public policy. Generals Valens and Cæcina spent theirs running the government, amassing their own ill-gotten fortunes and competing to see whose wealth and retinue could surpass his rival's.

The average Roman's impression of the new regime might be summed up in three words: "soldiers, soldiers, soldiers." They were everywhere — especially the foreign-speaking Gauls and Germans who gawked about the Forum in their long cloaks of animal skins, often stumbling and slipping on the greasy uneven cobblestones to the constant laughter of Romans. But their presence was more than as sightseers. The barracks were overflowing, and soldiers who couldn't find shelter in private homes were forced to camp among the public colonnades and temples. Some of the foreign auxiliaries settled along the Tiber, where the foul, still summer air began to take their toll on their health.

Why didn't they just go home? Because they expected bonuses. Vitellius kept finding reasons not to pay them, meaning that the only income some soldiers lived on were handouts that Valens and Cæcina proffered in exchange for their allegiance.

But this hadn't stopped Vitellius from spending some 900 million sesterces in public funds in his first three months, some of it for the most outlandish banquets in Roman history. His most conspicuous building project was new stables for chariot drivers and his most common expense was for shows of gladiators and wild beasts.

Cruelty had become part of Vitellius' daily routine as well. Inflicting torture on one's suspected enemies was now a sport — especially when it came to the creditors who had pressed him as a civilian. One of them, who had come to a morning reception, was sent off to be executed, only to be recalled immediately before the guards had dragged him too far. Then, as courtiers were praising the emperor's mercy, he gave orders to have the man killed in his presence because "it would be a feast for my eyes." Another, a knight, cried out as he was being taken off to execution, "You are my heir!" Vitellius compelled him to produce his will. Reading that the man had actually named one of his freedmen as co-heir, he ordered the freedman brought to him at once so that both men could be killed.

When results of the battle of Bedriacum reached Vespasian in Judea, he asked his troops to swear allegiance to Vitellius as he had to Galba and Otho. However, his tone was tepid this time. Some men remained silent and others muttered the words with pained expressions. By summer's end, his officers, with the relentlessness of a battering ram, were pounding him with pleas to abandon his pledge. Vitellius was much Vespasian's inferior as a military man, they argued. The Vitellian legions were a moral disgrace and hardly deserved to be considered the flower of Rome when the nine strong and disciplined legions of the east were the epitome of military professionalism.

But it seemed that the more they flattered and cajoled him, the more obstinate Vespasian became. For the old soldier knew that unlike the Vitellians, his own legions had no experience in civil war. He considered, too, that while he had at age 62 already lived a fulfilling life, challenging Vitellius would risk losing his two sons in the midst of their youth. Indeed, the general would often caution his eager young aides, "You simply don't understand that when one covets a throne there is no middle way between the zenith of success and headlong ruin."

But something else preyed on Vespasian's mind that had nothing to do with his own fortunes. A steady stream of visitors and dispatches from Rome brought disquieting news of aimless soldiers clogging the city streets, imperial indifference, contagious corruption, impending bankruptcy and the prospect that the empire might be wracked by another series of power struggles among whomever could commandeer a couple of legions and make the most extravagant promises to his men.

The moment of decision was probably forced on Vespasian when he came to Berytus to meet the Syrian governor Mucianus, who had traveled down from Antioch. Mucianus was Vespasian's opposite in many ways, an urbane, polished administrator who wore his patrician wealth regally. Yet, Mucianus had grown to respect the good natured, level-headed Vespasian and the two had fashioned a workable partnership in governing Syria.

Mucianus had also sworn allegiance to each new emperor. But now he had come to convince the man he admired greatly that the time had come to change course. In a carefully staged public reception that left Vespasian no more room than a wrestlers' pit to struggle with his conscience, Mucianus turned to the general and said:

> Everybody who plans some great exploit is bound to consider whether his project serves both the public interest and his own reputation, and whether it is easily practicable, or at any rate, not impossible. He must also weigh the advice he receives. Are those who offer it ready to run the risk themselves? And if fortune favors the supreme undertaking, who gains the supreme glory? I, myself, Vespasian, call you to the throne.

> You need not be afraid that I may seem to flatter you. It is more of an insult than a compliment to be chosen to succeed Vitellius. It is not against the powerful intellect of the deified Augustus that we are rising in revolt; not against the cautious prudence of the old Tiberius; nor even against a long-established imperial family like that of Gaius, Claudius or Nero. You even gave way to Galba's ancient lineage. To remain inactive any longer, to leave your country to ruin and pollution, would appear [to be] sheer sloth and cowardice, even if such slavery were as safe for you as it would be dishonorable.

> The time is long past when you could appear to be unambitious: the throne is now your only refuge.[102]

As for himself, Mucianus vowed that he would always be second to Vespasian. "I shall have such honor as you grant me," he said. "But of the risk and dangers, we will share the burden equally" (meaning that he was ready to lead the Syrian legions into Rome). It was this appeal that made Vespasian change his mind and never look back. On the same day, the Syrian legion commanders swore an oath to Vespasian and a few hours later Mucianus announced the decision to the public in the splendid theater Herod Agrippa I had built for the people of Berytus nearly 30 years before.

Once the decision was behind them, Vespasian and Mucianus put the following events into motion: They quickly secured the support of virtually every client state in the region. Of greatest concern was Herod Agrippa II, who was notified in Rome and managed to slip out from the Vitellians and board a ship bound for Syria.

A dispatch was sent to Tiberius Alexander, governor of Alexandria, asking for his support. The governor responded boldly, administering the oath to his two legions on the same day.

Vespasian gave his troops a small "donation" and announced that no more would be forthcoming. As one observer reported: "He had set his face with an admirable firmness against largess to the soldiers, and his army was the better for it."

The general agreed that Mucianus should lead his troops to Rome. Rather, he would go to Alexandria and from there take charge of the grain supply that would be allowed to go to Rome. It took 8,000 tons of grain per week to feed the city's 1 million people. If Vespasian couldn't win the minds of Romans, he knew how to persuade their stomachs.

Vespasian's soldiers were called Flavians, after the name of his ancestral house. As Mucianus prepared the bulk of the Flavian army in Syria, a young general was chosen to lead an invasion force in northern Italy aimed at creating a belt across the country that would eventually seal it off from help from Gaul and Germany. Antonius Primus, who headed the avant-garde, proved to be just as ambitious and reckless as Valens and Cæcina had been in the Vitellian cause. His orders were to march as far as the eastern Italian border and wait for reinforcements from Syria and other legions in the eastern provinces. But Antonius had his own agenda. In Nero's time he had been stripped of his senatorial rank and exiled for forging a will. Yet, by sheer determination and intrigue he had regained enough stature in time to secure command of the Seventh Legion from Galba. Described as "a man of great physical energy," this war was his chance to be one of the first men in Rome if he could win nods of Senate approval for his feats of glory. And it no doubt explains why he couldn't resist racing westward past the undefended borders, even though he had far outdistanced his primary sources of supply.

Meanwhile, Vitellius had managed to rouse the general Cæcina from his couch in Rome and send him north with a force that far exceeded the two legions of Antonius.

Ironically, the two collided only a few miles from the gory Po River battle site that had marked the Vitellian high point. But this time the staging ground was Cremona, a walled market town of some 30,000 that happened to be in the midst of a harvest festival. The Vitellians had used the thickly walled Cremona as a military base against Otho, and they remained popular among the local citizenry. So when the Flavians loomed into view, they were quickly hooted and jeered from the ramparts by the confident Vitellian troops and their supporters.

But they were no less avid than Antonius' men. Though they had marched all day and had no rest or food, the Flavians feared that if they didn't attack immediately their officers would negotiate with the city magistrates and wind up lining their own pockets with ransom.

Soon the troops were clamoring to get on with it. But Antonius went around among the companies, telling them why they should trust the planning and foresight of their generals. "The risks we face are obvious," he implored. "It is night. The enemy is behind walls. Are you going to begin storming the town when you can't possibly see where the ground is level and how high the walls are? How do you know whether to assault it with engines or showers of missiles, or with siege-works and mantlets? Are you going to break through the walls with swords and javelins? Why not wait one night until our siege engines arrive and carry the victory by force?"

With a rapid fire of questions like these Antonius managed to reduce an uproar to sullen muttering. But not for long. Some Flavian soldiers had captured a few Cremonian stragglers and learned something staggering. Only four or five Vitellian legions were actually inside Cremona. Another six legions were camped some 45 miles west of the city and would no doubt rush to its rescue once they learned of the invaders. "Storm the city!" the mutinous men began shouting again.

It was now about nine at night. The Vitellians inside the walls could have waited for reinforcements. They might even have settled for a good night's sleep then try to annihilate the Flavians the next day when they would be cold, stiff and hungry. But it was festival time and the city's population was swelled half again with visitors, all shouting their support for Vitellius. It wasn't long before the emboldened Vitellian soldiers rushed out from the walls in a furious, disorganized attack. From that point on the battle was a confused slaughter on both sides.

As fate would have it, the fighting took place during an eclipse of the moon, and it became so dark that one could barely see in front of him. Worse, both sides were dressed and armed alike. Standards were easily captured and trod upon. Even watchwords were quickly known and used by both sides. The result was one of the strangest battles in history. Dio Cassius reports that as the night wore on,

...one might have seen them sometimes fighting, sometimes

standing and leaning on their spears or even sitting down. Now they would all shout the name of Vespasian, and on the other side that of Vitellius, and they would challenge each other in turn, indulging in abuse or praise of one leader or the other.

One soldier might have a private conversation with an opponent: "Comrade, fellow citizen, what are we doing? Why are we fighting? Come over to my side!"

"No, indeed! You come to my side!"

But what is there surprising about this, considering that the women of the city in the course of the night brought food and drink to give the soldiers of Vitellius, only to find that after eating and drinking themselves, they passed the supplies on to their antagonists? One of them would call out the name of his adversary (for practically all knew one another) and would say: "Comrade, eat this. I give you, not a sword, but bread. Drink this that I hold out to you — not a shield, but a cup. Thus, whether you kill me or I you, we shall quit life more comfortably.[103]

The night was a standoff — until the moon began to emerge from its eclipse in eerie fullness. It shone behind the Flavians, magnifying the shadows of their men so that the Vitellians would take a shadow for substance and aim their missiles awry. Moreover, the moon shone brightly on the Vitellians and made them easier targets. At last Antonius was able to recognize his own men and firm up their ranks.

As dawn brightened the sky, a rumor spread (started by Antonius himself?) that Mucianus and his fresh legions from Syria would arrive at any moment. With that the Flavians fought all the harder and the Vitellian line became more ragged. Before long the Vitellian ranks disintegrated, with Flavians pursuing them along the main highway from Cremona.

When the bulk of Antonius' troops returned at last from their chase and viewed the walls of Cremona in the morning sunlight, they gaped at their challenge. In the previous summer's occupation, Vitellians had erected ramparts all around and further strengthened the fortifications. The Flavian troops had had no rest and scant food for over 24 hours. To storm the town now would be exhausting and perilous. To return to the camp at Bedriacum would involve an equally fatiguing march and undo their victory. Yet, if they tried to erect a camp in this place, it would be subject to a rain of missiles. But when officers weighed all these emotions, their thirst for plunder was greater than their thirst for water and rest.

A brief delay ensued while the Flavians scoured the carnage of the surrounding battlefield for pickaxes, mattocks and hooks and ladders. Then, holding these weapons under shields that were raised above their heads, they advanced in the well-known tortoise formation. But of course their opponents were Roman soldiers who knew what to expect: they rolled down huge masses of heavy stones. Whenever the tortoise withered under the barrage, the defenders thrust at it with lances and poles until the whole cover of shields was broken up. Then they mowed down the torn and bleeding soldiers below with another flurry of missiles.

Eventually the Vitellians, frustrated at seeing so many of their missiles glide off the tortoise, sent their largest catapult crashing down upon them. In an instant it scattered and crushed the men beneath it. But a part of the great engine had been attached to the ramparts by chains, and as it came thundering down, its heavy weight dragged the top of the ramparts down with it. Stones, timbers, men all came tumbling down atop the already crushed invaders in the throes of gruesome death. But even as the dust blinded and choked everyone, Flavian soldiers were beginning to pour through the gaping break in the wall that had been opened.

At that point, the Vitellian general Cæcina, whom the Senate had earlier made consul, appeared majestically in full consular regalia, surrounded by his lictors. It was obvious that he had done this to stand out from the crowd and assure that he would be taken directly to Antonius and granted asylum. But the sight of this posturing so inflamed his own soldiers that they broke ranks and had to be restrained from rushing on him — all of which accomplished Cæcina's objective. He was quickly delivered to Antonius and later sent to Vespasian.

And what of the unfortunate people of Cremona? All eyes were on Antonius for a sign of what he would decide. It came when he went to the baths to wash off the stains of blood from the battle. Criticizing the temperature of the water as too tepid, his aides heard him say, "Well, it won't be long before it's hot."

That is all it took for the soldiers to begin torching the city.

> Without any respect for age or for authority, they added rape to murder and murder to rape. Aged men and decrepit old women, who were worthless as booty, were hustled off

to make sport for them. Any grown girl or handsome youth who fell into their clutches was torn to pieces by the violence of rival rapists, leaving the plunderers themselves to cut each other's throats. Whoever carried off money or solid gold offerings in the temples was cut to pieces if he met others stronger than himself. Some, disdaining easy finds, hunted for hidden hoards and dug out buried treasure by flogging and torturing householders. They held torches in their hands and, having once secured their prize, would fling them wantonly into the empty houses and bare temples.[104]

One thing more. Antonius ordered that no citizen of Cremona was to be taken prisoner. This was both because there was revulsion among Romans against selling Italians into slavery and because Antonius probably wanted no witnesses to tell of his butchery. When it was over, some 32,000 civilians were slain — citizens of Cremona and neighboring Italians alike who had thought they were coming to a festival.

By December, A.D. 69, the Flavian forces were encamped less than 50 miles north of Rome and the city was showing signs of exhaustion. On December 18 a weary Vitellius had even mounted the rostrum in the Forum in an attempt to announce his abdication, but he'd been shouted down by his palace Prætorians and German mercenaries. The next day the out-of-control Germans chased some Flavian supporters up the sacred Capitoline Hill and into the temple Jupiter Optimus Maximus. When the terrified Flavians pushed statues and other monuments into the entranceway as a makeshift barricade, the thoughtless mercenaries torched and burned to the ground the building that had most symbolized Rome's glory for over 500 years.

By now Vitellius had little or no control over events. Agents of Vespasian had already tempted him by offering life-long sanctuary in the Campanian villa of his choice if he would surrender Rome without bloodshed. Discussions had even progressed to the number of slaves he would require and the size of his annual purse. That these plans never materialized is due to the fact that the emperor was under the thumb of the Prætorians and Germans who made up his palace guard and feared the loss of their high wages.

The palace guard was buttressed by the emperor's courtiers, who had so debauched Rome with their excesses that there was no way a successor could let them live. "Once the conqueror took the city, what could make him honor his promise?" they lectured him. "Neither Vespasian's friends nor army will feel their safety assured until their rival is dead. Did Julius Cæsar let Pompey live? Did Augustus allow Mark Anthony? Has Vespasian a loftier disposition? No! Think of your father's three consulships and all the honor your great house has won. Do not disgrace them. If we are defeated in battle, we will die, but at least it will be with honor."

So, they resolved to fight to the death, and the result was a hand-to-hand, street-to-street battle that nearly cost Rome its very life.

Some historians say the battle of Cremona was the strangest in history of the empire, but certainly the battle *within* Rome was the most appalling, because it clearly showed the rot that had eroded the city and the depths to which the people within it had fallen. The Saturnalia of December, with its nonstop drinking and playful reversal of master and slave rolls, was supposed to have ended, but one would not have known it from the uninterrupted debauchery.

> The people came out and watched the fighting, cheering and applauding now on one side, now the other, like spectators in a gladiatorial contest. Whenever one side gave ground and its soldiers hid in shops or some private house, [the spectators] clamored for them to be dragged out and slaughtered. In this way they got the greater part of plunder for themselves. For, while the soldiers were busy with the bloody work of massacre, the spoil fell to the crowd.

> The scene throughout the city was cruel and distorted. On the one side were fighting and wounded men, on the other baths and restaurants. Here lay heaps of bleeding dead, and close at hand were harlots and their ilk. All the vice and license of luxurious peace, and all the crime and horror of a captured town. You would have thought the city mad with fury and riotous with pleasure at the same time.

> Armies had fought in the city before this, twice when Sulla mastered Rome, once under Cinna — nor were there fewer horrors then. What was now so inhuman was peoples' indifference. Not for one minute did they interrupt their life of pleasure. The fighting was a new amusement for their holiday. Caring nothing for either party, they enjoyed them-

selves in riotous dissipation and took pleasure in their country's disaster.[105]

Eventually the Flavians wore down their outnumbered foe. Fifty thousand Vitellians and plain citizens lay dead. Everywhere the city was finally free of fighting except the Guards' camp just outside the Colline Gate. Trapped there were all the Germans and other soldiers whose dirty deeds on behalf of Vitellius had left them no alternative but to die fighting. When the camp gates were finally torn down, Tacitus reports, "Those remaining faced their foes in a body and fought, steeped in each other's blood, until the very last of them fell dead."

As soon as the city had been taken, Vitellius left the palace by a back way and was carried in a litter to his wife's family home on the Aventine. He intended to stay hidden for the day, then escape by night to his brother, who still commanded a small army in Campania. For reasons only Vitellius could tell us (perhaps the Flavians had learned of his location), he sneaked back to the nearly empty palace during the afternoon. There he wandered the deserted halls like a latter day Nero, no doubt mumbling to himself and dragging a flagon of wine with one hand.

His assailants searched there, too, of course. Just before they arrived, Vitellius put on a ragged slave's tunic and hid in a small dark storeroom in which the palace doorkeeper had kept his watchdog. When the soldiers came ransacking everything in the usual way, they dragged the forlorn-looking fat man from his hiding place and asked him his name. He gave a false one; but being soon recognized, he asked to be imprisoned because he had some valuable information regarding the safety of Vespasian.

The soldiers would have none of it. They tied his hands behind his back and put a rope around his neck. They pulled and prodded Vitellius all the way through the Forum towards the rostrum where he had addressed cheering crowds the previous July. Along his path, jeering people poked at him, hurled insults and covered him with garbage and feces. He was dragged up the rostrum, where his captors used the points of their swords to make him hold up his head as he watched them smashing his statues.

At one point a German soldier in the crowd shouted that he could not endure the sight. "I will help you the only way I can," he shouted. With that he leaped on the rostrum and stabbed his sword into Vitellius' ample stomach. Then he turned his sword on himself.

But Vitellius did not die of the wound immediately. As a soldier on the rostrum mocked him, he gasped weakly, "And yet, I was once your emperor." With that he was stabbed several more times and taken off to the Gemonian

Steps. After more torture there, he was killed and his body thrown down. Its head was cut off and carried about the city on pikes, as seemed to be the growing custom for honoring deposed emperors in the capital of the civilized world.

The death of Vitellius ended the war but did not inaugurate peace. The Flavian victors remained under arms.

Lucius Vitellius and his forces in Campania surrendered and their commander was executed.

Quite contrary to Vespasian's orders, the defeated Vitellians were hunted throughout the city and butchered wherever found. Streets were strewn with corpses, which bred rats and turned the air toxic.

On the pretext of hunting for hidden enemies, no one's door was left unopened and no privacy uninspected. Resistance was an excuse for murder.

Slaves betrayed masters for rewards.

Antonius Primus, whom it is said removed enough money and slaves from the imperial palace to make one think he was plundering Cremona, was made consul by the Senate. Domitian, the younger of Vespasian's two sons, was named consul-designate at age 18. He joined happily in the raping and looting — the first public display of character of a young man who would one day become emperor.

THE CHRISTIANS MIGHT have been akin to the trees that grew in the public gardens of Rome. When one of them flourished to the extent that its branches spread out across a road or over a courtyard wall, slaves of the prefecture would chop the tree back severely as if to warn it against ever growing again. But nature seems to tell such trees that they must now compensate by sending out new shoots and at a more vigorous rate than ever. It is always a reminder that the trunk is only the visible part of a broad, strong root system.

In the same vein, it would be inaccurate to think of all Christians as mortally wounded because Peter and Paul were cut down. Rome had been the trunk of the Christian tree only to the extent that Peter and Paul had both been there in their final years. The same analogy holds true for the Jewish Christians who had been centered in Jerusalem. The seizure of the temple by the Zealots and the rupture with Rome had felled the Jewish Christian trunk that had stood in Jerusalem; but because the leadership within Jerusalem still hadn't forbidden people from leaving the city until sometime in A.D. 69, the Jewish Christians decided to move out during the year. They put down new roots in Pella, some 50 miles to the northeast, and old ones were deepened in places like Antioch and Cæsarea.

327

And of course other roots had been long planted in other places — often in far-away lands beyond the reach of the Roman communications system. For instance, while Paul traveled throughout the western provinces, the apostle Thomas left his footprints well beyond Rome's easternmost reaches. Almost from the day after he had personally inspected the nail wounds on the risen Jesus, Thomas had set out to evangelize Parthia, often with Jude at his side, and had never returned.

The account of Thomas leads to a discussion of the twelve apostles (including Matthias, who replaced Judas) and their possible whereabouts as of A.D. 69. One knows what became of James because he was martyred in Jerusalem by Herod Agrippa I. The travels of Peter and John are known to some extent, but all the others remain the subject of speculation, oral tradition and/or controversial ancient manuscripts. Yet, against that sparse backdrop one can add some logic:

1. The resurrected Jesus stood among his disciples and charged them to "Go out into all the world and preach the good news to all creation." The persecutions that followed the stoning of Stephen and the execution of James surely dispersed any apostles who might have lingered in Jerusalem.

2. The growth of Christianity did not flow outward from Rome or any one source, suggesting that its seeds were planted in many places by traveling apostles.

3. There is no written or oral tradition that any of the apostles ever repudiated Jesus. On the contrary, it is probable that *all* either died as martyrs or lived their whole lives faithful to the gospel.

4. The respect of archeologists and scientists for oral tradition is growing — not declining — as new discoveries unfold. For example, the battle of Jotapata had been known for centuries only through the writings of Josephus. However, some ten years ago an Israeli archeological team discovered the actual site and the dig so far verifies everything the ancient historian wrote about Jotapata. Conversely, consider the evidence offered by the *lack* of any oral or written tradition. Paul, for example, wrote that he intended to push on to Spain, and some historians suggest that perhaps he did. And yet, these claims ring hollow because in a nation that is unrivaled for revering its saints with relics and statues, there are no sites, stories or lore about Paul ever being there.

So, how does one navigate through an admitted hazard — balancing the much more complete stories of Peter and Paul with the fragments of the others who most surely devoted their entire beings to the advancment of early Christianity? Texts and traditions probably offer a smorgasbord of fifty or so episodes and essays. What follows are a representative few that seem to be the most logical and likely.

Thomas headed for India, determined never to doubt his master again. One story Christians from the orient tell often is that Thomas's mission had taken him through Parthia, to Bactria and eventually to the Arabian isle of Socotra, where he now pondered entering India. It was probably in the last years of Claudius (not that a Roman emperor had any sway that far away). It was also a period in which the Buddhists of India were winning many converts among the Zoroastrians of eastern Parthia and the latter were showing their displeasure by invading several Indian border provinces.

Bloodshed was rampant, and the tradition says that Thomas was fearful for his life and doubtful that anyone would want to hear about a new religion when two others were vying for supremacy. But one night Jesus appeared to Thomas in a bedside vision. "Fear not, Thomas," he said. "Go into India and preach the Word there, for my grace is with thee."

The next day, the story goes, Thomas hired himself as a servant to an Indian merchant and sailed with him to the city of Cranganore on the southwestern coast. There Thomas sought out the king of that land, named Gondophares, and entered into his service. He must have had the king's ear, because the tradition continues that Thomas remained for years, converting several high-caste Hindu families, making some of the men priests and establishing seven houses of prayer. The area was somewhat isolated because it consisted of a flat coastal plain, hemmed in by steep mountains to the east. There, oblivious to the arguments over circumcision, dietary laws and other issues that divided western churches, the Indian church welcomed and tolerated all comers.

Thomas, the story continues, left this pleasant scene and embarked on the third leg of his life's journey: he went overland to China, where he built at least one house of prayer. Afterwards, he returned to India, settling in the eastern coastal city of Mylapore. According to a manuscript from Chaldea (where Thomas had once settled briefly) he built both a house of prayer and a house for himself, which the locals called the "house of the holy man."

The same source alleges that Thomas met a martyr's death not far from that house at the hands of leading local Brahmins.

> The envious Brahmins, who had been discredited before
> the king by the virtue of Thomas, went to kill him. Hearing
> that he was in the cave near the Little Mount (which at the
> time of the apostle was called Antenodur), they stood near

the slope of the mountain, where there was a narrow opening to let in a little light, and looking through it they found
the apostle on his knees with his eyes closed, in a rapture so
profound that he appeared to be dead. The Brahmins thrust
a lance through the opening and wounded him mortally. It
is not proved where exactly this place was, but all authorities are in accord in saying that it was on the slope of a
mountain. The wound was about half a span deep. When
Thomas sighed, all the murderers ran away and he in his
death agony got out of the cave and dragged himself down
to the Big Mount. And there he died. [106]

Thomas was buried at Mylapore, says the Chaldean report. The time
would have been equivalent to the eleventh year of Nero's reign. One
wonders if the apostle at that time even knew who ruled distant Rome.

As the stories of Thomas indicate, other disciples surely traveled equally great distances to preach in often-hostile lands. One would like to know
more, for instance, of the apostle Simon, the one-time Zealot (at least at the
time Jesus chose him as an apostle) who has been tracked through Egypt,
Libya, Carthage, Spain and then Britain. By one account, Simon got swallowed up in the vicious tribal rebellion that destroyed perhaps 200,000
Britons and Romans in the early years of Nero. But other reports say that
Simon fled from Britain and went on to Parthia, where he was martyred along
with the apostle Jude. All one can say is that there was once a record in the
Tabularium of Rome (which housed official archives) stating that in the last
year of Nero's reign the wife of Aulus Plautius, a Roman official in Britain,
was brought before a magistrate on charges of being a Christian. How did
she come to believe? Perhaps Simon should be given the benefit of the doubt
until proven otherwise.

The apostle Andrew is another such example. The younger brother of Peter
appears to have spent his earliest missionary years in Parthia, some of
them in the company of Bartholomew. But later, some say, he went to
Scythia and spent several years bravely preaching the gospel to the pirates
who ruled that part of the Black Sea and the wild, nomadic horsemen who
prevailed along its blustery shores.

The traditions agree that Andrew was martyred. But where? Some say
in Scythia. But there is also evidence that Andrew went on to Greece where
he met his death in the city of Patræ, the port city on the western side of the
Gulf of Corinth. It seems that Andrew's preaching had been instrumental
in making the wife of the Roman proconsul Ægeates a devout Christian. So

firmly did she refuse all his demands to recant that the exasperated proconsul ordered the apostle to renounce *his* faith before a public tribunal or face a severe scourging. Each man begged the other to recant, with Ægeates imploring Andrew not to lose his life and the apostle in turn beseeching the governor not to lose his soul.

At last Andrew was put to scourging. When he endured the rod in silence, the governor called for crucifixion — but of an unusual kind. The cross was to be in the shape of the letter X. In order to prolong Andrew's suffering — or perhaps to offer him still more time to repent — Andrew was tied — not nailed — to the cross by ropes at his wrists and ankles. According to an account by a first century Roman named Flamion, the apostle hung in a public place for some two days, preaching as he writhed in agony and pierced the hearts of the people who gathered before him. As the end drew near, the Roman recorded these words:

> Ye men that are here present, and women and children, old and young, bond and free, and all that will hear...take no heed of the vain deceit of this present life, but heed us rather who hang here for the Lord's sake and are about to depart out of this body. Renounce all lusts of this world, and condemn the worship of the abominable idols, and run unto the true worshipping of our God that lieth not, and make yourselves a temple pure and ready to receive the Word. Hasten to overtake my soul as it hastens toward heavenly things. In a word, despise all temporal things and establish your minds as men believing in Christ.[107]

Suddenly Ægeates himself rued what he had done and ordered his men to untie the ropes that bound his victim. But Andrew summoned all his strength and resisted them. "Oh, Jesus Christ," he shouted, "let not your adversary loose him that is hung upon thy grace. O Father, let not this small one humble any more him that hath known thy greatness."

With that he gave up the ghost as all about him wept and lamented. Flamion says it was the last day of November in the year of Galba, or a year and six months after Peter and Paul met their martyrdom.

By the end of Galba's reign it is probable that all of the original apostles save Matthew and John had died martyr's deaths. These two and the many other disciples who had been living witnesses to at least some portions of Jesus' ministry were now becoming quite elderly. After all, if a disciple were age 25 at the crucifixion of Jesus, he would be approaching 65 in the year of the four emperors. If he had been 35, as old or slightly older than Jesus, he would by now be well into a venerable age for the first century.

What a pity that so many apostles went to their reward without leaving a written account of what they witnessed. But by A.D. 69 it is likely that one gospel — Mark — was in circulation and possibly that of Matthew.

No one can say if Mark's account is the first witness to Jesus ever put in writing — only that it was the first one to be circulated among the Christians of Rome and the western provinces. In any case, who would be better qualified to write such a history? As stated earlier, John Mark and his mother lived in a large house in Jerusalem with their cousin Barnabas as a frequent visitor. This is the house where Christians were meeting when Peter and John were arrested for preaching in the temple, and some say it is also the same house with the "upper room" where the apostles gathered after Jesus' crucifixion. If Mark was but a lad at this time, he may well have been the boy who was with the disciples in the Garden of Gethsemane the night that Judas led the temple elders to arrest Jesus. In the scuffle that followed, one of the men grabbed at the boy's tunic, but he "fled naked," leaving the assailant with a handful of cloth. Since this seems to be a trivial detail to mention at such a dramatic moment, it may have been inserted simply because it was such a defining moment for the writer — Mark — himself.

In any event, the young Mark went on to become valuable as a missionary, especially because he seems to have spoken both Greek and Hebrew, having had a Jewish mother (hence the name John) and a Roman father (from whom came his second name Mark). Mark was always a favorite of Peter's and probably accompanied him to Babylon.

But Mark seems to have his own missionary story as well — in Alexandria and probably beginning in the fourth year of Nero, or A.D. 58. The story goes that he had broken the strap of his sandal during the journey and that the first thing he did after entering the city's eastern gate was to seek out a cobbler to mend it. When the cobbler took his awl to work on it, he accidentally pierced his hand and cried out, "Heis ho Theos" (God is one). Mark saw this as a sign that he might have a willing convert. He miraculously healed the man's wound and soon found that the cobbler was anxious to hear all that he said about Jesus and the new covenant. Before long, the man, whose name was Anianus, had taken Mark home with him to baptize his whole family.

Many more converts followed. Within several months so many people in Alexandria had been won over that Mark's renown began to put him at risk. Authorities had spread word that a Jew from Judea was preparing to incite a crowd to overthrow the city's pagan idols. Mark decided

it was time to leave until matters had calmed down, so he ordained Anianus bishop, along with three priests and seven deacons, to watch over
the congregation in his absence.

Exactly where Mark went immediately is unknown (one tradition says
Venice). But by A.D. 66 Mark had joined the Christians in Rome, most likely as a translator and amanuensis to Peter. It was probably when the apostle faced the possibility of arrest and even death at any time that Mark began
writing the gospel based on Peter's personal accounts. And in this account
was a prophecy that was now about to unfold all around them. The prophecy, Mark records, came when Jesus and his disciples had returned from the
temple on the first day of his fateful visit to Jerusalem. They had climbed
the Mount of Olives opposite the temple in the late afternoon, and as they
gazed down on its huge marble walls and glistening buildings, the disciples couldn't stop marveling about what splendid sights they had beheld.
It was then that Jesus said to them, "Do you see these great buildings? There
will not be left here one stone upon another that will not be thrown down!"

Peter, James and some others pressed him to tell more. "When will this
be?" they asked incredulously. "And what will be the sign when these
things are all to be accomplished?"

Instead of a simple answer, Jesus painted a much larger portrait of what
was to come after his mission on earth was over:

> Many will come in my name, saying, "I am he!" and they
> will lead many astray. And when you hear of wars and ru-
> mors of wars, do not be alarmed. These must take place, but
> the end is not yet. For nation will rise against nation, and
> kingdom against kingdom. There will be earthquakes in
> various places; there will be famines, this is but the begin-
> ning of the sufferings.

> But take heed for yourselves, for they will deliver you up to
> councils and you will be beaten in synagogues and you
> will stand before governors and kings for my sake to bear
> testimony before them (for) the gospel must be preached to
> all nations.

> And when they bring you to trial and deliver you up, do not
> be anxious beforehand what you are to say, but say whatev-
> er is given you in that hour; for it is not you who speak, but
> the Holy Spirit. And brother will deliver brother up to

death, and the father his child, and children will rise against parents and have them put to death, and you will be hated for my name's sake. But he who endures to the end will be saved.[108]

Sometime after Peter's martyrdom in Rome, perhaps even before, Mark returned to Alexandria and the church he had founded. To his delight, its numbers had multiplied to the point where they had organized a large communal compound in the suburban district of Baucalis, where cattle grazed by the seashore. While this community no doubt struck Alexandrians as strange and secretive, it seemed to exist peacefully enough. But there was something about the reappearance of John Mark, the founding patriarch, that again inflamed the local authorities — undoubtedly because the Jewish revolt in Jerusalem had given the Hellene majority in Alexandria an excuse to settle old scores with local Jews and any "splinter sects." Another irritant may have been Mark's gospel, which they could now read for themselves. In any event, word circulated that Mark was back and again intended to incite his Christians to topple all the statues of pagan deities they could find.

This was in the last year of Nero, almost a year after Peter and Paul had met martyrdom in Rome. The occasion was Easter, which fell on the same day as the festival of Serapis, honoring the consort of the Egyptian goddess Isis. A mob whipped itself up in the Serapion temple and then set out for Baucalis, where the Christians had begun celebrating Easter. Marching on the settlement, the hooligans seized Mark and carried him off to the road from which they had come. Mark by then was probably well over 50 and worn by years of travel. No one cared about that. They tied a rope around his neck, bound his hands, and had him dragged through the streets by horses. At nightfall, they grew weary of their prank and threw Mark into a jail, bloody and barely alive. The next morning they dragged him out again and made him suffer many hours of the same torture until he at last expired.

Mark's murderers had planned to cremate the torn and bloodied body, but a spring gale blew up so suddenly and brought such heavy torrents of rain with it that the mob quickly scattered. At nightfall some Christians from Baucalis crept into the street where the body lay and carried it off. A secret grave was dug beneath the altar of the house of prayer, and there the Christians buried another of the men who had witnessed the life of Jesus — scarcely a year after the Christians of Rome had buried Peter and Paul.

As already stated, by A.D. 69 all the apostles, save one or two, had already gone to their deaths preaching the gospel. Whether Matthew was still alive is simply unknown, although he may have perished not long after dictating his gospel in Antioch. If so, it would leave only John, who was probably the youngest of the apostles during Jesus' time.

Who would be a better living legacy of all Jesus said and all that happened in those years? John and his older brother James were the sons of Zebedee, a Galilean fisherman so prosperous that he employed servants in his work, had a second home in Jerusalem, and connections to its priestly families. John's mother, Salome, had accompanied Jesus' mother, Mary, to the tomb and was obviously her close companion. Moreover, John was often referred to as "the beloved disciple," or the "one Jesus loved." He was present at the transfiguration and sat at the right of Jesus at the last supper. He was present at his master's trial (perhaps due to his priestly connections) and stood at the foot of the cross, where the stricken Jesus told him to care for his mother, Mary. Afterward, John was Peter's tireless companion when preaching to the Jews by the temple gates.

John continued preaching in Judea for years, even after his brother James became the first apostle to meet martyrdom in the persecutions of King Herod Agrippa. It may have been then that he moved to Ephesus in Roman Asia. Or it may have been early in the reign of Nero, when the unscrupulous procurators began vexing the people beyond all endurance. Paul had already formed churches in Ephesus, and during his subsequent imprisonment in Cæsarea and Rome John would have been a welcome fortification to the faith. Ephesus would also be a more secure haven in which to honor his obligation to care for Mary.

If one assumes that Mary was perhaps 16 when she bore Jesus, she would have been just over 50 at the time of his crucifixion, around 65 at the time of Herod Agrippa's persecution and nearly 80 in the early years of Nero. Her husband Joseph had undoubtedly passed on many years before either of her probable departure dates for Ephesus. Although Mary was by then too old to have lived long in Ephesus under the wing of her kinsman, it would appear that the house where she lived was quickly made into a place of veneration by Christians from Asia Minor. Today a sixth century church stands on the same site.

By A.D. 69 John would have been around 70. He had not only become patriarch of the church at Ephesus, but was revered throughout the churches in the seven major cities of Asia Minor. Of all the apostles, only John would go on until the end of the century, still one of the "Sons of Thunder."

A.D. 70–71

THE JERUSALEM THAT TITUS and his four legions encountered in the early spring of A.D. 70 contained somewhere between 600,000 and 1 million permanent residents, depending on how many had fled or succumbed by then. But at this particular time the actual number of people within the walls was at least 2 million. The reason is that Titus came upon the city just before the Passover Festival, and so devout were Jewish visitors from all over the world that they came to their religious center even in such dire times as these.

The three legions that now plodded uphill from Cæsarea and other wintering camps to the north had at first been culled of their most seasoned veterans by the four legions that left for Rome with Mucianus. But these in turn were soon bolstered by absorbing 2,000 troops that had been led from Egypt by no less than Tiberius Alexander, the governor and enthusiastic supporter of Vespasian. To these could be added the many auxiliaries from loyal kingdoms as near as Herod Agrippa's and as distant as Macedonia. The most bloodthirsty of all were auxiliaries from the Syrian Hellenistic cities who had fought their Jewish neighbors so bitterly over the years.

As this force approached, the defenders who watched from the walls were dazzled at how the armor and shields of 80,000 soldiers sprayed glistening beams of reflected sunlight in all directions. More impressive was the precision and discipline of such a large force. First in the long winding train came the auxiliaries, followed by the engineers who prepared roads and measured out the camps. Then came the commander's luggage, Titus himself with a select body, followed by the horsemen and the pikesmen. After all these came the engines of war, the tribunes of the cohorts and their elect bodies, the ensigns and their eagles, and then the trumpeters. But all these were only the beginning of the column, for they were followed by an endless parade of foot soldiers marching six abreast, then their baggage and the mercenaries who had been hired to guard the rear.

On one hand, the fact that Vespasian and Titus felt compelled to muster 80,000 men against Jerusalem was a tribute to the thickness of its walls and the zeal of the men inside. Alexander the Great had used only 32,000 men to forge his vast empire, Julius Cæsar had invaded Britain with only 25,000 legionaries and Hannibal had 50,000 when he crossed the Alps to contest Rome at its doorstep. On the other hand, they didn't fully realize the divided and desperate state of the people within Jerusalem. What must have struck Titus first was the same awesome sight that had dazzled pilgrims for over 60 years: the huge white blocks of stone that had been fused into seamless city walls and the almost blinding light that lit up the late afternoon landscape as the declining sun shone on the great plates of gold that covered the exterior of the temple at its highest places. As for its marble facing, one traveler wrote that "the temple appeared to strangers, when they were coming at it from a distance, like a mountain covered with snow; for as those parts of it that were not gilt, they were exceedingly white."

As Titus approached from the north, he faced, if you will, the short side of a ragged rectangle that stretched just over four miles to encompass the city. The northern approach also put the Romans at the city's strongest point, for the natural elevation was further fortified by a succession of three walls.

The newest and outermost wall extended along the city's entire northern border, ran for a mile or so along the western boundary, and connected to an ancient wall that protected its western flank. The northern wall was the one that Herod Agrippa I had feverishly attempted to build until halted by a suspicious emperor Claudius 27 years before. Agrippa's purpose had been to enclose the homes, gardens and natural springs of the rapidly expanding "New City" to the north. The present defenders of Jerusalem had used the lull created by the Roman civil wars to justify Claudius' concerns: they built a wall 44 feet high that now stood in defiance of Roman authority.

The second, much older inner wall included Herod's palace and Upper City to the west. As it turned northeast it encompassed the Fortress Antonia, which had garrisoned Roman troops and housed their arsenal until the rebels captured it. Parts of its north and eastern faces were at the same time the walls of the temple itself.

The wall continued along the eastern and southern perimeters, through what is called the Lower City. But at these points Jerusalem was defended primarily by the fact that the land just outside these walls plunged sharply into the Kidron Valley below.

Some of the towers along the inner wall to the north were fortresses within themselves. For instance, the tower of Hippicus, just north of Herod's palace, was 44 feet on each side and rose 52 feet. It included a reservoir 35 feet deep, over which was built a two-story house. The nearby Tower of Phasælis had a cloister atop it, covered by bulwarks and breastworks. Above this was built another tower full of private living and bathing rooms. It was also adorned with battlements and turrets so that the whole thing stood 157 feet high and was often compared to the famous Pharos lighthouse that once stood in the harbor at Alexandria.

The defenders under arms numbered no more than 30,000 and would have been far less had it not been for the winter arrival of some 10,000 men led by one Simon of Gerasa.

Simon may have been the most ferocious brigand in Jewish history, having collected a rag-tag force of robbers, rebels and hungry escapees from towns recently stormed by the Roman invaders. When Simon and his "army" had arrived at the gates of Jerusalem the previous winter, they had invited its leaders to take one of two choices — either admit his men as leaders in the rebellion or face an invasion that would cripple the city before the Romans ever reached it.

Thus, until almost the very day that the Romans appeared, Jerusalem had been torn by the fighting of three factions. Simon of Gerasa occupied Herod's palace. John of Gischala and his Zealots occupied the lower temple precincts. A splinter group of Zealots, headed by the tenacious Eleazar, had fled to the upper precincts of the temple. Thus, for weeks Eleazar's men reigned down missiles on John's Zealots, who constantly skirmished with Simon on their other flank. All during this incessant melee pilgrims and priests came and went to the temple despite the fact that its courtyards were constantly strewn with the corpses of those who had been felled by stones and darts from the warring factions.

The Passover Feast in April had only intensified the temple traffic and the number of killings, as thousands of pious Jews from all over the empire came each day in order to be faithful to the ritual their forefathers had practiced for generations. To do so they had to brave the menacing scrutiny of Eleazar's guards, knowing that their sacrificial fees would probably wind up in some brigand's purse.

One might assume that at first sight of the Romans, the three factions would have united instantly in common bond. They did only to the extent that Eleazar made an uneasy truce with John and brought his 2,400 men back under Zealot command. Added to John's 6,000 men and 20 commanders, they controlled everything in and around the temple. Five hundred yards to the west, Herod's palace and the Upper City were controlled by Simon, who lived in the commodius Tower of Phasælis. Under Simon were 10,000 men and 50 commanders as well as 5,000 Idumeans, who paid them allegiance. While it is true that both Jewish factions were determined to fight Romans, they never ceased skirmishing within the city — even to the point of designating an area between their camps as a mutually convenient spot in which to vent their hostilities.

But many hours of tedious preparation came before the Romans hurled the first javelin. Titus began by uprooting all the gardens outside the walls and cutting down every tree in sight. Then the men set fire to all the suburbs around the walls. All of the timber and vegetation they could gather was used to start the piling up of crude embankments against the wall he intended to breach. To protect those who built the banks he stationed archers and engines that threw javelins, darts and stones. The engines were the army's finest, and could hurl a 60-pound stone for 400 yards.

Once the Romans finished their banks, they were able to bring battering rams up to the wall. Now the pounding reverberations of many engines filled the air night and day. After many hours the walls remained intact, but so frightened by now were John and Simon that they vowed to ignore their differences for the duration and concentrate their ire on the attackers below. Some of their bravest men hurdled over the ramparts and landed on the wooden and metal roofs that had been erected over the Roman rams and attacked the soldiers beneath them. Dozens more ran about the ramparts, flinging torches on the wooden engines. At one point when it seemed that the majority of Romans had retired to their camp, either out of weariness or perhaps to take a meal, the Jews poured out from their gates and descended on the few men who guarded the rams.

Before long the Romans had added another type of "weapon" that did as much damage as their siege engines. As the building of the earthen embankments began, Titus had ordered the construction of three wooden, iron-plated towers, each over 80 feet tall.

Once these were finished and put into place atop the banks, they allowed the Romans to hurl missiles down on the opposing ramparts without letup. Yet their height and iron sheeting were such as to render the Jewish darts ineffective. The result was that fewer defenders remained on the ramparts and no one now resisted the constant pounding of the rams. At the first breach in the wall's weakest point, the Romans poured through uncontested as the few remaining Jewish guards fled inside the second wall.

Thus, on April 22, just 15 days after their arrival, the Romans entered the outer city walls of Jerusalem and erected a new camp in the far northwest corner. Now they were in a position to contest simultaneously two key parts of the inner second wall: Simon's forces in Herod's Palace and John's commanding perch in the Fortress of Antonia and adjoining temple.

It took the Roman engines only five more days to breach the second wall. This happened about a thousand feet north of Herod's palace where the wall met the narrow streets in the Upper City populated by the many wool and fabric merchants. Titus could have cleared a larger opening and stormed his army through it, but he still hoped to gain a bloodless surrender by showing restraint. Thus, Titus entered the second wall with only a thousand armed men — all of them forbidden to kill anyone or set any buildings afire.

John and Simon perceived it as a sign of weakness that Titus knew he could not take the rest of the city. They also threatened death to anyone who said a word about surrender. Two things then happened. A large army of Simon rushed outside the wall and drove off the Romans who had been ordered to guard it until their comrades inside returned. Next, bands of Jewish soldiers burst forth from this house and that alleyway, ambushing the Romans as they wound their way through the narrow streets. As the disoriented Romans raced back and tried to funnel through the narrow breach in the wall, they would have been cut down had not Titus ordered his archers to stand in a solid row and fire at the attackers until everyone had gotten through to the other side.

The Jewish forces were jubilant, for they thought Titus would never again venture beyond the second wall. But the next day the Romans were back again, of course. For three days as they battered and charged, the Jews barred their entrance through the narrow breach by covering themselves with armor and literally stuffing their own bodies into the open space. But on the fourth day they broke under the incessant pressure and fled as the wall behind them came tumbling down. This time Titus demolished it from one end to the other. Soon his legions had struck new camps at the foot of both Herod's Palace and the Fortress of Antonia.

By now Titus could see for himself conditions that existed inside the walls. While the men of both Simon and John seemed healthy enough, it was obvious who held the food supplies and who did not. Outside the soldiery, the masses of Jerusalem were clearly suffering for want of nourishment. If the soldiers did not have enough to spare the populace, Titus reasoned, the time would come soon enough when they, too, had none.

So, the Roman commander decided to relax the siege for a while and give the people of Jerusalem time to let their stomachs influence their thinking. But four days came and went without even an offer to talk. Now Titus faced a crucial decision. He did not want to destroy the temple, but he could not leave Jerusalem without removing the force that now occupied it. To assault the temple and its massive, almost seamless stone walls would be long and difficult. When the siege had begun almost a month before, the Jews had brought out the catapults they had captured from the Fortress of Antonia. But they were untrained and clumsy in hurling stones. By this time they had much improved their skills and (the Romans counted 340 such engines along the walls) were making it much more dangerous for the attackers to raise banks than before.

Titus decided on one more attempt to negotiate. He sent Josephus himself to the walls to plead for a peaceful surrender. But at the sight of a Jewish general-turned-traitor the clamor and vilification was so hot that Josephus had to retreat quickly to avoid the hailstorm of darts and stones from above.

Now came a new tactic. Despite their increased isolation and the risks of getting caught, gnawing hunger still prompted many Jews to slip out of Jerusalem at night in search of anything edible in the steep valleys that surrounded the southern and eastern perimeters. Most were poor people who were deterred from deserting altogether by the certainty that John or Simon would kill their families inside if they did. Thus far Titus had chosen to overlook them. Now he dispatched regular cavalry patrols to scour the valleys and bring back anyone they could catch. In a given day they would snare over 500 Jews, and each day the soldiers would nail them to crosses that were rung about the perimeter of the temple wall. As Josephus witnessed: "Some they nailed one way, another after another way, to the crosses by way of jest, so that their multitude was so great that room was wanting for the crosses, and crosses wanting for the bodies."

Yet, there was no change in the Jews. Indeed, Simon and John merely pointed to the crosses as proof of what awaited all Jews within the walls.

The Romans had not been idle, however, during the two weeks that armed clashes had been suspended. The invaders had now finished building four towers at various points along the temple wall and were now ready to resume the assault.

But the Jews had not been idle, either. As the Romans were building a tower against the face of the Fortress of Antonia, John's men had been busy burrowing underneath its foundation. Indeed, their tunnel had extended beyond the walls and under the base of the earthen banks and Roman siege tower that stood atop it. As in constructing a mine, they had buttressed the top of their tunnel with large timbers. Only in this case they had first covered the supports with pitch and bitumen. Now the timber supports were lit afire as the Jews scurried out of their tunnel. Before long, and after the Romans had climbed into their new tower, the inflamed mine supports burned through and gave way. Without any notice, the earthen embankment collapsed into the mine tunnel below and the giant tower toppled over in a heap of dust and smoke. And there it continued to burn, for the Romans could not control the source of the fire.

When the Jews finally retired, nearly all the Roman towers and siege engines had been either badly burned or broken, and Titus was forced to call a meeting of his officers to re-assess their position. Without towers and rams, the risk of heavy casualties was too great to assault the temple. With absolutely no more trees or vegetation available around Jerusalem, finding replacement materials meant journeying at least 20 miles and back. Yet, Titus despaired of keeping so large an army idle for so long, and he worried that it would also diminish the glory of the triumph he envisioned in Rome.

The answer was to build another wall. This one would be earthen. It would cover the entire four-mile perimeter of the remaining Jewish defense line and it would be broken at intervals by 13 Roman garrisons. Each garrison would maintain 24-hour-a-day patrols atop the entire earthen works so that absolutely no one could get in or out.

If siege engines could not conquer Jerusalem, famine could.

The wall was finished in three days, as May turned to June and the scorching months of summer.

DURING THE EARLIER MONTHS of winter and early spring, Vespasian in Alexandria and Titus in Judea had more to show for their efforts than did the uneasy coalition that tried to rule Rome in their absence. The consul (and former general) Antonius Primus seemed more intent on amassing wealth and his co-ruler Domitian in collecting women. Meanwhile, the Senate argued endlessly about whether post-war retributions should be taken against this friend of Vitellius or that informer of Nero. Anguish mounted over a spreading revolt in Germany and the fact that Roman fortifications there had been reduced to older men and raw recruits when the flower of the legions had gone down to fight in Italy. Moreover, Rome was now feeling a serious grain shortage — ironic because it was Vespasian himself who caused it, thinking that he would be squeezing Vitellius into surrendering the city. Now his success had made victims of his own subjects.

When Mucianus finally arrived in early March, the ship at last had a captain — but at a price. The Senate returned to its fawning ways, as if it had just crowned a new emperor, and Mucianus himself seemed to expect it. In addition to accepting triumphal honors (which until then had been reserved for those who gain victories over *foreign* armies), Mucianus was liberal in telling the Senate, "It was I who had held the empire in the palm of my hand and gave it to Vespasian."

But Mucianus also provided the decisive leadership that Rome had needed. For instance, he quickly diminished the cult status that Antonius was gaining among his troops by moving his Seventh Legion to winter quarters in Pannonia. The best men in other units of Antonius were combed out and sent to the German front. He even managed to throw some cold water on Domitian. Only Mucianus could have risked writing a blunt letter to the lad's father. The dispatch documented the son's excesses, ranging from the pilfering of other men's wives to his insistence on being given command of the troops in Germany. The terse reply from Vespasian in Alexandria was this: "I thank, you, my son, for permitting me to hold office and that you have not yet dethroned me."

A popular story is that, upon reading this, a chastened Domitian sulked alone for weeks in a room of a country villa, using a sharpened stylus to spear flies for hours on end. Thus, when someone in town would ask, "Where is Domitian these days?" another would answer, "He's living alone without even a fly to keep him company."

Yet, it was not any one man who kept Rome from governing effectively and regaining its tarnished luster during these months; it was more a matter of money. The treasury was severely depleted by Nero and the succeeding wars, and there was no quick way to replenish it. One embarrassing reminder was the ugly charred shell of the Temple Jupiter Optimus Maximus atop Capitoline Hill. This had been the symbol of Rome's might; and now, when a chieftain in a backward part of Germany was asked why he decided to join the revolt, he answered that the Roman Empire was finished. Why? Because its leaders could not even afford to rebuild their most sacred temple.

343

Vespasian's last action in Egypt was to respond to a dispatch from Rome that the city's corn supply had dwindled to about ten days' worth. Despite the fact that the ocean winds were still unpredictable, the new emperor sent off a large fleet of corn ships. No doubt he would have wished to join them. Instead, by April Vespasian was back in Cæsarea, hoping that Titus might have finished his destruction of Jerusalem and departed with his father for a triumphant entry to Rome. But as we have seen, such an event was not even in sight.

So, embarking on as direct a route as the swirling winds of early spring would permit, Vespasian and a small party sailed a merchantman from Cæsarea to Lycia and then proceeded by both land and sea to the eastern Italian port of Brundisium. There, just as their predecessors had journeyed from Rome to meet the grieving family of Germanicus 44 years before, a delegation of senators and notables were on hand as he disembarked. Not among them was the young prætor-consul Domitian, who sent word to his father that he was ill.

Before the emperor had departed Cæsarea, Titus had begged him to be lenient with his younger brother. "Friendships can be extinguished by time, chance and misunderstandings," Titus had reportedly said, "but a man's own blood cannot be severed from him." Apparently Vespasian accepted this counsel, but I suspect Domitian was left to jab at many more flies with his stylus, because in the remainder of this year the focus shifted wholly to a very busy emperor and his attempts to pull Rome back from the edge of self-destruction.

Vespasian was swift in relieving internal dissension. He freed most of those who had been exiled by Nero. The properties of Otho, Vitellius and other fallen foes he left their kinsmen. He replenished the ranks of senators and knights, which had been depleted by years of murder and purge. The courts, which were so clogged with lawsuits that many litigants could not hope to have their cases heard in their lifetimes, were stripped of all but the most important cases by selecting commissioners by lot to decide on their own the most routine disputes.

However, rebuilding public works was the emperor's highest priority. He resumed work on a temple to the deified Claudius that had been begun by Agrippina but then destroyed by her son Nero. He began work on a new temple of Peace in the Forum as well as his grandest project of all, a new amphitheater on the grounds of the Golden House (which itself would soon be converted into a public bath). As for the many lots of ugly rubble that still remained from the great fire of six years before, the emperor ordered that anyone could seize and build upon them if the current owners failed to do so within a given date.

Of course the largest charred site of all was the temple atop the Capitoline, and to this Vespasian gave his highest priority. First, the blackened timbers and tiles were carted to the wharves and barged to the marshes of Ostia. Then on June 21, a clear bright day, the whole temple complex was decorated with chaplets and garlands. In marched soldiers — all chosen for having names of good omen — carrying branches of trees deemed to be equally propitious. Then came the Vestal Virgins, who cleansed it all by sprinkling fresh water from a spring or river. The Pontiff Maximus further purified the site by a solemn sacrifice of a pig, sheep and ox, then prayed to Jupiter, Juno and Minerva, the guardian deities of the empire, to shine their divine grace on the temple to be built there.

After the purification rite, an assemblage of nobles dragged a huge cornerstone into place. Gifts of gold and silver were thrown into the foundation trenches and over them were placed blocks of virgin ore, unscathed by any furnace, just as they had come from the womb of the earth.

Vespasian himself had led the stone laying, and now he took charge of restoring some 3,000 bronze tablets that had been destroyed in the blaze. These were the most priceless and ancient records of the empire, containing the decrees of the Senate from the city's foundation on such matters as alliances, treaties and honors to individuals.

The other side of the coin is that all these projects cost a great deal of money. And so Vespasian felt justified in openly selling positions ranging from stewardships to governorships. More than once he used treasury money to corner certain markets on commodities, then released supplies at a profit. One of his most unpopular acts was to rescind the exemption from taxes that Nero had so munificently (and thoughtlessly) granted to the Greek states of Achaia, Lycia, Rhodes and Samos. But even more unpopular in Rome was the nuisance of many small new taxes such as an unprecedented tax on use of public toilets. A story went around at the time that even Titus came to complain about it to his father, whereupon Vespasian held up a coin to his son's nose and asked if he found its odor offensive.

"Well, no, " said Titus. "Why?"

"Good, because it was made from urine," said his father with great delight.

Yet, it would seem that none of the fruits of all this public fund raising went to the emperor himself. His own lifestyle remained nearly as Spartan as his days as a field general. He rose before dawn and had usually completed his correspondence in time for a morning reception. His afternoons were typically spent in the Senate or courts, then at bath. He entertained often and was a cordial and gracious host. While he did not skimp on things like banquets, neither his personal dress nor behavior was lavish. And he detested foppery to the same degree than Nero loved it. Thus, when a young military officer, reeking with perfumes, came to thank him for receiving a commission, Vespasian drew back his head in disgust. "I would rather you had smelled of garlic," he said, and revoked the appointment.

BY MID-JULY THE ROMANS had finished raising banks again at the Tower of Antonia. To find materials for this painstaking task, detachments of soldiers had traveled with oxen and wagons 20 miles out from Jerusalem in all directions. Now, no tree remained standing anywhere within that distance. Suburbs that had once been adorned with pleasant gardens and groves were now a desolate desert, so that, as Josephus bemoaned, "any foreigner who had once seen Jerusalem in its splendor would fall to the ground in tears if he came upon it now."

The Roman earth banks were once again in place against the walls of the Fortress of Antonia, and both sides knew that the decisive moment of the war had arrived. All understood that if the Romans took Antonia, they would have access to the entire temple complex — and they would occupy higher ground because the old Roman citadel looked directly into the Court of Gentiles. But both sides knew as well that if the Jews could somehow destroy the towers and rebuilt siege engines, the Roman soldiers alone could not surmount the wall and would be forced to retire for lack of any more building materials.

For two days the rams battered against the walls of Antonia without effect. At that point the Romans took drastic action: they employed brigades of men to undermine the foundation stones of the fortress despite a constant rain of stones and darts all around them. As some men held shields aloft in an improvised tortoise formation, others would be crouched below digging or prying at the giant stones with crowbars. Although many men fell from the darts and stones, the Romans eventually succeeded in dislodging four large foundation blocks. Yet by the time they retired for the night, King Herod's already battered and undermined tower remained upright.

In the middle of the windless, starry night, Roman soldiers bolted from their cots as they heard a tremendous crash in the direction of the Fortress of Antonia. Grabbing their armor as they rushed to the camp perimeter, they saw a great cloud of dust and mound of rubble. The Tower of Antonia still stood, but the much-battered wall connecting it to another corner of the old Roman citadel had apparently been so underlain with tunnels from John's "surprise" of the previous month that it had finally toppled without further help.

Trumpeters blared as Roman soldiers formed up ranks, expecting this night to plunge through the opening and take the temple at last. But when they marched to the wall, and when the dust clouds cleared enough for them to see, they squinted in the moonlight and saw before them…yet another wall! John and his men, while fighting Romans and famine, had also managed to build a second wall connecting the gap left when the first wall fell. Titus and his men blinked in disbelief.

The Romans went back to bed dejected. But in the light of the next day they took a closer survey of the new wall and determined that, given its hasty construction, it probably was not as thick or sturdy as the first one. Eventually it might succumb to the rams.

And yet…Titus was feeling his men's frustration and fatigue at the many weeks of building, battering and digging. The time for a more dramatic solution had come at last, and those who had begged for a chance to show their valor would now have it.

Titus gathered men from every legion and gave them a rare oration. He began by calling it an "exhortation" and he quickly let them know it was about going over the wall they now faced. God himself had shown Romans the way to victory by making the first wall collapse, declared the young commander. Yet so far, it was "unbecoming" that men who were trained to conquer had been too often outshone by the "pure courage" of their opponents. Yes, he said, "we can wait until famine and fortune work their will, but we also have it in our power now…to gain all that we desire!"

Titus forthrightly acknowledged that the first ones over the wall would undoubtedly die, but to a soldier death in battle was preferable to death by another means.

But should a man survive the ordeal, Titus concluded, earthly rewards would be there as well.

Despite Cæsar's emotional exhortation, its conclusion drew no hurrahs — only a wall of petrified silence. At last Titus was rescued from his embarrassment when one man stepped forward. His name was Sabinus, a black-skinned, common foot soldier who served with the Syrian auxiliaries. He was already known for his courage in battle, yet one would not have expected it from his short and very lean stature.

"I will readily surrender myself up to thee, O Cæsar," he said, looking up at the thickly muscled commander. "I will first ascend the wall and I heartily wish that my fortune will follow my courage."

Eleven others were stirred by Sabinus' declaration, and soon they marched up to the edge of the new wall with shields raised over their heads. As they climbed their ladders, some of the twelve were quickly knocked off by darts and large stones. Sabinus, who was first, had already been hit by a few darts himself by the time he fought his way over the wall. At first the men on the ramparts were astonished by the fury of his fighting. Many others gave way because they thought Sabinus was merely the first in a tidal wave of Romans.

Sabinus was actually chasing several Jewish soldiers through the Court of Gentiles when he was knocked to the ground by a large stone. He managed to get to one knee and wounded several attackers with his sword. But another gash disabled his right hand, and now all he could do was lie on the ground and try to cover himself with his shield. But he was soon pierced by many more darts and died.

When it was over, three of his companions had been dashed to pieces by stones inside the walls. The eight others were wounded while climbing and were rescued by the Romans below.

Why this futile exercise? Where were the troops who were supposed to rally behind Sabinus? In a way, Sabinus did stir the men to victory for this reason: after two days of sulking in their shame and cowardice, some of them at last could stand it no more. As night fell, a dozen men who had been on forward guard duty at the Roman banks were quietly joined by two cavalrymen, a trumpeter and a standard-bearer from the Fifth Legion. Waiting until about nine o'clock, when they expected the Jewish guards to be nodding off, they sneaked through the ruins and up to the base of the Tower Antonia. The Romans quietly climbed the wall and cut the throats of the three sleeping guards. Then they ordered the trumpeter to sound a charge while they themselves yelled as loudly as they could.

The sound, of course, woke up the rest of the guards on the wall. Thinking this the beginning of a massive invasion, they scrambled down into the broad temple courtyard. When Titus heard the trumpet signal, he ordered everyone into their armor immediately and rushed them to the site. Soon Romans were pouring over the wall and Jewish reinforcements were coming from all parts of the city.

They converged in the middle between the Tower of Antonia and the steps of the temple itself. And there took place the most furious hand-to-hand warfare of the campaign. The Jews would drive the bulk of the Romans back towards the tower, only to be themselves pushed back to the steps of the temple. The clashing of swords and shouts of men made a deafening sound as it reverberated about the stone walls of the great enclosure.

The battle raged continuously until seven the next morning. Gradually, the zeal and courage that the Jews had somehow summoned from their starved bodies at the prospect of their temple being invaded proved too much for the Romans. The latter were forced back into the Fortress of

Antonia, where they were at least content to savor their new advantage of looking down on the temple courtyard.

The Jews, with an awesome courage that overcame their gnawing stomachs, had won the night valiantly. But they had already lost the days to come, for the Romans, in truth, had waged the battle with only a part of their army. Fresh reinforcements could now be brought up, and the next battle chosen at their convenience.

On August 6 Titus' spies informed him that the Jews — perhaps due to exhaustion — had stopped offering their daily temple sacrifice to God. And so the Roman commander decided to send Josephus to the walls once again.

With tears and groans, Josephus told those inside the walls that Cæsar had beseeched them to save the temple from fire by moving their men to another place of their own choosing and continue the battle there. Would they do so?

John of Gischala shouted back that the temple was in no danger because it was God's place and would be protected by him. To which Josephus sputtered with bitter invective,

> To be sure you have kept this city wonderfully pure for God's sake! The temple continues entirely unpolluted! Nor have you been guilty of any impiety against him for whose assistance you hope! He still receives his accustomed sacrifices! Vile wretch that thou art! If anyone would deprive you of your daily food, you would esteem him to be your enemy. But you hope to have that God for your supporter in this war whom you have deprived of his everlasting worship![109]

Josephus again said that if John would yet repent, " I dare venture to promise that the Romans will still forgive you."

But again all Josephus received back was more torment. In fact, it was evident to the Romans in the background that John's men were more interested in luring Josephus closer to the walls so that they might kill him with darts or somehow get their hands on his neck, for they saw him as the worst Jewish traitor of all. But Josephus turned their reproach back against them:

Josephus was sobbing, and in such great distress that Titus himself now stepped from the background. All about them in the outer courtyard were heaps of bodies from the all-night battle before. After staring up at John for some time, he held up his hand for silence and shouted, with Josephus interpreting his words, "Hasn't Rome given you permission to deny Gentiles your sanctuary on pain of death — even if they be Romans? Have not Romans respected its sanctity?

"Why do you now trample upon dead bodies in this temple? Why do you pollute this holy house with the blood of both foreigners and Jews? I appeal to the gods of my own country and to every god that ever had any regard for this place. I also appeal to my own army and to those Jews that are now with me, and even to yourselves, that I do not force you to defile this sanctuary. And if you will not but change the place whereon you will fight, no Roman shall either come near your sanctuary or offer any affront to it."

But Titus, too, was rebuked and refused. And as if to leave no doubt about it, John ordered that his largest catapults be positioned at the very gates of the temple. So Titus resigned his men to raising more banks — this time against the walls of the temple building that stood in the great outer courtyard.

On August 28, A.D. 70 Titus called a council of his legion commanders and tribunes. The temple siege had not gone well. The Roman rams had battered Herod's 14-foot-thick walls for six days with scarcely a shiver. Soldiers had tried to undermine the foundations of the massive north gate, but the gate held fast and many legionaries lay dead from the stones the Jews had flung constantly with their captured Roman catapults. Titus had even ordered an attack with ladders, but the Jews had flung his men back upon the hard pavement with many casualties. And now at this very moment, parts of the outer cloisters — the colonnades that lined the square courtyard perimeter — had been set afire. In one case a daring Jewish raiding party had torched the northwest cloisters in hopes it would spread to the adjacent Tower of Antonia. But neither were Romans blameless: they, too, had fired other parts of the cloisters, and Titus himself, in frustration, had ordered the temple gates set ablaze after his men failed to dislodge the foundations. Then, a day later, he changed his mind and had the fire extinguished.

The reason for the war council was Titus' own torment over the temple. And yet he could not ignore that it was a military sanctuary as well. Titus must have been well aware that he had already caused excessive casualties to his own men — by mounting ladders, for instance — when it was likely that burning the whole temple would facilitate its capture more than all their siege engines combined. What should he do?

Some of the commanders were adamant that the Jews would never cease rebelling as long as the temple stood. It was both their symbol of nationhood and their citadel of defiance, and it should be demolished as would any enemy stronghold under the rules of war.

"And yet," said Titus, "is it right that we should avenge ourselves on an inanimate object rather than the men themselves?" Consider as well, he added, that leaving the building intact would be a monument to the mighty dominions governed by Rome. His closest advisors agreed, and it was decided that early the next day the entire army would try to overwhelm the temple defenses and even bring up all their encampments on all sides of it if the struggle became protracted.

But the plan was never carried out. Later that same afternoon, a detachment of Roman soldiers was attempting, as Titus had ordered, to put out a fire that burned along one of the cloisters when a band of Jewish soldiers ran out from the temple and attacked them. After a few of them were killed, the Romans began to get the best of their assailants and drove them all the way back to the temple steps. But so incensed were some of them that they gave no thought to Titus' wishes. One soldier climbed on another's back with a lit torch and was able to heave it through a golden window that was open above them. The window happened to be at the end of a corridor that led to several rooms that ran along the north wall. Soon one could see smoke and flames billowing out from the upper windows and the people inside in an obvious state of great agitation.

The rest is a blur of confusion and conflicting recollections. The Roman version is that Titus was in his tent resting before his planned attack on the morrow. When an officer came running to tell him that the temple was afire, he hurried out all the way into its outer courtyard to see if it could be stopped. Behind him came most of his commanders, and after them, soldiers tying on their armor as they ran. No trumpets had sounded, no call to battle came, but at the sight of the flames, the soldiers let out a beastly roar and rushed forward. Perhaps some thought that some of their comrades had already launched a surprise attack and that they were now needed to join in. However, it seems more probable that this was a surge of blind fury brought by their long weeks of frustration and the fact that the temple may have contained more gold, silver and jewels than any building on earth save the temple of Saturn in Rome (and maybe not even *that* considering the low state of the state treasury). Thus, a mass of men — "each one's passion his only commander," as Josephus notes — blindly stampeded past their starving enemies through the charred temple gates and into the small inner courtyards. Behind them, more Romans ran from their camps, often falling amid the hot and smoking ruins of the outer cloisters as they scrambled towards the temple. The Jews inside were too busy defending themselves to put out fires. Outside, Titus stood shouting for the men to quench the fire, but they swept by him with fires of their own burning in their eyes. In fact, they soon lit even more parts of the temple ablaze.

As they stormed inside, the Romans found many of the people too weak even to fight. These quickly had their throats cut. Many Jews had chosen to say their farewell to the world on the altar, which lay in the Court of Priests just to the left of the entrance to the sanctuary. Within the first few minutes the altar was already piled with bodies, and a great quantity of blood ran down from it all the way to the entrance steps.

Titus, seeing that he had no control over the men inside, raced in with a few of his officers and ran to the sanctuary steps, thinking they might still save it. Since the fire was already raging around the rooms that faced the outer wall, Titus commanded a centurion and some of his men to beat soldiers with their staves — if for no other reason than to command their attention so he could address them. And yet, writes Josephus, "their passions and hatred of the Jews were too hard even for the regard they had for Cæsar" and the fear of disobeying his command.

Plunder drove them most of all, of course. The men had heard often that every room was full of money and even the walls plated with gold. Plunder they did, but they were denied much of it by their own disorganized fervor. Even as Titus implored them to leave the sanctuary intact, other fires were erupting all over the temple. Now the flames and smoke were spreading so wildly that Romans and Jews alike soon were pushing and shoving their way out of the temple. Among them was Titus himself, who just managed to run back through the front gates as the flaming support structure began to crash around him. All that now remained alive inside were a handful of brave priests. Those who didn't perish quickly climbed atop the sanctuary roof. As their last desperate measure they grabbed the spikes that were set in lead to deter birds and hurled them down on the Romans below.

Outside the temple the slaughter was even worse, because the Jews who fled now had Romans at their backs and the advancing legions in the courtyard in front of them. Those slain either in the temple or in the outer courtyard exceeded 10,000. Another 6,000 Jews — mostly women and children — had managed to find some relief cowering among the surrounding cloisters; but as the Roman officers were in the process of deciding to spare them, the soldiers had already begun slaughtering them like cattle.

Below, crowds of gaping Jews had gathered from all over the city. What they could see at the top of their highest hill was a blaze so huge that it seemed as if the entire city were on fire. But what they could hear was even more horrifying. Both the walls of the courtyard and the mountains to the east had an eerie way of echoing back great noises, and now the sound was like no other.

> The flame was carried a long way and made an echo, together with the groans of those that were being slain. Nor can one imagine anything greater or more terrible than this noise; for there was at once the shout of Roman legions, who were marching all together, and a sad clamor of the seditious, who were now surrounded with fire and sword. The people who were left were beaten back by the enemy...and made sad moans at the calamity they were under.

> The multitude that were in the city joined in this outcry with those who were upon the hill. Many of those who were worn away by the famine and their mouths almost closed, when they saw the fire of the holy house broke out into groans and outcries again.[110]

The next day, Titus strode among the charred and burning rubble and determined that nothing could be saved of the temple. That same day he ordered that fires be set to what remained of the cloisters as well as those small parts of the temple that had not already burned down. Perhaps the most convincing argument that Titus originally had not planned to destroy the temple is the fact that the treasury chambers burnt down along with everything else. According to Josephus, the losses included "an immense quantity of money, an immense number of garments and other precious goods there deposited."

One might think that it would take only a few more days to subdue the few sections of Jerusalem that remained in the hands of the rebels. In fact it would take the Romans an entire month. For example, building up banks against the high walls of Herod's palace (just 1,500 feet west of the temple) meant extending the search for materials to a 33-mile radius of the city. When the Roman rams finally knocked a hole in the palace wall and poured forth, they found many Jews already dead by their own swords and others too weak from hunger to resist. Even those in the great towers above also surrendered, causing Titus to exclaim, "It was none other than God who ejected the Jews out of these fortifications, for what could the hands of men or machines do to overthrow these towers?"

The Upper City was stormed and burned. But most often when the soldiers entered houses in search of plunder, "they found in them entire families of dead men, and the upper rooms full of corpses...of such as died in the famine," writes Josephus. "They stood in horror at such sights and went out without touching anything."

Some 2,000 persons were discovered hiding in subterranean caverns, together with as many corpses and a considerable treasure. John of Gischala was among them and sent word asking Cæsar's right hand of security. It was denied. Simon held out longer, but finally surfaced for want of food and was spotted wandering about in the streets of the Upper City. He was captured and preserved for a reason to be explained shortly.

Despite the fact that much of the temple treasury disappeared in the fire, Titus learned that great quantities had been hidden, and several priests were willing to tell him where in exchange for their lives. Plunder from other caches and deserters was so enormous that gold sold for about half its usual price throughout Syria for several months.

One of Titus' secretaries, a freedman named Fronto, was given the task of determining who should live or die. Some 40,000 persons — mostly those who had deserted prior to the temple destruction — were allowed freedom to live anywhere but Jerusalem. Fronto culled out 700 of the handsomest young men, to be reserved for the triumph in Rome. He marked 97,000 other adult males for slavery, some to be distributed to the provinces for gladiatorial and wild beast shows, but most to be sent to the mines of Egypt.

In all, it is estimated that 1,100,000 Jews perished from famine, disease or battle. No one in the first century could argue with Josephus when he wrote that this "exceeded all the destructions that either men or God ever brought upon the world" at any one time or place.

Titus now ordered the entire city and temple demolished with only a few exceptions. He left the inner west wall of the city and its three strongest towers (Phasælis, Hippicus and Mariamme). This he did for the convenience of housing a Roman garrison and to show posterity how well fortified a city he had conquered. But after the rest had been demolished, Josephus observed that "It was so thoroughly laid even with the ground by those who dug up to the foundation, that there was nothing left to make those who came thither believe it had ever been inhabited."

It would be two more years before the Romans could actually claim to have subdued the whole Jewish nation, for a thousand Sicarii still looked down defiantly from the mountaintop that Herod had leveled to build the fortress of Masada. Titus, in fact, marched right past it when he led his two legions on a farewell visit to Egypt as the year drew to a close. On the way they passed the forlorn scene of what had been Jerusalem. Titus claims to have despaired at seeing such a "melancholy site." Yet his father, at least, would have been soothed at learning that the tenth legion was busying itself uncovering a bonanza of gold and silver in the rubble.

In the spring of A.D. 71 Titus and his two legions sailed with their captives and booty from Alexandria to Rome, where the city was bedecked with flowers for a joint triumph — a long-delayed one to celebrate the emperor's civil war victories and the other the son's stupendous exploits in war.

First the soldiers marched in procession. On the Palatine Hill, Vespasian and Titus came out crowned with laurel, clothed in their purple-rimmed togas. They proceeded to where a walkway overlooked the Forum, where they were met by the Senate and equestrian leaders. After Vespasian gave a short speech and both men sacrificed, with their heads covered by priestly shawls, the soldiers gave up great shouts of acclamation. Then they were all sent off to a banquet provided by the emperor.

Now it was time to display the trophies that had come from Jerusalem. First came marchers carrying a variety of riches — silver, gold, ivory sculptures and jewels, giant purple wall hangings that had been embroidered in Babylonia, the golden table from the temple and the large golden menorah, or holder of seven candlesticks. The last of all the spoils was the temple ark, containing the Laws of the Jews. Later, Vespasian would build the Temple of Peace, which put these trophies on display for Romans and tourists to see for years to come.

Next marched the male captives from Jerusalem, all of them adorned in fine dress as well. But the greatest delight of the crowd was reserved for the great platforms, built by competing trade guilds, each carried by 60 or more bearers and depicting various scenes from the battles that Vespasian and Titus had fought throughout Judea. On this one the audience could see squadrons of enemies slain; on that one a stout wall battered by Roman siege engines; here an army pours through a breached wall; over there the replica of the Jewish temple actually burning with fire.

At the end of the procession trod Simon of Gerasa, led throughout by a rope over his head and exposed to the torments of the throng that pressed against him on the narrow parade path. Now came the last and most ritualistic part of the ceremony. The procession wound up to the steps of the Temple of Jupiter Capitoline, which was nearing full restoration. Here the crowds suddenly fell silent as an ancient Roman tradition unfolded. Simon was brought forward, standing proudly, quietly erect. Then an executioner swung a heavy sword and lopped off his head.

The triumph had ended, as rules of Roman warfare had long dictated. As the crowd at the temple let up a mighty cheer, the throngs below knew what it meant, and their roar cascaded across the Forum below, to the 30,000 in the Theater of Marcellus, and even across the Tiber to Trastevere, the crowded section of narrow alleys and strange food smells where thousands of Jews still attempted to ply their ancient trades.

EVERY JEW FROM SPAIN to Babylonia was affected by the destruction of Jerusalem in two ways. To the extent that they lived in isolated quarters amidst suspicious and unfriendly Gentiles, they could now expect more visible expressions of enmity and more risk to their personal safety. Thus, each time some legionary swaggered out of a tavern just as a Jew happened to pass by, there was always the instant possibility of a cursing that would spark a fight along with the usual crowds and riots and killings.

The second thing common to all Jewish adult males is that they no longer paid annual tribute to the temple in Jerusalem. Instead, they were now taxed an equivalent sum to support the temple of Jupiter Capitoline in Rome. Gone for centuries to come, along with the pilgrimages to the festivals of Passover and Pentecost, was the proud reassurance of having a central secular storehouse of wealth that gave evidence of a powerful religion and a great nation.

These changes were dramatic, to be sure, but beyond Judea the life of religious worship was changed little because the community synagogue, rabbi and elders remained the center of it. It was the Jews of Judea who now had to absorb these institutions themselves. With the obliteration of the temple and slaughter of so many eminent citizens, the Sanhedrin was no more and the influence of the priestly families was badly crippled. Even the Essene community at Qumran, a traditional refuge for priestly reflection, had been shattered and its buildings fired to the ground because one of the seven Jewish generals had been an Essene. The absence of temple ritual and its priests as a central authority placed these things in the hands of individual congregations and their rabbis, who were mostly Pharisees.

And as Jews re-established order among themselves, Jewish Christians were not a part of it. These Christians had fled Jerusalem well before the siege and now took pains to convince Roman authorities that they were in no way a sect of Judaism. So it is no wonder that Christians would be barred from the synagogue, if for no other reason than the risk that they might even be agents of Rome.

In any case, a movement had already begun to preserve and purify Jewish traditions. Even as Titus and his legions were breaking camp to leave the wreckage of Jerusalem, a group of surviving scholars had taken up residence in Jamnia, just 30 miles west where the coastal plain begins. They included priests who had fled early from the procurator Florus, Pharisees who had escaped the tyranny of John and Simon, and those who had been pardoned by Titus and his freedman Fronto in the aftermath of battle.

Their focus now was the Torah. Together the scholars began a long, painstaking effort to decide what scriptures it should include. Moreover, many versions of the Law had been in circulation throughout the world and the men at Jamnia wanted to arrive at a single authorized canon. When this was accomplished it would then be translated into Greek for the Jews of the Diaspora. All this would take years.

The men of Jamnia labored under the scrutiny of the Tenth Legion, now garrisoned in the towers of Herod that rose above the rubble of Jerusalem. But the scholars enjoyed at least some peace of mind: their project had received the personal blessing of Vespasian and Titus thanks to one man — the turncoat Josephus. Still only 33 and now consigned to the gardens of Titus' household, he would begin writing an account of the Jewish wars that would, unsurprisingly, extol the achievements of his Roman patron. After that Josephus would begin work on an extensive history of the Jewish people from the creation of mankind.

BY THE TIME THE ROMANS had begun the siege of Jerusalem, most of the Jewish Christians within the city had managed to flee it. Even as the battles raged, the Jewish Christian leaders of Judea had largely re-settled in Pella, which lay about 60 miles northeast of Jerusalem along the hogback ridge that overlooks the River Jordan and Samaria to the west. Their leader was now Symeon, who had presided over the community ever since James, the brother of Jesus, was killed. Under Symeon's guidance, the Christian communities in Judea and Samaria continued to grow in numbers — partly because the synagogues rejected Jewish Christians from their congregations.

This growth may also be due to the same reasons that had affected all Christians throughout the empire with the end of Nero, his persecutions, the civil war and the Jewish wars. With the peaceful reign of Vespasian came at least five important changes.

First, Christians now had more freedom to meet in the open. This is not to imply that Vespasian ever studied or encouraged Christianity. It stemmed simply from the fact that the emperor was even-tempered by nature and not disposed to disrupt those who didn't deliberately demean or threaten the gods of Rome.

This freedom was all the more possible because Christians were finally seen by the average Roman citizen as more distinct from Jews than before the war on Jerusalem. As noted earlier, the Jews themselves contributed to this when the Christians departed Jerusalem before the siege. Jews saw it as confirmation of their long-held suspicions that Christian ties to Jesus were stronger than to the Torah, and the bonds were broken when they didn't stay to share in the city's defense. Jews even found it irritating that Christian worship services continued to use Jewish traditions and quote rabbinical scripture. For example, Jesus was called the "Lamb of God" because he was crucified at the same time that thousands of Paschal lambs were being slaughtered for the Passover meal. And his blood, to Christians, represented much the same hope and protection as the blood of sacrificial lambs that was smeared on the doorways of Jewish homes. Jews were further rankled by the fact that Christians ceased to sacrifice lambs at Passover. Their Lamb of God had already been sacrificed.

Christians had their reasons for schism as well. Most viewed the destruction of the temple as God's punishment for rejecting the savior he had sent them. And when citizens throughout the empire harassed and made miserable their Jewish neighbors during the wars in Syria, Christians were quick to tell the persecutors that they were in no way associated with Judaism.

The second change in Vespasian's reign flows from the first one. As it became possible for Christians to become more visible, new leaders in the latter first century rose by necessity to walk in the footsteps of the original apostles and evangelists. Thus, the Christian Titus, who learned at the feet of Paul, now headed the churches of Crete. Timothy, Paul's companion from Asia Minor to Rome, was now called "bishop" of Ephesus (a title that surely would have been held by the venerable apostle John had it not been for his advanced age). Similarly, in Athens the patriarch was none other than the Æropagite Dionysius, who became the first Christian convert after Paul's address to the Athenians in the Areopagus, or chief meeting place. In Alexandria, the patriarch was the same Anianus, the cobbler who mended the sandal of Mark and then became his first convert. And in Rome, the bishop and principal minister of the gospel was Linus, who was soon recognized as such after the death of Peter and Paul.

The various titles associated with the above names were very new to Christian communities. They certainly suggest a tendency towards a formal hierarchy of authority, which helps explain the third major change during Vespasian's reign: the devolvement toward a uniform worship ritual. It was as if Christians had collectively come to the conclusion that if they were now deprived of Jesus and the apostles in the flesh, they must take their strength from common worship and a common effort to support evangelism beyond their immediate communities.

Ironically, as already noted, the early Christian worship service was structured much like that of a synagogue. Attendees began by reading passages of Jewish Scripture that had a bearing on their own people and problems. Yet they also read from the letters of Paul, Peter, the gospel according to Mark and other works (which, alas, seem to be written more by Jewish Christians than not). The same can held true for the hymns and psalms that were sung and said at various intervals in the service. Some were of Christian authorship, but most were taken from rabbinical scripture.

Each service also included several common prayers to God, and here the Christian was more apt to depart from the Jew. In the earliest years of the Christian house churches, a time was reserved in which people would pray in their own way at the same time. Some might be making esthetic utterances, as in a trance, or speaking in tongues, while others prayed aloud to ask God's blessing or offer him thanks. Some of this continued after A.D. 70, but prayer was more likely to be made by the leader of the church as the others listened in silence. Then the leader might ask if others had special prayers to offer. The congregation would then recite the Lord's Prayer, literally unchanged from the version said today.

Baptism could be part of a given service or reserved for special occasions. Again, this ritual seems to have been based on the Jewish rite of purification by water. But in another sense, the first century Christian, when being immersed, shared in the crucifixion of Jesus. And when he emerged from the water, he or she shared in Jesus' resurrection.

After all these things took place in a service, the head of the congregation, or perhaps an elder, would deliver a prepared oratory on some insights about the life of Jesus or how to lead a life of service to one's fellows. Yet the longest ritual of the service is what came next: the Lord's Supper. In this ritual was a distinctly Christian tradition unless compared to the meals that some of the temple priesthoods and trade guilds took together.

No persons could take part in the Lord's Supper unless they had declared themselves for Jesus and joined a particular congregation. The meal originated from the last night Jesus was with his disciples, when he took bread and said, "This is my body, which is broken for you." And after the meal he took some wine and said, "This cup is the new covenant in my blood. Do this, as often as you drink it, in remembrance of me."

This was a full meal in the first century, and more than once Paul had to remind congregations that it was intended to fulfill a spiritual need and not merely one's stomach. Yet, few churches of the day could say that they merely broke bread and served wine — and there are at least two good reasons why. Devout Christians were expected to fast on both Wednesdays and Fridays, and when Sunday came around people looked forward to a good meal, prepared by the women of the church, as much as they did a good sermon. In addition, the meal was often used to serve members who were poor or ill. In many churches it was the deacons' task to take part of the Sunday meal to the homes of members who couldn't attend.

The Lord's Supper typifies the fourth change in Christian churches that emerged in Vespasian's time: their growth as providers of care to the poor, the homeless, the elderly, widows, orphans and the afflicted. By this time, 40 years after the resurrection, the immediacy of the Parousia, or second coming of Jesus, had receded to the extent that few Christians were selling all their possessions and keeping watch for the final day of judgment. Yet, churches were sharing their resources like never before to reflect Jesus' love in acts of charity and compassion. Was a Christian traveler new to the city? Let him seek lodging in a Christian home. Was an old woman lonely? Let her seek comfort in a Christian congregation.

Public social services like these were much more unusual than today. The first century was still a world where rich men commonly abandoned enfeebled slaves and where the most a poor widow could hope for from her city magistrates was the bread dole and a slice of meat during a festival. Whereas people once saw Christians only as a strange group that performed suspicious rituals and banded together in self-defense, they could now be heard saying, even if begrudgingly, "Look how Christians love one another! Look how they care for each other!" They were amazed as well that a church could contain rich people, poor, women and slaves all behaving as equals. Indeed, where else would one find women leaders, as those who served as church deacons? Where else would there be an Order of Widows that visited the bedridden and helped to raise orphans?

Christians, of course, had always cared for one another; but in the grim days of Nero's persecutions, when whole families were shattered, their numbers did not necessarily grow. Now they *did,* and one result was that some churches became too large and busy to be contained in private homes and villas. Even the Lord's Supper had created problems — and resentment — when some were served in the homeowner's inner dining room while others had to eat outside at rough tables. And so, a few congregations in the provinces, where land was less dear, actually built or acquired separate buildings for their churches. In crowded cities, such as Rome, at least one church occupied several rooms on the ground floor of a large brick tenement and may even have held services in a basement grotto used for Mithraic rituals.

Growth is what the apostles sought, of course, when they spread the gospel, but it also brought a fifth change in the latter first century. The more the numbers, the greater propensity there was for debate, division, sects, false prophets and rivalries among competing personalities. Paul had written in his letter to the Romans that Gentile Christians were "a wild shoot grafted into the olive tree that is Israel." But without Paul or the other apostles to prune it when needed, the wild shoot grew in many directions after their passing. Thus, while most churches of Antioch considered themselves the fulfillment of Judaism, most of those in Asia Minor thought themselves a new religion. In Ephesus some church members stirred up a tempest by proclaiming that, since they had already been granted eternal life by God's grace, they saw no need to do good deeds or follow the Ten Commandments. Elsewhere in Asia, a few preachers stated that because Jesus was a spiritual being to begin with, he did not actually "die" on the cross and was therefore not resurrected. So why should they be willing to be martyrs?

In some churches, members argued about who had the more direct genealogy to the family line of Jesus. In Antioch, the churches had been dazzled by the magic tricks of Menander, a disciple of Simon the Magus, whom Peter tracked down in Rome and silenced. Now this successor again used more magic as he claimed to emulate the miracles of Jesus.

In Alexandria, a "Christian" named Cerinthus attracted a following by reciting tales of wonder that had been revealed to him by angels. When Christ returns to his kingdom, he proclaimed, it will be on earth, and Jerusalem will be reborn as a paradise of carnal pleasures, including a thousand years of uninterrupted wedding festivities.

Much more formidable, however, was the onslaught of philosophical schools, each with its body of literature and erudite teachers. One could, for instance, find many of Ebionites, who believed that Jesus was but a man, born of natural union, who elevated his ordinary circumstances merely by learning and growth of character. However, the most enduring "sect," if such it can be called, were the Gnostics. Knowledge of God, they argued, could be "earned" by study of many sources, of which Jesus was but one. To be sure, Jesus possessed a special knowledge, they said, but by learning his teachings, one could attain equality with him and even go on to loftier levels of excellence.

Some Christians bemoaned the fact that leadership in each church was passing from the hands of several elder members to men with more authoritative titles such as *pastor* and *presbyter* and *bishop*. The common need to sort out and give guidance regarding cases like the above is one more reason why Paul himself foresaw the need in his last days when he told Timothy:

> I charge you in the presence of God and of Christ Jesus who is to judge the living and the dead, and by his appearing and his kingdom: preach the word, be urgent in season and out of season, convince, rebuke and exhort. Be unfailing in patience and in teaching. For the time is coming when people will not endure sound teaching, but having itching ears they will accumulate for themselves teachers who suit their own likings and will turn away from listening to the truth and wander into myths. As for you, always be steady, endure suffering, do the work of an evangelist, fulfill your ministry.[111]

The main reason why Paul believed that ordinary men could carry on Christ's mission successfully against so many distractions was that the message itself is uncomplicated: salvation comes from God's grace to all who will simply believe in him, love him and love their neighbor. Paul and the other apostles believed that this one bright beacon would be sufficient to keep a congregation on course provided that the pastor and presbyters kept a firm hand on the tiller.

The winds that could blow this ship off course were the words of those who preached that only this man possessed the Truth or only that philosophy spoke the mind of God, or that God blessed this or that bodily nourishment. And again, Paul's reasoning was simple and clear: even the wisest of men is but a foolish child to God. If knowledge of God were a great river and the wisest of all philosophers were to dip into it, he could retain no more than a cupful.

But unlike knowledge, the first century apostles preached that what God *did* give man in boundless amounts is the power of love. Great men would inscribe their conquests on massive stele, but the only monument to early Christianity is the fact that the numbers of believers continued to grow despite persecution, superstition, wars and isolation. And this can only have been achieved by thousands of loving acts. It strongly suggests that after the centurion Cornelius met Paul in Cæsarea, certain Roman soldiers took on a new life among their ranks. When Jews despaired in the desert after begging the governor Petronius not to erect a colossal statue of Caligula in their temple, did Christians go among them soothing and listening? When Paul and Silas left Lystra after the earthquake, did the jailer they had baptized tell his neighbors of his experience? When all passengers aboard a ship-wrecked grain ship survived on Malta, how many must have thanked — and followed — the Christian prisoners who gave them courage and comfort? When Nero left cities and families in wreckage as he continued his artistic conquest of Greece, were there not Christians in their midst to show them a better life? Did not The Way spread from the sentries who guarded Paul in his Roman apartment and Peter in his dank cell in the Mamertine? When Jotapata and Jerusalem were surrounded and besieged, were there not Christians among them sharing their food and comforting the dying?

When they did, their message was not one of politics or philosophy, but a simple appeal. For as Paul wrote to the quarreling Corinthians many years before he was martyred:

> Love is patient and kind. Love is not jealous or boastful. It is not arrogant or rude. Love does not insist on its own way. It is not irritable or resentful. It does not rejoice at wrong, but rejoices in the right. Love bears all things, believes all things, hopes all things, endures all things.

> Love never ends. As for prophecy, it will pass away. As for tongues, they will cease. As for knowledge, it will pass away. For our knowledge is imperfect and our prophecy is imperfect. But when the perfect comes, the imperfect shall pass away.

> When I was a child, I spoke like a child. I thought like a child. I reasoned like a child. When I became a man I gave up childish ways. For now we see in a mirror dimly, but then face to face. Now I know in part. Then I will understand fully, even as I have been fully understood. So faith, hope and love abide — these three.

> But the greatest of these is love.[112]

EPILOGUE

THE FLAVIAN ERA DESERVED to have a happy ending. Vespasian, who earned his place in the pantheon of good emperors simply by restoring order from chaos, ruled nobly until dying peacefully in A.D. 79. Titus, who assumed the throne at age 40 and looked forward to a long and enlightened reign, reminds us that frailty rules the human condition. The conqueror of nations and slayer of dozens in hand to hand combat died only two years later of some ill-defined "distemper" (pneumonia?) after bathing in a frigid stream.

And so, Titus' 30-year-old profligate, probably paranoid brother Domitian wound up emperor of the Roman Empire and quickly followed in the footsteps of Caligula and Nero. Fittingly, the most memorable achievement of his 15-year reign was in building a new palace complex on the Palatine that may have been even more stupendous than Nero's Golden House.

Among Domitian's many victims throughout the empire were both Christians and Jews. The latter were often seized for not paying what had been the former temple tax to the rebuilding of the temple of Jupiter Capitoline. Christians were sometimes arrested for the same offense, which shows that many Roman officials continued to identify them as a Jewish sect.

However, both religions suffered even more because one of Domitian's primary tools for consolidating power was to strengthen the state religion and wipe out those who appeared to threaten it. Thus, Christians died by the thousands in purges and in gladiatorial shows at the newly built Flavian Amphitheater (which was not called the Coliseum until the Middle Ages).

Still, the numbers of Christians continued to grow everywhere. In fact, one reason for the persecutions was that Domitilla, a sister or cousin of Domitian, and her husband T. Flavius Clemens, a senator and consul, were identified as Christians and executed. Both were accused of practicing "atheism," which meant failure to worship the emperor and the pagan gods of Rome. One of the city's major catacombs bears the name Domitilla, and the rapid extension of these underground burial chambers further verifies the growing Christian population. Today, excavations of now-famous catacombs such as San Sebastiano, San Callisto, Domitilla and Priscilla have so far revealed a combined 360 miles of corridors, tombs and grottos.

The work of the post-temple Jewish scholars culminated in A.D. 100 when the Synod of Jamnia formally decided which books were to be accepted by all Jews as Holy Writ. A uniform version of the text was translated and circulated to Jewish communities of the Diaspora. Although Jews were without a geographical center, their communities prospered and in time many even returned to Jerusalem to replant their roots.

By the year A.D. 132 Jerusalem had again become such a Jewish stronghold that its citizens once more defied Rome, re-establishing the high priesthood and minting their own coins. And again the Roman legions came marching up from Antioch and Cæsarea. The Jewish defenders held out for three years, finally being reduced to a resistance movement that fought on from caves in the desert around the Dead Sea.

In its aftermath, Jerusalem was turned into a Roman provincial town and given the name of Colonia Ælia Capitolina. On the temple hill the Romans built a sanctuary honoring Jupiter Capitolinus, and on the traditional site of Calvary they built a temple to Venus. The city was populated with Romans, Greeks and people from the east. Jews were forbidden to enter it on pain of death.

As Jewish survivors again found themselves clustered in hundreds of ghettos across the empire, they redoubled their efforts to practice the same self-protective devices that had sustained them for over 30 centuries. Local rabbis exchanged information over a well-organized courier network called The Responsa. No Jewish community was to seek help from a Gentile government, so an extra layer of voluntary taxes was imposed on all members in order to support charity and universal education. To guard against further depopulation, the community was expected to provide a dowry to any eligible woman who couldn't afford one. And if a Jew were sold into slavery, the community nearest the slave owner was made responsible for buying his or her freedom within seven years. To further assure that the culture would continue intact, Jewish scholars compiled the first Hebrew dictionary and standardized the worship liturgy. Tolerance for dozens of finicky sects came to an end. Either you were in or out. And measures like these, more than any battle victories, sustained the Jews in the next 20 centuries.

I would like to conclude with some further words about the fates of the best-known apostles and, at the same time, about oral traditions that have been passed down through the centuries. Earlier, in the text, I wrote that oral traditions have a remarkable record of proving out. Luke provides us with a good example in one sense because there are absolutely no oral traditions about him. No city claims him other than his hometown of Philippi. No churches claim to have his bones or relics. Not even in *Acts* or the *Gospel of Luke* does the author himself offer a clue. And yet, even universal silence can be helpful in this case because it suggests that Luke probably returned to Philippi, remained an elder in his church and continued to be a practicing, compassionate physician.

At the other end of the spectrum, let us look more closely at the case of Peter, about whom there has been a very strong oral tradition. In the text I reported the tradition of the Catholic church — not corroborated by direct evidence — that Peter came to Rome with his wife and at least one daughter, Petronilla, who was said to be lame throughout life. By this account, he lived in Rome for a few years under the patronage of a wealthy senator named Pudens, whose family was baptized and whose home in the Subura was used for worship. The tradition gains credibility in that Paul's second letter to Timothy offers greetings from "Pudens," that the most ancient of active Roman parishes is St. Pudente in the former Subura, and that its church is named St. Pudentiana (after one of the senator's baptized daughters).

The only written confirmation of the above comes from the Christian bishop Eusebius writing over 200 years later, and most scholars are wary because many of his sources are works that have since disappeared with time. However, regardless of when Peter came to Rome and who came with him, I have no doubt that the apostle (who probably never heard himself called "the first pope") was crucified in the Circus of Caligula and Nero and that the "Vatican" neighborhood in which he was entombed is the same Vatican we now know as the Holy See.

The reason is that, unlike the case of Luke, time and science have given the oral tradition new life. In about A.D. 150 the tomb of Peter, across from the Vatican Circus, was buttressed with an ornamental and protective structure consisting of a roof and four white marble columns. The enclosure was called "The Trophy of Gaius," probably after a prominent churchman of the day who commissioned the work. When the emperor Constantine decided to build the first St. Peter's Basilica in A.D. 326, he could have made his engineers' job easier by choosing any of the many perfectly level sites available in the Vatican neighborhood. Instead, he insisted that the enormous slab that was to anchor the cathedral be exactly where a hillside, first century necropolis was located. It meant not only excavating and removing tons of earth, but informing hundreds of very unhappy families that they would have to move the graves of their loved ones elsewhere.

The whole purpose of this massive engineering feat was to situate the altar of the basilica directly over the Trophy of Gaius, which lay at the base of the hill. Since a city block or two of crypts were on the same level as the Trophy of Gaius, or grave of St. Peter, they were allowed to remain — and to be permanently "entombed" under the foundation of the basilica.

In 1506, when the present St. Peter's replaced the aging basilica, the new altar was placed in precisely the same spot.

In 1939 Pope Pius XII ordered some probing excavations below St. Peter's as he sought to find suitable space for his own burial place. This led to an announcement in 1950 that the excavators had not only uncovered an entire street of the first century necropolis, but the "Trophy," the tomb below it, and part of the red wall behind the tomb.

Visiting the ancient necropolis beneath the Vatican is available to anyone who can advance a legitimate academic reason, provide ample advance notice and be ready to bend with the winds and whims of the Vatican bureaucracy. It is a stirring experience, and partially because it lends new respect for an ancient tradition.

At the far end of the spectrum one can find whole sets of oral-written traditions in conflict with other sets — and they directly collide in the case of the apostle John. Eusebius and others say that the youngest apostle went to Ephesus with the mother of Jesus and lived a Christian patriarch until age 100, or the end of the century itself.

Did he? Some modern scholars have latched onto some fourth-to-sixth century references that say he perished in A.D. 42 with his brother James in the persecutions of Herod Agrippa I. Yet, neither *Acts* (A.D. 70?) nor Eusebius, who wrote around A.D. 320, give it a notion.

Next, this question: Did an aging John actually write the fourth gospel? If so, why did he wait so long? Again, Eusebius offers a simple answer:

> The three gospels, already written, were in general circulation and copies had come into John's hands. He welcomed them, we are told, and confirmed their accuracy, but remarked that the narrative only lacked the story of what Christ had done first of all at the beginning of his mission.

> This tradition is undoubtedly true. Anyone can see that the three evangelists have recorded the doings of the Savior for only one year, following the consignment of John the Baptist to prison, and that they indicated the very fact at the beginning of the narrative....

> Thus, John in his gospel narrative records what Christ did when the Baptist had not yet been thrown into gaol, while the other three evangelists described what happened after the Baptist's consignment to prison. Once this is grasped, there no longer appears to be a discrepancy between the gospels, because John's deals with the early stages of Christ's career and others cover the last period of his story....[113]

And now the final question: Did the apostle John write the Biblical *Book of Revelation* as well? Here we run into the claim that Ephesus was also the home of one John the Elder, a Jewish-Christian from Jerusalem, but quite a different man than the apostle John. All that we can say for sure is that a certain John was tortured in Rome by the emperor Domitian and then banished to the Greek isle of Patmos somewhere around A.D. 95. And there he wrote the apocryphal polemic, *Revelation*, the last book accepted into the Christian New Testament. Drenched in mystic symbolism, the book forecasts a day in which Nero will rise again at the head of a Parthian army that will vanquish the evil Rome, only to be overcome in the end by the heavenly forces of Jesus.

We know nothing about John the Elder except that he seems to have immigrated from Jerusalem and knew little about Rome (describing it as a port city that will be swallowed up by a big wave, for example). But we also know that John the apostle: (1) wrote his gospel in a different style than *Revelation*, (2) did not preach rebellion against official Rome; (3) could not conceivably, after learning what Nero had done to the apostles James, Peter, Paul and countless Christians, have championed the notion of a dead emperor leading Rome's worst enemy into battle.

John the Elder, whom no one in the first century ever mentions, may well have written *Revelation*, and this author would frankly prefer to hope it was not John the Apostle. For the John in my mind is the same one who, according to the bishop Eusebius, approached his one hundredth year and the end of a century in unbroken devotion to the master he had dropped everything to follow in Galilee so long before. This was a time when the arrival of Ebionites, Gnostics, Cerinthians, Nicolaitans and many more splinter sects began to justify the words of Jesus that "many will come in my name, claiming 'I am the Christ' and deceiving many." But as their philosophical gibberish confused the faithful, the aging John seemed to make their choice ever simpler. As Eusebius reports, "He became so old and frail that he could no longer walk and had to be carried to meetings and services. All he could manage to say was: 'My little children, love one another'"

But in those few words the old "Son of Thunder" had managed to distill the faith and the power of the Christian message.

APPENDIX I

ENDNOTES

For complete references to the works cited in these notes, see the Suggested Reading list on p. 375.

1. *Acts*, 2:17–18.
2. Eusebius, *The History of the Church*, p. 38.
3. Ibid, p. 39.
4. Tacitus, *The Annals of Imperial Rome*, p. 209.
5. Suetonius, *The Lives of the Twelve Cæsars*, p. 153.
6. Tacitus, p. 211.
7. Suetonius, p. 170.
8. *Acts*, 26:16–18.
9. Philostratus, *Apollonius of Tyana*, Book 1, p. 17.
10. Bradford, *Paul the Traveller*, p. 90
11. Ibid, p. 90.
12. Ibid. p. 90.
13. *Romans*, 1:22–24.

14. British Museum Papyrus No. 1911. Cited in *Roman Civilization*, p. 366–67.
15. *Roman Civilization*, p. 368. See also Josephus, *Antiquities of the Jews*, p. 578.
16. Juvenal, *Satires*, VI, as quoted by Grant's *Twelve Cæsars*, p. 145.
17. *Acts*, 13:26–34.
18. Onesiphorus' description of Paul outside Iconium is taken from *The Acts of Paul*, written in A.D. 160 and translated by M.R. James in *The Apocryphal New Testament* (Oxford, 1924).
19. *Acts*, 15:6–11.
20. Ibid, 15: 16–18.
21. Ibid, 15:22–29.
22. Ibid, 17:22–31.
23. *Thessalonians*, 4:16–22.
24. *Morals*, p.278–79.
25. *Galatians*, 1:6-10.
26. Ibid, 3:1–5.
27. Ibid, 5:14–24.
28. *1 Corinthians*, 1:12–17.
29. Ibid, 1:20–25.
30. Ibid, 2:1–4.
31. Ibid, 3:2–6.
32. Ibid, 5:11–12.
33. Ibid, 6:7–11.
34. Ibid, 8:10–12.
35. Ibid, 11:4–7.
36. Ibid, 11:20–29.
37. Ibid, 14:7–9.
38. Ibid, 13:1–3.
39. Ibid, 15:12–19.
40. Ibid, 15:35–53.
41. Ibid 15:54–58.
42. *2 Corinthians*, 11:19–29.
43. Ibid, 12:2–5.
44. Ibid, 12:8–10.
45. Ibid, 9:2–3.
46. Ibid, 11:21–22.
47. Suetonius, p. 258–259.
48. *Romans*, 1:8–14.
49. *Acts*, 20:22–35.

50. Ibid, 24:11–21.
51. Dio Cassius, Book 62, p. 71.
52. Tacitus, *Annals*, p. 333–34.
53. *Acts*, 26:9–18.
54. *Romans*, 1:21–25.
55. Ibid, 3:9
56. Ibid, 3:21–26.
57. Ibid, 5:1–5.
58. Ibid, 6:2–14.
59. Ibid, 8:37–39.
60. Seneca, *Four Tragedies and Octavia*, p. 274.
61. Eusebius, p. 59.
62. *James*, 4:8–10.
63. Ibid, 5:1–3.
64. Ibid, 2:14–26.
65. *Ephesians*, 2:10.
66. *James*, 5:8–9.
67. Eusebius, p. 59-60.
68. *Acts*, 28:26–27.
69. *Philippians*, 1:12–14.
70. Ibid, 1:27, 2:1–18.
71. *Romans*, 13:1–4.
72. *Colossians*, 1:15–20.
73. *Philippians*, 1:22–26.
74. Tacitus, *Annals*, p. 362.
75. Suetonius, p. 269.
76. *II Timothy*, 4:6–8.
77. Ibid, 2:1–3.
78. Ibid, 3:12–15, 4:1–5.
79. Dio Cassius, Book 62, p. 157.
80. Josephus, *Life of Flavius Josephus*, p. 2.
81. Josephus, *Wars of the Jews*, p. 713.
82. Ibid, p. 722.
83. Ibid, p. 724
84. Ibid, p. 728.
85. Ibid. p. 729.
86. Ibid. p. 730.
87. Fasola, *Peter and Paul in Rome*, p. 72.
88. Ibid. pp. 84–86.
89. *I Peter*, 1:3–7

90. Ibid, 1:18–25.
91. Ibid, 2:12–17.
92. Ibid, 4:7–18.
93. Dio Cassius, Book 62, p. 151-53
94. Speech from an inscription in the town of Acræphiæ (modern Karditza), quoted in *Roman Civilization*, p. 394-95.
95. Dio Cassius, Book 62, p. 175.
96. Josephus, *Wars*, p. 736.
97. Ibid, p. 745.
98. Ibid, p. 747.
99. Ibid, p. 753.
100. Ibid, p. 754.
101. Tacitus, *The Histories*, p. 98.
102. Ibid, p. 101
103. Dio Cassius, Book 64, pp. 241–43.
104. Tacitus, *Histories*, pp.136–37.
105. Tacitus, *Histories*, p. 168.
106. McBirnie, *Search for the Twelve Apostles*, p. 160 (quoting from the book, *The Traditions of the St. Thomas Christians*).
107. Lockyer, *All the Apostles of the Bible*, p. 248.
108. *Matthew*, 24:5–8.
109. Josephus, *Wars*, p. 813.
110. Ibid. p. 823.
111. *II Timothy*, 4:1–5.
112. *I Corinthians*, 13:1–13
113. Eusebius, p. 87.

Appendix II

Suggested Reading

ANCIENT SOURCES
The primary sources for this book were ancients who lived during or not long after the first century. They are:

Dio Cassius. *Roman History*, Books 56–60. Trans. Earnest Cary. Cambridge, MA: Harvard University Press, 1994.

_____. *Roman History*, Books 61–70. Trans. Earnest Cary. Cambridge, MA: Harvard University Press, 1995.

Eusebius. *The History of the Church from Christ to Constantine*. Trans. G.A. Williamson. Ed. Andrew Louth. London: Penguin Books Ltd., 1989.

Holy Bible, Revised Standard Version. New York: Thomas Nelson & Sons, 1953.

Lucan. *Lucan*. Trans. J. D. Duff. Cambridge, MA. Cambridge, MA: Harvard University Press, 1986.

Petronius. *Satyricon*. Trans. Michæl Heseltine and W.H. D. Rouse. Cambridge, MA. Harvard University Press, 1987. 497 pp. (The volume also contains Seneca's brief *Apocolocyntosis*, a satirical account of how the gods on Mount Olympus greeted the newly-deified Claudius.)

Philo. *The Embassy to Gaius* (Vol. X in the works of Philo). Trans. F. H. Colson. Cambridge, MA: Harvard University Press, 1991.

Philostratus, Flavius. *The Life of Apollonius of Tyana*, Vols. I and II. Trans. F. C. Conybeare. Cambridge, MA: Harvard University Press, 1989.

Pliny (The Younger). *Letters and Panegyricus* (Vol. I). Trans. Betty Radice. Ed. G.P. Goold. Cambridge, MA: Harvard University Press, 1989.

Seneca, Lucius Annæus. *Four Tragedies and Octavia*. Trans. E.F. Watling. Harmondsworth, Middlesex, England: Penguin Books Ltd., 1984.

Seneca, Lucius Annæus. *Morals*. Trans. and Ed. Sir Roger L'Estrange. New York: A.L. Burt Company Publishers, n.d.

Suetonius (Gaius Tranquillus). *The Lives of the Twelve Cæsars*. Trans. and ed. Joseph Gavorse, New York, Modern Library Inc., 1959.

Tacitus, Publius Cornelius. *The Annals of Imperial Rome*. Trans. Michæl Grant. Harmondsworth, Middlesex, England: Penguin Books Ltd., 1956.

_____. *The Histories*. Trans. W.H. Fyfe. Ed. D.S. Levene. Oxford: Oxford University Press, 1997.

Whiston, A.M., trans. And ed. *The Life and Works of Flavius Josephus*. (Complete works, with seven dissertations). New York: Holt, Rinehart and Winston, 1977.

MODERN RESOURCES

Aharoni, Yohanan and Michæl Avi-Yonah, eds. *The Macmillan Bible Atlas*. New York: Macmillan Publishing Co. Inc., 1968.

Balsdon, J.P.V.D. *Romans and Aliens*. Chapel Hill, NC: The University of North Carolina Press, 1979.

Basso, Michele. *Guide to the Vatican Necropolis*. Rome: Fabbrica of St. Peter's, the Vatican, 1986.

Bradford, Ernle. *Paul the Traveller*. New York: Macmillan Publishing Co. Inc., 1976.

Barrett, Anthony A. *Agrippina: Sex, Power and Politics in the Early Empire*. New Haven and London: Yale University Press, 1996.

Boyle, Leonard. *A Short Guide to St. Clement's*. Rome: Collegio San Clemente, 1989.

Brilliant, Richard. *Pompeii A.D. 79*. New York: Clarkson N. Potter Inc., Publishers, and the American Museum of Natural History, 1979.

Crowe, Jerome. *From Jerusalem to Antioch*. Collegeville, MN: The Liturgical Press, 1997.

Cwiekowski, Frederick J. *The Beginnings of the Church*. Mahwah, NJ: Paulist Press, 1988.

Dimont, Max I., *Jews, God and History*. New York: Penguin Books U.S.A. Inc., 1994

Durant, Will. *Cæsar and Christ*. New York: Simon and Schuster, 1944.

Earl, Donald. *The Age of Augustus*. New York: Crown Publishers, 1968.

Fasola, Umberto M., *Peter and Paul in Rome*. Rome: Vision Editrice, 1983.

Feldman, Louis H., *Jew & Gentile in the Ancient World*. Princeton, NJ: Princeton University Press, 1993.

Filson, Floyd V. *A New Testament History*. Philadelphia: The Westminster Press, 1964.

Freely, John. *Classical Turkey*. London: Penguin Books, 1991.

_____. *Western Mediterranean Coast of Turkey*. Istanbul: Sev Matbaacilik ve Yayincilik A.S., 1997.

Goodspeed, J. Edgar. *Paul*. Nashville and New York: Abingdon Press, 1947.

Grant, Michæl. *Herod the Great*. New York: American Heritage Press, 1971.

_____. *The Army of the Cæsars*. New York: Charles Scribner's Sons, 1974.

_____, ed. *Latin Literature*. Harmondsworth, Middlesex, England: Penguin Classics, 1958.

Guignebert, Charles. *The Jewish World in the Time of Jesus*. New Hyde Park, NY: University Books, 1968.

Holum, Kenneth G., et al. *King Herod's Dream: Cæsarea on the Sea*. New York: W.W. Norton & Co., 1988.

Hornblower, Simon and Anthony Spawforth, eds. *The Oxford Classical Dictionary*. Oxford: Oxford University Press, 1996.

Landels, J. G. *Engineering in the Ancient World*. Berkeley, CA: University of California Press, 1978.

Lewis, Naphtali. *Life in Egypt Under Roman Rule*. Oxford: Clarendon Press, 1983.

Lewis, Naphtali and Meyer Reinhold, eds. *Roman Civilization. Sourcebook II: The Empire*. New York: Harper & Row, Publishers, 1955.

Locker, Herbert. *All the Apostles of the Bible*. Grand Rapids, MI: Zondervan Publishing House, 1972.

Marks, RCA. *Christianity in the Roman World*. New York: Charles Scriber's Sons, 1974.

Martini, Carl M. *The Testimony of St. Paul*. Trans. Susan Leslie. New York: Crossroads Publishing Company, 1981.

Mason, Steve. *Josephus and the New Testament*. Peabody, MA: Hendrickson Publishers Inc., 1992.

McBirnie, William Steuart. *The Search for the Twelve Apostles*. Wheaton, IL: Tyndale House Publishers Inc., 1973.

Monate, Claude. *The Search for Ancient Rome*. London: Thames and Hudson, 1999.

Pagels, Elaine. *The Gnostic Gospels*. New York: Random House, 1979.

Quispel, Gilles. *The Secret Book of Revelation*. New York: McGraw-Hill Book Company, 1979.

Rowley, Harold H., ed., et al. *New Atlas of the Bible*. Garden City, NY: Doubleday & Company Inc., 1969.

Segala, Elisabetta and Sciortino, Ida. *Domvs Avrea*. Milan: Electa and Soprintendenza Archeologica di Roma, 1999. .

Wilson, A.N. *Paul: The Mind of the Apostle*. New York: W.W. Norton & Company, 1997.

APPENDIX III

MODERN NAMES & LOCATIONS OF ANCIENT PLACES

Names not followed by parentheses are cities. Places described only as "sites" today have neither permanent populations nor significant ruins.

1st Century Name ....**Present Name and Location**

Achaia (Roman province) ....Greece
Adiabene (kingdom) ....NE Iraq–NW Iran
Adramyttium ....Edremit, W Turkey
Ægæ ....Yumurtalik, SE Turkey
Alba Longa ....Castel Gandolfo, Central Italy
Alesia ....Alise-Ste. Reine, France
Alexandria ....Alexandria, N Egypt
Amphidpolis ....Amfipolis, NE Greece
Attalia ....Antalya, S Turkey
Antium ....Anzio, W central Italy
Antioch (Syrian) ....Antakya, E Turkey
Albania (kingdom) ....Azerbaijan, N Iran

Alexander Troas ....Ruins near Bozcaada, NW Turkey
Anthedon ....Site near Gaza, Israel
Apennines (mountains) ....N central Italy
Apollonia ....Apollonia, NE Greece
Arcadia (region) ....Central Peloponnesus, Greece
Ardea..Site W of Rome, Italy
Armenia (kingdom) ....Armenia–NE Turkey
Artaxta ....Site near Yerevan, Armenia
Ascalon ....Ashquelon, SW Israel
Asia (Roman Province) ....W Turkey
Asphaltitis (lake) ....Dead Sea, SE Israel-SW Jordan
Assos ....Behramkale, W Turkey
Athens...Athens, Greece
Avernus (lake)..Averno, SW Italy
Babylonia (region)..Central Iraq
Bactria ....Tajikistan-Uzbekistan
Baucalis.............................Site in or near Alexanrdia, Egypt
Baiæ...Baia, W central Italy
Bedriacum ....Site in N Italy
Berytus..Beirut, Lebanon
Bethoron ....Bayt Ur al Fawqa, near Jerusalem, Israel
Betheunabris...........................Ruins at Tall Nimrin, W Jordan
Bithynia (Roman province)...........................N central Turkey
Bœotia (region) ....Central Greece
Boroea ....Veroia, N Greece
Brixellum ....Site on Po R., N Italy
Britain (region)...England
Brundisium ....Brindisi, SE Italy
Cæsarea............................Ruins near Horbat Qesari, Israel
Camerium..Site NE of Rome
Campania (region) ....W central Italy
Camulodunum ....Colchester, England
Cappadocia (Roman province) ....E Turkey
Capri (island) ....Capri, off SW Italy
Capua ....Capua, W central Italy
Carthage ....Carthage, N Tunisia
Castores.......................................Site near Cremona, N Italy
Caystrus (river).......................Kucuk Menderes, W Turkey
Cenchreæ ....Cenchreæ, SE Greece
Chalcis (city state).......................................Chalcis, N Syria

Chaldea (region) ....S Iraq-Kuwait-Iran
Chios (island)...Chios, Greece, off W Turkey
Cilicia (region)...SE Turkey
Cilician Gates (mtn. pass) ....N of Tarsus, SE Turkey
Colossæ ....Site in S central Turkey
Cordova ....Cordova, Spain
Corinth ....Korinthos, Greece
Cos (island) ....Kos, Greece, off SW Turkey
Cranganore ....Site on Malabar coast, W India
Cremona...Cremona, N central Italy
Crete (Roman province)...Crete
Ctesiphon ....Ruins SE of Baghdad, Iraq
Cyprus (Roman province) ....Cyprus
Cyndus (river)...SE Turkey
Cyrene..Ruins at Shahhatat, Libya
Dacia (region) ....N Romania
Dalmatia (Roman province) ....Croatia and some contingent areas
Damascus...Damascus, Syria
Delphi ....Ruins at Delfol, central Greece
Derbe...Site near Karaman, S central Turkey
Divodurum ....Site in N France
Edessa (city-state)...Urfa, SE Turkey
Edom (region) ....S Israel and Jordan
Engaddi...En Gedi, SE Israel
Ephesus ....Ruins near Kusadasi, W Turkey.
Eturia (region) ....Tuscany - Lazio, N Italy
Euboea (island) ....Evvoia, E Greece
Euphrates (river) ....Runs through Syria and Iraq
Fair Havens (harbor) ....S Crete
Fucine Lake ....Site N of Rome, Italy
Gabao ....Site NW of Jerusalem, Israel
Gadara ....Umm Qays, NW Jordan
Galilee (region) ....N Israel
Gamala..Site near E Israel-W Jordan border
Ganges (river)...E India
Gangites (river) ....Struma R.(?), NE Greece
Gaul (Roman province) ....Alpine Italy N through W France
Gaulanitis (region) ....S Syria, N Jordan
Gaza (region) ....Gaza Strip, SW Israel
Gennesaret (lake) ....Sea of Galilee, N Israel

Geresa	Jarash (W Jordan)
Gerizzim (mountain)	At Jabal at Tur, Samaria, central Israel
Ginæ	Site in Samaria, Israel
Gischala	Jish, NW Israel
Gophna	Site (?) N of Jerusalem, Israel
Herculaneum	Ruins in W Italy
Herodium	Tal Horodos, S Israel
Hostilia	Site E of Cremona, N Italy
Hyacrania	Al Mird, E of Jerusalem
Iberia (kingdom)	Georgia
Iconium	Konya, S Turkey
Idumea (region)	Southern Israel
Illyricum (Roman province)	Nations along NE Adriatic Sea
India (region)	India
Issus	Site near Adana, SE Turkey
Jamnia	Near Yavne, Israel
Japha	Site W of Nazareth, Israel
Jericho	Ariha, E central Israel
Jerusalem	Jerusalem, Israel
Joppa	Yafo. Abuts Tel Aviv, Israel
Jotapata	Ruins, S of Sakhnin, N Israel
Judea (region)	Central Israel
Lake Bolhe (lake)	Limni Volvi, NE Greece
Lasea	Site in S Crete
Lesbos (island)	Greece, off SW Turkey
Leucas (island)	Levkas, off W Greece
Libya (nation)	Libya
Londinium	London, England
Lower Germany (Rom. prov.)	Germany N of Rhine
Lucania (region)	S Campania and Lucania, Italy
Lugdunum	Lyon, France
Lycaonia (region)	SE Turkey
Lydda	Lod, near Tel Aviv, Israel
Lydia (region)	W Turkey
Lystra	Site near Konya, S central Turkey
Macedonia	Macdeonia and N Greece
Macherus	Mukawir, SW Jordan
Malea (cape)	Akra Maleas, S Greece
Masada (fortress)	Ruins in S Israel
Massilia	Marseille, France

Mauretania ....Morocco and W Algeria
Melita (island) ....Malta
Mesopotamia (region) ....Tigris, Euphrates valleys, Iraq
Miletus ....Yemkoy, W Turkey
Misenum ....Site near Pozzuoli, W Italy
Mitylene ....Mitilini, Isle of Lesbos, Greece
Moesia (region) ....N Bulgaria, E Serbia
Mount Gerzzim (mountain) ....Samaria, central Israel
Mount Ida (mountain) ....NW Turkey
MountOlympus (mountain) ....Oros Olympos, NE Greece
Myra ....Kale, S Turkey
Mysia (region) ....NW Turkey
Nabatea (region) ....S Israel–W Jordan
Narbonese Gaul (region)..S E France
Neopolis ....Site near Amfipolis, S Greece
Neapolis..Naples, Italy
Nola..Nola, W Italy
Numidia (Roman province) ....E Algeria-W Tunisia
Ocriculum ....Site near Otricoli, Umbria, Italy
Ostia..Ostia, W central Italy
Pandateria (isle) ....Pantellaria, off W Italy
Pannonia (Roman province) ....W Hungary and Serbia
Paphos ....Paphos, SW Cyprus
Parthia (empire) ....E Syria to India
Patara ....Ruins near Kinik, S Turkey
Patræ ....Patrai, W central Greece
Peloponnese (region)..Peloponnesus, S Greece
Perea (region) ....W Jordan
Perga ....Site near Antalya, S central Turkey
Pergamum ....Bergama, W Turkey
Persia (empire)..Iran
Philadelphia ....Amman, Jordan
Philippi..Site N of Amfipolis, Greece
Phœnix..Site in SW Crete
Piræus..Piræus, SE Greece
Pisidia (region) ....S central Turkey
Pisidian Antioch..S central Turkey
Placentia ....Placenza, N central Italy
Pompeii ....Ruins in W Italy
Pontia (isle)..Ponza, off W Italy

Ptolemais	Akko, NWIsrael
Puteoli	Puzzuoli, SW Italy
Ravenna	Ravenna, NE Italy
Rhegium	Reggio di Calabria, S Italy
Rhodes (city)	Rhodes
Rhodes (island)	Rhodes, Greek isle S of Turkish coast
Salamis	Salamis, eastern Cyprus
Samaria (region)	Central Israel
Samos (island)	Samos, Greek isle W of Turkish coast
Samothrace (island)	Samothrace, NE Greece
Scythia (region)	S Ukraine to Caspian Sea in Russia
Scythopolis,	Bet Shean, E Israel
Sebaste	Shomron, in Samarian Israel
Seleucia	Samandagi, SE Turkey
Sepphoris	Zippori, NW Israel
Sidon	Sidon, Lebanon
Socotra	Suqutra, off SE Yemen
Spain (Roman province)	Spain and Portugal
Sparta (city-state)	Sparti, S Greece
Syracuse	Siracusa, Sicily, Italy
Syria (Roman province)	S Turkey S to Egypt
Tarracina	Terracina, W Italy
Taricheæ	Site near Migdal, NW Israel
Tarsus	Tarsus, SE Turkey
Taurus (mountains)	Toros Daglari, SE Turkey
Tenedos (island)	Bozcaada, off NW Turkey
Thasos (island)	Thasos, NE Greece
Thessalonica	Thessaloniki, NE Greece
Thrace (region)	S Bulgaria–N Greece–WTurkey
Tigranocerta	Silvan, E Turkey
Tiberias	Teverya, N central Israel
Tirathaba	Near Khirbat Balatah, central Israel
Trachonitis	NE Israel, SW Syria
Trastevere (neighborhood)	Trastevere, Rome, Italy
Troy	Ruins near Truva, W Turkey
Tusculum	Site near Frascati, SE of Rome, Italy
Tyana	Ruins at Nigde, central Turkey
Tyre	Tyre, Lebanon
Upper Germany (Rom. prov.)	Germany S of Rhine R.
Venice	Venezia, NE Italy

Modern Names & Locations of Ancient Places

Appendix IV

Who's Who

Below are thumbnail profiles – largely genealogical – of persons who influenced Christianity in the years immediately following the crucifixion of Jesus. Page numbers in parenthesis indicate the first mention of their names.

Some persons have been omitted from the list simply because there is no information about them beyond what is already described in the text.

Abraham (*c.* 1500–2000 B.C.), first patriarch and progenitor of the Hebrews (p. 119).

Acte, Claudia. Allegedly descended from the kings of Pergamum in Asia Minor, she came to Nero as a freedwoman and became his mistress. Gradually supplanted by Sabina Poppæa from 58 on, but it was she who later deposited Nero's remains in his Domitii family tomb (p. 183).

Agabus, Jewish Christian prophet who, in A.D. 58 came from Jerusalem to Cæsarea to warn Paul that the Jewish Sanhedrin would persecute him if he entered the holy city (p. 192).

Agrippina, Julia (The Younger) (A.D. 15–59), eldest daughter of Germanicus and Agrippina. Sister of the emperor Gaius Caligula. Betrothed in A.D. 28 to C. Domitius Ahenobarbus and bore him one son (the future emperor Nero) in 37 (p.124).

Agrippina, Vipsania (The Elder) (14 B.C.–A.D. 33), daughter of Vipsanius Agrippa and Julia (daughter of Augustus). Married Germanicus around A.D. 5 and bore him nine children, including the future emperor Gaius Caligula and Julia Agrippina, mother of the emperor Nero (p. 6).

Albinus, Roman procurator of Judea A.D. 62–63. Censured the high priest Ananus for ordering the death of James, brother of Jesus (p. 235).

Alexander the Great (356–323 B.C.), son of Philip, king of Macedon. Educated by Aristotle. Brought most of Greece under his control before setting eastward on a path of conquest that left its mark on the future political administrations of the Ægean, Syria, Egypt and lands as far as Parthia and India. (p. 4).

Alexander, Tiberius, named procurator of Egypt by Nero in A.D. 62. First to declare his legions for Vespasian in July 69. Served under Titus during siege of Jerusalem in 70. (p. 264).

Ananias, citizen of Damascus, then an Arab-ruled city of the Decapolis. Instructed by the voice of Jesus to meet and care for Saul (Paul) on the latter's arrival there as a newly-converted Christian (p. 34).

Anianus, a cobbler in Alexandria who, according to tradition, became Mark's first Christian convert in the Egyptian capital around A.D. 58. Became first bishop of Alexandria some four years later when Mark was forced to leave (p. 332).

Ananus (the Younger), high priest of Jerusalem and son of a high priest of the same name. Soon after taking office in A.D. 62 he ordered the execution of Jesus' brother James. Later removed from office, but re-asserted himself during the Jewish rebellion against Rome (p.231).

Andrew, apostle of Jesus. Raised in Bethsaida, Galilee. Younger brother of Simon Peter. Tradition has him evangelizing in Scythia (on the Black Sea) and later in Patræ (in southwestern Greece) (p. 89).

Anicetus. (*d.* A.D. 70?), freedman and early tutor of Nero. Later prefect of the fleet at Misenum and conspirator in the murder of the emperor's his mother Agrippina. (p. 201).

Antonia (36 B.C.–A.D. 37), younger daughter of Mark Anthony and Octavia (sister of Augustus). Married Nero Claudius Drusus (the brother of Tiberius) and bore Germanicus, Livia Julia and the future emperor Claudius. Widowed in 9 B.C., she reigned over the royal household, rearing her grandson Gaius Caligula, among others (p. 7).

Apollos, Jewish Christian from Alexandria who attracted a large following as an evangelical preacher who traveled widely throughout Syria and Asia Minor during A.D. 50–70 (p. 161).

Aquila, Jewish Christian who plied tent and sail making trade with wife Priscilla in Rome. Settled in Corinth around A.D. 50 after Claudius expelled the Jews from the capital. Converted by Paul in Corinth and later helped the apostle settle in Ephesus (p. 146).

Archelaus, (40? B.C.–A.D. 6?), son of Herod the Great. Named ethnarch by Augustus on the king's death and given the lands of Judea, Samaria and Idumea, he governed so poorly that the emperor yielded to petitions by both Jews and Samaritans to resume direct Roman administration of the region. Archelaus was banished to Gaul in A.D. 6. (p. 12).

Aretus (9 B.C.–A.D. 39), fourth of several Arab kings of this name to rule Nabatea (southeast of Judea) and several cities of the Decapolis (including Damascus). His daughter married Herod Antipas, son of Herod the Great and ruler of Galilee and Perea, and who summarily divorced her in 27 (p. 23).

Aristarchus, Christian of Thessalonica in Macedonia. Assisted Paul in

Ephesus, then accompanied him on the embassy to Jerusalem. Stayed with Paul through much of his confinement in Cæsarea and Rome (p. 164).

Aristobulus IV (*d.* 6 B.C.). Son of Herod the Great and Mariamme. Brother of Alexander III. Father of Herod Agrippa I and Herodias (p. 41).

Artabanus III (*d.* A.D. 38), king of Parthia from around A.D. 10 to his death. Won the throne in a civil war (p. 8).

Augustus, Octavian Cæsar (63 B.C.–A.D. 14), grandnephew of Julius Cæsar and his closest male relative when the dictator was assassinated in 44 B.C. At age 19, led the dead Cæsar's adherents in various skirmishes and alliances, culminating in a co-consulship with Mark Anthony in which the latter ruled Egypt and the East. But the frail partnership ended with a naval battle in 31 B.C., leaving Octavian as Imperator of all Rome. His remaining 45 years of rule were marked by consolidation of imperial power and sweeping administrative reforms (p. xvi).

Barnabas, Jewish Christian disciple. Native of Cyprus. Resident of Jerusalem, then of Antioch. Accompanied the apostle Paul on two of his missionary journeys. Cousin of John Mark (p. 61).

Bartholomew, apostle of Jesus. Reportedly traveled to Parthia and India, eventually settling in Armenia (p. 89).

Bernice (*b.* A.D. 28), daughter of Herod Agrippa I. Married her uncle Herod, king of Chalcis in 46. Upon his death in 48 she lived with her brother, Herod Agrippa II and was active in ruling Judea. Supported Flavian cause and became Titus' consort when he was in Judea (67–70) and later in Rome (p. 185).

Brittanicus, Tiberius Claudius Cæsar (A.D. 41–55). Son of Claudius and Valeria Messalina, surnamed Germanicus, but "Brittanicus" was added after Claudius invaded Britain. (p. 97).

Burrus, Sextus Afranius (*d.* A.D. 62), equestrian from Narbonese Gaul who served Livia, Tiberius and Claudius. Picked by Agrippina the

Younger to become Prefect of the Prætorian Guard. Acted with Seneca as unofficial co-regent in the first years of Nero's reign (p. 142).

Cæcina, Aulus (*d.* A.D. 79). Supported Galba's revolt against Nero in A.D. 68 and was rewarded with legionary command of Upper Germany. Then helped instigate Vitellius' bid for power, leading his army in the invasion of Italy and becoming consul in 69. (p. 315).

Callistus, Julius Gaius (*d.* A.D. 52), influential freedman of the emperor Gaius (p.111).

Calpurnius Piso, Gaius (38 B.C.?– A.D. 20), Roman consul in A.D. 7. Named by Tiberius as governor of Syria in A.D. 27 to advise and monitor the militarily ambitious Germanicus. After well-publicized acrimony between them, Tiberius' adopted son died under mysterious circumstances and Piso was tried in Rome for his murder. As the trial turned ugly and Tiberius withheld his support, Piso committed suicide (p. 4).

Cestius Gallus, Gaius (*d.* A.D. 67), son of a consul and himself a suffect (temporary) consul in A.D. 42. Governor of Syria 65–67. Failed in a siege of Jerusalem in 66 (p. 257).

Cicero, Marcus Tullius (104–43 B.C.), Roman lawyer, orator, politician and philosopher. As consul in 63 B.C., exposed a conspiracy led by the senator Cataline and caused his execution. Later, he severely criticized Mark Anthony, only to be led to his own execution when Octavian and Anthony combined forces to share rule of the Roman Empire (p. 288).

Claudius, Tiberius Nero Germanicus (10 B.C.–A.D. 54). Youngest child of Nero Claudius Drusus and Antonia. Became consul in A.D. 37 under his nephew Gaius Caligula and emperor in 41 upon the latter's assassination. Consul four times thereafter and censor in 47–48. Married Messalina, who bore him Brittanicus and Octavia. Upon her death, married Julia Agrippina the Younger, mother of Nero (p. 42).

Corbulo, Gnæus Domitius (*d.* A.D. 66), Roman patrician, career soldier. Legate of Lower Germany (A.D. 47). Proconsul of Asia under Claudius (50?). Became legate of Cappadocia and Galatia (58) in war with Parthia over control of Armenia. Made legate of Syria in 63. Daughter Domitia Longina became wife of the future emperor Domitian in 70 (p. 158).

Cornelius, Roman centurion, garrisoned in Cæsarea. Visited and baptized with his family by the apostle Peter in A.D. 37 or 38 (p. 69).

Croesus, last king of Lydia (560–546 B.C.). Used some of his great wealth to expand the temple of Artemis at Ephesus. Lost his throne when the Persians under Cyrus invaded his capital of Sardis, but later became friend and counselor to Cyrus (p. 161).

Cumanus, Roman procurator of Judea A.D. 50–52 or 53. Recalled to Rome for trial after mishandling control of animosities between Samaria and Galilee (p. 127).

David (1027?–968 B.C.). From Bethlehem in Judah. Rose quickly in the court of Saul, married the king's daughter, led defeat of the rival Philistines, became king in 990 and brought contentious Judah and Israel under a single reign for the first time. Organized civil administration into 12 districts (p. 13).

Demetrius. Maker of tin and silver souvenirs in Ephesus during Paul's long stay in the Asian port city. Apparent head of the metal workers trade guild that tried to expel the apostle (p. 164).

Dionysius, a member of the Areopagus (the highest law court of Athens) who was converted by Paul. Later became the first bishop of Athens (p. 358).

Domitian, Titus Flavius, (A.D. 51–96), youngest son of the emperor Vespasian. Brother of Titus. At age 20, took part in the triumph of Vespasian and Titus marking victory in the Jewish war. Became emperor in 81 on Titus' sudden death. Ruled for 15 years. Married Domitilla (p. 327).

Domitilla, Flavia, niece of the emperor Domitian. In A.D. 95 she was exiled and her husband, the consul Flavius Clemens, executed for "atheism," which many sources interpret to mean Christianity (p. 365).

Drusus, Julius Cæsar (13 B.C.–A.D. 23), only surviving son of Tiberius and his first wife Vipsania. Married Germanicus' sister Livilla. Commanded legions in Pannonia and Illyricum, becoming consul in A.D. 15 (the year after his father became emperor) and again in 21. Father of Julius Cæsar Nero (Gemellus), heir to Tiberius until poisoned by rivals (p. 6).

Drusus, Julius Cæsar II (A.D. 7–33), second surviving son of Germanicus and Agrippina the Elder (p.26).

Drusus, Nero Claudius (38–9 B.C.), popular son of Livia and Tiberius Claudius Nero. Born just after she divorced her husband to marry Octavian. Drusus and his brother Tiberius became the princeps' chief commanders in subduing unruly client states. Married Antonia and fathered Germanicus, Livia Julia and the future emperor Claudius. Died in a German military camp at age 47 after being thrown from a horse (p. 3).

Eleazer, chief scribe at the Jewish temple around A.D. 56–58 and later head of a Zealot faction that commanded a portion of Jerusalem just before and during the Roman invasion in 70 (p. 235).

Epaphras, elder of the church at Colossæ who came to Rome during Paul's confinement seeking the apostle's advice about tensions within his congregation (p. 239).

Epaphroditus, member of the church of Philippi in Macedonia. Met Paul upon his arrival in Rome and served as his assistant until forced home by illness (p. 223).

Eusebius (A.D. 260–339), Biblical scholar, bishop of Cæsarea from 313–339 and contemporary of the Emperor Constantine. Attended the Council of Nicæa in 325 and delivered a speech at dedication of the Church of the Holy Sepulcher at Jerusalem in 335 (p. 22).

Fadus, Cuspius, Roman procurator of Judea, A.D. 44–49 or 50. Installed soon after the death of King Herod Agrippa I (p. 99).

Felix, Claudius. Brother of Antonius Pallas (financial secretary to Claudius). One of his three wives was a daughter of Anthony and

Cleopatra. Another was Drusilla, sister of Jewish king Herod Agrippa II. Procurator of Judea in A.D. 52–58 or 59. Presided over Paul's public hearing in Cæsarea (p.145).

Festus, Portius (*d.* A.D. 62), procurator of Judea A.D. 60–62 and successor to Felix. Heard the case of the apostle Paul and sent him to Rome for trial (p. 212).

Flaccus, A. Avillius, prefect of Egypt under the emperors Tiberius and Gaius. Instigated or acquiesced to a violent persecution of the large Jewish community in Alexandria for not paying proper homage to Gaius upon his ascendancy (p. 53).

Florus, Gessius, Roman knight who married Cleopatra, friend of Nero wife Poppæa Sabina. Named procurator of Judea in A.D. 64 and precipitated its suicidal insurrection in 66 (p. 235).

Gaius, Christian church leader from Derbe in Pamphylia. Assisted Paul in Ephesus, then joined his "embassy" to Jerusalem (p. 164).

Gaius Julius Cæsar (Caligula) (A.D. 12–41), son of Germanicus and Agrippina the Elder. Grandson of Antonia and nephew of Claudius. Formally adopted by the emperor Tiberius in A.D. 37 as his successor just before his death the same year (p. 26).

Galba, Servius Sulpicius (3 B.C.–A.D. 69), emperor A.D. 68–69. From patrician family close to the empress Livia. Governor of Aquitania and consul (A.D. 33), governor of Upper Germany (40–42), proconsul of Africa (44–45) and Spain (60–68). Rebelled against Nero and proclaimed himself emperor in same year (p. 297).

Gallio, L. Junius (*d.* A.D. 65). Born Annæus Novatus, brother of philosopher L. Annæus Seneca, but changed name in adulthood when adopted by the orator and senator L. Junius Gallio. As proconsul of Achaia in A.D. 52 he heard a case against the apostle Paul (p. 148).

Gamaliel (*c.* 20 B.C.–A.D. 50?), rabbi and scholar in Jerusalem. President of the Sanhedrim at one point. Head of the temple rabbinical college during Paul's tenure there as a student (p. 21).

"Gemellus," Julius Cæsar Nero (A.D. 19–37), son of Drusus (Tiberius' son) and Julia Livilla. Joint heir to the throne of Tiberius. But upon the emperor's death he was adopted by Gaius, then forced to take his own life in the same year (p. 27).

Germanicus, Julius Cæsar (15 B.C.–A.D. 20), elder son of Antonia (daughter of Mark Anthony) and Drusus (brother of Tiberius). Married Agrippina the Elder, who bore him nine children. Those surviving infancy were Nero Julius Cæsar, Drusus Julius Cæsar, Gaius (the emperor), Agrippina the Younger (mother of Nero), Drusilla and Julia. Adopted by Tiberius as heir-apparent, but succumbed mysteriously (to poison?) in Syria at age 35 (p. 3).

Hannibal III (247–183 B.C.), general of Carthage. Invaded Italy in 218 B.C. after crossing the Alps with a force of elephants and 40,000 men. Despite several victories, he was unable to capture Rome. Later, when Rome invaded Carthage, Hannibal fled to the Seleucid kingdom of Antiochus III. After confronting the Romans again and suffering defeat, he committed suicide (p. 337).

Helius, freedman of Nero. Placed in charge of affairs at Rome during Nero's tour of Greece (A.D. 66–68). Probably responsible for the deaths of the apostles Peter and Paul (p. 261).

Herod Agrippa I (10 B.C.–A.D. 44). Son of Aristobulus IV and grandson of Herod the Great. Reared in Rome with his sister Herodias under the patronage of Antonia. Boyhood friend of her son Claudius (p.23).

Herod Agrippa II, Marcus Julius (A.D. 27–100?). Son of Herod Agrippa I and great- grandson of Herod the Great. Raised largely in Rome at the palace of Claudius. Named king of Chalcis in A.D. 50, along with the right to name Jewish high priests. His realm expanded by Claudius and Nero (p. 98).

Herod Antipas, (B.C. 30?–A.D. 40?), son of Herod the Great. Named by Augustus as tetrarch of Galilee and Perea. Married daughter of Aretus IV, king of neighboring Nabatea. Later divorced her to marry Herodias, sister of his brother Philip. Responsible for the executions of John the Baptist and Jesus (p. 12).

Herod the Great (73–4 B.C.), son of an Idumean administrator, Herod rose to become tetrarch of Judea under Mark Anthony and Cleopatra, then switched his allegiance when rival Octavian began winning the struggle for Rome. Married Mariamme of Jewish royal Hasmonean line (37 B.C.) along with at least nine other wives from various ethic groups in Judea. Upon his death, Augustus divided the kingdom among sons Archelaus, Herod Antipas and Philip (p. xvii).

Herodias (12 B.C.?–A.D. 41?), granddaughter of Herod the Great. Daughter of Aristobulus IV. Sister of Herod Agrippa I. Married her uncle, Herod Philip (King of Chalcis) and divorced him to marry another uncle, Herod Antipas (p. 23).

James (*d*. A.D. 42), apostle of Jesus. Son of Zebedee and Mary Salome. Elder brother of the apostle John (p. 87).

James (the Just) (*d*. A.D. 62). Matthew (13:53–58) mentions him first (the eldest?) among four brothers of Jesus (the others: Joseph, Simon and Jude) and more than one unnamed sisters. Came to Jerusalem in A.D. 35 or 36 to assume leadership of the Jewish Christians (p. 62).

John (A.D. 7?–100?), apostle of Jesus. Son of Zebedee and Mary Salome. Younger brother of the apostle James. Preached with Peter in Jerusalem, probably moved to Ephesus in A.D. 42–43. Guardian of Jesus' mother, Mary, after A.D. 30 (p. 16).

John the Baptist (6 B.C.?–A.D. 28 or 29), son of Elizabeth, who was cousin of Jesus' mother Mary. Preacher/prophet who baptized thousands (including Jesus), calling for repentance to prepare for the arrival of the Jewish Messiah, the Kingdom of God and the Last Judgment. Abducted and murdered by the tetrarch Herod Antipas after condemning the ruler's marriage to his niece Herodias (p. 23).

John of Gischala, brigand and foe of Josephus during fortification of Galilee in A.D. 66–67. Escaped to Jerusalem and became leader of one of the defending factions in the siege of the city in A.D. 70 (p. 270).

Jona, father of the apostles Peter and Andrew. A fisherman of Bethsaida in Galilee (p. 86).

Jonathan (*d.* A.D. 54 or 55). Served as high priest in Jerusalem (part of the term with Ananias). Survived a trial or hearing in Rome under Claudius. Assassinated early in Nero's reign by the Sicarii (p. 186).

Josephus, Flavius (A.D. 37–100?), Jewish priest of aristocratic descent and Pharisaic education. Named by Jewish resistance leaders as governor-general of Galilee in A.D. 67 or 68. Captured by Vespasian in 69 and lived in Rome under Flavian patronage, writing *The Jewish War* (75–79) and *Antiquities of the Jews* (p. 59).

Julia III (B.C. 39–A.D. 14), daughter of Octavian Cæsar Augustus and his first wife, Scribonia. Married successively to Marcellus, Agrippa, then Tiberius. Mother of Gaius Cæsar, Lucius Cæsar and Agrippa Postumus (all of whom died in early manhood). Her fourth child, Agrippina, married Germanicus and gave birth to the future emperor Gaius (Caligula) and eight other children (see Agrippina I). In her later years Julia was banished by her father for her scandalous conduct with men and wine. Died in exile (p. 3).

Julius Cæsar, Gaius (100–44 B.C.). Descendant of a venerable patrician family, Cæsar began as military tribune and quickly rose to become Pontifex Maximus (chief religious official) and architect of many Senate reforms. Formed the First Triumvirate in 60 B.C. with Pompey and Crassus. Conquered Gaul and Britain for Rome in 58–49 B.C. Defeated Pompey in 48 and returned to Rome as "dictator for life." Assassinated by senators who feared his excessive power (p. 146).

Linus. Christian leader during Paul's stay in Rome (cited by the apostle in Timothy II) and bishop of Rome after the deaths of Peter and Paul (p. 358).

Livia Drusilla, (58 B.C.–A.D. 29). Wed to a senator who fought on the side defeated by Octavian, the comely Livia was pursued by the young emperor and persuaded (compelled?) to marry him in A.D. 39. With her came her four-year-old son Tiberius and the still unborn Drusus. She bore Augustus no children of his own, but became widely revered a model of patrician Roman propriety, dignity, intelligence and tact. Some, however, say she ruthlessly manipulated events that led her son Tiberius to the throne over various grandsons of Augustus by his previous marriage (p. 2).

Livilla, Julia (13 B.C.–A.D. 32?), daughter of Drusus and Antonia; sister of Germanicus and Claudius. Married Drusus, the son of the emperor Tiberius, and bore Julius Cæsar Nero, better known as Gemellus (p. 6).

Locusta, an infamous poisoner, of Gallic origin, who was employed by Agrippina the Younger to poison Claudius and by Nero to murder Brittanicus, the son of Claudius (p. 153).

Luke, Gentile Christian physician and writer from Philippi in Macedonia. Accompanied Paul to Philippi, Corinth, Cæsarea and Rome. Author of the Gospel of Luke and of Acts (p. 130).

Lysias, Claudius, Roman tribune (colonel) in charge of the Fortress of Antonia at the time of Paul's visit to Jerusalem during the Passover of A.D. 58 or 59 (p. 194).

Macro, Quintus Nævius Sertorius (d. A.D. 38). Became Prætorian Prefect after he conspired with Tiberius to overthrow his commander Sejanus in A.D. 31. Later helped maneuver Gaius Caligula into position as his successor (p. 7).

Manæn, a Jewish Christian leader in Antioch. May have been a boyhood friend of the Jewish tetrarch Herod Antipas (p. 92).

Manahem, Jewish brigand and outlaw who briefly joined the Jewish rebel forces in Jerusalem (A.D. 66), but soon proclaimed himself king and was murdered by rival factions in the same year (p. 263).

Mariamme (d. 29 B.C.), granddaughter of the Hasmonean Jewish king Hycrannus II. Wed to Herod in 37 B.C. Mother of Aristobulus IV (father of Herod Agrippa I) and Alexander III. Executed by Herod in 29 B.C., followed by murder of both sons in 6 B.C. (p.11).

Mark Anthony (83–31 B.C.), commander and ally of Julius Cæsar. Combined with Octavian to defeat Brutus and Cassius, who assassinated the dictator in 44 B.C. Married Octavian's sister Octavia, then deserted both for Cleopatra and an attempt to rule the western part of the Roman Empire from Egypt. Committed suicide after losing the decisive naval Battle of Actium (p. 42).

Mark, John (A.D. 16?–69?). Son of Mary (of Jerusalem), cousin of Barnabas and companion of the apostle Paul on his first missionary journey. Probably accompanied Peter to Rome in the early sixties A.D, where he wrote the Gospel of Mark. Reportedly went on to form churches in Alexandria (p. 88).

Mary, Mother of John Mark. Cousin of Barnabas. Her home in Jerusalem was used by followers of Jesus in the period following the crucifixion and possibly provided the Biblical "upper room" for the Last Supper (p. 88).

Mary Salome, wife of Zebedee and mother of the apostles James and John. One of the women who anointed the body of Jesus after the crucifixion (p. 87).

Matthias, apostle of Jesus, chosen to replace Judas Iscariot following his suicide (p. 18).

Messalina, Valeria (A.D. 18?–48), great-granddaughter of Augustus' sister Octavia and daughter of Domitia Lepida. Married in A.D. 39 to the emperor Claudius, her second cousin. Bore him two children, Claudia Octavia and Britannicus (p. 97).

Moses (*c.* 13th century B.C.), Hebrew orphan who was brought up in the royal Egyptian court. Prophet and leader in liberating the Jewish people from bondage to Pharaoh Ramses II. During a prolonged, nomadic desert existence, God revealed himself to Moses on Mt. Sinai, gave him the Ten Commandments and led the Hebrews to Canaan, "the Promised Land," (p. 193).

Mucianus, Gaius Licinius (*d.* A.D. 77?), patrician and thrice suffect (temporary) consul of Rome. Served under Corbulo (58) and then governor of Lycia-Pamphylia. Named governor of Syria by Nero at the same time Vespasian was assigned to quell Judea. Persuaded Vespasian to revolt against Nero and remained his most prominent ally (p. 318).

Narcissus (*d.* A.D. 54), politically and financially powerful freedman and secretary to the emperor Claudius. Saluted by the Senate for exposing the infidelities of the empress Messalina (p. 111).

Nero, Lucius Domitius Ahenobarbus Claudius Cæsar (A.D. 37–68), son of C. Domitius Ahenobarbus and Julia Agrippina (daughter of Germanicus). Tutored by Lucius Annæus Seneca, whom his mother recalled from exile. Wed to the emperor Claudius' daughter Octavia. Assumed the throne in 54 when his adoptive father was poisoned. (p. 124).

Nero, Julius Cæsar (A.D. 6–31), eldest of the three sons of Germanicus and Agrippina to survive infancy. After the death of Tiberius in A.D. 23 he became, at 17, the next in succession to the Principate (p. 7).

Octavia, Claudia (A.D. 40?–62), daughter of Messalina and the emperor Claudius. Married Agrippina's son, Nero, in 53. (p. 97).

Onesimus, a young slave who ran away from his master, Philemon, in Laodicea, to join Paul in Rome around A.D. 62–63 (p. 237).

Otho, Marcus Salvius (A.D. 32–69), second husband of Poppæa Sabina and close friend of Nero. Sent to Lusitania as governor in 58 and remained until 68. Overthrew Galba in 69 and hailed as emperor (p. 183).

Pætus, Cæsennius Lucius, Roman patrician and general. Consul A.D. 61. Named legate of mission to subdue Armenia in 62, but returned to Rome in disgrace. Named governor of Syria by Vespasian in 70, perhaps because he was married to Flavia Sabina, the emperor's niece (p. 230).

Pallas, Marcus Antonius (d. A.D. 62?), long-time freedman of Antonia, then financial secretary of her son, the emperor Claudius. Brother of the Judean procurator Felix. Ally (and presumed lover of) Agrippina the Younger in her effort to wed Claudius (p. 111).

Paul (Saul), (A.D. 4?–67?), apostle of Jesus, primarily to the Gentile world. Son of a tent and sail maker from Tarsus in the province of Cilicia. Educated at temple rabbinical college in Jerusalem. A sister was known to live in Jerusalem (p. 33).

Peter, Simon (also Simeon or Cephas) (d. 67?), apostle of Jesus. Raised in Bethsaida, Galilee. Elder brother of the apostle Andrew. Apostle to chief Jewish population centers of Jerusalem, Antioch, Babylon and Rome (p. 18).

Petronilla, daughter of the apostle Peter, according to Roman Catholic tradition. Said to have accompanied him to Rome (p. 284).

Petronius, Publius, Roman augur from A.D. 7, proconsul of Asia (29–35?) and legate of Syria 39–42. Sympathized with the Jews in resisting the erection of a statue of Gaius Caligula in the temple at Jerusalem (p. 54).

Philemon, a church leader of Laodicea in Asia Minor, owner of the runaway slave Onesimus, and recipient of a Pauline epistle around A.D. 62 (p. 240).

Philip (the Evangelist), a member of the early Christian Council of Seven who settled in Samaria around A.D. 33–35 and preached The Way. Hosted and assisted Paul at Cæsarea around A.D. 58 and during his subsequent confinement there. Philip had four daughters, all known as prophets (p. 35).

Philip, apostle of Jesus. One of the least known among the 12 apostles, except that he, like Peter and Andrew, had been a fisherman in Bethsaida, Galilee (p. 89).

Philip, (d. A.D. 34), son of Herod the Great. Upon the latter's death, named by Augustus as tetrarch of the northern Jewish territories, including Batanea, Trachonitis, and Gaulanitis. Founded the city of Cæsarea Philippi (p. 12).

Philip II of Macedonia (382–336 B.C.). After inheriting a kingdom nearly dissolved by civil war, he built an aggressive military force that subjugated many states surrounding Macedonia. Despite stormy, often estranged relations with his son Alexander, the latter became king on Philip's death and made Macedonia the center of an empire unprecedented in breadth (p. 131).

Philo, philosopher, writer and political leader of Alexandria, Egypt. Brother of Alexander the alabarch. Represented the persecuted Jewish community in an embassy to the emperor Gaius (p. 48).

Phoebe, a Christian deaconess in Corinth who carried Paul's letter to the Romans by ship to Rome (p. 188).

Piso, Gaius Calpurnius (*d.* A.D. 65), respected Roman aristocrat chosen to succeed Nero had the conspiracy plot of A.D. 65 succeeded (p. 250).

Plautius, Lateranus (*d.* A.D. 65), nephew of Aulus Plautius, who led Claudius' invasion of Britain in A.D. 44. Deprived of senatorial rank in 48 as a lover of Messalina. Restored by Nero in 55. Executed for his role in the conspiracy against Nero (p. 250).

Plautus, Rubellius (*d.* A.D. 62), son of C. Rubellius Blandus and Julia, granddaughter of the emperor Tiberius. Viewed by Nero as a possible consort for his mother Agrippina, and thus banished – then executed (p. 226).

Pompeius (Pompey), Magnus Gnæus (106 B.C.–48), equestrian soldier who rose to commander under the dictator Sulla. Achieved two triumphs (for conquests in Africa and Spain), then stamped out piracy in the Mediterranean. Sent to eastern provinces with unprecedented powers, where he subdued Armenia, annexed Syria and established Roman administration of Judea. In B.C. 59 formed ruling coalition with Julius Cæsar and Crassus. When the fragile alliance crumbled, Pompey lost to Cæsar in a decisive battle and fled to Egypt, where he was stabbed to death (p. 230).

Pontius Pilate, Roman prefect of Judea in A.D. 26–36, who acquiesced to the crucifixion of Jesus during the Passover of 30. Recalled to Rome in 36 for ruthless repression of Samaritans (p.14).

Poppæa Sabina (*d.* A.D. 65). Granddaughter of a Roman consul, C. Poppæus Sabinus. Married first to a Prætorian prefect under Claudius. Became mistress of Nero in 58 while wed to the future emperor Otho. Married Nero in 63 and bore him a daughter, Claudia, who died at four months. Known to have Jewish sympathies, but also thought to have helped secure the appointment of the repressive Gessius Florus as procurator of Judea in 64 (p. 183).

Priscilla, Jewish Christian of Rome who ran sail and tentmaking business with husband Aquila. Moved to Corinth around A.D. 50 when

Claudius expelled the Jews from Rome. Helped support Paul and form churches in Corinth and Ephesus (p. 146).

Primus, Antonius Marcus (A.D. 20–97?). Born in Narbonese Gaul. Career Roman military officer. Supported Galba and won command of Pannonia. Declared for Vespasian in 69, led invasion of Italy and captured Rome. Retired as provincial governor (p. 320).

Pudens. According to Roman Catholic tradition, a wealthy senator who sponsored or hosted Peter in Rome and allowed his home to be used for Christian worship. Paul's second letter to Timothy sends greetings from a "Pudens." Pudente today remains the name of a Catholic parish in Rome (p. 284).

Secundus, a Christian leader from Thessalonica. Part of the group (with his fellow churchman Aristarchus) that accompanied Paul to Cæsarea and Jerusalem to deliver famine relief funds for the Jewish Christians of Jerusalem (p. 189).

Sejanus, Lucius Ælius (11? B.C.–A.D. 31). Joined his equestrian father as co-prefect of the Prætorian Guard in A.D. 14 and became sole commander when his father was named prefect of Egypt (p. 5).

Seleucus, Nicator I (358–281 B.C.), fought under Alexander the Great and inherited Babylonia and other eastern conquered lands upon the king's untimely death. Conquered Syria and founded Antioch as one of his royal capitals (p. 90).

Seneca, Lucius Annæus (4 B.C.?–A.D. 65), son of a wealthy equestrian from Cordoba, Spain. Brother of Junius Gallio, proconsul of Asia and of Annæus Mela, father of the poet Lucan. Married Pompeia Paulina and had one son, who died in A.D. 41. Tutored Nero as a boy and became a chief minister once Nero assumed the throne in 54. Author of many plays and philosophical essays (p. 141).

Silas (Silvanus), Jewish Christian from Jerusalem. Accompanied Paul to Antioch and then on his second missionary journey. Also probable that he was later in Rome (A.D. 65?) and helped Peter write Peter I (p. 120).

Silius, Gaius (A.D. 17?–48). Grandson of a Roman consul and son of a senator who was put to death by Tiberius for befriending Sejanus. Was consul-designate when he "wedded" Messalina, the wife of Claudius, in a public ceremony and was put to death (p. 110).

Simeon Niger, Christian leader in Antioch. Tradition says he is the same man who was ordered to carry the cross of Jesus in Jerusalem (p. 92).

Simon of Gerasa. (*d*. A.D. 71), Galilean warlord and brigand during the rebellion against Rome (A.D. 66–70). Amassed a large "army" in Idumea and forced his way into Jerusalem. Led one of the major defending factions in the siege of Jerusalem (p. 338).

Simon the Magician (*c*. A.D. 32–52), a traveling charismatic magician or charlatan who once offered the apostle Peter money to infuse him with the Holy Spirit. Tradition has him later performing in Rome (A.D. 40–42?) (p. 35).

Simon (the Zealot), apostle of Jesus. Oral traditions report his missionary activities in Egypt, Libya, Carthage, Spain and Britain (p. 89).

Solomon, (*d*. 922 B.C.), son of David and his successor as king of Judah-Israel 972–922 B.C. Known for his wise judicial decisions, but also for massive public works projects and expansion of trade. Strengthened Jerusalem and built the first temple (p. 13).

Sopater, a Christian elder from the church in Macedonia. A member of the group that accompanied Paul to Cæsarea and Jerusalem to deliver famine relief funds for the Jewish Christians of Jerusalem (p. 189).

Sporus, an adolescent boy whom Nero made into a eunuch, then took as a "wife." Accompanied the emperor during his tour of Greece (A.D. 66–68) and was addressed as "Lady Sporus" (p. 261).

Stephen (A.D. 4?–33 or 34). A Hellenic Christian in Jerusalem. Named to the Council of Seven, an administrative group that distributed food, clothing, etc. to needy Christians. Stoned on orders of the Sanhedrin for zealous preaching (p. 32).

Symeon, the successor to James the Just (in A.D. 62) as leader of the Jewish Christian church in Jerusalem (p. 357).

Tabitha, Jewish Christian woman of Joppa in Judea. Raised from the dead by the apostle Peter in A.D. 37 or 38 (p. 68).

Tertullian, Quintus Septimius Florens, (A.D. *c.* 160–240). Born around Carthage, son of a centurion. Orator and writer, steeped in the spirit of the Christian martyrs. Defended Christianity against pagan charges of atheism and magic. Devoted self to study of Christian ethical problems. Joined the Montanists, who believed they received direction directly from the Holy Spirit (p. 22).

Thaddeus, apostle of Jesus. Reported by the historians Eusebius and Tertullian to have borne a letter from Jesus to the king of Edessa (p. 89).

Thomas, apostle of Jesus, referred to as "the twin" in John. Reportedly went east to Parthia, India and China, where he died a martyr (p. 89).

Tiberius Julius Cæsar Augustus, (42 B.C.–A.D. 37), son of Livia, who divorced her husband and married Augustus when Tiberius was four and she was pregnant with his brother Drusus. Adopted as Augustus' heir in A.D. 4. Served many military commands. Became emperor at 56 and served 14–37, during the ministry and crucifixion of Jesus. (p. 2).

Tigellinus, Ofonius (*d.* A.D. 69), a Sicilian commoner brought up in the household of Gaius. Made sole Prætorian Prefect by Nero in A.D. 62 and served as the emperor's instrument in executing "enemies" of the state. Forced to commit suicide during reign of Otho (p. 224).

Timothy (*c.* A.D. 49–90?). Raised in Lystra, in Lycaonia, son of a Gentile father and Jewish mother. Accompanied Paul on his second missionary journey, then to Macedonia, Corinth, Cæsarea and Rome. Became bishop of Ephesus after Paul's death (p. 129).

Tiridates, brother of Vologeses I, king of Parthia, who set him on the throne of Armenia in A.D. 54. In 66 he visited Rome to acknowledge Nero's hegemony (p. 231).

Titus, Christian missionary with Paul in Ephesus. Also assisted Paul during his confinement in Rome. Later became head of the church in Crete, according to the historian Eusebius (p. 174).

Titus Flavius Vespasian (A.D. 39–81), eldest son of the emperor Vespasian. Reared in the royal court with Brittanicus, son of Claudius. Began career as military tribune in Germany and Britain. Joined his father in A.D. 66 to suppress the Jewish revolt. Led the siege of Jerusalem. Became emperor upon father's death in 79 (p. 272).

Torquatus, Decimus Julius Silanus (*d.* A.D. 64), consul A.D. 53. Forced to commit suicide because he could boast of descent from Augustus (p. 252).

Trophimus. Joined Tychicus (see below) in Paul's delegation of Christian churches to deliver famine relief funds to the Jewish Christians of Jerusalem in A.D. 58 (p. 189).

Tychicus. Represented the Ægean coastal cities of Asia (along with Trophimus) in the delegation that accompanied Paul to bring famine relief funds to the Jewish Christians of Jerusalem. Later joined Paul in Rome and delivered the apostles letters to Asian churches (p. 189).

Valens, Fabius (*d.* A.D. 70), an equestrian officer who supported Galba in his revolt against Nero (A.D. 68), then helped proclaim Vitellius emperor while in Upper Germany. Led Vitellian forces in decisive Battle of Bedriacum (p. 315).

Vespasian, Titus Flavius (9 B.C.–A.D. 79). Born at Sabine Reate, Italy, to a tax collector (although his mother's brother was a senator). Began career of soldiering as military tribune. Rose within the legions under patronage of Narcissus, freedman of Claudius. Took part in invasion of Britain. Became proconsul of Africa in 62. Named by Nero to suppress Jewish rebellion in 66. Hailed by his troops as emperor in 69. Father (with Flavia Domitilla, who died before his accession) of the emperors Titus (79–81) and Domitian (81–96) and a daughter, Flavia Domitilla (p. 267).

Vindex, Julius Gaius, descended from kings of Aquitania and son of Roman senator. Governor of Gaul when he revolted against Nero in A.D. 68 (p. 296).

Vipsania, Agrippina (*d.* A.D. 20), first wife of Tiberius and mother of his only son, Nero Claudius Drusus (p.2).

Vinius, Titus (*d.* A.D. 69), long-time military associate of Galba and his co-consul in A.D. 69 when the latter became emperor (p. 314).

Vitellius, Aulus (A.D. 15–69), son of Lucius Vitellius. Consul in 48 and then proconsul of Africa. Named governor of Lower Germany in 68 by the emperor Galba. Became emperor in 69 (p. 314).

Vitellius, Lucius (5 B.C.?–A.D. 55?), prominent patrician politician. Consul in A.D. 34 and twice thereafter. Confidant to emperors Tiberius, Gaius Caligula and Claudius. Legate (governor) of Syria 35–37. Temporary ruler of Rome when Claudius left to invade Britain in 43. Father of emperor Aulus Vitellius (p. 31).

Vologeses I, king of Parthia A.D. 51 or 52 to 79 or 80. In 54 he thrust his brother Tiridates III on the throne of Armenia, causing prolonged hostilities with Rome (p. 230).

Zebedee, a fisherman from Bethsaida in Galilee and probably a merchant as well. Father of the apostles James and John. Husband of Mary Salome, who traveled often with Jesus. (p. 86).

Appendix v
Maps

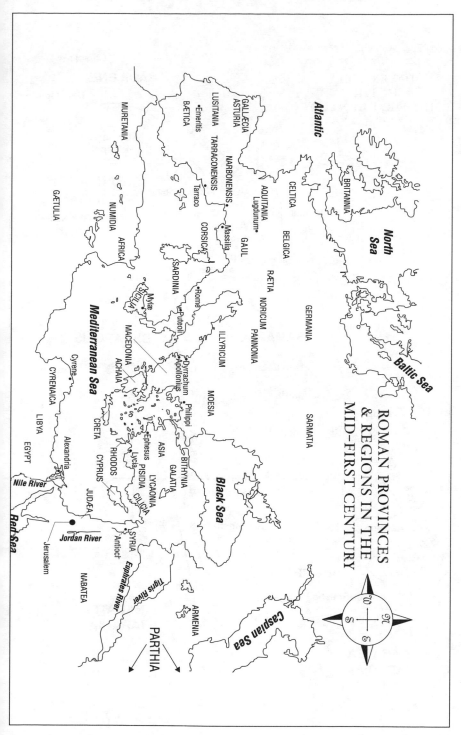

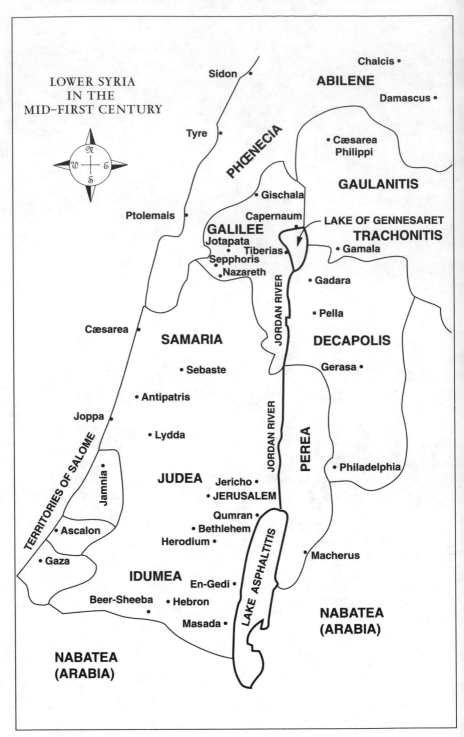

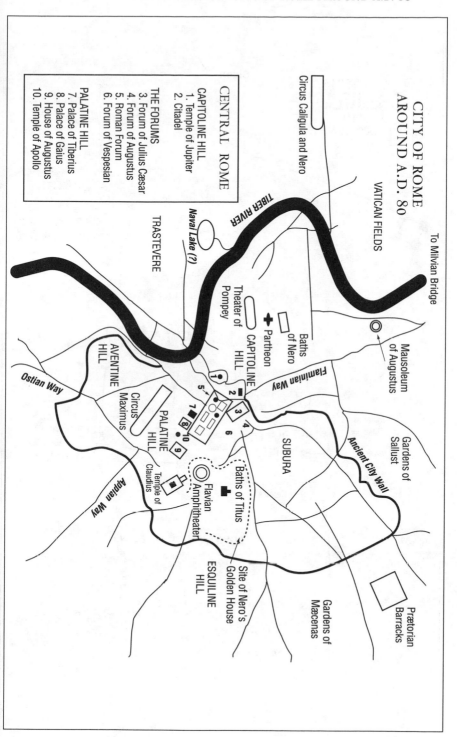

CITY OF ROME
AROUND A.D. 80

To Milvian Bridge

VATICAN FIELDS

Circus Caligula and Nero

Mausoleum
of Augustus

TIBER RIVER

Naval Lake (?)

TRASTEVERE

Baths
of Nero

Theater of
Pompey

Pantheon

CAPITOLINE
HILL

Flaminian Way

Gardens of
Sallust

Ostian Way

AVENTINE
HILL

Circus
Maximus

PALATINE
HILL

SUBURA

Ancient City Wall

Appian Way

Temple of
Claudius

Flavian
Amphitheater

Baths
of Titus

Site of Nero's
Golden House

ESQUILINE
HILL

Gardens of
Maecenas

Prætorian
Barracks

CENTRAL ROME

CAPITOLINE HILL
1. Temple of Jupiter
2. Citadel

THE FORUMS
3. Forum of Julius Cæsar
4. Forum of Augustus
5. Roman Forum
6. Forum of Vespesian

PALATINE HILL
7. Palace of Tiberius
8. Palace of Gaius
9. House of Augustus
10. Temple of Apollo

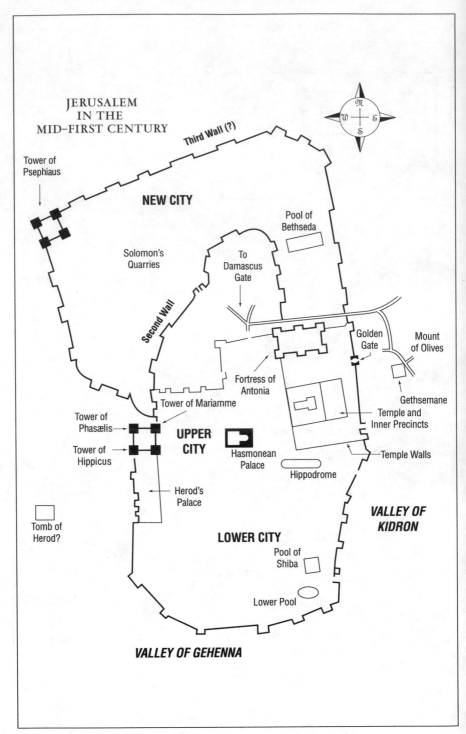

JERUSALEM
IN THE
MID-FIRST CENTURY

Third Wall (?)

Tower of
Psephiaus

NEW CITY

Pool of
Bethseda

Solomon's
Quarries

To
Damascus
Gate

Second Wall

Golden
Gate

Mount
of Olives

Fortress of
Antonia

Gethsemane

Tower of Mariamme

Temple and
Inner Precincts

Tower of
Phasælis

UPPER
CITY

Tower of
Hippicus

Hasmonean
Palace

Temple Walls

Herod's
Palace

Hippodrome

Tomb of
Herod?

VALLEY OF
KIDRON

LOWER CITY

Pool of
Shiba

Lower Pool

VALLEY OF GEHENNA

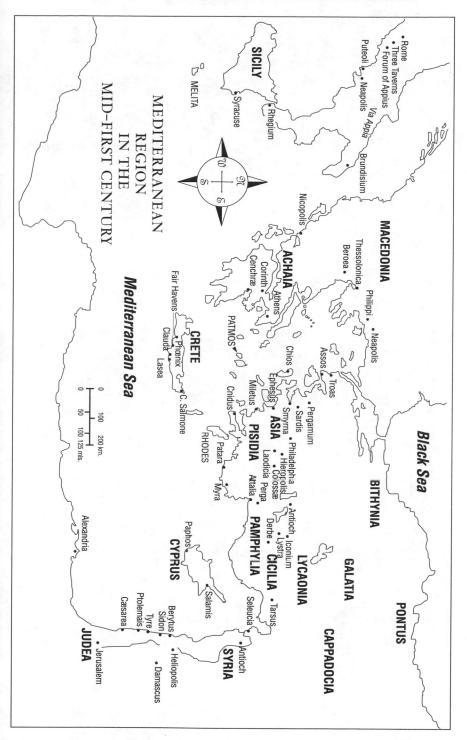

MEDITERRANEAN
REGION
IN THE
MID-FIRST CENTURY

Mediterranean Sea

Black Sea

SICILY
MELITA
Rome
Three Taverns
Forum of Appius
Puteoli
Neapolis
Via Appia
Brundisium
Syracuse
Rhegium

MACEDONIA
ACHAIA
Nicopolis
Thessalonica
Beroea
Philippi
Neapolis
Corinth
Cenchræ
Athens

CRETE
Fair Havens
Phenix
Clauda
Lasea
C. Salmone
PATMOS

Chios
Assos
Troas
Cnidus
Miletus
Ephesus
Sardis
Smyrna
Philadelphia
Pergamum
RHODES
Patara
Myra
Attalia
Perga
Laodicea
Hierapolis
Colossæ

ASIA
PISIDIA
PAMPHYLIA
LYCAONIA
Antioch
Iconium
Lystra
Derbe
CILICIA
Tarsus
Seleucia
Antioch

BITHYNIA
GALATIA
CAPPADOCIA
PONTUS

CYPRUS
Paphos
Salamis

SYRIA
Berytus
Sidon
Tyre
Ptolemais
Cæsarea
Heliopolis
Damascus

JUDEA
Jerusalem

Alexandria

0   50   100 200 km.
0   50   100 125 mls.

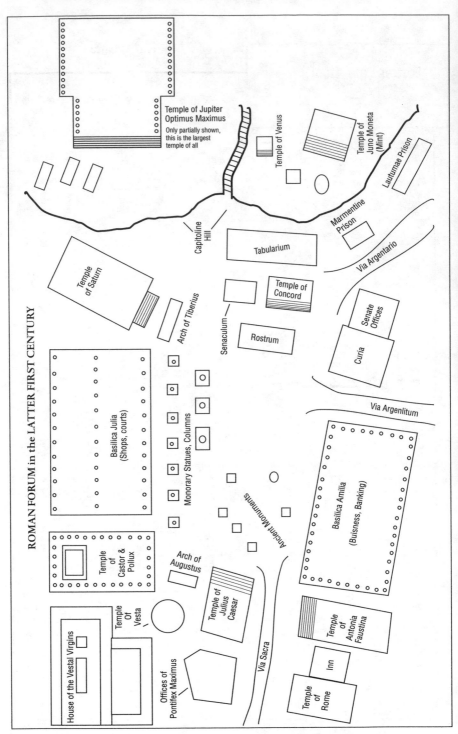

ROMAN FORUM in the LATTER FIRST CENTURY

Temple of Jupiter Optimus Maximus
Only partially shown, this is the largest temple of all

Temple of Venus

Temple of Juno Moneta (Mint)

Lautumae Prison

Marmentine Prison

Capitoline Hill

Tabularium

Via Argentario

Temple of Saturn

Arch of Tiberius

Temple of Concord

Senate Offices

Senaculum

Rostrum

Curia

Basilica Julia (Shops, courts)

Monorary Statues, Columns

Via Argenlitum

Basilica Amilia (Buisness, Banking)

Temple of Castor & Pollux

Arch of Augustus

Ancient Monuments

House of the Vestal Virgins

Temple Of Vesta

Offices of Pontifex Maximus

Temple of Julius Caesar

Via Sacra

Temple of Antonia Faustina

Inn

Temple of Rome

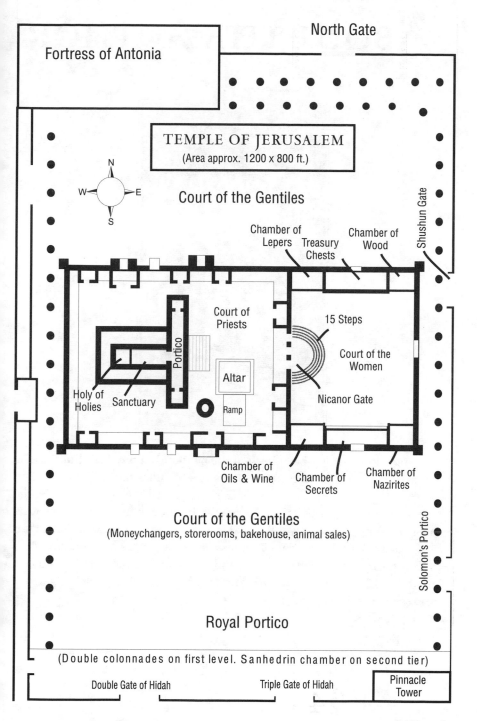

North Gate

Fortress of Antonia

TEMPLE OF JERUSALEM
(Area approx. 1200 x 800 ft.)

N
W   E
S

Court of the Gentiles

Shushun Gate

Chamber of
Lepers   Treasury
Chests

Chamber of
Wood

Court of
Priests

15 Steps

Portico

Court of the
Women

Altar

Holy of
Holies   Sanctuary

Ramp

Nicanor Gate

Chamber of
Oils & Wine

Chamber of
Secrets

Chamber of
Nazirites

Court of the Gentiles
(Moneychangers, storerooms, bakehouse, animal sales)

Solomon's Portico

Royal Portico

(Double colonnades on first level. Sanhedrin chamber on second tier)

Double Gate of Hidah   Triple Gate of Hidah

Pinnacle
Tower

ABOUT THE AUTHOR

Writing and reporting have been at the heart of Jim Snyder's life since he graduated from Northwestern University's Medill School of Journalism in 1958. While studying for his master's in political science at The George Washington University, he served as a Washington corespondent for several business magazines. Over the next 25 years he would write for more than 100 magazines ranging from business newsmagazines and medical journals to the *Harvard Business Review* and *Parade* magazine. More recently, he served as Chairman / CEO of a company that founded seven magazines and several related conferences.

Having also served as a Presbyterian elder and church officer for many years, Snyder has had a deepening interest in early Christian history that led him to visit and study nearly all of the first century sites mentioned in this book. Snyder and his wife Sue live in Jupiter, Florida.